The end of history:
An essay on modern Hegelianism

History ended, according to Hegel according to Kojève, with the establishment and proliferation in Europe of states organized along Napoleonic lines: rational, bureaucratic, homogeneous, atheist. This state lives in some tension with the popular slogan that helped give it birth: Liberty, Equality, Fraternity. But there is now also totalitarianism – the only new kind of regime, according to Arendt, created since the national state. Man is now in charge of nature, technology, and society; much of political life has become a gavotte elaborating the meaning of the Napoleonic model.

This interpretation, however opposed it seems to common sense, has been influential, particularly in France where the course of existentialism is unintelligible without taking it into account. Professor Cooper argues that it is inherently plausible and examines the arguments of Hegel and Kojève to reveal its consistency and explanatory power. And he applies it to more contemporary events – the experience of the atomic bomb, the Gulag system of extermination, and the growth of multinational corporations.

The work concludes by pulling together the presuppositions and theories of the totalitarian system, the Hegelian version of the Napoleonic state, and our contemporary technological society. Overall, the reader will find here a complete and challenging presentation of how the modern world understands its collective life.

BARRY COOPER is a member of the Department of Political Science at the University of Calgary.

BARRY COOPER

The End of History:
An essay on
modern Hegelianism

UNIVERSITY OF TORONTO PRESS

Toronto Buffalo London

For Catherine
ἕως κόρακες λευκοὶ γένωνται

© University of Toronto Press 1984
Toronto Buffalo London
Printed in Canada

ISBN 0-8020-5625-3

Canadian Cataloguing in Publication Data

Cooper, Barry, 1943–
The end of history : an essay on modern Hegelianism
Includes index.
ISBN 0-8020-5625-3

1. Hegel, Georg Wilhelm Friedrich, 1770–1831 – Influence.
2. Kojève, Alexandre, 1902–1968. Introduction à la
lecture de Hegel. I. Title.
B2948.C66 1983   193   C83-099039-9

A note on the cover: 'The owl of Minerva spreads its wings only with the
falling of the dusk' (see p 245).

This book has been published with the help of
a grant from the Social Science Federation of Canada,
using funds provided by the Social Sciences and
Humanities Research Council of Canada, and a grant from
the Publications Fund of University of Toronto Press.

Contents

Preface

This essay originated in an earlier study I did on Merleau-Ponty. One fine day, about half-way through, the sun came out, and I saw that Kojève's lectures on Hegel were very important. They also provide the intellectual horizon for much of Sartre's work and also for Camus's *The Rebel*. But I was attracted to Kojève by more than his intrinsic importance. For some time the dispute between Kojève and Leo Strauss about a forgotten text of a forgotten classical writer had been a source of puzzlement. Like many Canadians, I read as much as I could of George Grant's writing. What he had said of Kojève and Strauss added to my interest in Kojève. I had long been curious about Strauss and his pupils and thought that I might gain some understanding of Strauss's work from reading one of the few critics of Strauss from whom one might learn anything. And finally, I had been successful in the past at finding a place at the table set by the Canadian and French governments for academics with a taste for the intellectual banquets served by each other's countrymen. That is, fortune, in several senses, was important in seducing my attention to Kojève. I believe this happens a lot.

The origins, then, were unsystematic. The result, at least in intention, is less so. It is first of all about the contemporary world and how to understand it. Next it is about Kojève's book on Hegel. Finally it is about Hegel. This is why there is a wide variation in the number of notes to each chapter: I have been most thorough about contemporary evidence and least about scholarly disputes centred upon recondite aspects of Hegel's text. The premise, which is tested or justified by the essay as a whole, is that Hegel, as interpreted by Kojève, makes sense of our present social and political life in a systematic and comprehensive way. Whether our present social and political life can make sense of any kind, of course, is quite another matter. I happen to think it can. Reading Kojève has helped me come to that understanding. End of apology.

There are a few technical questions that should be mentioned. Capitalization is always a problem when moving from German conventions to English ones. I have written in English. From time to time when a peculiar German or French word or phrase is important for the argument I have included it. Translation is always interpretation, and this concession to pedantry simply acknowledges as much. In the text, the first page reference to works cited in the list of abbreviations is to the original edition, and the second is to the translation, if there is one. Where both the English and the original are numbered by paragraphs, only one reference is given. I also consulted the old translation of Hegel's *Phänomenologie des Geistes* by J.B. Baillie, *The Phenomenology of Mind* [1910] (New York: Harper Torch Books, 1967). In some ways it is superior to Miller's version since Baillie was alive to the religious sensibilities of Hegel.

Thanks are owed not only to the taxpayers of Canada and France, but also to numerous friends and several classes of students who, I am sure, have grown weary of the end of history, a response that is perfectly meet. Leah Bradshaw, Zdravko Planinc, Tom Darby, Brian Metcalfe, and Debbie Samuel Hobson have been especially helpful in their remarks on various aspects of the text. I have also benefited from conversations with Abraham Rotstein, Ed Andrew, and George Grant. I met neither Kojève nor Strauss. Several of their acquaintances, many of whom knew them both, answered my impertinent questions. I would like to thank in particular Nina Ivanoff, Jean Cassou, Stanley Rosen, Pierre Labourie, Georges Canguilhem, Pierre Berteaux, Rayond Aron, Jacques d'Hondt, Mme Pierre Kaan, Gaston Fessard sj, and Allan Bloom. As ever, George Blount, Bobsy, and Jake made their own distinctive contributions. From Pokhara toward Anapurna and the gleaming Fish-tail, Machhapuchare, I talked with Charles Taylor on high-altitude Hegelian themes and learned that disagreements and resistances were also a way toward the sunlight. Larry MacDonald and John Parry scrubbed away editorially, and I am grateful.

BC
May 1983

Abbreviations

Dok   G.W.F. Hegel, *Dokumente zu Hegels Entwicklung*, ed J. Hoffmeister, Stuttgart, Fromann, 1936

GA I   Aleksandr Solzhenitsyn, *The Gulag Archipelago, 1918–1956. An Experiment in Literary Investigation*, vol I, tr Thomas P. Whitney, New York, Harper & Row, 1973

GA II   Ibid vol II, tr Thomas P. Whitney, New York, Harper & Row, 1975

GA III Ibid vol III, tr Harry Willetts New York, Harper & Row, 1976

HPW   *Hegel's Political Writings*, tr T.M. Knox, Oxford, Clarendon, 1964

IH   Alexandre Kojève, *Introduction à la lecture de Hegel*, Paris, Gallimard, 1947 *Introduction to the Reading of Hegel* tr James H. Nichols jr, ed Allan Bloom New York, Basic Books, 1969

Lev   Thomas Hobbes, *Leviathan*, ed M. Oakeshott, Oxford, Blackwell, n.d.

OT   Leo Strauss, *De La Tyrannie*, Paris, Gallimard, 1954 *On Tyranny*, Ithaca, Cornell University Press, 1963

PhG   G.W.F. Hegel, *Phänomenologie des Geistes*, ed J. Hoffmeister, Hamburg, Meiner, 1952 *The Phenomenology of Spirit*, tr A.V. Miller, Oxford, Oxford University Press, 1977

RPhil G.W.F. Hegel, *Grundlinien der Philosophie des Rechts*, Frankfurt, Suhrkamp Verlag, 1970 *Philosophy of Right*, tr T.M. Knox, Oxford, Clarendon, 1952

VPG   G.W.F. Hegel, *Vorlesungen über die Philosophie der Geschichte*, Stuttgart, Philipp Reclam, 1961 *The Philosophy of History*, tr J. Sibree, New York, Dover, 1956

THE END OF HISTORY

French Revolution. Trace back the ideas and it becomes the consummation of history.

Lord Acton, University Library, Cambridge. Add. mss, 4922

Je sais bien que... toute notre époque – que ce soit par la logique ou par l'épistémologie, que ce soit par Marx ou par Nietzsche – essaie d'échapper à Hegel... Mais échapper réellement à Hegel suppose exactement ce qu'il en coûte de se détacher de lui ; cela suppose de savoir jusqu'où Hegel, insidieusement peut-être, s'est approché de nous ; cela suppose de savoir, dans ce qui nous permet de penser contre Hegel, ce qui est encore hégélien ; et de mesurer en quoi notre recours contre lui est encore peut-être une ruse qu'il nous oppose et au terme de laquelle il nous attend immobile et ailleurs.

Michel Foucault, Leçon inaugurale

'You can blame me for Alexander and Caesar, the Hohenstaufens and Teutonic Knights, even for Napoleon and Wilhelm II, but not for Hitler and Stalin. There I disclaim responsibility. Their crimes were none of my doing. The present is not mine. My book is closed; my history is done.'

At that I cried, 'No friend Flounder. No! The book goes on, and so does history.'

Günter Grass, The Flounder

Dr. Sherman A. Thomas, the Washington, D.C. physician who was accused of killing a Canada goose with a golf club on the 17th green of the Bethesda Country Club in May, has been fined $500 for violating federal hunting laws. As Thomas paid the fine by check at a Baltimore courthouse, he mystified the court clerk with this cryptic remark: 'This is the end of history. Do you want to handle history?'

Boston Globe, 17 August 1979

Introduction

The following study is an essay, an imperfect and partial composition, but suitable for the present topic. The usual scholarly paraphernalia can be minimized, subtle qualifications and second thoughts may be dispensed with. An essay presents a point of view, not new information. It pushes investigation and argument to an extreme, and it does so in a mood of great confidence.

The essay is centred on one book, Alexandre Kojève's *Introduction à la Lecture de Hegel*. Kojève's book consists chiefly in a detailed commentary on Hegel's *Phänomenologie des Geistes*. Scholars have disputed Kojève's interpretation. It is not balanced. It is not fair. It is a wilful distortion of Hegel's meaning, a cunning reading that finds in the text what the commentator put there. None of that concerns us directly. The Hegel scholars are probably correct to say that Kojève has vulgarized Hegel. So far as political science is concerned, that is not necessarily a fault, nor does it detract from the value of his argument. Perhaps, however, the scholarly detraction of Kojève's interpretation is but the reflection of self-righteous anger at the desecration of a mystery.

Hegel has, for a long time, been considered as one full of secrets. A modern commentator on his language, for example, remarked that Hegel's argument called into question the traditional understanding of what philosophic discourse is.[1] It has been said, quite rightly I think, that Hegel wrote in code. Kojève's importance in this regard is that he decoded Hegel.[2] By turning Hegel's encoded wisdom into a straightforward, almost common-sense idiom, Kojève has made it widely accessible. Now it may be judged, mocked, laughed at, hated, by nearly anyone. Moreover, Kojève showed on sound Hegelian grounds (cf *PhG* 58–9:44–5) why this is an appropriate fate for Hegel's teaching. As much as possible, therefore, I avoid the question of whether his decoding is valid. An essay, unlike the science of wisdom, is not incomplete for being founded on an unexamined premise. The initial premise of this study is that Kojève's interpretation is sound. One of the purposes of this essay is, as it were, to decode Kojève, to turn Kojève's allusions and suggestions into a coherent argument, to secularize the mystery of Kojève and expose the prose behind his poetic charm and extravagant irony.

The thesis is that Kojève's account of Hegel is coherent and comprehensive. What it accounts for is modern self-consciousness. That is, the content of Kojève's interpretation expresses the self-understanding of modernity. It presents the aims and premises of the modern world. What we are concerned with, then, is not so much Hegel, the great German philosopher and man of letters, as the extent to which Kojève's interpretation brings to light specific aspects of contemporary, modern life that otherwise might be overlooked. As one of the most competent and judicious Hegel scholars has said, 'One finds in Kojève's work the Hegelian reflection of *contemporary* thought.'[3] One should ask, therefore, not whether Kojève has got his Hegel right, but whether contemporary modern life, especially political life, is post-historical in Kojève's sense. During the course of the argument it is assumed that readers are intelligent enough to draw the obvious conclusions. Not until the final chapter is any extended attention devoted to the contemporary manifestations of Hegel's political science. The greater part of the study is a presentation and justification of Kojève's interpretation by reference to Hegel's texts. In this introduction, only the briefest hint may be given to indicate that the enterprise is not utterly futile.

Surely the topic, the end of history, appears bizarre. Some preliminary clarifications are therefore in order. The term does not refer to the extinction of the species, universal entropy, or any similar state of affairs. 'To exit from history,' wrote Henri Lefebvre, 'at the theoretical level, is first of all to turn back towards history in a general retrospective; it is to *totalize* history by thought; it is to take up once more *historicity* itself, and yet as a matter that has been overcome.'[4] The end of history is a theoretical or interpretative matter involving a certain way of thinking; it has been discussed at some length, and a conventional vocabulary has been agreed upon.[5] Thought, and its manifestation or appearance as discourse, are understood to be a Hegelian 'act of negation.' Thought 'negates' finite things by turning them into concepts, the proper medium of discourse. Philosophy is the coherent and systematic accumulation of ever more general concepts, which is to say, a speech or discourse. If *all* concepts and *all* philosophical discourse are intelligibly integrated, one has thereby elevated a series of discontinuous and multiple (philosophical) speeches into aspects, or parts, or moments of a single, de-finite, de-terminate system, which, it is also agreed, is called wisdom. In his 'dialogue' with Lefebvre, Kostas Axelos was even more explicit: history was over because 'everything having been said, in a certain language ... is there anything still to say? And in what language?'[6] The logic of the problem is then straightforward: having negated finitude (that is, nature, time, human action and passion, history, etc), discourse can transform these phenomena into concepts, which are integrated as moments of the system. Everything having been said and done, these doings and sayings may be totally accounted for in the one system of science or wisdom.

Scholarly readers of Hegel have often pondered the effects of Hegel's 'ladder to the absolute standpoint' (*PhG* 25ff:15ff). Hans-Georg Gadamer, for example, noted that a careful reading of Hegel's text 'has the remarkable consequence that precisely that which one extracts in painstaking attempts at interpretation of the section which one is reading, is stated explicitly in the next section. Every reader of Hegel has this experience: the more he explicates the content of a particular train of thought which he has before him, the more certain he can be that the explication will follow in the next section of Hegel's text.'[7] After about six hundred pages the text comes to an end and everything is explained, including the beginning. Indeed, the end is a return to the beginning.

For Kojève and for wise Hegelians everywhere, this circularity is proof of Hegel's wisdom: nothing is outside, nothing is excluded, everything is taken care of. Hegel scholars, however, have raised objections. In her recent book, for example, Judith Shklar wrote: 'Hegel offers no argument for or against any of his selections, choices, and imputations. We can take or leave his account of the experiences of consciousness.' She criticized Hegel for leaving us 'at the end of an era.' This was said to be a mistake because 'the actualization of knowledge, the creation of unity in social action, was still in the future of the "world-spirit." Behaviour had not yet caught up with knowledge. It evidently has not done so yet.' Kojève would disagree. The task of behaviour is not to catch up with knowledge; knowledge makes sense of behaviour, that is, shows or brings to light its reasonableness. Moreover, while Hegel left us at the end of an era, he did not err, because in fact he left us at the end of the final era, when the world-spirit had been fully unfolded and so had no future. Knowledge and social action, wisdom and power, would henceforth be united. Shklar, however, could imagine Hegel in error because she considered history 'the imposition of present, self-generated concepts and purposes upon a chosen past.' Consequently, she feared 'a threat of arbitrariness' and sought salvation 'from that danger by the communal character of both the recollected past and the activity of remembering it.'[8] The obvious Kojèvian response would be that, while truth is one, errors are multiple: no wonder Shklar preferred communal pluralism.

In a similar vein, Gadamer noted that post-Hegelian philosophy must take place outside the Hegelian circle of wisdom. According to him, it has taken place largely outside what is commonly called philosophy, and certainly outside academic philosophy. Gadamer mentioned Schopenhauer and Kierkegaard, Marx and Nietzsche, along with the great novelists and poets. But *were* they outside the circle of science? 'Concisely stated, the issue here is whether or not the comprehensive mediation of every conceivable path of thought, which Hegel undertook, might not of necessity give the lie to every attempt to break out of the circle of reflection in which thought thinks itself.'[9] More explicitly, Gérard Lebrun said it was impossible to judge Hegel's discourse except on Hegelian terms; Roger Garaudy maintained the opposite, that remaining within the circle was a sure way to avoid understanding.[10] These are difficult hermeneutical problems. Fortunately, they can be avoided, or at least postponed, by making the assumption indicated above: Hegel's discourse is a complete and self-perpetuating activity that follows from itself. There is no creation from nothing, as in the Biblical myth. Rather creation, or the whole of being, includes nothing. Hegel's account of the whole, then, is without presupposition, complete, and eternal. There are certain difficulties with the shining concept of completed and perfected discourse, but they are merely logical. Since they touch the present topic hardly at all I discuss them briefly in the epilogue, for it is by no means obvious that humans require logically coherent discourse to interpret their own doings to themselves. I contend, in short, that the end of history is a symbol fully adequate to express the meaning of our present age.

A second aspect of the end of history concerns the genesis and nature of the final, perfect, and complete regime described by Hegelian science. In common with many others, Hegel organized a vast amount of historical data on a single line of time that issued in the virtual, if not actual, present. His argument provides a more or less coherent account of the entirety of Western (and now ecumenic) political and spiritual development. Accordingly, it is a major component in our contemporary self-understanding and our contemporary self-consciousness. It is difficult to deny that we habitually and unthinkingly interpret our own history as the development of freedom. Conventionally we begin the story in the ancient Near East (with perhaps a brief glance at the exotica of the Far East) and proceed to Greece, Rome, medieval Christendom the Italian renaissance, the Protestant reformation, the Enlightenment, the French Revolution, and its aftermath. We do not usually reflect on the form in which the argument is cast: we do not wonder whether it makes sense to talk of meaning revealing itself (or being brought to light by us) in terms of a plausibly constructed (or discovered) single line of time. Normally, we do not raise the question of whether we construct, that is, invent, this time-line or discover an already existing one. If historical sequence is not meaningful, one might ask, what is? A more tractable question to consider concerns the easy placement of ourselves in the aftermath of the French Revolution. In doing so we assume, as did Hegel, the meaningfulness of historical sequence.

Hegel's most accessible work, *The Philosophy of History*, ended with an account of the empirical triumph of liberalism. Now, the task of a Hegelian sage is to account for the historical rationality of the actually existing world. Kojève and, for the sake of discussion, the present author and reader can adopt the role and continue the story to include events after 14 November 1831, when Hegel, the first and paradigmatic sage, died. That is one meaning of the Hegelian 'we' about which scholars have disputed.[11] Liberalism, however, is not the clearest of concepts. Perhaps one should not call it a concept at all but rather a collection of opinions that optimally expressed a complex of sentiments at the time of its origin but subsequently was overtaken by events. In this way, liberalism has been forced to change and alter its content in order to reveal the meaning of a new configuration of events as being contiguous with the earlier, optimally true, opinion. The original political liberal calling himself by that name was a member of a constitutional party in the Spanish parliament of 1812 who was opposed to the restoration of the old regime. The same decade saw the introduction of the term 'conservative' by Chateaubriand. Later revolutionary shocks overwhelmed both conservatism and restoration as plausible political ideas. Under the impact of the industrial revolution, the revolutions of 1848, European imperialism, the Russian and Nazi revolutions, the revolution of rising expectations, and so forth, liberals, in the nineteenth-century sense, have taken the role originally played by conservatives. It seems quite reasonable, then, to argue that liberalism, whether in its nineteenth- or twentieth-century form, is a phase of a continuing revolutionary movement. The dramatic beginning of that movement is 1789.

So far as its spiritual content is concerned, liberalism holds that dogmatic intellectual authority in matters of religion and science restricts knowledge. Hence there must be a separation of church and state, with religious practice having the status of a private activity, like golf. Politically, liberalism is opposed to executive encroachment upon the judiciary or upon the legislative branch. A liberal constitution, therefore, is characterized by an authentic (though not necessarily legal) separation of powers. Socially, a liberal is offended by the privileges granted under the old regime to members of the clergy and to the nobility; one's position in a liberal society is to be a reflection of one's achievement, of the actualization of one's potentialities. This is done chiefly within that sphere of life Hegel identified as civil society. But it is exactly here that liberals are opposed by socialists, who point out the contradiction between the aspirations of liberalism and the result: a class society where certain members are prohibited from actualizing their potentialities. The liberal replies that this is an abuse no different in principle from the abuses of the old regime. Thus, one finds a stalemate so far as principles are concerned, and debate turns upon tactics.

The opposition between liberalism and socialism (including Marx's variety of socialism) is not, by this account, fundamental. Tactical differences may be profound and the pragmatic results may even be violent, but that is not in itself evidence of fundamental disagreement. A fundamental disagreement would be involved, for example, if one side upheld the privileges of the nobility or of the clergy or denied that the highest goals in life could be gained by self-actualization. Indeed one might say that a fundamental disagreement would call the entire realm of politics and worldly activity into question as the source and purpose of human meaning. As Leo Strauss has observed, 'The conservatism of our age is identical with what originally was liberalism, more or less modified by changes in the direction of present-day liberalism. One could go further and say that much of what goes now by the name of conservatism has in the last analysis a common root with present-day liberalism and even with Communism.'[12] What present-day conservatives, present-day liberals, and present-day socialists share are not simply common roots in the modern break with antiquity, but a common goal as well. The utter implausibility of creating a regime the political principles of which offended those of the French Revolution is what makes Hegel's political argument the sole context for debate, and what makes all subsequent political discussion confined to tactics. One again assumes, of course, the comprehensiveness of Hegel's discourse, at least to the extent that Hegel has provided the most complete and coherent account of the contemporary political world. Whether one is in favour of or against the regime that Kojève called the universal and homogeneous state is a matter of indifference if the principles of this liberal-conservative-socialism exhaust all reasonable grounds for discussion.

It would clearly be an exaggeration to say that Kojève is unknown to English-speaking political science. Yet it is certainly true that his is a familiar name only to specialists and to a small circle, many of whose members were pupils, or pupils of pupils, of Leo Strauss. Kojève was more widely known in France, though as late as 1961 Amié Patri found it necessary to throw light on the 'unknown Superior' of progressive Parisian intellectuals.[13] A short biographical note is therefore in order.

Aleksandr Kojevnikoff was born in Moscow in 1902. He left the Soviet Union at age 18 to study philosophy at Heidelberg and Berlin and received his doctorate in 1926. He studied with, or at least listened to, Jaspers, Husserl, and Heidegger; he travelled extensively in Italy studying art history and in 1928 arrived in Paris to begin the study of Eastern religions, especially Buddhism, at the École pratique des hautes études. During the ten or so years following his departure from Russia Kojève had been supported by a wealthy uncle. When his relative's business went bankrupt, necessity forced Kojève to earn his bread, and he accepted a teaching post in 1930 at the École. Until the outbreak of war he expounded Hegel's *Phenomenology* and pursued more or less orthodox academic activities. He reviewed books for the new and philosophically exciting *Recherches philosophiques*, published the occasional article, and with Henri Corbin translated *Die Sozialistische Idee* of Henri de Man into French after it had been banned in Germany.

His lectures on Hegel are rightly celebrated. Stanley Rosen has written, correctly in my view, that 'one can say with no fear of exaggeration that Kojève's interpretation of Hegel is among the two or three most important of our century and in my opinion among that of others, perhaps the best single work ever written on Hegel.'[14] It was, moreover, influential: 'Through his Paris lectures on the *Phänomenologie des Geistes* he bound two decades of French philosophizing to Hegel and, in general, left a stronger mark on Hegel research than, for instance, Croce, with his distinction between the living and the dead in Hegelian philosophy.'[15] Among Kojève's auditors were the most innovative and intelligent minds of his generation: Raymond Aron, Jean-Paul Sartre, Georges

Bataille, Alexandre Koyré, Maurice Merleau-Ponty, Brice Parain, Jacques Lacan, Raymond Polin, Raymond Queneau, Rogert Caillois, Pierre Klossowsky, Pierre Uri, Robert Marjolin, André Breton, Gaston Fessard SJ, Tran duc-Thao.

Following the defeat of France, Kojève was demobilized from the army. From 1941 to 1944 he lived in Marseilles where he joined the resistance. He served as a liaison and courier for the group 'Combat.' He did not serve in the maquis, the armed resistance, though his work involved great personal risk. He also undertook propaganda operations directed against Asiatic troops from the Soviet Union whom the Nazis had been able to recruit but whom they did not entirely trust and so used only as occupation forces. Evidently Kojève was adept at recruiting these 'Mongolians,' as they were called, as well as other Russian soldiers, to desert and joint the resistance.[16] After the war, Robert Marjolin persuaded him to join the Ministère de l'Économie et des Finances. His work took him to North Africa, the Middle East, eastern Europe, and Japan. Raymond Aron said he was the *éminence grise* of the ministry; certainly he was an important negotiator.[17] Kojève died in Brussels on 3 June 1968, following an address to the delegates to the GATT negotiations. He was a chevalier of the Legion of Honour.

Finally in this introduction I should say something about the organization of this essay. It is in many ways a large sandwich. The filling, chapters 3 through 6, deals with Kojève's discussion. However, I begin in chapter 1 with a sketch of what I understand modernity to mean. There are countless definitions of modernity and modernism around, and reference could be made to any number of poets, painters, songwriters, philosophers, historians, or what-have-you for evidence to uphold one's preference. A political scientist, however, is in part at least constrained by a received tradition. And in any case I believe that one of the important tasks of political science is to connect the non-discursive practices of public men to the discursive practices of political thinkers. Obviously political actors reflect upon policy and sometimes commit their reflections to print. One can learn a great deal about Canadian politics, for example, from reading Mackenzie King's *Industry and Humanity* or by examining the written works of Pierre Trudeau. So much is common sense. In addition, however, there are great texts that express the experience of great minds. These works illuminate much more than the concerns of the hour. Of this class of writing the greatest example in the English language is Hobbes's *Leviathan*. Like all writing, it is a product of circumstance; but it is also a work that still expresses much of our current experience. The most important political aspect of that experience, I believe, is the advent of totalitarian political practice, a novel political regime, as Hannah Arendt argued, but one whose essential features were indicated in *Leviathan*. I begin, then, with Hobbes as the theorist of political modernity and, as it were, a prelude to the song of Kojève's Hegel.

Chapter 2 introduces Kojève. It has become more or less widely known that Kojève had a great influence. It is less well known that he developed his interpretation of Hegel within a peculiar and unusual academic context. In this chapter, then, I discuss his work in the 1930s as a specific response to a set of problems raised in an incomplete way first by Jean Wahl and then more adequately by Alexandre Koyré. By the standards of the day Wahl and Koyré were brilliant and imaginative in their approach to Hegel. Kojève's resolution of the problems they were intelligent and sensitive enough to discover was stunning and audacious, evidence, I believe, of his authentic greatness.

Kojève, I said, was the centre, the filling of the sandwich. Hobbes is a beginning, one of the pieces of bread. If Kojève's interpretation is sound, it ought to be able to account satisfactorily for our contemporary present. The other piece of bread reviews three prominent features of post-Hegelian political practice: the emergence of multinational enterprises as the successors to nineteenth-century colonial imperialism, the system of Soviet concentration camps, and the supersession of them both in the technological society. Other interpretations of these phenomena are, of course, possible. Some, indeed, may be more persuasive. But I know of none comprehensive enough to integrate these admittedly diverse phenomena into a believable configuration of meaning. This is no more than one ought expect from a discourse that claims to unite what is actual and what is rational.[18] In chapter 8, then, I endeavour to give a believable Hegelian or Kojèvian interpretation of our present actuality.

All discourses, it seems, are limited. In a brief epilogue I try to show the limitations of Kojève's interpretation. These limitations do not cast doubt on the original premise, that Kojève's Hegelianism is a comprehensive account of modernity. On the contrary, the limitations of Kojève's interpretation express, I believe, the limitations of modern self-understanding. If we refuse to take refuge in the discourses of the past, if we refuse to pretend, for example, that we are polis-dwelling pagans or subjects of the *sacrum imperium*, then we must come to understand the truth of our existence by way of our modernity. That means, I believe, that we must understand the meaning of the Gulag, of atomic weapons, of microprocessors, quark flavours, and McDonald's restaurants. One way – and I do not say the *only* way – is to proceed by way of Kojève and his limitations. Nothing is gained by understanding modernity from the outside except moral superiority and the fraudulence of a good conscience.

1

The legacy of Hobbes

It has become a commonplace, a platitude, to describe or deplore the crisis of 'our times,' of 'modernity,' of 'western civilization,' and so on. To be modern apparently means that what is new is preferred to what is old and that what is constructed by human beings is more meaningful than what was once thought to be given by nature or by God.[1] Adopting the modern attitude allows one to consider one's self as autonomous, independent of nature (or God), and free to create whatever meanings one will. The intellectual vision of modernity is most perfectly expressed by the term 'science,' which connotes technical mastery resulting in a human regime of freedom. What is indicated by the term 'crisis,' however, is not first of all this vision and the complex of sentiments, attitudes, arguments, and hopes that make it a reasonable object of belief. Rather, it is the disproportion between the vision or model and the experienced reality of everyday modern life.

A problem therefore arises: either the vision of modernity cannot be achieved or the present achievement brings to light aspects of modernity that were previously unnoticed or obscured. Placing the accent on the first formulation, one may conclude that, since mastery over nature (or God) cannot be obtained, neither can the sought-for regime of freedom. Placing the accent on the second, one may conclude that what mastery we have gained must be partial, that partial mastery results in the devastation and depredation of what once was indicated by the term 'nature' (or by 'impiety' with respect to God), and that the political regime resulting from this activity is sterile, narcissistic, empty, nihilist, tyrannical, etc., even while celebrating itself as free. Either approach indicates a crisis. Taken together they indicate the general interpretative strategy used in this essay: an argument may be judged not only by its coherence and logic, but also by its vulgar, public consequences. The more vulgar the consequences, the easier it is to establish the meaning of an argument. By looking to the consequences of an action one also may learn whether its justification in speech is simply an ideological pretext, an uncritical opinion, an outright fantasy, a secret doctrine, or in fact a common-sense observation or genuine theoretical insight.

No doubt the most vulgar and public fact of this century is the number of human deaths caused by human beings. The actual number, around 100 million, is comparable only to deaths caused by plague or disease. This parallel may lead one to embrace a comforting fatalism: having gained some control over the violence of nature, one may believe that some unknown god has mysteriously compelled human beings to produce directly a massive number of corpses in ghastly tribute. One must not, however, invoke such gods prematurely, that is, before attempting to understand the matter. Here one turns for guidance to the work of Hannah Arendt, of contemporary political scientists the one most devoted to common sense. In *The Origins of Totalitarianism*, she described in an uncompromising way the political face of the contemporary crisis, the new regime of modern political man.[2]

Totalitarianism

Arendt emphasized two constituent elements, anti-semitism and imperialism. The sheer stupidity and ugliness of anti-semitism is not of importance here, but its relationship to nineteenth-century nation-states. The chief contradiction of modern republican regimes is between formal, legal, and political equality, and social or class inequality.[3] All citizens were equal as citizens, but the most important status in one's life was economic or social and was defined by one's class and its hierarchic relationship to other classes. Jewish existence as a group in society, however, could occur within any class; equally anomalous, the political position of Jews was specially defined either by certain privileges or by specific emancipation laws. That is, unlike other groups, Jews were defined mainly by politics and not by society. By the end of the eighteenth century the aristocracy, especially on the continent, was no longer able or willing to act as the ruling political class. No other existing class took its place. Politically speaking, the nobility, content in attending to its economic interests, behaved like the bourgeoisie. The consequences were, first, that the split within the political community between the state and society widened and, second, that the state transformed itself into a large-scale economic enterprise. Since the bourgeoisie (which included, for present purposes, the nobility) was devoted to 'private enterprise' rather than state finance, the Jews alone were available to finance initial state activity. In return, the state granted protection and privilege. Beginning in the mid-nineteenth century, and increasingly with later imperialist expansion, the rational calculative bourgeois came to see that their own private interests were tied up with those of the state. Accordingly, when the state became economically interesting, the position of Jews in state finance was altered. More important, however, when succeeding strata of the bourgeoisie came into conflict with the state, whether over the interest of the state in regulating their affairs or over their interest in taking over profitable state affairs, they became anti-semitic 'because the only social group which seemed to represent the state were the Jews.'[4] Beginning in the mid-nineteenth century with the nobility, anti-semitism eventually was adopted by the masses of poorer bourgeois. The twentieth-century consequences are well known.

The role of the bourgeoisie in the second constituent element of totalitarianism, imperialism, was equally important.[5] The historical dynamics are clear enough. The bourgeoisie aspired to direct political power only when the established structures showed themselves unable fully to serve bourgeois interests in an expanding economy. 'Expansion,' the key term, fit or expressed the reality of industrial growth, the ever-increasing production of consumer goods and services. 'Imperialism,' Arendt wrote, 'is not empire building and expansion is not conquest.'[6] Territorial acquisition was not followed by political integration, and the inhabitants of the acquired territories were not turned into citizens. What was gained for the imperialist bourgeoisie was simply freedom to operate upon raw materials, some of them natural, some of them human, some for production, some for consumption, and some indeed even for the defence of the former homeland. However, there were limits to freedom and expansion. As we now know, but as our predecessors apparently did not, it is possible to reach a material limit to growth. At first, though, the limits were political.

The goal of imperialist businessmen was not short-term looting and plunder and certainly not assimilation, but the acquisition of endless business opportunities. The novelty of the overriding principle of imperialism, that expansion was the highest political goal, was a result of its being derived from the sphere of economic activities. To an earlier age, sheer expansion and growth would not have been political principles at all. It should occasion no surprise, then, that the activities of business-

men, which gave historical force to the new principles, were in conflict
with the existing historical form of the nation-state, which was based on
the notion that its citizens constituted a coherent people living within a
known and stable legal structure. When the alternatives appeared to be a
tremendous loss of national wealth or a vast increase, it does not seem
mysterious that national governments were persuaded to export domestic instruments of violence on behalf of these same businessmen. That is,
the contradiction between imperialism and the existence of the nation-
state was not immediately obvious since the new formulas were first put
into operation overseas. Yet, in trying to serve the nation's interest, governments created a new class of armed and unarmed bureaucrats, legally
and physically removed from other national institutions. Let loose upon
the world, these new power-brokers were completely incapable of founding external political regimes.[7] Their aim, like that of the imperialist
businessmen, was expansion moderated by no overriding interest or
limit. It took the form of unlimited acquisition of power rather than of
capital, but the two goals were in no way incompatible. Power became
the most important category of political thought when it was exported
from the nation it was to serve; its unlimited expansion, initially in the
hands of expatriate administrators, was the first expression of bourgeois
rule. Moderation, therefore, became the political virtue most conspicu-
ously absent.

The political emancipation of the bourgeoisie through the imperialist
movement had several additional implications. Content with any state
that protected its property, the bourgeoisie tended historically to support
essentially a police state, Kant's 'night watchman.' Anything more than
the police (and the armed forces) amounted to interference with the
highest goals of life and was in any case unproductive and wasteful, the
appropriate object for righteous resentment. Now, the essential feature
of police or military rule is that it governs by administrative fiat directly
backed by violence rather than by law and the visible responsibility of
speech, argument, and political assembly. Accordingly, bourgeois imperialist rule became government by bureaucratic decree. The great advantage of rule by decree is its unambiguous, imperative mood. Moreover,
the anonymity of its origin coupled to the absence of any mediation
between justification and application provides the administrator with
unparalleled efficiency in exacting compliance. There could be no argument because there is no information to base it on: rules are rules. They
can be followed or broken, not discussed.

Those to whom rules were initially applied were natives. Though there is no logical connection between racism and administration, it is understandable that the overseas bureaucrats saw themselves fated by nature or by history to rule their racial inferiors.[8] Just as in the formation of the new bodies politic administrative regulation began to replace the legal and constitutional structure of the state, so race took the place of nationality. The process of administrative racism was most advanced in the non-European world, but it turned out to be a temporary measure, an expedient justification for repression of natives made necessary by still-imperfect administrative strategies. The odium of racial vanity and the eventually unsatisfactory (because temporary) rewards of glory and triumph over a particular population on behalf of another particular population could be overcome only by identifying one's activity with universal forces. In this way, the imperialist became a functionary of the historical process itself, the tangible result of which was immediately obvious in the extension of rules. The sole theoretical limit to expansion was provided by the globe, the *ecumene*. As in post-Hellenic times, the world was seen as an object of conquest, not the home of mankind.

A final implication of imperialist administration is that if one were seriously to search for power after power, the inherent instability of political life must result in the destruction of all political communities. But here one moves from questions of the genesis of totalitarianism to the question of its essential features.

Concentration camps, extermination camps, destructive labour camps, all have been prominent institutions in totalitarian regimes. They have long been linked to colonies and sometimes have been equated with them.[9] More is involved than a vague intuition and the knowledge that the first camps were used by British imperialists or that a policy of 'administrative massacres' was discussed as a means of retaining India within the British Empire. One need not go so far as André Glucksmann, who saw in the 'SS Archipelago' the 'despotism of manufacture and of imperial colonialism,'[10] to recognize that imperialism was at least a 'preparatory stage for coming catastrophes.'[11] Its intermediate status, moreover, allows one to identify other totalitarian elements in pre-imperialist European history. 'Read *The Gulag Archipelago* with care and one is seized with a sense of *déjà-vu* and *déjà entendu*. The countryside is depopulated, the workers are shut away, the elite is purged and trained. From the start, these are the means that each epoch has used to civilise a part of Europe.'[12] In other words, in the camps one can concentrate history and time as well as bodies and space. The greatness of the Soviet achievement in this respect is to have compressed three centuries of Western criminality into the short period of fifty years. Totalitarianism proper, then, while having certain features all its own, also expressed the perfection of those principles of rule discovered by the bourgeoisie during its imperialist phase; only now they would be directed against their authors.

The most important material condition for totalitarian rule is the availability of very large numbers of 'superfluous' or 'paranthropoid' masses.[13] Masses are not mobs, though like mobs they must be led, or rather organized, by 'strong men.' Members of a mob at least have aggregated individual (if lawless) interests; masses do not. They are isolated, resentful, embittered human beings, their selflessness born not from a sense of sacrifice but a sense that nothing, including themselves, is worth anything.

The leader is at once irreplaceable, the embodiment of a universal will, and at the same time a sheer contingent particular: anyone could do the job, anyone can succeed to it. His will, being the embodiment of universality, is always right. Or rather, the question of rightness cannot be raised since no standards of truth independent of his will exist. Yet no one is responsible for anything, not even the leader, since his will is not, properly speaking, his own, but the expression of fate. In such a regime the masses are both gullible and cynical: they are deceived and they know it, like children watching television advertising. But it hardly matters; nothing does. In any case, they are suspect, since the leader's will may change and they may start to think. There is always the possibility of a 'secret exchange of thought.'[14] The model totalitarian citizen is therefore a kind of Pavlovian bundle of responses.

Pavlov's dogs did not roam Russian streets but were carefully trained in laboratories. The human equivalent is the camp. Only there, through the instrumentalities of terror, can one actualize the genuine homogeneity needed to create and maintain the perfect mass man, 'the horizon of the deracinated, abstract, and equalized humanity, which the smiling Princes would like to make into the material of their Power.'[15] The ideal inmate, like the ideal citizen, has neither a will of his own nor the capacity to make decisions; moreover, the guards are trained equally well not to think, simply to accept 'that this was the way it had to be and that the person who gave them their orders was always right.'[16] The result for prisoners and guards alike was akin to that achieved by Pavlov: the extinction of spontaneity.

The final addition made by totalitarianism to the already impressive achievements of imperialism was to render self-conscious the principles of domination. This was the purpose of ideology.

Ideology

The term 'ideology,' a nineteenth-century neologism, seems to imply that 'ideas' can serve as the topic for *logoi*, for scientific speeches. This, however, is deceptive.[17] Where hematology is the scientific discourse about real blood or theology about real gods and not the 'idea' of blood or the gods, the ideology of race or history is not speech about real races or real histories. Nazis and Stalinists are not cultural anthropologists and historiographers. Rather, they treat an 'idea' as if it were a self-evident reality. By making deductions from it as if it were a premise, and then acting upon the deductions as if they were policy instructions, the 'proof' of the 'idea' is obtained. For example, since the Soviet system is best, without it the Moscow subway would never have been built. If one knows (or might find out) that there exists a subway in Toronto, one might begin to wonder if ways other than the Bolshevik were possible. But this cannot 'logically' be. In order for it to remain impossible, the Toronto subway must not exist. If it is destroyed, it won't. Thus, the Toronto subway must be destroyed. Or: since Poles are an inferior 'race,' they do not have fully developed intellects. This may be proved by noting the absence of a Polish intelligensia. The proof will be valid when no Polish intellectuals exist. Thus, all Polish intellectuals must be destroyed. Moreover, one may reverse the procedure: since Viet Cong soldiers follow Mao's teaching that they should move among peasants as fish in the sea, they must die when the sea dries up. Thus, the Viet Cong will be defeated when all the Vietnamese peasants are put into camps. Because the logic of deduction is endless, consistent, and eventually all-inclusive, one 'idea' is enough to explain everything that needs to be explained. It will be proof-tested against the intrusions of mere experienced realities.

Ideologies, according to Hannah Arendt, have three characteristically totalitarian features.[18] First, they are concerned with time as history, that is, with the unstable creation of meaning and not with standards or norms. All past historical events can be explained, the significance of the present can be fully known, the future reliably predicted. Of course, tomorrow the actual content of the ideology may change, but that is to be expected: tomorrow is another day, new 'truths' were forming in the dark, etc. Second, ideological deductions are abstract in the sense that the impact of actual worldly events is completely unpredictable. Ideology is independent of our ordinary perceptions of reality because it serves as the arbiter of them, fits them into a context, and endows them with meaning. Once one learns not to trust one's sense-perceptions, apparent meanings are dissolved, and everything seems to mean something else. Third, there is a moment of restoration following the dissolution just indicated. Now the facts are reordered and made consistent with the initial premise. Whether the consistency is syllogistic or dialectic is a matter of style since nothing in the world corresponds to it anyhow. By combining the element of self-generated movement with that of a single self-evident premise, this third aspect synthesizes the other two. Ideological violation of common sense and one's ordinary experience of the world would remain a human oddity but for the uncomfortable observation that movement and instability are the common and exhaustive experiences of mass life. When everything in the world seems in flux then one must seek consistency elsewhere. The purity of logical argument is an obvious place to look.

The pervasive unreality of ideology is its greatest strength. By revealing the meaning of the whole of history but at the same time acknowledging the need to undertake 'next tasks,' the conformity of ideology with actuality is indefinitely deferred, the next tasks remain, the movement continues. Ideology, then, is the immediate and direct expression of the instability of genesis. Its logical structure, however, gives it the semblance of complete immobility. It is a kind of counterfeit wisdom, the 'truth' of which is guaranteed not by the persuasive stability of its discursive contents but by a frenetic conformity exacted by violence.

Solzhenitsyn is no doubt correct to observe of ideology that it 'gives evildoing its long-sought justification and gives the evildoer the necessary steadfastness and determination ... Thanks to ideology, the twentieth century was fated to experience evildoing on a scale calculated in the millions.'[19] One may specify its nature more precisely: 'Die and die again, and cause death around you, for absolute death is the objective present of humanity.'[20] The most important practical consequence of ideology, namely death, appears in two distinct forms. The first and most explicit proceeds from the conspiratorial nature of totalitarian movements: those within the conspiracy appropriate all meaning to themselves, and those outside are 'dead' or 'dying.' Consequently, it matters not if the movement demands the actual death of one of its members: the movement embodies all life, and the member is necessarily touched with its immortality, whatever his or her personal fate. With death at the centre of its own operations, the movement necessarily is incapable of dying. The second form is made manifest by the declaration that those outside are already virtually dead, so that their actual murder is a mere formality. The execution of the opponents of the regime amounts to fulfilling the prophecy of their necessary demise. For the ideologist, the actual deaths of the 'dying' groups (Jews, Kulaks, Viet Cong) simply affords 'proof' of the 'truth.'

There is a further step. What is involved in ideological calculation is not simply a matter of killers using transparently self-serving alibis to excuse themselves. There is nothing new in that. What is new is that they invent 'enemies' precisely in order to be able to declare them 'dying' or 'dead' and so embark on the grisly process of 'proof.' Here the key factor is the claim to consistent, scientific, logical predictability. The end product of ideological deduction, which can be practically perfected only in the camps, is the extinction of plurality, thought, spontaneity, unpredictability, heterogeneity, and freedom of any kind whatsoever. Everyone in the world is a suspect because anyone might think, and who knows what their thoughts might be?

The addition of ideology to the ecumenic aspirations of imperialist expansion has the consequence of rendering unimportant the geographic limitations of the globe – or of the expanded, unearthly *ecumene* of outer space. Real geographic limits of earthly space are overcome when they are transformed into the indefinite limits of history. Ideology effects a translation of space into time and thereby appears to give a lease to indefinite expansion. Henceforth, the establishment of a totalitarian regime is an infinite historical task because its spatial universality can be taken for granted. Since it is the *sole* task of an expansionist regime, one may as easily call its purpose post-historical.

The argument concerning the genesis and nature of the crisis of 'modernity,' at least in its political form, namely totalitarianism, may be summarized as follows: when the economic drives of the bourgeoisie burst the integument of the nation-state, expansion, as Cecil Rhodes averred, became everything. The world, especially outside Europe, was conceived as raw material, unclaimed real estate that promised rich rewards if properly managed by an appropriate police procedure. The extension of the rule of Europeans over natives, who in no way could be assimilated to the European nation-state, necessarily meant their oppression as inferior 'races.' European nations were likewise transformed into 'races' so that neither ruler nor ruled were people in any political sense. Both expressed 'natural' data and the brute necessity of fate. Consequently,

the universality implied by the term 'mankind,' which extended historically to a legendary and unknown beginning and an equally unknown
end, as well as geographically to the limits of the inhabited world, was
eclipsed. It was replaced with the ersatz universality of bureaucratic gen-
erality, rule backed by violence and terror, a magical identification of
administrative action with the forces of history itself that, for the actors,
was a great spy-game of endless ulterior motives in endless movement.
And it all made perfect sense: the only way to rule without colonizing
and populating a territory is by means of armed bureaucracy; the only
principle available to justify it was racism; no criteria of right or wrong
could possibly override the inexorable orders of fate.

The political consequence for the Europeans was the end of the meaningful but limited particularity of the nation-state, of the comity of European powers, and of the intrinsic moderation of a balance among them.
The reimportation to western Europe of previously external extrava-
gances and superfluities, centred upon such matters as annihilation of
enemies or compelling them to surrender unconditionally, can be seen
easily enough as early as 1914–18. The aftermath we know only too well:
statelessness and refugee camps; the liquidation of society based on class
interests as a result of inflation, unemployment, war, and civil terror;
and its replacement with a classless society of brutalized, lonely, gullible,
anomic, resentful, alienated, suspicious masses, interested in nothing
and fit only for the impotent enjoyment of an ideological rage, the immediate intention of which is the destruction of spontaneity, and the ultimate product of which is torture and death.

Ideology and theory

The preceding sections dealt chiefly with the consequences of a specific
configuration of prior political and economic actions, with a succession
of historical phenomena and their apparent meaning. The point was
made earlier that the interpretative strategy employed in this essay is
governed by the observation that political theory and political action are
intelligibly linked. The argument has frequently been made that political
actors often follow certain 'philosophies' such as liberalism or socialism
or conservatism. Governed by a double intention of guiding political
action and of providing an interpretation of it, these 'isms' are more
accurately called 'ideologies' than 'philosophies' or 'theories.' One must
therefore distinguish between a theory and an ideology.

A first approximation would emphasize the different animating intentions. In contrast to ideology, theory has no aim beyond understanding. That is, whereas ideologies are, and understand themselves to be, elements of political reality as well as interpretations of it, theories are, and understand themselves to be, simply interpretations. It has just been argued that modern political reality, or if one prefers the modern component of contemporary political reality, is constituted by totalitarian political action and ideological self-interpretation of it. For political theory, the entire complex is an object standing in need of interpretative understanding. The relationship between political theory and political action that is emphasized here, then, is not that political actions may be inspired by theory or ideology but that theory, in part at least, is a coherent presentation of the sense or meaning of political action. That the meaning of theory is not exhausted by the foregoing remarks is suggested by the observation that, willy-nilly, the theorist too is a part of political reality. Accordingly, a theoretical interpretation may well conflict with the self-interpretation of society, whether that self-interpretation is ideological in the modern sense or not.

The conflict of interpretation is a familiar theme to political science: no one is ignorant of the fate of Socrates. The practical dilemmas of this conflict and its characteristic solutions may be summarized as follows. Under conditions of social and political upheaval, the fundamental problems of political life appear in practical form to everybody. Those are times when the insights of political scientists would be especially helpful. In fact, it is a time when such people are in the greatest physical danger. Political upheaval means that individuals fight one another; they fight not simply from sheer self-interest or the desire to dominate, but also and more importantly on grounds of reasons for their actions, opinions about the justness of their cause, and so on. For the political scientist, however, their justifications often seem to be the intellectual expressions of the disorder of the times that is made more strenuously manifest in violence. The political scientist, then, claims to see a broader world than the partisan. As proof, he can render an account of the antagonists that is more comprehensive than they can of themselves, of each other, or of him. Unfortunately, his insights are not likely to be accepted with good grace. In the excitement of violent action, the participant expects everyone to choose sides. Yet the political scientist is quite likely to refuse, because the issue does not warrant the risk of his own life, and he knows that it is the element of risk, not the nobility of his justice, that accounts for the compulsiveness of the partisan. For the partisan, on the contrary, it is easier to accept opposition than contempt, so the wider horizons of the political scientist become the occasion of a public scandal.

When the public stage is dominated by zealots ready to kill and risk their lives for their faith, the political scientist is turned into a private individual lacking an audience before which he could gain recognition for his insights. He knows that if he tried he would gain only the resentment of a disordered world that hates what it cannot understand. The safe thing to do would be to keep silent. Unfortunately, this is not always possible. Totalitarians, of course, would extinguish thought of any sort, and so actively must track it down; and ordinary tyrants seek to learn the opinions of even their passive subjects. However, the initiative may come from the other side, since, as I said, the political scientist too is a part of reality. Indeed, following this argument, he is a more vital part than the public representatives who surround him. Furthermore, his insights are not simply neutral pieces of information about the world. They have practical implications, not least of which is that the political scientist experiences an obligation to gain public recognition for his insights.

But the public is not necessarily one's contemporaries, especially when they are burning with various enthusiasms. The public indeed may not yet exist. Perhaps one's writing will contribute to its formation. Here one encounters the problem of rhetoric: how does one address a non-receptive and maybe non-existent public? This can be a delicate problem in a demotic and not particularly courageous time; historically a common way of dealing with this question of rhetoric is to write in code. Then only the few who care to read carefully, to reflect on what they have read, and to draw the intended conclusions, will constitute a public.[21] These few, one may say, are a competent public. They can recognize the political scientist's insights because, like him, they have the courage and intelligence to forsake the thrill of action in order to pursue a more astringent satisfaction. Of course, this means that they do not directly 'do' anything, in the strong sense of the term. Whether their inaction is ultimately satisfying is a question that may safely be left open.

A major contention of this essay is that Hegel was one of those who wrote in code. The sharpness of debate over the meaning of Hegelian science at least confirms the likelihood of this contention. A second contention is that Alexandre Kojève's *Introduction à la lecture de Hegel* deciphered Hegel in a way that is of particular importance to a political science concerned with the political phenomena described earlier. There is widespread scholarly agreement, to say nothing of Hegel's own words, that his political theory marked a phase of the Western crisis of which the most visible contemporary manifestation was the French Revolution. Kojève's interpretation of Hegel is contemporary with its totalitarian phase.[22] Of course there is an abyss between the active brutality of revolutionary or totalitarian politics and the work of the scholars of Jena or Paris. The time is long past when one would seriously debate whether Hegel was a Prussian chauvinist, let alone a 'contributor' to totalitarianism. My contention is different: it is that Hegel's political teaching, as interpreted by Kojève and summarized by the phrase 'the end of history,' expresses the purposes and ideals of modern civilization for both bourgeois capitalists and bourgeois socialists (including that aspect of modernity, identified as totalitarianism) with an unequalled depth, coherence, clarity, and exhaustiveness.

The assumption of the present essay is that theory is the articulation and interpretation of action. Because it transforms the doings of people into speech, it is as much a part of political reality as the actions themselves. The particular contents of any political theory, therefore, are historical because occasioned by events. But so too are the particular contents of ideology, mysticism, myth, revelation, gnosis, and magic. These forms of speech also provide a historically conditioned meaning to events. While it is true that one can trace the ultimate difference between theory and ideology to distinctive experiences, the difference stressed here is derivative, found at the discursive surface of speech rather than in its animating depths. Theoretical discourse appears both open and coherent. It is coherent in that it is not arbitrary nonsense. Things follow one from another. But the same can be said of the other forms of speech. The difference between them lies in the question of openness. In principle, nothing is prohibited, no premise cannot be questioned, no experience is excluded from consideration. This *via negativa*, this unspecifiable movement toward greater horizons, expresses the rational aim of theory. Accordingly, theoretical discourse transcends the occasion of its origin. Like all speech, it gives sense to activities that do not speak for themselves. It must, therefore, be superior or transcendent to brute, inarticulate doings. But, in addition, theoretical speech tends to transform itself into speech about speech, which in turn is about deeds. This second transcendence, which is a self-transcendence, is the distinctive feature of theory. Theory does not just express or articulate the sense of events, it justifies itself as interpretation, as speech. There is thus a double movement. From its own depth, theory provides an account of its own basis; toward its own goal, it provides an account of its own purpose. Self-justification is the equivalent of intentional self-transcendence.

These abstruse remarks have a particular application. Hegel's political science is certainly 'theory' in the sense that it aims at providing a coherent interpretation of events. Whether in addition it is open to the full range of human experiences is a central issue in all interpretations of his texts. Indeed, it is the central issue of interpretative disagreements in general. We shall leave further consideration of this question until the argument and consequences of Hegel's political teaching have been presented. One thing ought be made plain at the start: Hegel's approval or disapproval of totalitarianism is not at issue. He would doubtless dismiss such a question as moralistic nonsense anyhow.

The crisis I have repeatedly mentioned certainly originated long before Hegel's time, and Hegel was hardly the first to have noticed it. In the previous section I followed Hannah Arendt in emphasizing the political emancipation of the bourgeoisie as a major constituent element. Now, we have just argued about why political theory is likely to attain its full amplitude of a science of man in society during times of crisis. Given the focus chosen, it is fitting to turn to 'the only great philosopher to whom the bourgeoisie can rightly and exclusively lay claim, even if his principles were not recognized by the bourgeois class for a long time,'[23] namely Hobbes, to uncover in pure form the principles by which the bourgeoisie lived. As Bernard-Henri Lévy rightly observed, 'At the basis of every political philosophy known to this day, there always lurks the shadow of Hobbes, and at its conclusion, some sort of Hegelianism.'[24]

Hobbes's new political science

Contemporary with Kojève's study of Hegel, Leo Strauss published a study of Hobbes.[25] He presented Hobbes's innovations within a context of 'traditional natural law' as expounded chiefly in the political science of Plato and Aristotle. Traditional natural law, Strauss argued, was constituted by a body of precepts to which rational men owed obedience. That is, traditional natural law was a pre-existent, 'objective' order, morally binding upon human will. In contrast, modern natural law, as expounded by Hobbes,[26] originates in human will, that is, in passion coupled to imagination, and is constituted by an unstable series of 'subjective' rights, or claims, or desires. The premise of modern natural law, and with it of modern political science, is the rejection of the morality of obedience.

More was involved in this shift than a new perspective on traditional patterns of human behaviour. For example, there was no implication in traditional political science that obedience to rational precepts was ever widespread. On the contrary, it was generally acknowledged that the non-philosophical majority did not obey the principles of reason, did not love virtue, justice, goodness, beauty, etc, for their own sake but (if at all) for conventional rewards: the high opinion, esteem, and recognition they got from others for appearing to act virtuously, justly, and so on. The novelty of modern political science on this question lay in its contention that nobody, whether a philosopher or a non-philosopher, really obeyed the precepts of reason or truly conformed their actions to a pre-existent natural order. The modern argument contends not simply that men have always rejected nature, reason, and so forth. This rejection has always been part of human life. Indeed, to be disobedient was, by the standards of pre-modern political science, to reveal oneself as immoral, irrational, unjust, or perverted. The modern position is more radical: it denies that the order of nature can be grasped by reason in such a way that reason mediates human existence and guides human conduct. The modern argument roundly declares that the things to which the words referred do not exist.

This is an ontological, not just an empirical or psychological, assertion. Not surprisingly, discussion on this point is enormously complicated. One may expect, however, that whatever the merits of pre-modern political science, it is unlikely that those who rejected it were simply wicked or stupid. They may have had a point. Consider Strauss's argument: an important difference between Hobbes and Aristotle, he said at one point, can be captured by the contrast between Aristotle's remark that man is not the most excellent (*mē to ariston*) thing in the cosmos (*EN* 1141a3) with Hobbes's view that man is the 'most excellent work of nature' (*Lev* Intro, 5).[27] For Hobbes, that is, the most excellent is not an 'eternal' order, which, so to say, does not 'exist.' For Aristotle, the most excellent, apparently, is the eternal. But the eternal was never held to exist in the same way as human things do. One wonders how the two are compared, how the most excellent eternal can ever be in the same comparative context as the existing human. Whatever the non-existence of eternity is taken to be or to mean, one cannot help but be sympathetic to modern political science for doubting that it was adequately described by the term 'nature.'

This sympathy is not an index of condescending generosity. Rather, it recognizes the difficulty in accounting for non-existent realities (such as eternity) when the vocabulary of philosophic speech had turned into dogmatic hieroglyphs (*Lev* VIII 51). Fortunately we need not pursue this vexing question further: what does seem beyond controversy is that when the symbolism of nature hardened into dogma, lively minds sought meaning in history.

The search was neither simple nor devoid of contradiction. To begin with, history had not been ignored by pre-modern political science. It was used to illustrate norms or standards said already to be in existence and capable of apprehension by reason. That is, history was a servant to philosophy, rather like rhetoric in that it might be useful in persuading the non-philosophic to orthodoxy. The modern view was different. A greater interest in human over eternal things and a disinclination to believe that anybody actually lived in obedience to eternal, rationally apprehended precepts led people to see in history not just a storehouse of examples but the expression of norms. This change meant not that the 'lessons' of history were easier to obey but that obedience was unnecessary. Historical generalizations inductively apprehended could also serve as norms. Moreover, they were self-justifying because they recorded the successful actualization of aims, intentions, designs, and plans. As Strauss remarked, 'If discovery of the norms is in any way expected from history, then – explicitly or implicitly – moral goodness must have been identified with success, and virtue with prudence.'[28] Once the rules for success were formulated, the new political science was able to supersede history, to transform, abolish, and elevate it as an independent enterprise. Henceforth, political science carried its historical 'lessons' within its own concepts. In short, through its own successes, history had provided the norms of the new political science. The new political scientist was simply an onlooker, a historian who viewed the course of history and reproduced its meaning. Such a political science may properly be called the result of a historical dialectic. Its weakness, as judged by pre-modern political science, was that its norms, being unstable, were not norms at all. This is a question to which we shall return in the following chapter.

In terms of traditional natural law and traditional political science, it was nothing short of miraculous that history, the coming to be and passing away of human things, an expression of the instability of genesis, could produce of itself form, standard, and measure. Equally miraculous for the older political science was the way that order, stability, morality, and reasonableness were produced from what had been seen up to then as the chaos of passions. We shall consider first, following Hobbes's own plan in *Leviathan*, his theory 'of man,' and second, his theory 'of commonwealth.'[29]

Hobbes's anthropology

All human action or 'motion' is a mechanical response to external stimuli. Motion toward the cause of the stimulus is called 'appetite,' away from it is called 'aversion.' One loves and calls 'good' the objects of appetite, hates and calls 'evil' the objects of aversion. The mechanical superiority of humans over animals results from their greater ability to reckon and imagine, that is, to see the connections between cause and effect. Thus can they anticipate the consequences of actions and imaginatively experience appetite or aversion. The means to obtain a future apparent good by following one's appetites are called 'powers.' These may be natural and limited, such as strength, eloquence, and nobility, or, like 'riches, reputation, friends, and the secret workings of God, which men call good luck,' they may be instrumental in gaining further powers. 'For the nature of power, is in this point, like to fame, increasing as it proceeds' (*Lev* X 56). Felicity comes from success in obtaining good things, 'that is to say, continual prospering.' It is necessarily confined to this life 'because life itself is but motion,' because 'there is no such thing as perpetual tranquillity of mind, while we live here,' because the alleged joys by which God rewards the pious are unknowable so that 'the word of Schoolmen *beatifical vision* is unintelligible' (VI 39), and because death is simply the absence of desire (VIII 46). Felicity therefore cannot be 'the repose of a mind satisfied,' because such a mind would be dead. And indeed 'the old moral philosophers' were wrong to speak of an utmost end or greatest good by which desires could be ordered: instead there is only progress from one object of desire to another, with the first the means to the second.

Consequently, there are competition and contention. The final source of this contradiction is human plurality: men, not man, inhabit the world. 'And as in other things, so in men, not the seller, but the buyer determines the price. For let a man, as most men do, rate themselves at the highest value they can; yet their true value is no more than it is esteemed by others' (X 57). The first and most important inclination of human beings is 'a perpetual and restless desire for power after power, that ceaseth only in death' (XI 64). The process is endless not because desires cannot finally be sated or because men are incapable of moderation but because they cannot be assured of the power they have or of the goods they enjoy by it, save by the acquisition of more. Competition inclines to contention and war, especially competition in praise and the attaining of glory.

Men are more or less equal in physical or mental endowment, but are exactly equal in the qualities that matter—their desire or hope for good things and their ability to kill in order to get them—because the weakest has strength enough to do in the strongest, 'either by secret machination, or by confederacy with others' (XIII 80). Should two desire the same thing, either because it is necessary to their preservation or merely because they wish to enjoy it, they become enemies. Thus are men diffident one of another. Their mutual distrust can be overcome only if, by force or wiles, one of them attains mastery, eventually mastery over as many others as possible: 'This is no more than his own conservation requireth, and is generally allowed.' In addition, however, there are some, 'taking pleasure in contemplating their own power in the acts of conquest, which they pursue farther than their security requires,' whose aggressiveness poses a threat. In response, even those who 'would be glad to be at ease within modest bounds' must act to increase their power too. 'And by consequence such augmentation of dominion over men being necessary to a man's conservation, it ought to be allowed him' (XIII 81). In short, aggressive expansion follows of necessity from competition and diffidence. And finally, men quarrel over esteem or recognition. In the absence of a common power to overawe all men, they come to grief, 'for every man looketh that his companion should value him, at the same rate he sets upon himself.'

The state of war exists so long as human passions are not kept in check. War is not simply the act of fighting to the death, but includes as well 'the known disposition thereto.' Under such conditions, whether they consist in actual fighting or an attitude of competition, suspicion, and pride, life is hard. There is a diminution of industry, agriculture, trade, architecture, travel, knowledge of foreign parts, historiography, arts, letters, and social intercourse, 'and which is worst of all, [there is] continual fear, and danger of violent death; and the life of man, solitary, poor, nasty, brutish, and short' (XIII 82).[30] This state or condition of nature is not an actual historical phase in the evolution of political life but indicates rather a potential for disorder into which common life may at any time relapse when men are overcome with pride and vanity. Savages of seventeenth-century America apparently lived in that brutish manner. More importantly for non-savage man, 'it may be perceived what manner of life there would be, were there no common power to fear, by the manner of life, which men that have formerly lived under a peaceful government, use to degenerate into, in a civil war' (XIII 83). This is why people lock their doors. In any event a state of nature is often actualized in war between sovereigns, even while this same sovereignty establishes and ensures domestic order. One implication at least is clear: if men are by nature warlike, they are by nature neither just nor unjust. By nature, 'nothing can be unjust. The notions of right and wrong, justice and injustice have there no place. Where there is no common power, there is no law: where no law, no injustice. Force, and fraud, are in war the two cardinal virtues' (XIII 83). Justice, then, must be conventional, artificial, historical.

It is plain that Hobbes's analysis of competition moves far beyond the vulgarity of bourgeois desires for consumer goods. To glory in one's power means more than to enjoy abundance. The true joy for man 'consisteth in comparing himself with other men; [he] can relish nothing but what is eminent' (XVII 111). Life, in effect, is a rat race. 'But this race we must suppose to have no other goal, nor other garland, but being foremost.' In the race, 'continually to be out-gone, is misery. Continually to out-go the next before is felicity. And to forsake the course, is to die.'[31] The limit is reached when one competes with God. This is madness, pride in excess. Often it begins as inspiration: one is lucky enough to find an error in the opinion of others, 'and not knowing, or not remembering, by what conduct of reason, they came to so singular truth ... they presently admire themselves, as being in the special grace of God Almighty, who hath revealed the same to them supernaturally, by his Spirit.' When such persons combine together their madness constitutes 'the seditious roaring of a troubled nation.' At its limit the madman identifies himself with God the father (VIII 47–8).

Hobbes's idiom was theological, as was the seditious roaring of his times. The significance of his analysis was that it dissected a political myth. Very little interpretative ingenuity is needed to transform the continuum of pride, which extends from the plain madness of identifying oneself with God to the milder madness of divine inspiration, into contemporary terms where the plainly mad are political saviours and the milder ones simply profess the one and only truth.

The derivation of political order

If men were simply striving continually to out-do one another, the war of all against all would be endless. Yet men seem not to be condemned in perpetuity to an actual condition of war. We come, then, to the second major topic of Hobbes's political science, his derivation of political order, the artifice of justice and law, from man's prepolitical bellicose nature. Earlier, following Strauss, I noted that Hobbes's political science included a dialectic whereby history ceased to be a storehouse of examples and instead managed to extrude its own norms and standards. A similar dialectic, equally miraculous for traditional political science, accounts for the creation of the political community. Unlike Grotius, for example, Hobbes did not invent a convenient 'social instinct,' but relied, consistently enough, on passion. The chief passion, equal in force to pride and equally natural, is the fear of violent death at the hands of another.[32] That violent death is an evil no one denies; that it is the greatest evil presupposes that men are absolutely mortal, that death is final annihilation, and that men are equal as potential murderers.

Some of the elements in, and conditions for, the dialectic of pride and fear have already been indicated. Men are by nature vain, so they strive to out-do one another, to have their sense of superiority recognized and confirmed. Vanity is a psychic not a somatic quality, as is the feeling of superiority. It is a simple matter to imagine onself master of the world, forgetting altogether about bodies. To move beyond this subjectively certain but imaginary world, reality must intrude upon it. The real, Spinoza said, resists. Thus must the world somehow destroy vain imaginings by reminding men of the thing they, in their vanity, forgot: that they have bodies susceptible to hurt and injury. But pain alone would teach men only that they were constrained by physical limitations; their pride and vanity might well survive unimpaired. Accordingly, they must be injured spiritually or intellectually as well.

Reason, as has been explained, is for Hobbes the ability to see the connections between cause and effect, to 'reckon upon consequences.' Just as those who are blind from birth have no idea at all of light, 'and no man conceives in his imagination any greater light, than he hath at some time or other perceived by his outward senses: so also is it ... of the light of the understanding, that no man can conceive there is any greater degree of it, than that which he hath already attained unto.' Consequently, 'it comes to pass, that men have no other means to acknowledge their own darkness, but only by reasoning from the unforseen mischances, that befall them in their ways' (XLIV 397–8). That is, the limit of one's intellectual superiority, the true centre of vanity and pride, is experienced only in the breakdown of one's power of reckoning. Unforseen mischance, especially mortal danger, which is a threat to one's physical body, alone can destroy the dreams of vanity and render natural man into political man.

This dialectical supersession takes place in the following fashion. By nature, men imagine themselves superior. But they cannot know this for certain unless others acknowledge their superiority. Accordingly, they demand their superiority be appropriately recognized. If the demand is refused they are offended; if taken seriously, the other, an equal, is insulted. One or another is slighted, resents it, and seeks revenge. The reckless avenger cares not for his own life but that the other acknowledge his error and submit. It is a serious business because distinct and particular material bodies (and not simply the imagination of one of them) are in contrary motion against one another. 'From the beginning of the conflict the two opponents have, without realizing and forseeing it, completely left the imaginary world.'[33] The clash of bodies provides the sought-for resistance of reality in the form of undeniable physical pain, which eventually induces fear for one's life. Things are serious indeed. Revenge is put aside (I haven't just been insulted; he's trying to kill me!) and is replaced with hatred. Not submission but extermination is now the object of the fight. Thus does natural man stumble upon fear of violent death at another's hand; thus does the *summum malum* become the centre of coherence and order for human life, replacing the 'unintelligible' *summum bonum* of the old moral philosophers and schoolmen.

Let us consider the outcome further. Fear for his life turned one of the combatants away from the vanity of triumph. He retires, leaves victory to his foe, and preserves his life. For his part, the victor has his confirmation of superiority and for that reason finds it dishonourable to kill his now beaten and actually unequal former enemy. The honourable victor becomes master of a vanquished and dishonoured slave. As Strauss pointed out, this natural 'state,' namely despotism, is akin to that other natural 'state' patriarchy.[34] But despotic patriarchy is unstable. Nature does not replicate exactly: the issue of a courageous despot may be a coward, and dishonoured slaves may breed honourable children. Consequently, each generation seems called upon to refound the despotic regime. Or rather, since generations overlap, a despotic regime seems to imply little more than the repressive interlude in a continuing civil war.

An artificial rather than a natural state overcomes this defect. This 'commonwealth by institution' is created when *both* combatants are terrified and 'choose their sovereign ... for fear of one another' (xx 130). That is, both no longer simply and immediately see an enemy to be killed; both see the appearance of death mediated by the shape of the foe. This cathartic experience of the threat of death teaches them that it, not the human foe, is the real enemy. Their pride and vanity overcome in this way, the two former foes find themselves predisposed to trust one another in an alliance against their common enemy, the threat of violent death.

Hobbes recapitulated this argument in the vocabulary of natural law. The Right of Nature, *jus naturale*, he said, referred to the absolute freedom, derived from the natural condition of man, that an individual has to preserve his life. As this condition is never utterly abolished, even if it is superseded in an artificial state, neither is the Right of Nature ever entirely destroyed. A law of nature, *lex naturalis*, is any rule, discovered by reason, inspired by the experience of fear of death, and having as its purpose the preservation of life in society. 'It is a precept, or general rule of reason, that every man, ought to endeavour peace, as far as he has hope of attaining it; and when he cannot obtain it, that he may seek, and use, all helps, and advantages of war.' This first natural law, which is conditional, contains within it natural right, which is not. A second is like unto it: 'that a man be willing, when others are so too, as far-forth, as for peace and defence of himself he shall think it necessary, to lay down his right to all things; and be contented with so much liberty against other men, as he would allow other men against himself' (XIV 85). A transferring of rights by promissory contract is merely a moral obligation. But 'nothing is more easily broken that a man's word' (XIV 86), so that morally binding promises expressed by the laws of nature 'of themselves, without the terror of some power, to cause them to be observed, are contrary to our natural passions, that carry us to partiality, pride, revenge, and the like. And covenants, without the sword, are but words, and of no strength to secure a man at all' (XVII 109). Accordingly, everyone covenants with everyone else 'as if every man should say to every man, I authorize and give up my right of governing myself, to this man, or to this assembly of men, on this condition, that thou give up thy right to him, and authorize all his actions in a like manner.' Having done so, thereby is created 'that great Leviathan, or rather, to speak more reverently ... that *mortal god*, to which we owe under the *immortal God*, our peace and defence' (XVII 112). The one to whom rights have been so transferred is called 'Sovereign,' whether it be a single man or a larger or smaller assembly.

Central to Hobbes's analysis of the generation of Leviathan from the covenant is the concept of person. 'A *person* is he, whose words or actions are considered, either as his own, or as representing the words or actions of another man, or of any other thing, to whom they are attributed, whether truly or by fiction' (XVI 105). Persons may be natural and self-representing, or they may be artificial or feigned, as when representing the words and actions of others. Hobbes used the term with etymological strictness. The Latin *persona* and Greek *prosopon* connote appearance, mask, disguise, meanings also present in the archaic English verb *personate* and the contemporary *impersonate*.

Hobbes's purpose in taking such care in making the meaning of the term explicit is that it allowed him to separate the visible and evident plurality of bodies from the invisible realm of psychic truth. In a natural condition, the inner truth of the individual soul, namely the passions of pride and vanity, is outwardly represented by equally individual bodily conflict and verbal threat. With the creation of the Leviathan, and the transfer of natural right to the Sovereign, the inner realm of individual passion is transferred to the new person. No longer do the individual units of pride and vanity have any standing: they are all superseded by the Sovereign representative. 'For it is the unity of the representer, not the unity of the represented, that maketh the person one. And it is the representer that beareth the person, and but one person: and *unity*, cannot otherwise be understood in multitude' (XVI 107). Hence, the only way to achieve those things that reason, that is, foresight and reckoning, indicate are worth gaining, namely safety, commodious living, and equitable reward for industriousness, 'is, to confer all their power and strength upon one man, or upon one assembly of men, that may reduce all their wills, by plurality of voices, unto one will: which is as much as to say, to appoint one man, or assembly of men, to bear their person.' The one who bears the person of the many acts on their behalf and submits 'their wills every one to his will, and their judgments to his judgment. This is more than consent, or concord; it is a real unity of them all, in one and the same person.' Authorized by the covenant, to which every particular individual agreed, the universal Sovereign 'hath the use of so much power and strength conferred upon him that by terror thereof, he is enabled to form the wills of them all, to peace at home, and mutual aid against their enemies abroad. And in him consisteth the essence of the commonwealth' (XVII 112). Individual persons have dissolvd their personalities into the person of the Sovereign, creating thereby a new mystical body and fulfilling God's word to Job (41, 34): 'He beholdeth all high things: he is a king over all the children of pride.'

Religion and self-consciousness

The remainder of *Leviathan* made explicit the implications of Hobbes's evocation. One series of arguments explained the Sovereign's law. These may be summarized as a literalist's rendering of the common-law fiction that the king can do no wrong. Having transferred right to the Sovereign, a dissatisfied subject has no right of rebellion. The charge of tyranny is empty and shows no more than that the discontented are oppressed or 'mislike' their government. In sum, 'nothing the Sovereign representative can do to a subject, on what pretence soever, can properly be called injustice or injury; because every subject is author of every act the sovereign doth' (XXI 139). The universal end or purpose of the Sovereign, being the safety of the people, yet requires particular institutions to be established in service to that end. Of these, legal equality, public charity, and choice of counsellors on the basis of merit are likely to commend themselves to moderns. There are others, equally required, though less likely to receive general acclaim. For Hobbes's citizens 'it is not enough for a man to labour for the maintenance of his life; but also to fight if need be, for the securing of his labour.' Indeed, under some circumstances, 'for such as have strong bodies ... they are to be forced to work' (XXX 224–7).

A second set of arguments was directed against the chief cause of political disturbance in his day, religious factionalism. They make explicit Hobbes's intention, thinly veiled in the preceding quotation, and may be summarized as a justification of spiritual or intellectual uniformity, which, once attained, would bring peace. First Hobbes dealt with the question of worship. Reason directs men to worship God not just in secret but 'especially, in public, and in the sight of men.'[35] Moreover 'the greatest worship of all' is 'obedience to his laws, that is, in this case to the laws of nature.' Accordingly, as 'a commonwealth is but one person, it ought also to exhibit to God but one worship ... And this is public worship; the property whereof, is to be uniform' (XXXI 239–40). What makes a commonwealth Christian is the will of the Sovereign. Second, then, is the question of the institutions of worship. A church (not *the* Church) is 'a company of men professing Christian religion, united in the person of one sovereign, at whose command they ought to assemble, and without whose authority they ought not to assemble.' Any who assemble for worship or for any other purpose without warrant from the Sovereign do so unlawfully. If a church is able to command, judge, absolve, condemn, or do anything else, it is only because it is first of all a civil commonwealth consisting, *per accidens*, of Christian individuals. It is 'called a civil state, for that the subjects are men: and a Church, for that the subjects thereof are Christians.' 'Temporal' and 'spiritual' are but two words, diabolically intended 'to make men see double and mistake their lawful sovereign.' In fact, there exists 'no other government, in this life, neither of state, nor religion, but temporal' (XXXIX 305–6). Miracles are, Hobbes granted, works of God. But they are easily counterfeited by clever men, so recourse must be had to public authority to discriminate between the true and the fake. A similar though more cautious argument disposed of the political significance of any realm beyond the earthly, such as would be intended by the words 'external life, hell, salvation, the world to come, and redemption' (XXXVIII). The other side of this doctrine is that faith is untouched by persecution, being a gift of God (XLII 327).

Next in importance after public worship and the institutional status of a church is the question of scriptural (or any other) interpretation. To begin with, as the Sovereign is the sole legislator, he alone defines, by law, the canon (XXIII 246). In this same capacity, it is up to the Sovereign 'to appoint judges and interpreters of the canonical Scriptures' and to ensure that excommunication means punishment, not words. 'In sum, he hath the supreme power in all causes, as well ecclesiastical as civil, as far as concerneth actions and words, for those only are known and may be accused; and of that which cannot be accused, there is no judge at all but God, that knoweth the heart' (XLII 361). And knowledge of the heart has no political significance unless it issues in words or actions. In effect, the Sovereign's control over the interpretation of scripture is just a special case of his control of opinion. 'For the actions of men proceed from their opinions; and in the well-governing of opinions, consisteth the well-governing of men's actions, in order to their peace and concord.' Thus does the Sovereign decide what opinions and teachings are conducive to peace, who is to be allowed to address what assemblies on what topics, who is to publish what doctrines in books. None of this power can possibly interfere with truth, 'for doctrine repugnant to peace, can no more be true, than peace and concord can be against the law of nature' (XIII 116).

Two additional observations can be made, on Hobbes's destruction of religion and on his substitute for it. Religion is confined to human beings and owes its origin to specifically human qualities. These are, as we already know, the capacities for imagining and reckoning. When they are combined in such a way that the capacities for imagining what is likely (and adverse) exceed the capacity to reckon upon a successful course of action, religion is generated (XII). 'And this fear of things invisible, is the natural seed of that, which every one in himself calleth religion.' Having observed 'this seed of religion,' some men nourish it and tend its development; they give anxiety over the future a legal form and use it to rule over others (XI 69). These people are of the kingdom of darkness, 'a confederacy of deceivers, that to obtain dominion over men in the present world, endeavour by dark and erroneous doctrines, to extinguish in them the light, both of nature, and of the gospel; and so to disprepare them for the kingdom of God to come' (XLIV 397). The greatest error preached by such deceivers is that the kingdom of God is not 'to come' but already in place in the form of the church to which they belong. In fact, the kingdom of God, instituted between God and Moses, passed away with the election, by the people, of Saul (XXXV). Afterwards there was no kingdom of God in the world, nor will there be until the second coming. 'Which second coming not yet being, the kingdom of God is not yet come, and we are not now under any other kings by pact, but our civil sovereigns' (XLIV 399). In other words, if the kingdom of God has any meaning, it will appear only with the second coming. Meanwhile, anyone who presumes to speak on behalf of that kingdom is a fraud in his own right and a dangerous one for not admitting his true motive, 'to obtain domination over men in the present world.' And as for the Church of Rome, 'from the time that the Bishop of Rome had gotten to be acknowledged for bishop universal, by pretence of succession to St Peter, their whole hierarchy, or kingdom of darkness, may be compared not unfitly to the *kingdom of fairies*; that is, to the old wives' *fables* in England, concerning ghosts and spirits, and the feats they play in the night,' for 'the Papacy is no other than the ghost of the deceased Roman empire, sitting crowned upon the grave thereof' (XLVII 457).

Having reduced the children of pride to humility, Leviathan might well allow them to go in peace and serve the Lord. Yet, theirs is humility untouched by love, a combination of external compliance and internal resentment, as though the crushing terror of Leviathan had no other object but to awaken the pride of rebellion. Rebellion, however, would be futile, because there is no 'beyond' that might be invoked to justify it. Hobbes did not wish to found a new religion. Indeed, the most obvious teaching to be found in *Leviathan* is that religion, if it is anything more than a ministry of the State, is a kind of politics, a politics of darkness, duplicity, and fraud, and it should be treated that way. If the pope commands any divisions, he does so as a secular not as a spiritual power. Indeed, there is no spiritual unity of mankind beyond the legally closed sovereign units. Hobbes did not seek simply to replace religion, though one can discover in his work an argument that one day religion would become superfluous. Or, what amounts to the same thing, for some, such as himself, religion was already superseded.

For Hobbes, religion results from an intellectual error or a failure in one's capacity to reckon. Perhaps failure is inevitable, perhaps not. In any event, Hobbes 'denied the existence of a tension between the truth of the soul and the truth of society; the content of Scripture, in his opinion, coincided in substance with the truth of Hobbes.'[36] As Strauss argued, the principle of Hobbes's morality (and, one would add, his political science) is self-consciousness.[37] Certainly this is implied by his teaching on religion. If religious belief is generated as Hobbes indicated, an awareness of the principle of religion already overcomes its charm. Self-consciousness is likewise implied in the constituent elements of Hobbes's political science: the moment of fear is an immediate expression of one's indubitable knowledge of one's own weakness; the moment of pride similarly expresses one's knowledge of one's competitive place in the great race. And Hobbes's achieved and completed political science must itself be understood as a form of self-consciousness.

As the mighty Leviathan was generated from man's natural condition, so, by laying bare the origins and history of previously authoritative beliefs, including religious beliefs, does *Leviathan* provide a true and final understanding of political life. Historical criticism shows that so-called eternal or superhuman limits were set by men. The truth of the matter is that no order binds men from the origin or the end of all things; the proof of that truth is in the evidence of progress. 'Time, and industry, produce every day new knowledge,' Hobbes said. And just as 'the art of well building is derived from principles of reason, observed by industrious men ... long after mankind began, though poorly, to build: so, long time after men have begun to constitute commonwealths, imperfect, and apt to relapse into disorder, there may be principles of reason be found out, by industrious meditation, to make their contribution, excepting by external violence, everlasting. And such are those which I have in this discourse set forth' (XXX 220). Hobbes's principles of politics are the endpoint of progress inasmuch as they result in an everlasting constitution. Hobbes's principles, therefore, are a suitable replacement for the 'eternal' verities of the old moral philosophers. It is true, of course, that everlasting principles are not eternal since they had a historical origin. However, from the time they have been formulated and are in place, the distinction between eternal and everlasting is indiscernible. The difference between Hobbes's principles and earlier formulations is that his are physically rather than morally binding.

Hobbes's achievement in explicitly delimiting the principles of reason that will result in an everlasting constitution is based on a very specific understanding of philosophy, namely, 'the knowledge acquired by reasoning, from the manner of the generation of any thing, to the properties: or from the properties, to some possible way of generation of the same; to the end to be able to produce, as far as matter, and human force permit, such effects as human life requireth' (XLVI 435). Once the chain of cause and effect and the manner of generation have been discovered, which it is Hobbes's claim to have done, it is clear, as he said in the following paragraph, that the importance given to prudence by the old moral philosophers was a mistake. Once upon a time prudence may have been needed, as knowledge acquired by reasoning was defective or imperfect. But no more. The task of political science is no longer to evoke a noetic ikon of the best regime but to establish a program 'as far as matter, and human force permit' to realize that regime. The new political science, as Strauss observed, is essentially technical, its practitioners political technicians, which is to say ideologists, according to the argument made earlier.[38] In short, the supersession of prudence as a political virtue is simply a supersession of the past. Yet Hobbes's 'end of history,' his everlasting constitution, is no more than a claim based upon calculative reason. Unlike Hegel, who made the same claim, Hobbes did not provide the historical evidence, the picture gallery of historical deeds and speeches, that would have rendered it more convincing.

Technical achievements, as distinct from scientific ones, are intended for use. *Leviathan*, unlike Aristotle's *Politics* or Plato's *Republic*; was intended to be practical. At the end of part II (XXI 241), Hobbes explained his purposes at some length. Considering how different his doctrine is from political practice and how much learning is required of administrators of the sovereign power, Hobbes wrote, 'I am at the point of believing this by labour, as useless, as the commonwealth of Plato.' Not so, however. Sovereigns and the principal ministers need not know anything of mathematics save that the study of it ought be encouraged. Thus the education of rulers is greatly simplified: 'The science of natural justice, is the only science necessary.' Moreover, this science has, for the first time, in Hobbes's work, been rigorously set forth and the theorems of protection and obedience finally proved. Consequently, he wrote, 'I recover some hope, that one time or other, this writing will fall into the hands of a sovereign, who will consider it himself (for it is short, and I think clear), without the help of any interested, or envious interpreter; and by the exercise of entire sovereignty, in protecting the public teaching of it, convert this truth of speculation, into the utility of practice.'

The unity of theory and practice, however, does not come easily. There are, for example, all those tiresome old moral philosophers whose teaching is still alive in the several realms of darkness. Thus, the propagation of Hobbes's truth is first of all a practical problem. The majority of mankind, he said, through necessity, covetousness, superfluity, or sloth, 'being diverted from the deep meditation and the learning of truth ... requireth, receive the notions of their duty, chiefly from divines in the pulpit.' And the divines (and lawyers) receive instruction from the universities. 'It is therefore manifest, that the instruction of the people, dependeth wholly, on the right teaching of youth in the universities. But are not, may some man say, the universities of England learned enough already to do that? or is it you, will undertake to teach the universities? Hard questions' (XXX 225). 'Who will teach the teachers?' asked Hegel's most famous pupil, Karl Marx. Hobbes knew the answer was not impossible. To the first query he replied: 'it is most certain, that they [i.e. the universities] have not been sufficiently instructed ... But to the latter question, it is not fit, nor needful for me to say either aye, or no: for any man that sees what I am doing, may easily perceive what I think.' Lest his readers stupidly misconstrue his modesty and reticence, Hobbes later made his position quite plain. After castigating in detail the universities for teaching not philosophy but Aristotelity (XLVI 439ff), he remarks that 'there is nothing in this whole discourse, nor in that I writ before of the same subject in Latin, as far as I can perceive, contrary either to the Word of God, or to good manners; or to the disturbance of the public tranquillity. Therefore I think it may be profitably printed, and more profitably taught in the Universities, in case they also think so, to whom the judgment of the same belongeth' (Conclusion, 467).

Hobbes's legacy

Hobbes's discourse on civil and ecclesiastical government was 'occasioned by the disorders of the present time' (Conclusion, 467). It serves, in this respect, not as justification for one or another form of seventeenth-century absolutism but as evidence of the strength of the new spirituality that must be subdued if any social life is to be possible: only fear of violent death can tame the newly liberated passions; only total control over body and soul can achieve peace. As Eric Voegelin observed, the Leviathan 'adumbrates a component in totalitarianism which comes to the fore when a group of Gnostic activists actually achieves the monopoly of existential representation in a historical society.'[39] That component is the most prominent feature of Hobbes's evocation, the ruthless suppression of resistance created in part by the Sovereign.

The features of the Leviathan that ensure the intolerability of resistance may be briefly recapitulated. First, there is no natural order by which an existing political regime might be measured. There is no 'higher justice' by the invocation of which rebellion or disobedience might be justified. There is no 'beyond,' no isles of the blessed, to which the just who may be badly treated 'here below' may hope to repair in post-existence, there to gain their final reward for righteousness. In a competitive society of individuals, equal in their power to kill one another, success is a matter of chance, of 'the secret working of God, which men call good luck.' Those who fail, who are unlucky, are out of the race and so also out of society. The poor are therefore indistinguishable from the criminal, fit only to be shut away from society, along with the mad. Both virtue and vice have been swallowed by luck or fate, and no one is responsible for anything. Charity, for example, is replaced by social welfare, which means not simply medicare but also forced labour, censorship prior to publication, the suppression of the difference between church and state in a form of compulsory public worship,[40] and, one assumes, the mandatory study of Hobbes's works in both Latin and English. All of this is predicated upon the transfer of individual powers to the person of the Sovereign, whose will is law, who is the real unity of the commonwealth because he commands universal obedience.

Second, the same features of Leviathan that ensure the impossibility of resistance also ensure the impossibility of any political community at all. Based on a transfer of power, not legal right, to the person of the Sovereign, the Leviathan attains no more than a monopoly on killing (in exchange, it is true, for a conditional assurance that one will not be killed). Law is simply administrative decree backed by state power, and obedience to it is simply conformity. Shut off from a political community or 'public thing' in the sense of 'traditional natural law' of the old moral philosophers, one can gain a sense of one's place in the world only by comparing oneself competitively with others, but only privately, alone, and in one's own mind, not publicly by appearing before them as a person in one's own right. Indeed, one never appears as a public person, since the Sovereign alone monopolizes public personality. Consequently, no bonds based upon human commonality can be formed, no likemindedness or political friendship is possible since these cannot be achieved alone. This is why no one need be loyal to one's defeated country, why slaves have no obligations to anybody, and so on. In short, the attitudes of the Sovereign's subjects ensure that any temporary alliance can easily be destroyed.

The picture, and its many contradictions, are changed, however, if one understands that Hobbes 'depicts the features of man according to the needs of the Leviathan.'[41] Then, presumably, it all makes a kind of sense. Having broken the pride of individuals, the Sovereign can himself absorb the force of that pride. The individual no longer exists in a natural condition, though the person of the Sovereign does, so far as other sovereigns are concerned. In this way begins a repetition of the process that created the Sovereign, only this time the individuals are sovereign themselves, at least at the outset. That Hobbes has provided a justification for imperialism is obvious. He has also established a necessary prerequisite for racism, the abolition of mankind as a meaningful symbol of human comity. There is, for example, no international law, since foreigners are outside the contract and on that account in a state of nature or war with parties to the contract. Nations, in effect, become tribes based upon 'natural' differences. The eventual outcome is the establishment of a single, ecumenic Leviathan, and the process leading to its creation is war.

In the conflict of Leviathans we have moved from an analysis of 'human nature' in its bourgeois form to the course of bourgeois history. The inconsistency in a theory that promises safety in the form of submission inspired by fear – for no one can at the same time feel safe and afraid – has already been indicated at some length: since power is by nature a means, any political order based upon it is unstable because inherently expansive. Taken as an end, that is, power is a self-perpetuating process that, as Hobbes rightly indicated, 'ceaseth only in death.' In fact, death is its only product.

One ought not conclude from this that Hobbes's 'philosophy of power' was simply a 'philosophy of death' even if the latter was contained in the former. Rather, as numerous commentators, who otherwise have very little in common, have shown, Hobbes expressed the political needs of the new and rising bourgeoisie. The most important belief of this class is that the highest human good is served by endless accumulation of property. Yet, if seriously pursued the endless accumulation of property turns into the endless accumulation of power in order to make that property secure. The conclusion was obvious: a new body politic would have to be created to take the new political realities into account. 'What he actually achieved was a picture of man as he ought to become and ought to behave if he wanted to fit into the coming bourgeois society.'[42]

The historical event that conditioned Hobbes's theory was the English Revolution, not the 'rise of the bourgeoisie,' a term that would have been meaningless to him and about the precise historical meaning of which much contemporary ink has been spilled. The significance of the English Revolution is also in dispute. However, it seems to belong to a series of events the other important elements of which are the American, French, Russian, and perhaps the German National Socialist revolutions. Taken as an intelligible configuration, and including the imperialism of nineteenth-century Europe, the increasing modernness or radicalness of the process is evident. The Puritans still saw themselves as Christians; English society recovered its political culture and settled down to a couple of centuries of peaceful rule by a parliamentary aristocracy. The National Socialist revolution in twentieth-century Germany in contrast 'brought for the first time into full play economic materialism, racist biology, corrupt psychology, scientism, and technological ruthlessness—in brief, modernity without restraint.'[43] Somewhere in the middle may be ranged the French, and Russian ones. For Hobbes, however, there obviously could be no pattern, but simply the English events themselves. In effect, for later political science, he was arguing on the basis of too small a data base. Accordingly, he cast his argument in the form of an analysis of human nature, a quasi-eternal structure of passions, drives, and mechanisms. But as Strauss has argued, by denying an eternal order by which human reason was guided one inevitably casts into doubt the power of reason as compared to the passions. Philosophy then turned for guidance to history, the arena where passions above all were displayed, only subsequently to be itself historicized. Hegel's political science was deliberately or self-consciously historical, and his data included the American and especially the French revolutions. With Kojève's interpretation of Hegel, the full range of historical evidence was available, and his work reflected the richer historical circumstances provided by the passage of additional time.

Hegel and Kojève took up and perfected Hobbes's concern with order and the meaning of modern revolutionary politics. In addition, they overcame the limitation of Hobbes's understanding of his own achievement. As has been shown, Hobbes was content simply to claim that his political science was the end-product of intellectual progress. But he did not trouble to refute his predecessors or show how their opinions had been superseded. In short, Hobbes did not prove, on the basis of argument or historical evidence, that his political science was final. According to Kojève, Hegel overcame these defects – and if Hegel did not, Kojève himself surely did – by accounting for the whole of human history and thereby overcoming the dilemmas of historicism. In Strauss's language, Hegel intended to resolve the *querelle des anciens et des modernes* by his Science of Wisdom. Now we turn to the implications of this achievement.

2

Historical consciousness

The dilemma of historicism

Whether or not human being is also trans-historical, it is indubitably historical. Historical existence is a problem, a dilemma, a predicament. On the one hand one must act 'in' history, but on the other one must rise above the stream of events in order to understand the sense and direction of one's action. One needs a perspective beyond the fashions and prejudices of the day in order to see them for what they are, yet it is always difficult to know whether one has simply exchanged one prejudice for another. Of course one may object that there is nothing new in this: truth has never come easy. The swiftness of contemporary changes may signify no more than that the difficulty of gaining a proper perspective is more acute than in former times. Perhaps. But there is an alternative understanding that may be identified as historical scepticism or historicism. From the observation that what is true today seems false tomorrow one can draw the sceptical conclusion that the meaning of history is no more than the conflict of opinions and that there are no stable criteria by which a choice can be made between them. If this is so, it doesn't much matter what opinions one holds, and the result, as Stanley Rosen has argued, is nihilism.[1]

The movement of consciousness toward nihilism unfolds in three typical stages.[2] Reflecting upon the absence of unquestionable truth in the present age, the historically self-conscious modern individual also recalls that great deeds have been inspired by great faith. Lacking such a faith today, knowing indeed that it is impossible, one knows also that nothing can be done. One has reached the stage of sceptical paralysis. It is possible to remain here, a nay-sayer, a prophet of decline and decadence. Alternatively, one may seek escape not through a recovery of faith but in the invention of an ersatz faith. One believes that one believes (but one doesn't). Like paralysis, it is doomed to collapse. One is always aware that the story has been made up for ulterior purposes; one can never avoid the fundamental awareness that commitment does not create truth. Eventually, one may achieve a synthesis of the two prior moments in ideological fanaticism. Ideology is not a pragmatic and ersatz faith but a real one, believed in because it is true, not true simply because one happens to espouse it. Moreover, as was argued in the first chapter, even if it is not historically or factually true it can serve as a program of action that may become actually true. And yet, at the same time, the ideological believer knows that his truth is only programmatic and not yet fully and absolutely true. Ideology, as was argued earlier, is necessarily activist, aggressive, fanatical. The end-point of historical self-consciousness, then, seems to be the armed *divertissements* of world-conquering ideologues. Whether it is inevitable that one move from historical self-consciousness to historicism or historical scepticism and then to ideological political action may be doubted. There is no doubt, however, that many modern individuals have done so. Let us consider further what this modern self-understanding involves.

'Historicism' is a term to which many meanings have been attached.[3] Early in this century it was used in a polemical way to describe the illegitimate use of historical knowledge to answer non-historical and chiefly moral questions. Later it was removed from the heat of moral debate and expounded as a methodological possibility, useful within certain limits. Methodological debates, however, have a tendency to turn into ontological ones. Then they become fierce or at least very serious, because being itself is held to be at issue. Leo Strauss compressed the two dimensions of the question. Historicism, he said, is 'the assertion that the fundamental distinction between philosophical and historical questions cannot in the last analysis be maintained.'[4]

The implications of Strauss's distinction centre upon two different sorts of discourse, the philosophical and the historical, and their relationship, if any. In the tradition of *philosophia perennis*, discussed earlier as an aspect of pre-modern political science, history and philosophy are related only accidentally. History is a storehouse of examples, but it has no further ontological significance and is not, of itself, meaningful. Meaning, on the contrary, is provided by the discourse for which history provides rhetorical confirmation through illustrations. History, to use a famous image, is a cave from which the philosopher seeks to escape.

Until the philosopher has gained (somehow) entrance into an eternal realm, he has not gained truth. If this truth is timeless, and if it is accessible to human beings, then human beings must have a capacity that is itself also timeless. That is, human being is a 'nature' that is not significantly influenced by history. By 'significantly influenced' is meant influenced in such a way that access to eternal or timeless or 'metaphysical' truth is made impossible. Strauss confined the topic to historical questions rather than answers. If one seeks answers, to be given only questions in response to questions can be frustrating and dissatisfying. Perhaps this is inevitable, but it does not constitute a decisive refutation, on its own grounds, of *philosophia perennis*. The incompleteness of philosophical answers, or the possibility of asking one additional question (without repeating an earlier one), is held to be only accidentally a consequence of one's historical circumstance. The essential or fundamental defect is held to lie in the inability of the discussants to comply with the eternal, universal standards of rational discourse. The failure may be repeated innumerable times, but it is not for that reason to be blamed upon the historical condition of the discussants. After all, they can correct one another by pointing out and rectifying errors in reasoning. In this way one can assert that the universe of philosophical discourse is one, eternal and timeless.

In contrast, the possibility of *philosophia perennis* may be denied, and with it the anthropology of human nature. Human beings have no capacity for apprehending eternal truths. On the contrary, they are involved 'essentially' in the world; human being is first and last a being-in-the-world. Involvement extends to knowledge of the world as well. Thus, both the world and discourse about it are historical. If one adopts this position, *philosophia perennis* appears as a temporary opinion. It claimed to be independent of the world, and it claimed to be able to judge the world truly on the basis of that independence, for true standards were to be found nowhere in the world. Abandoning those claims, philosophy henceforth must be concerned not with timeless truths so-called but with the history of beliefs in standards alleged by believers to be true and independent of the world. Accordingly, philosophy, that is, philosophers, must become as involved in the world as are other human beings. Or rather, they *are* as involved, and they had better wake up to the fact. Moreover, if they are to remain philosophers, they must practise the same discrimination and judgment as did their predecessors within the tradition of *philosophia perennis*, but they must do so on the basis not of eternal verities or the 'ideas' of the good, the true, and the beautiful, but on the basis of history. Here one sees the real sharpness of Strauss's point.

If philosophers face up to the world and to themselves as beings-in-the-world, the historicist argues, they must recognize that theirs is a historical world. Claims to truth change. Philosophical discourses conflict. Since the eternal realm of *philosophia perennis*, the single universe of philosophic discourse, is gone, no appeal to eternal standards is possible. Moreover, this universe of discourse is *really* gone. It is not still there, merely out of our feeble or defective sight. And it is *gone*, which is to say that once upon a time it was not gone. In this lies the difference between ordinary relativism and historicism. The relativist argues that there are no eternal verities and never have been; the historicist argues that once upon a time the eternal verities were eternal verities, but no longer. The difference is analogous to that between the fool who says in his heart, 'There is no God,' and Nietzsche's madman who said, 'God is dead, and we have murdered him.' Once upon a time, that is, God was alive. But then, if the eternal verities have (somehow) gone, how can the philosophers do their job? If the claim of *philosophia perennis* to transcendent, eternal, timeless truth is an illusion that has finally been unmasked, how can philosophy distinguish truth from falsehood?

Hegel's answer, restated most emphatically by Kojève, was that the philosopher can understand history only if history is over, if all historical human possibilities have been achieved, and all interpretative discourse has been completed. That is, all possible questions have been answered, and in the right order. The end of history, then, is also the end of philosophy: wisdom has been actualized. The actualization of the end of history in the end of philosophy would overcome the merely logical contradictions of historicism. The only problem seems to be how to gain that end. First, however, historicism must be seen as a problem or a dilemma standing in need of resolution. It is to that topic that we now turn. We shall examine briefly the arguments of Jean Wahl and Alexandre Koyré insofar as they bear upon the Hegelian themes taken up by Kojève. The balance of this chapter may also serve as a general introduction to the broad foundations of French Hegelianism, which is still very much alive, as they were laid during the 1930s.[5] Inasmuch as a century of scholarship has failed to reach agreement on the 'meaning(s)' of Hegel, one may be excused as no more than prudent if one avoids judgment as to the truth or fidelity of the interpretations considered. And in any case, one of the most important claims made, by the close of the 1930s, was that Hegelianism, the system of Science, made its own claim to truth independent of the intentions of its author.

Hegel in France

The French discovery of Hegel did not occur during the 1930s or even during the twentieth century. Hegelian 'traces' have recently been found in the writing of Victor Cousin, a 'French' Stefan George, Mallarmé, Villiers de l'Isle-Adam, Caro, Taine, and Renan, but, as did certain twentieth-century surealists, Hegel was not studied so much as appropriated for purposes that were far from philosophical.[6] Furthermore, with philosophy faculties ruled by Descartes and Kant and with the history faculties closed to anything like Hegel's philosophy of history, he was virtually excluded from the academy. Writing of the mid-nineteenth century, Koyré observed: 'Hegelianism therefore suffered the worst disgrace that might befall a doctrine for which the verdict of history had been erected into the supreme standard of judgment': it was ignored.[7] Not until the centenary year of 1870 can one speak of a serious interest in Hegel, and even then notice of him was an occasion for lamenting the recent defeat of French arms and the general decadence of Berlin following the death of Schelling. Most Frenchmen would no doubt have shared the sentiments, if not the style, of Ernest Hello, who declared: 'Satan and Hegel give forth the same cry: "Being and Nothingness are identical."'[8]

Until well into the twentieth century the sole French Hegelian, properly speaking, was Lucien Herr, but he was able to publish only a single article, in *Grande Encyclopédie*.[9] Consequently, where Hegel was mentioned at all, it was simply as a figure in the broad sweep of German intellectual history; in this vein the most intellectually competent writing was devoted to simple summaries that attempted to rectify the more gross but conventional misinterpretations that had lain undetected and uncorrected for over half a century.[10] The result was that Hegel, no longer in league with the devil, was now seen as the ultimate Kantian.[11]

Following the First World War, Hegel's work, with the sole exception of Emile Meyerson's study of *Philosophy of Nature*, was included in the virtual eclipse of all things German.[12] Thus, it was not until 1927 that Victor Basch began to combat the prejudice that Hegel was 'the very precursor of barbaric, imperialist pan-Germanism' and a Prussian militarist of the same cast as Treitschke. Basch concluded that while certain passages taken out of context could be forced to read as supporting pan-Germanism, as a whole Hegel's political thought 'is radically repugnant to everything that is pan-Germanism, imperialism, or even excessive nationalism' and certainly had nothing to do with fascism.[13] A more positive note was struck in Charles Andler's lectures in 1929 and 1931 at the Collège de France on Hegel's *Phenomenology* and in the collection published in the special issue of the *Revue de Métaphysique et de Morale* in 1931.[14] What these studies have in common, and what marks them off from the analyses that followed, is that they dealt with Hegel primarily as philosophical idealist. Hegelian texts concerned with perception, sense-certainty, consciousness, and so on, were analysed no differently than texts of Kant, Spinoza, or Descartes that apparently treated the same topics. Hegel was understood as the author of certain (rather abstract) doctrines. The task of the interpreter was little more than one of intellectual dissection; there seemed to be no question of Hegel's teaching ever moving the souls of his readers or, indeed, of his intending to touch upon the problems of morality, politics, and religion that concern most people. As late as 1945 the history of philosophy as taught in the University of Paris ended with Kant. Yet at the same time, when writers took stock of the configuration of French ideas following the Second World War, they invariably noted, and often deplored, the influence of Hegel.[15] Today Hegel, or perhaps the Marxian-existentialist Hegel, has become what Kant had been. The new orthodoxy, as Kojève had promised, consists in repeating the moments of the System.[16]

Jean Wahl and the unhappy consciousness

Because he contested the traditional assumptions about the proper way to read Hegel, Jean Wahl's study of the unhappy consciousness in *Phenomenology* has rightly been called 'the first important study of "French Hegelianism."'[17] In a series of papers published during the late 1920s and subsequently incorporated in his book, Wahl proposed to defend the then unusual thesis that Hegel was concerned more with moral and religious problems that with intellectual ones; full weight, he said, must be given to the theological, romantic, and quasi-mystical meditations that lay behind the philosophical formulas. 'What Hegel dealt with in the *Phenomenology* were not philosophies but ways of living; or rather, the two were not separated.' He was concerned with 'the categories of practical life: service, recognition of service, sacrifice.' Hegel's overriding preoccupation was one of philosophical and religious estrangement and diremption as well as of the way it could be overcome. The unhappy consciousness, according to Wahl, was an initial moment in this process.

'For the beginning of philosophy, as of religion, is less wonder than non-satisfaction and a tattered consciousness.'[18] Hence, the unhappy consciousness was the incarnation of negativity in the philosopher's life, the motor that inspired him to act with a view toward reconciliation, not least of all by redeeming his own non-satisfaction.

Religion, or rather biblical religion, was the greatest expression of existential diremption as well as of the greatest effort to overcome the 'boredom of the world.' The infinite distance between the Lord of History and his servants, as found in the Old Testament, was mediated by Jesus, 'the priest of religion of man – the man-God is above all a man.'[19] Sin could be overcome only 'by the death of a God,' and Christ's death 'only suppresses what is nothingness; it is the mediation, the reconciliation of the subject with the absolute.' Thus, Hegel's meditation on the verse from Luther's hymn, 'God Himself has died,' resulted in his understanding Jesus as the happy consciousness that had overcome the unhappiness of Judaism. Yet, Jesus *suffered*, so that 'at the very moment when he personifies the happy consciousness, Jesus is still an unhappy consciousness. Nothing else conforms so well to Hegelianism as this idea.'[20] That this reconciliation, the famed rose at the heart of the cross, was imperfect was shown in the subsequent development of Christianity. While it was true that the death of the man-God Jesus overcame the separation between divine Master and human Servant, the unity achieved in the mystical body of Christ was but a preparation for the even greater separation that crystallized as the alliance and division of Church and State. Through its own spiritual intensity, the Church became, as with the Jews, a small group, separated from God and other men; free individuality was crushed, as with the Jews, and God was worshipped as Master of Heaven and Earth; Jesus seemed to have come in vain. But Christianity was not just a repetition of Judaic unhappiness, for the 'moment' of Jesus was historically crucial. Christianity was 'the religion of unhappiness'; and though 'the Christian Church is the consciousness of the unhappy consciousness'[21] for that very reason it was *directed* toward happiness.

At the same time, Christianity was *only* directed toward happiness, just as its separation from God was *only* directed toward a reconciliation that was itself eschatological. The great flaw in Christianity, the reason for its inability to attain the goal toward which it moved, lay in the passion of Jesus, the redemptive suffering of the man-God. For Hegel, heroes alone could achieve reconciliation, and heroes do not emerge from passion and suffering but from great and noble action.[22]

Since the origin of philosophy, as of religion, was held to be radical non-satisfaction, one may discover a movement parallel to the dialectic of the unhappy consciousness in philosophy. In particular, Kantian consciousness was also unhappy 'insofar as this latter is a struggle against nature and is dominated by the category of Master and Slave ... The Kantian is his own slave' and hence equivalent to the Jew and the medieval (or Roman Catholic) Christian: 'The Kantian thing-in-itself remains a beyond, like the Jewish God.'[23] Kantian morality was a bourgeois, servile morality, a kind of martyr's passion without the bother of suffering. Just as Christianity remained an unhappy consciousness even while being opposed to the unhappy consciousness of Judaism, so too were the opponents of Kant, namely the romantics, Fichte, and the 'beautiful soul,' united with him in virtue of a common dualism: taken together they illuminated the problem but did not overcome it.[24] The religious and the philosophical were, according to Wahl's Hegel, aspects of the same incomplete historical self-consciousness. Only 'philosophy,' or more precisely 'science,' could unite the two.

It is for this reason, according to Wahl, that Hegel undertook the study of the unhappy consciousness. Wahl's argument is straightforward: only when consciousness has descended to the absolute depths of separation could it recover its own unity. The death of the man-God Jesus was genuine mediation and a genuine sanctification, but an 'imperfect' one. The 'perfect' death of God is not one of actual suffering and passion but rather is pre-eminently a 'consciousness of death,' a 'negativity.' Now, 'negativity' is a 'philosophical' or scientific term, and hence can be grasped within 'the idea of the concept.' By the transformation of Christ's passion into the idea of negativity, 'reflection provides its own reconciliation with destiny.'[25] The unhappy consciousness became a 'moment' in the immanent dialectic of Spirit, a 'necessary element of the happy consciousness, being identical in its essence with the very movement of the dialectic.' Or again: 'The sentiment of the loss of life is the knowledge, and possession of life. We are led back to the idea that, by the negation of the negation [i.e. by negating the original diremption], one arrives at the true. By losing one's life, one gains it. The genuine concept is the negation of its own negation; and Spirit, leaving itself, returns to itself.'[26] *This* reconciliation was a genuine or 'perfect' reconciliation because it knew itself to be a final reconciliation. And it did so because it had actively overcome the most radical possible separation that followed the passion and death of God.

Hegel's conception of his own efforts or, better, of the efforts of Spirit that appeared in his work effected a transformation of the history of Spirit before his time. In particular, Wahl pointed out, Protestantism became 'a kind of second revelation, a sort of primitive Hegelianism.' Protestantism had destroyed forever the 'beauty and sacrality of the world,' and only Hegelianism could overcome the diremption that followed upon the (necessary) destructive work of Luther. 'The moment is coming when a universal and truly philosophical religion will appear; then will be revealed the genuine spirit of religion that, following the same laws of history, could not have shown itself at an earlier moment, but that was present in them as a germ. Then the third religion will be achieved, the second good news that will fill in the lacunae and the textual lapses of the first.'[27] Hegelianism was to be the completion of the 'thought' of Christ as well as of Luther because their 'thought' could be integrated into the System of Science as 'moments' of the self-mediation of Spirit.

Koyré's criticism

Wahl's study raised quite as many questions as it attempted to resolve. How could Hegel's writing a book serve to overcome the diremption and boredom of the world? Even if he had overcome his own non-satisfaction, how was Hegel any different from, say, an Epicurean who on his own terms was 'happy' but according to Hegel was only at a stage on the way of the unfolding of Spirit? Would a Jew or a Christian recognize his or her religious experience as 'painful' and 'unhappy'? And if so would Hegelian 'reconciliation' be persuasive? What would this 'reconciliation' mean for the concrete, actual person who, as Kant had pointed out in a similar context, was certain only of his own death? Indeed, the greatest part of Wahl's book, as Koyré remarked in a review, dealt with a renascent unhappiness that drove consciousness to even greater division; but if this were so, Hegel would have never escaped a kind of cosmic melancholy, not even far enough to give it a name.[28] Wahl did not deal explicitly with these (and no doubt many other) questions, although he did make a few remarks that pointed in the direction that later Hegelians followed.

It was, Wahl said, 'in the essence of Christianity that Hegel found the explanation of those separations, of those disturbances that were before his eyes when he examined the state of his own country. Or rather, there is an exact analogy between the moment when Hegelian thought developed and the moment when Christ lived.'[29] Christ's appearance at the time when Roman imperial rule had destroyed the parochial deities of its subject peoples was exactly analogous to Hegel's appearance in the wake of the spiritual havoc of the Reformation and the Enlightenment, which is to say that there was an internal link binding political events to the realm of the Spirit as it became self-conscious in persons such as Jesus and Hegel. Wahl did not consider what this link might have been or what the relation was between self-conscious Spirit in Jesus and the historical events such as the military campaigns that destroyed the independence of the various cities and nations that Rome incorporated into its organization.

However history as a *Schachtbank* was reconciled to the redemptive reconciliation that appeared in the consciousness of Jesus and Hegel, there can be no doubt that the two elements were 'moments' of a dialectical process immanent to Spirit itself, Precisely, religion was a moment (*a*) of a kind of transcendence, insofar as its contents are externalized as grace, communion, forgiveness, and so on. But *qua* external, it could be brought within consciousness as a separate and distinct moment (*b*):

The unhappy consciousness is religious insofar as it remains at the moment of transcendence [i.e. at *a*] and does not grasp that, implicitly, it has surpassed this moment [i.e. to *b*]. When consciousness will attain the affirmation of its unity in its very duality, what was the source of its unhappiness [i.e. *a*] will turn into the source of its happiness, and the three levels [of the Father, Son, and Holy Spirit] that characterize the religion of the incarnation allow it to go beyond its starting point, which is the religion of opposition, to its end point, which is absolute religion. This same passage from opposition to union, insofar as neither the one nor the other of these moments is negated, but on the contrary are both conserved, is what constitutes Spirit.[30]

By grasping within the idea of the concept the succession of moments of Spirit, Hegel had as it were given a complete account of God. At the same time, since his reconciliation was intended to overcome the diremption that followed the redemptive death of the man-God, Christ, Hegel had given a complete account of man: 'It is life, Spirit, the essence of man, that shows us what is the essence of God.' That is, Hegel's account of Spirit was essentially an anthropology.

Wahl did not explicate the connection between his anthropological reading of Hegel's speculations on Christianity and the immanent meaning of history expressed as events by concrete and particular individuals.

Nevertheless, the great significance of the book, as Salvadori pointed out, was its 'concrete' reading of Hegel. Wahl sought for the first time 'the mystical intuition and emotional warmth' that nourished the linguistic formulas.[31] Yet it was exactly this aspect of Wahl's book, his search for the human, concrete person, that prompted Koyré's most important critical remarks.

'M. Wahl,' Koyré said, 'likes the young Hegel, the romantic Hegel. That is understandable. At a later date Hegel is not very likeable. But does the romantic Hegel give us anything more than Hölderlin or Novalis? I think not. And, something more important, neither Hegel nor his contemporaries thought so ... What is true for Hegel, what is the *real* Hegel, is the *Logic*, the eternal cyclical movement of thought, the *Selbstbewegung des Begriffs*.'[32] In any case, Koyré said, the search for the concrete person behind the author was misguided: Hegel's 'unhappiness,' his 'tragedy,' was not genuinely lived anyhow but was just a moment of 'thought.' 'How could he have lived a tragedy, a real despair? Did he not know that the battle was only a fake one? And that his God, eternally moving and making himself, is at the same time eternally completed? A struggle whose victory is assured and even eternally won – is that a tragic struggle?' Of course, suffering and tragedy were necessary fuel for the movement of Spirit, but 'for God – and also for Hegel – tragedy is *already* overcome.' God eternally makes the rounds of the stages of his own self-movement, but is also eternally at his goal, 'and Hegel *knows* he is going to arrive precisely because he is already there.' According to Koyré, Hegel's greatness lay not in the human 'warmth' of his experience but in his 'inhuman frigidity. Not in the fact that later on he called "concept" what he had first called "love," but, on the contrary, in the fact that what he had begun by calling "love" he ended by calling "concept."'[33]

Koyré's remarks were not all critical. Nevertheless, his criticism reflected his judgment of what interpretative procedures should be avoided. Specifically, his insistence upon the 'synthetical' aspect of Hegel's thought was the result of his own antipathy to the elements of Dilthey's interpretative method that he found in Wahl's book. He objected, that is, to Wahl's insistence that *Phenomenology* should be read in the light of *Early Theological Writings*; Koyré's reason for objecting was that he saw in Wahl's remark an untenable interpretative principle, that the metaphysical ground of *Phenomenology* was to be discovered through an examination of its genesis in the historically prior texts.[34] His own interpretation would try to avoid this mistake.

Koyré's Hegel studies

Wahl's unorthodox view of Hegel may have been influenced by his earlier work on Kierkegaard, William James, and Bergson, none of whom was particularly welcome within the walls of the Sorbonne either.[35] Likewise, Koyré's early work, with the exception of his thesis on Descartes, was equally foreign to the philosophy faculty. The fact that the locus of Hegelian studies was outside the regular structure of academic philosophy is of some importance, especially for understanding Koyré and Kojève.

Koyré had left Russia before the First World War to study with Husserl, publishing at this time a number of articles on mathematical topics. Following his service as a volunteer in the French army, he studied at the École pratique des hautes études, in the general area of the history and philosophy of religion. In 1922 he published his thesis, and the following year he organized a course on the religious doctrines of Schleiermacher and Schelling. For the next two years Koyré continued a course on German speculative mysticism, adding Oettinger, Fichte, Och, Spalding, and the romantics. By 1926, he had reached Hegel, and using *Early Theological Writings* as a departure point he devoted the course to an analysis of the unhappy consciousness and the concept of mediation.

In these lectures Koyré developed the view of Hegel that formed the basis for his criticism of Wahl. Specifically, he insisted upon the radical immanentism of Hegel's religious opinions by arguing that since the unhappy consciousness was a substitute for sin 'the specifically religious idea of sin has no place in Hegel's system.' Thus, he said, the unhappy consciousness was contained as a negative moment of Absolute Spirit, within which it was nevertheless eternally surmounted. The following understanding of the Absolute Spirit was therefore implied: it was 'a perfect living personality, eternally complete and eternally completing itself,' and it indicated 'the conception of a real history of spirit realizing itself in the history of the world and in humanity that was reproducing the atemporal evolution of God unfolding in Time.'[36] We shall consider the meaning of this phrase shortly. Before doing so, however, we must note that from 1928 to 1932 Koyré devoted much of his attention to German and Russian mystics of the seventeenth and eighteenth centuries as well as to the murky amalgam of mysticism, alchemy, and theology known today as the 'origins of modern science.' The significance of these studies, along with his studies of Anselm and Boehme, as Yvon Belaval has said, was that Koyré became highly sensitive to the terminological subtleties of a very peculiar kind of writing.[37]

Koyré applied this skill to an analysis of Hegel's vocabulary, and in 1931 his preliminary conclusions were published. Hegel was difficult to understand, he began, not only because he was untranslatable but because even for a German he was often unintelligible. No doubt Hegel would have been amused by the complaint, Koyré said, since he claimed that the System was the form of a newer, more contemporary stage of Spirit; but he would also have been annoyed, since he considered the language he used to be necessary to render his experience intelligible. Two preliminary aspects of Hegel's language were significant: first, the changing sense of Hegel's terminology simply reflected its closeness to the ever-deepening experience it tried to articulate, its 'concreteness' in Wahl words. Second, Hegel used the 'living' vernacular and sought to bring out the hidden connotations of words. 'This speech [*langue* = *Sprache*], the speech in which Absolute Spirit is expressed, is the speech of philosophy, or more exactly, the speech of a people who have raised themselves to the level of philosophy, whose civilization has been lifted to the level of absolute knowledge, which was, Hegel firmly believed, realized by the dialectical logic that he elaborated.'[38] The terms 'dialectical language' and 'dialectical logic' were meant not simply to contrast with 'abstract' language and mathematical logic; they meant also 'belonging to a dialect.' As dialectical in this second sense, Hegel's language was 'a dialectical synthesis of diverse significations incarnate in words.' That is why, Koyré said, the best commentary on Hegel would be a historical dictionary of the German language.

Hegel did not simply engage in word play. He did not hold to any superstition concerning the 'primitive meaning' (*Ur-sinn*) of a term. Why then did he employ a kind of vernacular etymology in his philosophical writings? Because, Koyré said, his 'ultimate ambition was to unite dialectically rest and movement and to connect time to eternity by his notion of atemporal becoming.' All the levels that Spirit encountered in its development were real and necessary; 'each and every one forms the total experience of spirit, and within this total experience all are preserved in memory.' Each level forms an 'inamissible possession' that recovered the anterior forms of its own becoming as its own depth. 'And this is why Hegelian concepts ... appear as a disconcerting collection of historical significations realized in experience. In Hegel's thought the eternal concept is related directly and essentially to history and time.'[39] Hegel's terminology was thus intended to articulate both sides of the 'identity of time and eternity,' that is, to reflect the real value of historical evolution as the inamissible depth of the eternal concept.

In considering commentaries upon philosophical texts, one should always distinguish a paraphrase from an interpretation. Koyré had no doubt provided an accurate paraphrase of the Hegelian texts he quoted, but it is not clear what is meant by a phrase such as 'the eternal concept is related directly and essentially to history and time.' What is 'the atemporal evolution of God unfolding in Time'? The question bothered Koyré as well, for he asked: 'Is one within eternity or within time?' He gave what seemed to be the only possible answer: 'One is, *bien entendu*, within them both, for time alone allows the realization of dialectical development since alone, being negation and death, it is also the source of movement and life.' Koyré did not use the phrase '*bien entendu*' very frequently; and in this instance it is not particularly appropriate, since the sentence in which it occurs is far from self-evident. One may view Koyré's '*bien entendu*' as an indication that, while 'of course' Hegel had *declared* the synthesis of *logos* and history to be present in his own writings, Koyré had not (yet) accounted in his own mind for the meaning of that alleged synthesis. Thus, a few pages later, Koyré made an equally obscure paraphrastic remark: 'Time is, in fact, the being-there of the *Aufheben* itself. History and history alone realizes Spirit. History alone allows, or more exactly, it alone *is* the growth of spirit becoming itself, enriching itself in its becoming with all the wealth it carries within itself, for history, which is Spirit, is also victory over time, victory over negation and death, which time carries within it. It realizes, so far as we are capable of it, the *nunc aeternitatis* of the eternal present. History is the life of the Spirit in itself; it is its own being, and no longer just its being-there. For history is not preoccupied with the past. It surmounts it as it surmounts time.'[40]

Koyré had avoided the traces of historicism he found in Wahl's analysis; moreover, he had given a believable account of the difficulty in understanding 'concretely' Hegel's terminology. But the price he paid was to paraphrase rather than interpret the text.[41] Furthermore, Koyré was probably aware that his treatment was incomplete, for a few years later, following the publication of Lasson's edition of the Jena writings, he returned to the same question of historicity, having in the mean time written several studies in the history of science.

During the academic year 1932–3 Koyré again gave a course on Hegel, now as director of the newly formed XVI Section, 'Histoire des Idées religieuses dans l'Europe moderne.' Lasson's texts and Nohl's edition of *Early Theological Writings* (which Koyré observed could be more accurately entitled *Early Anti-Theological Writings*) were used. He described the course as follows: 'As it appears in these writings, the method of Hegel seems to be that of a phenomenological description of consciousness; during this period the problems upon which he meditated seem to have been the relationships between the finite and infinite (their mutual implication), and between eternity and time. It is the discovery of the dialectical nature of Time that, permitting Hegel to identify logic and history, made possible two studies of Hegel's Jena writings based on the topics covered in the course.'[42]

Hegel at Jena

Both papers began by referring to the difficulty of understanding Hegel, to 'the impression of being present as the astonished and impotent witness of an amazing acrobatics or a kind of sorcery.' One questions, *sotto voce*, whether this 'spiritual magic' means anything at all: 'one is astonished, amazed; one goes no further.' One of the reasons for this initial reaction, Koyré said, was that Hegel 'thinks in a circle' rather than in a straight line; Hegel took his own crack about Schelling, that he carried on his philosophical education in public, so seriously that only with difficulty could one piece together the scaffolding that once undergirded the system. The importance of the Jena writings is that they constitute the dismantled or at least forgotten scaffolding for *Phenomenology*. In particular, they document the transformation of a philosophy of nature into a philosophy of the concept of nature. More generally, Hegel's philosophy of nature was turned into a phenomenology of space and especially of time.[43]

The first paper continued Koyré's analysis of Hegel's language, this time in the light of the 'grave danger' of 'reducing philosophy to phenomenology, of substituting for things their concepts.'[44] Rather than a philosophy of nature one finds a description of the space and time of human beings; rather than a critique of language one finds the description of the linguistic world, 'the sole incarnation of the logos that Hegel acknowledged.' Thus, Hegel 'could criticize the bad use of language – that of his contemporaries – but not language itself. Language, word and thought, *sermo* and *verbum*, is spiritual reality. Language can be abstract, sick, and dying. The history of language and the life of language is at the same time the history of the life of Spirit.'[45] But, while the common or supraindividual existence of language rendered the individual by comparison so much more 'factic, contingent, and unessential,' it was still true that there was no 'language' as such, but only languages. Language was not simply Spirit, but also the expression of the 'spirit of a people.' Hence, a 'true' language was possible only amid a 'true people.' Such a notion of language, Koyré remarked, amounts to a transformation of Kant's problem concerning the conditions for the possibility of science. For Hegel it was 'included in the conditions of existence of a true people, whose most important conditions are political: the existence of a state, of a police, of a system of justice and a government. Philosophy of Spirit degenerates into philosophy of the State.' Now one knows the tree by the fruit it bears. Accordingly, the people and the State that have produced the truest philosophy will clearly be the truest people and theirs the truest State. Since 'from all evidence, his own philosophy was to Hegel the truest of the true,' the conclusion was obvious: the condition for the truth of the System is the political progress from ancient polis to modern state. 'As early as Jena he was, in Spirit, at Berlin.'[46]

Koyré's greatest efforts were devoted not to an explication of the political implications of Hegel's account of language, but to his phenomenology of time and human historicity. Hegel's discussion of time used Christian theological terms, but it was inspired by a 'profound irreligiosity.' The crucial difference was that 'the theological dialectic is a dialectic of the non-temporal while the historical dialectic is that of time. The one implies the primacy of the past, since within the *nunc aeternitatis* everything is already realized; the other, the primacy of the future, since within the historical *nunc* the present has no meaning save by its relation to a future that it projects ahead of itself, that it announces, and that it will realize by suppressing.'[47] Hegel's discussion, Koyré said, was simply in terms of the *nunc*, grasped by a phenomenology of 'internal time-consciousness' that excluded the eternal as abstract. 'The dialectic of time is the dialectic of man. It is because man is essentially dialectical, which is to say essentially a negator, that the dialectic of history – nay, history itself – is possible. Because man says *no* to his now – or to himself – he has a future. Because he negates himself he has a past. Because he is time – and not just temporal – he also has a *present*, a present victorious over the past.' The present, a 'now' inclining toward the future as well as uniting and embracing (but not suppressing) the past, is already an instant of eternity. 'Every *nunc* is a *nunc aeternitatis*, for eternity is time itself, the eternal movement of spirit.'[48]

Koyré had again reached the central problem of Hegelian historical consciousness, the point where the interpenetration of time and eternity (or atemporal becoming) was an analytical problem. This time he was not content to paraphrase Hegel but tried to resolve the seeming dilemma. Or rather, he argued that the dilemma was real and unresolvable, an aporia or paradox that was self-cancelling. As a result, the Hegelian System was declared to be 'dead, quite dead.'[49] If, he said, 'time is dialectical and if it is constructed *on the basis of the future* it is – whatever Hegel may say – eternally incomplete. Even more, the present itself – which is the formerly of the future – is nothing that might be grasped. For though Spirit can, in fact, make the past present, it can do so only with the help of the future.' Consequently, while 'the dialectical nature of time alone makes possible a philosophy of history, at the same time the temporal nature of the dialectic makes it impossible. For philosophy of history, whether we like it or not, is a halting place.' This is so because *philosophy* of history is not itself history, but the articulation of a *logos*, a coherent discourse in the present about the past with the help of the future, in the sense that 'doing' a philosophy of history, either by writing it down or by speaking, 'takes' time. Meanwhile the history about which the discourse was delivered has itself changed.

'One cannot foresee the future,' Koyré went on, so that every philosophy of history will be incomplete. And 'since the Hegelian dialectic, the expression of the creative role of negation, expresses the future at the same time as it expresses freedom,' it does not allow us to foresee the future either. Therefore, 'the synthesis is unforeseeable: one cannot construct it; one can only analyse it. Philosophy of history – and likewise Hegelian philosophy, the 'System' – would be possible only if history were terminated, if there were no further future, if time could be stopped.'[50] Now if Hegelian time is human time, if eternity is as it were swallowed in the perpetual unfolding of Spirit, if man 'is the being who exists only within the continual transformation of the future within the now, and who ceases to be the day when he has no future, when nothing further is to come, when everything has already come, when everything is already "accomplished,"'[51] then the condition for the completion of the System is the abolition of man and the swallowing of time by eternity.

Koyré concluded by reflecting that perhaps Hegel accepted the condition that history had been terminated and time had stopped. 'It is even possible that he believed that it was not only the essential condition for the system – for it is only at dusk that the owls of Minerva begin their flight – but also that this essential condition was *already* realized, that history was effectively completed, and just for that reason he was able –

he had been able – to complete it.'[52] One may recall Koyré's opening remark, that reading Hegel imparts a disturbing sense of 'attending upon a kind of sorcery or spiritual magic.' Nevertheless, between his apparent awareness of Hegel's 'spiritual magic' and the open act of thematic analysis fell the shadow of Hegel's stature as a philosopher in the traditional sense. It was as if Koyré were too much a gentleman to dispute so grand a reputation.

Kojève's interpretative principles

Wahl suggested an anthropological reading of Hegel's Christianity, and Koyré made it thematic. Together they argued, in effect, that an anthropological and immanentist reading led to a blending of eternity and time. This, they felt, was impossible. Kojève disagreed and sought to overcome the dilemma that Koyré emphasized. In addition, and the two questions are related, he took up the matter raised by both Wahl and Koyré but developed by neither of them of the relationship between concrete events such as the Roman and Napoleonic empires and the self-consciousness of individuals such as Jesus and Hegel. This section deals briefly with Kojève's methodological and interpretative principles. Much, no doubt, will appear to be contentious, even nonsense. But no one, not even Hegel, can say everything at once. The concluding pages of this chapter, then, may be considered as an introduction to Kojève's rhetoric as much as to his argument. One must grow accustomed to discussion of such oddities as the universal and homogeneous state, post-historical life, the System of Science. In the following chapters his argument is considered in more detail.

When in December 1933 Koyré left Paris to teach a term at the University of Cairo, Kojève was nominated to continue his course. As he explained in the *Annuaire*, it had 'been conceived as a continuation of M. Koyré's course on Hegel's religious philosophy' given the previous year. 'M. Koyré has analysed the texts prior to the *Phänomenologie des Geistes*. I have devoted my class to the study of the *Phänomenologie* by following M. Koyré's method of interpretation and basing myself on the central ideas of his course.'[53] Kojève had followed Koyré in another sense as well: he too was a Russian émigré who had spent some time studying in Germany. He was also widely read in the history of Russian theological and philosophical speculation, though unlike Koyré relatively little of his work was published.[54] And finally, like Koyré, Kojève was a philosophical opponent of Dilthey's *Lebensphilosophie*, and it is perhaps in that context that we might most easily see how he began to resolve the problems raised by the other two.

According to Kojève, Dilthey was the first philosophically talented thinker who had ceased to believe in philosophy as the description of the one and only world that was true in the emphatic sense of being independent of the historical and psychological situation of the philosopher. In place of philosophy as understood by the great philosophers, Dilthey sought to substitute his version of historicism. This led to two distinct kinds of 'philosophy of philosophy.' 'Either it will be "axiomatic philosophy," a construction of logically possible systems of philosophy, beginning with different geometries,' in which case the result will be at best an interesting but frivolous game with a philosophical *form*, or this 'philosophy of philosophy' will be 'a history and psychology of philosophy, and if you like, a philosophy of this history and psychology; a philosophical description not of the object of philosophy, but of descriptions of this object as proposed in the course of history and of the personal motives for these descriptions,'[55] in which case, while it may be serious, the *contents* of philosophy will have been extracted and turned into raw material for a wholly extra-philosophical and simply historical endeavour.

The most troubling aspect of Dilthey's approach was that it was essentially parasitic: 'The "philosophers" who no longer believe in philosophy can only "philosophize" because there have been philosophers who believed in the absolute truth of their systems.'[56] One could of course talk of *Weltanschauungen*, but Dilthey's *Weltanschauungsphilosophie* was a kind of *Weltanschauung* without a *Welt*, that is, an activity that simply related prior *Weltanschauungen* to their respective 'worlds.' In contrast, philosophy 'could almost be called a "world" without a *Weltanschauung*.' To illustrate, Kojève proposed to compare Dilthey's concept of *Weltanschauung* with Heidegger's concept of *Befindlichkeit*, which Kojève translated as the 'emotional attitude that a person takes to the world.' Philosophy is related to *Befindlichkeit* first of all as phenomenology. 'As such, philosophy begins by understanding the *Befindlichkeit* as it is, that is, precisely as a *subjective attitude* in an objectively real world ... Next, phenomenological philosophy describes the *Befindlichkeit* ... as it is present to itself, and not as it appears in and for the empirical consciousness of such and such a concrete individual who realizes it in space-time' (which was the first step). Then, phenomenological philosophy accounts for the contents of the attitude: 'It describes the world as it is revealed in the envisaged attitude, but without raising the question of the objective reality of this world, in contrast to the *Weltanschauung*, which affirms implicity its objective reality.' This far Kojève's 'philosophy' looks like *Weltanschauungsphilosophie* plus Husserl's *epoche*. The crucial difference came when the Husserlian 'brackets' were removed: 'As for philosophy properly speaking (based on phenomenology and, in the end, resulting in ontology), it wonders what must be the *real* or *objective* world such that this subjective attitude might be possible and that it could *appear* there where it does. Finally, ontology in the strict sense of the term raises the question relative to the structure of *Being* as such,' including both the being of the world and the attitude that is realized in it by revealing it to be what it is. Here, Kojève said, is the central philosophical problem: 'In order to be able to reveal the being of *everything* that is, of Being as *simply Being*, it is necessary, to begin with, to analyze the *totality* of subjective *attitudes* (whether real or possible) that reveal different aspects of existing being.'[57] Kojève added that Hegel claimed to have done precisely that in his *Phenomenology*. Dilthey's error, or the error of historicism generally, was to declare that all discourse that claimed to account for the nature of things, Being, the Real, etc., was no more than a historically contingent statement, a convention that several or perhaps all people at a particular time (which could last several centuries) agreed to call 'the nature of things,' 'Being,' etc. But if this were true it would also apply to *Lebensphilosophie*, in which case it would not be true. But if it were not true, then there might be a discourse about the nature of things, Being, etc., that was not merely a conventional agreement. In short, Kojève simply reduced Dilthey's historicism to a form of relativism.

And yet, Kojève said, Dilthey was on the right track with his concern for life, history, concrete individuals, and so on. Dilthey was right to dismiss the prejudices of *philosophia perennis*, the traditional notion of a timeless, essential, ahistorical human nature; but he was wrong to dismiss as well the notion of a single universe of rational discourse since inevitably the result was to collapse *Lebensphilosophie* in self-contradiction. In Kojève's words, history, concrete individuality, life, etc. 'only become truly philosophical when they are integrated into an ontological "System" that realized the traditional programme of philosophy.'[58] And that program, the program of *philosophia perennis*, was precisely to give an exhaustive and complete account of the nature of things, Being, etc. In order to realize that program there must be one universe of discourse, which Dilthey's *Lebensphilosophie* denied. Kojève therefore had to affirm that there existed a single universe of discourse, so as not to repeat Dilthey's error, but that it was not eternal in the traditional philosophical sense and did not require the postulate of an unchanging human nature, both of which assumptions, Kojève agreed, Dilthey had shown were untenable. Such a text, Kojève said, was Hegel's *Encyclopaedia*, indubitably historical, not eternal, but also complete. Before dismissing Kojève's claim as preposterous, an outrage to common sense, let us see what this claim means.

Hegel's phenomenological method

Two aspects of Hegel's argument are important in this context, the character of his method and the understanding of the nature of things, Being, etc. that this method both presupposes and brings to light. As did Koyré, Kojève several times mentioned that Hegel's method was phenomenological in the contemporary sense of providing an account of what appears, of strict description of 'the things themselves,' of revealing without prejudice or preconception what is 'there,' and so on.[59] So much is at least probable from the title of Hegel's work *The Phenomenology of Spirit*. But what, then, for Hegel, is dialectic? For surely the conventional reading of Hegel is not wrong to link his philosophy closely to dialectics or 'the' dialectic or to a dialectical method. Indeed, according to Kojève, Hegel's method, while remaining phenomenological, is nevertheless closely tied to dialectics. Here Kojève referred to section 79 of the third edition of Hegel's *Logic*; we shall consider his remarks in more detail shortly. For the moment we may simply note that, according to Kojève's interpretation, dialectic is an ontological category: Being, the nature of things, etc., is itself dialectical.

Assuming, then, that Being is dialectical, there is no reason to think that the method that brings the dialectical nature of Being to light is necessarily dialectical. In the introduction to *Phenomenology* Hegel explained at some length that it was unnecessary to bring external criteria of truth to bear on the topic under investigation because such criteria or standards in fact would exist only in the consciousness that is doing the investigation. Or, to put it another way, there is no point adhering to external criteria when the topic under investigation is those criteria. Because, Hegel said, consciousness is both consciousness of an object, consciousness of what for it is true, real, etc., *and* consciousness itself, consciousness of its knowledge of truth, there is no place but consciousness for these allegedly external standards to be lodged. Accordingly, there is no real testing of facts against standards, since both are present in consciousness. 'Consciousness verifies itself and all that is left for us to do is purely to look on (*das reine Zusehen*)' (*PhG* 72:54). There is, then, textual evidence for Kojève's view that Hegel's method is phenomenological and that his writing serves as a 'perfectly flat and indefinitely extended mirror' (*IH* 453:176) where Being, the Real, etc. is reflected. Thus, if Hegel's System is in any way dialectical, this is because it reflects the dialectical movement of Being of which it is a part and which it experiences by 'looking on' without any preconceived method or criteria.

As for a dialectical method properly speaking, according to Kojève, it is nothing other than discussion. Hegel simply repeated the coherent discussions of philosophy and reported the outcome in his own comprehensive discourse. Taken by itself, each philosophy was indeed dialectical, but only because the reality it expressed was also dialectical. That is, philosophy was the 'superstructure' of historical reality, but one that revealed its meaning. Hence, to understand in a full and comprehensive way the history of philosophy is to understand the meaning of history. Taken by itself, the dialectic or discussion of historical reality is carried on not with words and the clash of options but 'with clubs and swords or cannons on the one hand, and with hammers and sickles or machines on the other' (*IH* 461:185). So long as reality remained dialectical or historical, the account of it would be partial or provisional since what was accounted for was in the process of change. The 'corrections' administered by successive philosophers to the discourse of their predecessors reflected actual historical changes and the movement toward more perfect historical realities. The traditional or pre-Hegelian assumption that a rational human nature was required to participate in a single universe of discourse turns out to have been an 'ideal' or an anticipation of the actual completion of philosophical discourse in Hegel's system. Once the real dialectic of history stopped, philosophy could abandon its heretofore appropriate dialectical method and become phenomenological.

But how do we know when history is over? If history is the story of human transformations of what is given, where there is nothing to transform, nothing to negate, no action in the strong sense of the term, then there is no novelty introduced to the world, no creations, nothing to do – except, of course, understand that there is nothing to do. But understanding is not acting; understanding changes nothing but just 'looks on.' Nobody acts and changes anything because the given reality is completely satisfying. History is stopped. All human possibilities are, and are known to be, exhausted. And this is known because it is known what man is – that is, what he has become. And one can know this only if history is completed. And history is completed only if man has nothing more to do, etc. We are caught in a circular argument.

For Hegel (and Kojève), however, this is not so much a limitation to the argument as a proof of its truth. Just as a tree can be described by proceeding methodically to describe roots, trunk, branches, and leaves, so too does one account for history by the methodical description of the notorious succession of thesis, antithesis, synthesis (which can serve as a new thesis, and so on). Hegel avoided the impasse of historicism, according to Kojève, by ending up where he started, so that if one wanted to continue speaking one would simply repeat what had already been said, just as, once having exhaustively described a tree, all one can do is describe it again. If the description is indeed exhaustive, nothing can possibly be added, and it is 'eternal.' The 'tree' in this instance, however, is history, or rather 'conceptual history,' *begriffne Geschichte*, so that the 'eternity' involved might better be described as post-temporal or post-historical. Several questions have doubtless occurred to many. Did Hegel really account for all possible attitudes? Are all human desires exhausted in the desire for recognition? Did Hegel truly add nothing of his own to his descriptions? We will postpone these questions until after we have considered his argument in detail. For the moment it is enough that we see what is involved in the notion that Hegel's method was purely descriptive or phenomenological.

Dialectical structure of being

Like all genuine philosophy, Kojève said, Hegel's System of Science was developed on three distinct but hierarchically related levels. The first or 'phenomenological' level described the totality of real Being as it appears to real human beings, who are really part of the Being they speak about. The philosopher does not stop there, however: he is also interested in knowing what the real natural and human World must be in actuality, *Wirklichkeit*, in order to appear as it does. This level was called by Kojève 'metaphysical' and was contained in Hegel's later books, *Philosophy of Spirit* and *Philosophy of Nature*. Beyond the metaphysical level is what Kojève called the 'ontological' level, which is concerned with knowing what Being itself must be in order that it actualize itself in the real World, as described 'metaphysically,' which appears to human beings as they are described in *Phenomenology*. Hegel's 'ontology' is contained in his *Logic*. Considered objectively, phenomenology is derivative;

but subjectively it is the only one to be described directly and for which evidence appears. In this section, we shall review Kojève's summary of Hegel's ontology insofar as it is contained in Hegel's definition of dialectic.

As mentioned earlier, section 79 et seq of *Logic* provides a description of the threefold structure of revealed being. The familiar triad, Being for-itself, Being in-itself, and Being in-and-for-itself, is also present in the Discourse that correctly reveals that structure.

The first aspect of complete Discourse, which corresponds to abstract Understanding, *Verstehen*, describes Being abstractly in accordance with the principle of Identity. This is not wrong, since Being is, indeed, what it is. Yet this conception is insufficient inasmuch as it is a mere tautology and not a discourse, properly speaking. As soon as the thought of Understanding seeks to say something, it must introduce alterity, which contradicts identity, and so falsifies its own abstract truth. If the discourse of Understanding cancels itself – and we shall see this again in our consideration of chapter III of *Phenomenology* – then the concept of Being it upholds must be inadequate. 'Hence one must surpass Understanding to reveal real Being in its totality. Or, more exactly, the thought of Understanding is surpassed because the discursive self-revelation of Being reveals not only its Identity with itself but also its other fundamental ontological aspects' (*IH* 472:198). Thus does thought move from Understanding, *Verstehen*, to Reason, *Vernunft*.

The second and negative constituent element or 'moment' of revealed Being, which Kojève called 'negatively rational thought' or 'negative Reason,' identified the process of negation of determinate entities revealed by the first constituent element, Understanding. Reason, *Vernunft*, does not import negativity from the outside; rather, Being itself implies besides Identity, which ensures that every being remains identical to itself, a second primordial ontological category, Negativity, which ensures that every being can become other than itself. Real Being, accordingly, is both Identity and Negativity, both given-Being, *Sein*, or Nature, and also Becoming, *Werden*, History. For Understanding it is of course impossible to be oneself at the same time as being other than oneself. For Reason, however, all that is involved is the introduction of time into the static panorama of Being revealed by the first constituent element. Thus consciousness is for the first time explicitly and focally introduced. Henceforth the attitude that consciousness has actively taken up and assumed must never be ignored. For the individual human being, one exists (as one has been) for oneself (now). In contrast to existence for oneself (or, more generally, Being for-itself), the existence of simply self-identical being is in itself or for-others (who are themselves conscious).

So, Being that is both Identity and Negativity is more than Being that is simply Identity. It has a degree of freedom with respect to Being that is identical with itself in that it can identify with that Being without having to be it. For example, I can identify with my cat, Bobsy's bar in Longview, a fire hydrant in Singapore, the Calgary Tower, the bridge at Clare College, and so on, without becoming any of these things because I can form and possess the adequate concept of them through my discourse, all the while retaining the concept of myself in my memory. In other words, with this second ontological category we have a discourse that reveals static given-Being by negating it but also preserves the negated given-Being as an ideal or meaning.

Being is not yet adequately described by the two categories so far discussed. To repeat the simple objection of Understanding, Being cannot both be Identity and Negativity; and likewise for Being taken as Negativity, it must negate itself and 'be' pure Nothingness, *Nichts*, or it must become the same as itself through its self-negation, which would return us once again to static Identity and to Understanding. In other words, Being is neither Identity nor Negativity taken separately nor taken merely as juxtaposed. It is both taken together, what Kojève called Totality, and it is this aspect of Being that is revealed by 'positively rational thought' or positive Reason. 'It is as Totality that Being is truly and fully dialectical. But it is a dialectical Totality and not a tautological identity because it is also Negativity. Totality is the unifying-unity of Identity and Negativity: it is affirmation by negation' (*IH* 466:202). Totality is therefore conscious Being – or rather, since this Being can negate itself as well as external givens, it is self-conscious Being, Being in-and-for-itself. In *Phenomenology* Hegel called it *Geist*, Spirit, in *Encyclopaedia*, absolute Concept or Idea. Spirit, then, is split by Negativity into given-Being and the contrary that reveals the meaning of that Being; but it becomes reconciled to itself again when the Totality of Being is fully, exhaustively, and correctly revealed by a total discourse. This discourse, as we shall see in more detail in the next chapter, is Wisdom, the speech of the Sage, the System of Science.

Kojève summarized his interpretation of Hegel's ontology as follows. 'The Thesis describes the *given* material against which action is to be applied, the Antithesis reveals this *action* itself as well as the thought that animates it (the "project"), while the Synthesis makes visible the result of this action, namely the completed and objectively real *work* (*Werk*).

This work *is*, just as the initial given; only it exists not as *given* but as *created* by the active negation of the given' (*IH* 481:207).

The transformation of Being in-itself by Being for-itself into Being in-and-for-itself does not happen all at once. It 'takes' time to eliminate all the givens from a product. Certain elements of any particular Synthesis (save the last) will be simply givens. Thus, any Synthesis (save the last) may serve as a Thesis. Generally speaking, the process as a whole by which the element of givenness is eliminated and transformed into a product is History. Until there exists a product, described by a Synthesis, that implies *no* givens whatsoever that could be created into products by negating action, History continues. The final product, so far as we are concerned, is the universal and homogeneous State; the final Synthesis is Hegel's System of Science.

To put it in another but equivalent way, Hegel's philosophy is dialectical specifically because it tries to account for man insofar as human being is irreducibly different from all that is Nature. Nature is what it is; man by comparison is free to become what he may be by transforming what is. That is, he is both independent of Nature, since he can act on (and into) it, and he is dependent on Nature, since his action must make an impression on something. Freedom, Kojève said, preserves itself by perpetual creation, namely History. What distinguishes man from nature, therefore, is historicity. Hence to account fully for man is to account for History, which we know must be concluded if the account is truly to be full and adequate.

Hegel's anthropology

We come, then, to a synthesis of the last two sections, the phenomenological dialectic. Or rather, since this topic is treated in the entirety of *Phenomenology*, we come to a preliminary remark concerning the phenomenological dialectic. From the foregoing two sections we know that we are concerned at the phenomenological level with the meaning of Being as it appears to man, which necessarily involves an account of human being, an anthropology, an ontology of man. We also know that what is dialectical is the concrete real, 'the Real-revealed-by-a-discourse and Discourse-revealing-a-real' (*IH* 455:178), or Totality, total and final Synthesis, Spirit.

This 'thing,' revealed Being, which is indicated by the above terms, all of which are rigorously equivalent, has, clearly, two constituent elements: 'Being as *revealed* (Identity, Thesis) and Being as *revealing* (Negativity, Antithesis). Consequently, at the metaphysical level two Worlds that are inseparable but essentially different must be distinguished: the natural World and the historical or human World. Finally, the phenomenological level is constituted by the reflection of *natural* empirical existence within *human* empirical existence (external-Consciousness, *Bewusstsein)'(IH* 488:216). Now, we know that the specifically dialectical constituent element of Totality is Negativity, and that, taken by itself, Identity is in no way dialectical. Accordingly, when one moves from this ontological level to the metaphysical, it follows that the Real is dialectical because of the human or historical World and that Nature (including the postulate of an 'ideal' of a 'human nature' evoked by pre-Hegelian philosophers in order to correct one another) is of itself in no way dialectical. Likewise at the phenomenological level, man, being dialectical, imparts a dialectical element to natural phenomena because they appear to him – as, for example, they do in the natural sciences. Thus, Hegel's discussion of the 'dialectic of Nature' in chapter 5 A a of *Phenomenology* was according to Kojève not about a dialectic of nature, which is impossible nonsense, but properly speaking a description of the vitalistic experience of Nature by a bourgeois Schellingian intellectual. Of course Hegel may have thought he was describing a dialectic of nature, but this was an error.[60] In short, the phenomenological dialectic is a dialectic of human existence. We shall therefore consider the appearance of Hegel's three ontological and metaphysical categories, namely Being in-itself, Being for-itself, and Being in-and-for-itself, insofar as they also constitute the fundamental categories of his anthropology.

There is nothing particularly complicated in this. Identity, or Being in-itself, appears in Man as his biological life, his animality, and in general every aspect of human being that is inherited, from genes to jeans and money. Negativity, or Being for-itself, appears in Man as free creative action, specifically, in the activities of fighting for prestige and of labouring. Totality, or Being in-and-for-itself, appears in Man as historicity that preserves continuity in memory even while becoming other than what it was. Kojève does a masterly job ringing the rather complicated changes on the interrelations of these formal elements. Little more than a demonstration of his intellectual dexterity, which surely is undoubted even by his severest critics, would be served by reproducing the details of his argument. Accordingly, we shall content ourselves with the results.

Man, according to Kojève's Hegel, is a free, historical, mortal individual. By his action man negates what is given but creates at the same time a product that is preserved historically. The inseparability of freedom and historicity is obvious enough: there is history, properly speaking, that is, unforeseen creative evolution, only where there are free actors, and freedom can be actualized only by the creation of a historical world. In addition, however, man is an individual, a unique particular that is nevertheless potentially recognizable by all other individuals as identical with them. The historical manifestation of Individuality is the active realization of the desire for recognition. Necessarily this process of realization takes place in society or under the aegis of a state; but so long as that state is not homogeneous, it will not be Individuality that gains recognition but only one or another inherited given (family, money, race, gender, etc.), and so long as it is not universal, Individuality is not recognized by all, but only by a particular group. This is why modern, post-historical men who seriously desire universal recognition most often attempt to conquer the world.

However that may be, the full realization of Individuality, occurring within the universal and homogeneous State, simultaneously concludes History since now man will be able to be fully and completely satisfied and will have no need to negate his own final product. The three categories, Individuality, Freedom, and History, which are the anthropological equivalents of Identity, Negativity, and Totality, Thesis, Antithesis, Synthesis, etc., are obviously bound together: 'Man cannot "appear" as an individual without "manifesting" himself as a free agent of History; he can "reveal" himself as free only by "appearing" as an historical individual; and he can "manifest" himself historically only on condition that he "appears" in his individual freedom or his free individuality' (IH 508–9:238). In short, an individual is necessarily historical and therefore free; likewise, a historical being is always freely striving to be an individual. In other words, Man is a dialectical being in his empirical, phenomenal existence, his Dasein.

In section 81 of Encyclopaedia Hegel said that everything that is finite is an act of self-supersession or dialectical self-overcoming, Selbstaufhebung. Kojève would correct this to say that only a finite entity can be dialectical; that is, even though not all finite entities are dialectical, all dialectical ones are finite. We have just seen that, according to Hegel, man is a dialectical being. It follows that man is also finite. The finitude of being appears to man, on the human, phenomenal level, as death, his own individual death. Thus, 'an historical free individual is necessarily mortal, and a truly mortal being is always an historical, free individual' (IH 512:242). Again Kojève went through the variations and interrelationships of these four elements, and there is no need to repeat here what he said.

One aspect of human finiteness should be mentioned, however, because of its direct political significance. Because man dies fully and completely, with no 'afterlife' and no 'Beyond' where failures 'here below' could be redeemed, his actual participation in History is serious. Man alone, through his free individual acts, creates History, and he alone looks on, knowing he may fail, knowing he must die. Yet failure is simply unrealized possibility, so that if men did not fail there would be nothing new to do. That is, once a man is truly successful, in the sense that he has exhausted all human possibilities, there is nothing further for anyone else to do but copy his success. However that may be, History, which is the story of failures redeemed not by God in the Beyond but by other, later men acting here below, is possible and can be concluded only because of death. If, as Hegel argued, the end of History means human satisfaction, one can say that, by understanding fully his own death, and thereby knowing himself to be a free, historical individual, man becomes conscious of a self that has no desire to become other than as it is. Such a self has no reason to change, and change is impossible anyhow. We have only what 'appears' to be change but what in reality is no more than a shifting of perspective or a recombination of the same things that have already appeared. Once again, therefore, history is over.

Historical consciousness: a summary

We began this chapter with a consideration of modern historical consciousness. The predicament of our self-understanding is that most of us tend to consider our lives exhaustively ordered by our own actions. Yet we also desire to know if our actions make sense, are right, just, etc., and we seem to have a great deal of difficulty discovering standards by which to measure them. Not everyone is historically self-conscious, of course, but not everyone is modern either. For a non-modern, non-historically minded person, the dilemmas of historicism are self-generated fallacies. Such a one would, no doubt, offer the following advice: give up your historical preoccupations and recover the eternal verities, truth, beauty, justice, piety, etc., that your own attitude obscures. The historically minded, however, find such advice, even if well meant, difficult or impossible to follow. For them more is involved than a change of heart: they want reasons too. Moreover, they have their own reasons to believe that if the non-modern believer in the eternal verities would just have a change of heart he would no longer believe. We shall consider in detail below Kojève's argument about why belief in eternal verities has become impossible for modern individuals. One thing at least seems clear: no amount of argument based upon non-modern assumptions about eternal verities is going to carry much weight for modern historically minded individuals. If anything will be persuasive it will be history itself, the actual unfolding of what, for the non-modern tradition of *philosophia perennis* is nihilism. But nothing can be guaranteed since everything is in question.

The context within which this version of the war between ancients and moderns takes place is indicated approximately by the term 'French Hegelianism.' In effect, we confine ourselves to a consideration, more or less on its own terms, of the strategy and tactics of the modern camp. Jean Wahl began his study of the 'concrete' at a time when French philosophy was a march toward Kant's *Critiques*. Thus, his study of the unhappy consciousness, Koyré's use of Husserl's insights into consciousness of time, and Kojève's remarkable synthesis all appeared as daringly unorthodox adventures. Moreover, the power of their intellects, the sheer competence of their work, ensured that Hegel would not be ignored. No doubt Hyppolite's translation of *Phenomenology* and his detailed commentary were important in gaining academic respectability for Hegel, but it was the more exciting and 'existential' Hegel who came to light during the 1930s that seems to have had the greatest impact.

We began with a selective reading of *Le Malheur de la conscience dans la philosophie de Hegel* because it was the first book published in France to argue that Hegel was in no way an abstract thinker. According to Wahl, *Phenomenology* was concerned with questions of a practical, moral, religious, and political nature. More specifically, he said that Hegel sought, through his System of Science, to overcome the diremption, unhappiness, and boredom of his own epoch by providing a conceptual account of the appearance of disorder in the actual events of history. Wahl had made a significant discovery about Hegel's motivations and intentions. But it was precisely the warmth of this flesh-and-blood Hegel that Koyré wished to discount in favour of the cold logician.

Koyré raised an important methodological objection to Wahl's procedure as well: the key to the meaning of Hegel's later writings did not lie in his unpublished juvenilia. The later writings should be examined on their own, with a view to grasping the argument itself and not its motivation. When Koyré applied his own approach to Hegel's texts the results were, so far as the notion of history was concerned, rather surprising. He avoided any trace of historicism, which Wahl apparently did not, but at the cost of leaving Hegel's account of the relationship of eternity to time (or as Kojève would say, of the Concept to History) obscure, not to say unintelligible. The problem, very clearly, was that if Hegel had written a philosophy of history, that is, a coherent account of the temporal doings of man, history would in principle have been concluded. This Koyré refused to accept. Whatever their differences, Wahl and Koyré had had the important insight that Hegel's *Phenomenology* did not deal simply with consciousness as a sort of epistemological problem and was not merely the first part of a grand intellectual arabesque parading under the pretentious colours of 'German idealism.' It dealt with history in the most comprehensive sense, with the actions and words of mankind, including those philosophic speeches that attempted to account comprehensively for human deeds.

Kojève's interpretation began more or less where Wahl's and Koyré's left off. Like Koyré, he accepted the description of Hegel's book implied by its title. *Phenomenology of Spirit* was a coherent discourse, a logos, concerned with the appearance, the phenomena, of the concrete real Spirit. Necessarily all spiritual phenomena have appeared, or else a coherent account of them would be incomplete, and the book could not serve as an introduction to the System of Science or Wisdom.

Hegel's method could be phenomenological and still account for the entirety of history because Being was dialectical. According to Kojève it was dialectical in its non-apparent structure, but more important for our purposes it was dialectical in its historical appearance. In Kojève's own words, 'To say that Being is dialectical is to say first of all (on the onto-logical level) that it is a *Totality* that implies *Identity* and *Negativity*. Next it is to say (on the metaphysical level) that Being is realized not only as the *Natural World*, but also as a *historical* (or human) *World*, these two Worlds exhausting the totality of the objective-real (there is no divine World). Finally it is to say (on the phenomenological level) that the objective-real empirically-exists and appears not only as inanimate thing, as plant and animal, but also as *free, historical*, essentially temporal or *mortal, individual* (who *fights* and who *labours*). Or, in other words: to say that there is *Totality* or *Mediation*, or *dialectical-Supersession*, is to say that in addition to *given-Being* there is also *creative-Action* that ends in a *Product*' (*IH* 527–8:259).

In a formal or abstract logical sense, Kojève had overcome the difficulties raised by Koyré. According to Kojève, there was one universe of discourse, the System of Science. Hence the self-contradiction of historicism was overcome. But it was a human, historical creation and not an imaginary ideal that philosophers sought but never achieved. The historical condition for writing the System of Science was that all human potentialities had been fulfilled, that history was over. The proof that this was so is found in the empirical existence of *Encyclopedia*. However, contrary to common sense it may seem, the notion of an end to history has its own coherence. But mere coherence, as Hegel would be the first to acknowledge, is insufficient. We also require evidence and a detailed argument. This is presented in the following chapters.

3

How history ended

Kojève's 'correction' of Hegel

Kojève's book *Introduction à la lecture de Hegel* was not written as a book but consists rather of lecture notes and transcripts of lectures delivered over six academic years in the Section des sciences religieuses of the École pratique des hautes études between 1933 and 1939.[1] The greatest amount of time appears to have been devoted to chapter 6, on the dialectic of historical reality, and to chapter 8, on the post-historical attitude, the attitude of the Wise Man or Sage. During the early years Kojève completed a special study of the significance of death, to which we shall turn shortly, and another, referred to above, on Hegel's method. These early studies were placed by the editor, Raymond Queneau, in appendices along with an analytical table of contents of *Phenomenology*.[2] According to Kojève, *Phenomenology* was divided into two parts. The first discussed the constituent elements of existence, of which there were three classes: cognitive, emotional, and active. The second dealt with concrete existential attitudes, of which there were three classes: apolitical attitudes, political attitudes, and the post-historical attitude of the Sage. The three years between 1933–4 and 1935–6, the accounts of which constitute about one-eighth of the text, Kojève devoted to an intensive, almost line-by-line exegesis of passages from the first six chapters of *Phenomenology*. Thereafter his remarks were freer, contained more allusions to contemporary affairs, and were more confidently asserted. One may conclude that, beginning about 1936, with the commentary on subdivision B of chapter 6, Kojève tended to combine his own analysis and argument with his exegesis of Hegel's text.[3]

It was Hegel himself who provided sufficient warrant for Kojève's procedure. Toward the end of the Preface to *Phenomenology*, he reflected on his own role as author of what he realized was an unconventional book, a book unlikely to find favour with very many philosophers or theologians. He took some comfort, he said, in the conviction that 'it is in the nature of truth to squeeze its way through [into public acceptance] when its time has come; it appears only when this time has come, and so never appears too early nor ever finds a public not ripe to receive it.' Certain self-styled 'representatives' of the public might object to Hegel's book because they were incapable of grasping absolute Knowledge. But they, he said, 'are like the dead burying their dead,' which implied that Hegel was the new Redeemer, and that we are to follow him, as the crowds followed Jesus, and be healed (cf Matt 8:18–22). However that may be, the appearance of Truth at its proper time meant that 'the share of the particular individual in the total work of the Spirit is very small.' He is no more than the occasion for the appearance of universal truth, even though 'he must become and do what he can' (*PhG* 58–9:44–5). And this is why, according to Kojève, there was nothing illegitimate about his 'corrections,' and in no way could they be considered a falsification of Hegel's word. In short, although the System of Science, Wisdom, is the result of the efforts of somebody called Hegel – he does what he can – those efforts simply fulfil the labour of Spirit, patiently prepared throughout the course of history.

A very important consequence followed: because Science or Wisdom is singular and also universal,[4] it may be that the formulation provided on the occasion of its first articulation was incomplete or perhaps inconsistent. For example, Kojève spent some time, and not without embarrassment, correcting Hegel's inconsistencies regarding Nature. Our review of Hegel's phenomenological method and the dialectic of Being or the Real showed that, in the strict or narrow sense, the constituent element of Negativity is 'there' because Man is present in Reality. Any description of Nature that does not take this into account, then, is bound to be abstract. The 'discourse' of subatomic physics, for example, describes matter in terms of tendencies to exist and probability waves, which is to say, interconnections between the experimental situation and its measurement. This is not a description of 'things' by words that are meaningful; it is a display of probabilities by means of an algorithm. In other words, there is no revealing of the Real, no Truth, properly speaking in the specialized, abstract 'discourse' of physics (*IH* 453–5:177–8). When one moves from the realm of algorithms to 'things,' one must, as one researcher in high-energy theoretical physics said, employ a highly 'unscientific' vocabulary of myth and imagery.[5] The reason for this, according to Hegel's argument in *Phenomenology* (e.g. *PhG* 563 ll21–5:492 ll8–12), is that natural being is in no way dialectical. It is determined only by the category of Identity (*IH* 474 n1:199 n10). In Kojève's view, this was the correct understanding of Nature. In *Encyclopaedia* (section 81 n1), however, Hegel said that sheer finitude gave rise to dialectic inasmuch as what is finite is also transient and changing. Here he explicitly declared that physical elements, planetary motion, meteorological processes, and the basis of every natural change that 'forces nature out of itself' are evidence of a natural dialectic. This, Kojève said, was a regrettable error.[6] Let us see why.

We saw in chapter 2 that revealed Being in its totality was dialectical, but also that Totality was constituted of 1 / a purely identical natural reality that does not supersede itself dialectically and contains no novelty in its motion, and 2 / a human, negating, reality that supersedes both itself and what is naturally given to it. Through the dialectical supersession of the given there exist novelty and speech that discloses or reveals the product. In this way, then, concrete Reality, Reality revealed by discourse, is indeed dialectical. But just because the Totality is dialectical it by no means follows that each of its constituent elements must also be. To believe that everything that is is in the same way is a prejudice in favour of what Kojève called 'ontological monism.' Here were two symmetrical errors. On the one hand it was wrong to follow the Greeks, who discovered Nature and the ontological category of Identity and talk about human beings having an immutable nature – a slavish nature, for example.[7] On the other hand, it was wrong to follow Hegel, who, upon discovery of the ontological categories of Negativity and Totality on the basis of his analysis of human being, applied this anthropological ontology to Nature. 'Therefore,' Kojève concluded, 'it seems necessary to distinguish within the dialectical ontology of revealed Being or Spirit (dominated by the category of Totality), a non-dialectical ontology (of Greek and traditional inspiration) of nature (dominated by the category of Identity), and a dialectical ontology (of Hegelian inspiration, but modified as a result [of this argument]) of Man or History (dominated by the category of Negativity)' (*IH* 486n:213n; cf also *IH* 575n).

Kojève's correction of Hegel on this point did not mean that natural changes are inexplicable. What Hegel said in *Encyclopaedia* is, of course, incontrovertible: there are cosmic changes. These changes, however, are not linear but cyclical, as the old question of the chicken and the egg shows. And as for evolution, even if one does not accept that modification of the genetic text by the deletion, substitution, or scrambling of one or more pairs of nucleotides in DNA is random,[8] there are vastly different orders of time involved in the natural evolution of organisms and in, say, the 'evolution' of a chair from an oak tree. Whatever the time of the evolutionary cosmos may be, it is not history (IH 378:147). The same argument applies a fortiori to any unified theory of particles and forces that would predict the eventual evaporation of the universe into photons, electrons, muons, neutrinos, and what-not.

There is another even more serious reason to reject Hegel's notion of a dialectic of nature: it would make Wisdom unrealizable. We noted in chapter 2, and will see in more detail below, that Wisdom is necessarily circular and can come into being, so far as man is concerned, only at the end of History. So long as man changes and introduces novelty into the world he creates himself as other than what he currently is; thus, any historical account of what man is is already out of date and must be seen as a provisional truth. But if Nature as well as Man were historical, then truth, science, and Wisdom would be possible only at the end of time, including the time of the cosmos. And as for those changes in nature that took place in history, that is, before the end of time, they would be utterly unintelligible. If the stones and animals and bodies of ancient Egypt had changed as much as its architecture or religion, we would not be able to recognize the Egyptians as human. Even if they are not conscious as we are,[9] the different between modern men and ancient Egyptians is not a difference of species. On the contrary, it is precisely the abiding identity of the natural substratum of human being that allows the differences of human historicity to appear, and eventually to be grasped conceptually – at the end of History (cf IH 486–7n:214n).

If, as Kojève argued, the notion of a dialectic of natural being as presented in Encyclopaedia is 'absurd,' what is to be made of the vitalistic and allegedly phenomenological biology found in chapter 5 A a of Phenomenology? In this section, Hegel was referring to Schelling's Philosophy of Nature. Schelling thought he had provided a metaphysics of Nature, and Hegel allowed in this passage that he had given only a phenomenology of Nature. Hegel's error, Kojève said, though not as bad as Schelling's, was still an error. The best that can be said for it is that it expressed Hegel's Schellingian imagination. For 'us' who are properly Hegelians (as Hegel in this passage was not), it must be considered an element in the phenomenology of human (not natural) Being. What

Hegel truly did in chapter 5 A a was describe a bourgeois intellectual who devoted his life to the observation of Nature and interpreted his observations in a vitalistic way. Understood in this way, Hegel's description would be perfectly acceptable (*IH* 490:218).

The significance of Kojève's corrections, no less than the closing words of Hegel's preface quoted above, is that priority must be given to the appearance of Truth in the System and not to its author, a mere vessel and agent of Spirit. So far as Kojève's writing is concerned, the question of the validity of his interpretation of *Hegel* does not even arise.[10] When the System and not its (first) author is seen to be fundamental, Hegel becomes simply the first example of the Sage. 'To tell the truth,' Kojève remarked, 'the Sage is no longer an "individual" in the sense that he would be essentially different than all others. If Wisdom consists in the possession of Truth (which is *one* and which is the *same* for Hegel and for all his readers), then one Sage does not differ in any way from another Sage' (*IH* 508 n1:238 n30). There is, therefore, nothing personal in Kojève's 'corrections' of Hegel: they are both creatures of the System. That is why, for example, Kojève characterized one of his later books as a third introduction to the System of Science.[11] The other two, presumably, were his earlier *Introduction à la lecture de Hegel* and *Phenomenology of Spirit* itself.

Methodological objections have been raised against such an assertion. We shall consider them further at the end of this essay and will examine them now only to suggest a Hegelian or Kojèian response. Stanley Rosen, who has read both Hegel and Kojève with more care than any other writer with whom I am acquainted, expressed what is probably a widely held criticism. Summarizing chapter 5 B, he wrote: 'The initial discovery of self-consciousness in the struggle for recognition is continuously being lost, acquired, and lost again, until such time as the individual acquired *Self-Knowledge*, or recognition that self-consciousness is the manifestation of Absolute Spirit.' Nevertheless, he went on, 'there is no explanation in the *Phenomenology* of how the "two" selves are able to recognize each other in their initial encounter. In order for one self to recognize himself reflected in the other, he must already be acquainted with or conscious of himself.'[12] That is, Hegel wished to prove what in fact he presupposed.

There can be two responses to this observation. But first one must characterize Hegel's peculiar rhetoric. In effect, Hegel presented his argument from two different perspectives. The first is a phenomenology of consciousness as it attains an increasingly comprehensive knowledge

of itself and the world, as it grows wiser with experience. From this perspective one might reply that the origin of recognition is necessarily
veiled in silence because at that 'moment' of proto-consciousness no discourse was possible. One is dealing, in effect, with a myth of genesis that,
like all such stories, must be believed in if it is to be taken as true. As a
myth, it is expressed in the form of representational religious imagery,
not discursive speech or concepts. Consequently it is, of itself, impervious to merely logical objections. Hegel's second perspective is not really
a perspective or standpoint, but Wisdom, and he is not arguing so much
as revealing the truth as it really is. In this respect his discourse amounts
to an expression of the identity and differentiation of the Absolute, or
Totality. As Rosen remarked in his conclusion: 'In the last analysis, then,
no explanation can be given of the "origin" of self-consciousness, because in the last analysis self-consciousness does not originate.'[13] In the
language used above, Hegel and Kojève (or rather, the structure of their
self-consciousness in its opposition and comprehension) are creatures of
the one System of Science. Accordingly it is enough for the Sage to know
the fact that recognition *did* occur. We shall return to this problem
shortly. However, we must begin with 'natural' consciousness and the
proto-consciousness of desire.[14]

Desire and natural consciousness

The central doctrine of Kojève's interpretation, reiterated several times
during the course of his 600-page book, and stated with engaging simplicity in its opening sentence, is: 'Man is self-consciousness' (*IH* 11:3).
What is not or not yet self-conscious is not human, and what pretends to
a status above or beyond self-consciousness is not real, but merely an
aspect or moment of consciousness becoming conscious of itself, which
happens to be imaginary. The implications of the ultimacy of self-consciousness constitute the general topic of Kojève's book.

One becomes self-conscious when one says 'I' and understands thereby
that one's consciousness is set apart from what is non-consciousness. The
logically first step, namely the sensuous apprehension of a sheer 'this-
ness' is, however, prior to speech and understanding, for as Hegel said 'it
simply is impossible for us ever to say or express in words any sensuous
given-Being that we *mean*' (*PhG* 82:60). One may conceive of a condition
where one is unaware of the distinction between one's self (or consciousness) and one's surroundings (or given-Being). Kojève called this
condition one of 'absorption' by a not-yet self-conscious subject in and

by an object, and he identified this state of consciousness as 'contemplation.' So understood, contemplation is hardly the goal of consciousness,
and even less of philosophical consciousness, but rather amounts to a
condition prior even to a diffuse somatic awareness and virtually indistinguishable from that of a simple metabolizing organism or even a
stone.

Unless one is comatose or dead one does not remain 'absorbed.' The
'spell' of this attitude is eventually pierced by desire, first of all by the
'natural desire' to eat and so preserve one's body, to eat rather than be
eaten. War is therefore more fundamental than peace. The relation
between man and nature is adequately expressed by modern technological physics, which in turn serves as the chief weapon by which war upon
nature is waged. In short, the first act of hostility is eating, and the first
awareness of the precariousness of life is felt as the desire for, which is to
say, a lack of, food. War is natural even though it is directed against
nature. As with Hobbes, nature is but matter in motion; it can be measured, and thereby understood, and tamed. The human spirit, from the
start, and even before it is properly speaking human, exists in hostile
surroundings. The natural imperatives of survival mean that human
beings must take action against nature.

Desire, then, reveals to a subject that it is distinct from the objects that
surround it. Now, we know that consciousness is distinct from non-con-
scious being, what, following Kojève, we may call given-Being (Sein).
Accordingly, self-consciousness presupposes desire. That is, of course, a
tedious way to say that human beings are biologically alive and that they
maintain their lives through metabolism. This formulation brings to
light an important principle: desire leads to action (not 'contemplative'
absorption), and action, or 'negation,' to a twofold result. On the one
hand an object is destroyed, but on the other hand a subject, that is, a being
that senses itself independent, autonomous, and no longer absorbed by
things, is created and preserved. 'Generally speaking, the Ego of Desire is
an emptiness that receives a real positive content only by negating action
that satisfies Desire by destroying, transforming, and "assimilating" the
desired non-Ego' (IH 12:4). In this first instance the object negated was
naturally existing food, vegetables, for example, and the subject created
was equally natural. The awareness of itself that this bovine animal has
was called by Kojève 'Sentiment-of-Self,' a 'natural consciousness,' or a
non-reflective feeling of selfhood (see PhG 165f:132f; 196:157). The
rhythmic changes of contemplation and desire, which appear as a cycle
of hunger and feeding that in turn temporarily results in satisfaction,

may continue indefinitely and may never lead to self-consciousness. The 'struggle for existence,' a primitive war with nature, does no more than produce animals and a natural animal awareness.

Yet within animal consciousness necessarily lies the potential of human or self-consciousness. The single degree of freedom that lifts desire from contemplative absorption to activity inevitably awakens spiritual as well as physical appetites. As did Glaukon, we forsake the natural, healthy city, despising it as fit for pigs, and seek that satisfaction of desire the first appearance of which is the luxury of fine food. Before considering the aspects of this process that are important for our purposes, we shall briefly consider its development as necessity or inevitability. That is, we look at it first from the 'perspective' of the Sage; we presume to be wise. Then we may consider this paradigm of the human spirit as it develops historically.

Consciousness and self-consciousness

Part A of Hegel's *Phenomenology*, under the general head of 'consciousness,' deals with the movement from sense-certainty, the lowest, poorest, and most abstract stage of consciousness, by way of perception to analytical thought. The move from sense-certainty to perception, as Merleau-Ponty pointed out at great length in his own *Phenomenology*, involves consciousness in ambiguities: we lose touch with the things of the world by grasping after their truth. To perceive – in German, *wahrnehmen*, to take truly – implies both the universality of *true* perception and the particularity or subjectivity of the *perceiver*, the one who 'takes' the truth. The ambiguity or internal dialectic of perception leads consciousness to the resolution of analytical thought, what Hegel called understanding, *Verstand*. One finds in effect a recapitulation of Hobbes's 'epistemology.'

Having lost the sense-certainties of seeing and hearing, etc., in the ambiguities of perception, consciousness now formalizes the results of perception, eventually as a legal structure. The instability of the things of the world as given to perception is replaced by the (presumed or assumed) stability of scientific laws constructed on the basis of an indubitable method. Just as critics of modern behavioural political science have pointed to the one-sidedness of holding method to be the key to the truth about political things, so Hegel analysed (with great wit, one may add) the puzzles of its own making that consciousness encounters when it transforms the fluctuating meanings or properties grasped in perception into the quiet concepts of analytical science. But this scientific world is 'inverted' or 'upside-down' in that laws (eventually one law, the law of laws or the Concept of law) are completely detached from things and yet are considered to be the utmost in clarity about things. Furthermore, the clarity of laws is said to increase precisely as they grow distant from things; final clarity reposes in mathematical form. This is called 'explanation,' a self-satisfying activity, Hegel said, 'because in it consciousness is, as it were, directly talking to itself, enjoying only itself; even though it appears to be busied with something else it is in fact occupied only with itself' (*PhG* 127:101). That consciousness is *merely* self-satisfied proves its inadequacy, but that it is *self*-satisfied opens a new horizon.

Heretofore consciousness has been directed at externalities. Only with awareness of the contradictions of the inverted world of scientific analysis does consciousness also encounter itself and enter thereby the 'native realm of truth' (*PhG* 134:104). When consciousness first enters its native land, however, it is as a stranger: understanding is as much an alienation from the world as it is a discovery and experience of itself. By emerging from the rhythm of desire and 'contemplation' to reflect on the meaning of that rhythm, one eventually attains the analytic understanding of scientific laws. Yet consciousness understands itself in terms of those laws as radically not at home in the world. Accordingly, the chief task of consciousness will have to be a recovery or reappropriation of the world it has lost, a reappropriation that brings it home to the native realm of truth. We have summarized from the 'perspective' of the Sage the epistemological dead end attained by analytical thought, the creation of abstract, detached, and clear laws that correspond to no things. It is equivalent to the initial experiences of consciousness as a metabolizing ego, an endless and meaningless rhythm of inversions. The next step, evidently, is to learn 'what consciousness knows in knowing itself' (*PhG* 129:103).

Conceptually, this development of consciousness moves the discussion from the cognitive to the active element of human existence. We have seen that consciousness develops in opposition to externalities; but now we know from the dialectic of the inverted world that the 'objects' of the world are also internal to consciousness. Consciousness 'posits' or perhaps invents the objects of its desire. Implicitly or unselfconsciously, therefore, consciousness as animality *now* appears already to have posited the 'object' of biological life inasmuch as the appropriation of the object (its negation by eating, for example) serves to sustain and preserve consciousness, and thereby shows to consciousness itself that it exists as an independent life.

Destruction of the external object gives consciousness a self-certainty, it is true, but also the awareness of the independence of the object, so that consciousness simply reproduces (or posits) the object and the desire to negate it. However, since desire *qua* desire is not an object but a lack, an emptiness, the presence of an absence, to transcend this merely vital dialectic self-consciousness must desire something other than the mere object, namely 'the essence of Desire' (*PhG* 139:109). In other words, if self-certainty comes from the supersession (*Aufhebung*) of an other, and if this other is simply an object or given-Being, then self-consciousness appears condemned to the endless rhythms of mere life. But if this were so, if existence had not even attained Hobbes's state of nature, then the stage of sentiment-of-self would have been final. But it is not, for 'we,' who *ex hypothesi* have adopted the attitude of a Hegelian Sage, who *ex hypothesi* are wise, *are* self-conscious. In order to become so (or, *ex hypothesi*, to *have* become so) we must have encountered another Other, that is, an Other that is other than given-Being, and *this* Other is another self-consciousness.

This is what Hegel says: self-consciousness can obtain satisfaction only when the Other to be negated is not simply independent but rather carries out its own self-negation within itself, for then 'it is *in itself* the Negative, and must be for the Other what it is [for itself]' (*PhG* 139:109). *This* Other desires what *Ego* desires; hence Other is the same as Ego (since both desire the same 'thing,' namely the desire of the other) and Ego is other than itself (since it posits its own satisfaction in the desire of the Other). Thus, Hegel concluded: 'Self-consciousness achieves its satisfaction only in an other self-consciousness' (*PhG* 139:110). So now, for the first time, we have one self-consciousness encountering another self-consciousness, making of each an 'object' mutually. This amounts to a 'duplication of self-consciousnesses,' for as we have just seen, 'when self-consciousness is an object it is just as much Ego' (*PhG* 140:110). It is apparent that a condition for the mutual encounter of self-consciousnesses in the manner just indicated is that they be in spatial proximity. It would seem, therefore, that self-consciousnesses, having experienced the biological dialectic, exist in herds, as do certain animals. One may conceive of their 'speech' as akin to the waggle dance of the honeybee.

When this situation obtains, we have at hand the Concept of Spirit, and ahead the experience of what Spirit is, namely 'the unity of different independent self-consciousnesses as that, in their very opposition as perfectly free and independent self-consciousnesses, are united as constituent elements of Spirit: *Ego* that is *We*, and *We* that is *Ego*' (*PhG* 140:110).

Thus does consciousness first find its turning-point in self-consciousness, understood as Spirit, leaving behind both immediate sense-certainty and the supersensuous void of analytical understanding. Now self-consciousness 'steps forth into the spiritual daylight of the present' (*PhG* 140:111).

The pure Concept of Recognition

Before describing how self-consciousnesses appear to each other, Hegel outlined what he called the pure Concept of Recognition (*PhG* 143:112). As with the discussion of Consciousness and Self-consciousness just completed, the discussion of recognition is also presented from the 'perspective' of the Sage.

'Self-consciousness,' Hegel said, 'exists in and for itself while, and owing to the fact that, it exists for another self-consciousness in that way; i.e., it exists [in and for itself] only in being Recognized' (*PhG* 141:111). The constituent elements or 'moments' of the pure Concept of Recognition are as follows:

1 / Self-consciousness faces another self-consciousness, having come outside of itself. This results in (a) a loss of self since it sees itself as an Other, and (b) a supersession (*Aufhebung*) of the other since it does not see the Other as essential-Being but rather sees only itself in the Other.

2 / Self-consciousness now must supersede this otherness of itself obtained in 'moment' 1. It does so (a) by superseding the Other so as to gain self-certainty as essential-Being and (b) by superseding its own self, for this other (by moment 1b) is itself.

3 / This twofold supersession of the twofold otherness of self-consciousness is at the same time a twofold return to itself because (a) by supersession 2a, which was a supersession of its own otherness, i.e. 1a, it is reconciled with itself; and (b) by supersession 2b, which returns otherness to the other self-consciousness, i.e. 1b, it in turn supersedes the being of itself in the Other and so lets it go free.

This process has been presented as the activity of one self-consciousness, but it also describes the activity of the other; it is a double process of two self-consciousnesses with each seeing the other do exactly as it does. Thus consciousness both is and is not immediately itself, just as the Other is both for itself and for the first consciousness. Each, Hegel said, mediates the other, in its externalization, to itself, which mediation unites each to itself; and each is also an immediate essential-Being for itself thanks to this same mediation: 'They *recognize* themselves, as *mutually recognizing one another*' (*PhG* 143:112).[15] This complex but logically impeccable account of the pure Concept of Recognition has provided a permanent acquisition so far as Kojève's general argument is concerned: from it we learn that any one self-consciousness will never be satisfied until all self-consciousnesses recognize each other mutually.[16]

We said above that Hegel developed his argument from two 'perspectives,' the one being the comprehensive or absolute standpoint of the retrospective Sage, the other being the increasingly adequate or comprehensive standpoint of consciousness as it develops itself, as it climbs the ladder to the absolute standpoint of Wisdom. We turn now to the second perspective and a series of 'impure' accounts. The first of these, fundamental for Kojève's interpretation, is the 'myth' of Master and Slave.[17]

Primordial encounter of two self-consciousnesses

In the beginning, as noted earlier, self-consciousness comes into being when it says 'I' and grasps itself as sheer or immediate being for itself. Everything else is an inessential object. But some of these 'objects' also happen to be self-conscious; they do not appear that way to each other, however, because they have not externalized, through mediation, the immediate being for self that they are. Consequently, they do not appear to be anything other than given-Being. Each is certain of itself but only internally or subjectively; the other appears, so to speak, as food, an element in the biological 'struggle for life.' This subjective certainty can become true, revealed, or objective, according to the argument explicating the pure Concept of Recognition, only when each is for the other what the other is for it. And the most obvious thing that each is for itself is an individual living being. Accordingly, this must be negated in the primordial encounter of two self-consciousnesses. As Kojève remarked, 'All animal Desires are in the last analysis a function of the desire it has to preserve its life' (*IH* 14:7), so specifically human desire must subordinate the desire for preservation to its own proper ends. What is specifically human, namely self-consciousness, can appear only if this basic animal desire is suppressed or negated. Thus, self-consciousness must show itself to be unattached to life.

Or rather, both self-consciousnesses must so appear. Such an appearance is necessarily a twofold activity, by Ego and Other, in the shape of a fight. As with Hobbes, both must initially be willing to risk their own lives in order to seek the other's death. In this relationship, both attempt to raise their subjective certainty of self to the truth of appearance in the world. On the one side, risk raises self-consciousness above the mere given-Being of biological life and shows to self-consciousness that there is nothing in life it could not negate; on the other, to seek the other's death shows self-consciousness that it regards the other, which is its own externalized essential-being, as no more significant than its immediate self.

To seek the death of the other at the risk of one's own life is to act in such a way that one accepts with no reservations the reality of death, the finitude of human being. It is not necessary to accept the implication of one's act right away. Nevertheless, its effective significance is plain: 'By voluntarily accepting the danger of death in a Struggle for pure prestige [i.e. for Recognition], Man appears for the first time within the natural World; and by resigning himself to death by revealing it through his discourse, Man finally attains absolute Knowledge or Wisdom, and in this way completes History' (IH 540). In other words, consciousness of death, implied by the primordial anthropogenic actions, when fully and completely grasped, is Hegelian Wisdom. Or, as Hegel remarked on another occasion,[18] death is absolute labour inasmuch as it supersedes determinate particularity. Whereas soldiers may sacrifice themselves for the state, the non-combatant must gain consciousness of universality by way of speculation. Both forms of absolute labour, namely death in the service of Napoleon's revolutionary army and Hegel's absolute Knowledge or Wisdom, are apparently equivalent.

The importance of death

The argument that death is absolute and universal is essentially Hobbesian: all human beings die. Consideration of this fact has the same immediacy for Hegelian consciousness as the immediate fear of death at the hands of another has for Hobbes. The argument that absolute Knowledge or Science is equivalent is more complex.

The first element in this argument, which we shall consider in more detail below, is that philosophy is a search for Wisdom, and Wisdom is full and complete self-consciousness. The evidence that one is Wise is an ability to account for oneself, that is, one's actions, *and* to account for this ability, that is, one's words. Now, in the course of reflecting upon his own philosophical discourse, Hegel remarked that what is involved is an activity of separating that requires the strength, *Kraft*, and labour, *Arbeit*, of the Understanding. The Understanding, he said, is the greatest, most miraculous, indeed, absolute power, *der verwundersamsten und grössten, oder vielnehr der absoluten Macht* (*PhG* 29:18). In this context 'Understanding' meant the specifically human ability to speak analytically and separate the constituent elements of the Totality of Being. The meanings revealed by speech occur over a more or less extended period of time – hence they are an activity or a labour that requires strength. Even more, the Totality of Being is one and inseparable even while containing within itself the constituent element of Negativity. Thus, the separation achieved by speech may indeed be called miraculous, and the power that works the miracle, absolute. This power is, of course, the human ability to abstract from the *hic et nunc* and create a concept. It is absolute in that no real forces can stop it, but it is not for that reason merely fictitious because conceptual plans may be preludes to real technical transformations of the given. Granted, then, that the separation of meanings from their given, natural instantiation and support requires the laborious activity of the Understanding endowed with absolute, awesome, or miraculous power, and that philosophy must account for it, how is that equivalent to death on the field of honour?

We may summarize Hegel's argument, as given in the remainder of the paragraph cited earlier, as follows.

1 / Understanding separates meaning from its natural support and gives it an empirical existence, *Dasein*, as a word or discourse. *Qua* meaningful word, this *Dasein* is unconstrained by limitations that beset other empirically existing entities. For example, the empirically existing word 'dodo' exists now, whereas the large bird, formerly of Mauritius, does not. This 'miracle,' Hegel said, is the manifestation of the prodigious power of the Negative, *die ungeheur Macht des Negativen*, which in turn engenders thought, Understanding, discourse. But discourse must, of course, belong to an empirically existing human Self, a man who appears in the World as a speaker. Thus: the miracle of discourse, of which philosophy must render an account, is no different from the miracle of the empirical existence of Man in the World.

2 / Man, we know from the argument presented in chapter 2, is not a given-being, but the incarnation of Negativity. Ontologically, Negativity is actualized as Action; metaphysically, the true being of Man is his action; phenomenologically action appears as struggle and labour. Action nihilates Being, which means that it must also nihilate itself (as it, too, is a being). But if the nihilation of Action were totally without Being of any kind, it would be pure Nothingness; yet it *is*, in some sense. And that

sense, according to Kojève, is finitude. Action, therefore, is finite. Ontologically, Negativity is the finitude of Being; metaphysically, the historical World, created by Action, has a beginning, which we will discuss shortly, and an end; phenomenologically, the instantiation whose very being is the activities of struggle and labour appears to itself and to others as mortal.

3 / Accordingly, Death is what the unactuality of Negativity *is* (*PhG* 29:19). Kojève commented: 'But if man is Action, and if Action is Negativity "appearing" as Death, Man is, in his human or speaking existence, but a *death*, more or less deferred and self-conscious' (*IH* 548).

4 / It follows that to give an account of Discourse, of man the speaker, is to accept death and describe its significance. According to Hegel, this had not been done before. Death is the most terrifying thing and its acceptance requires the greatest strength, a strength that is missing from the cultivation of mere beauty, *die kraftlose Schönheit*. In contrast, 'the life of the Spirit' does not shrink before death. Spirit, we know from the argument of chapter 2, is revealed Being, Being revealed by speech; the *life* of Spirit is, therefore, the empirically existing and fully self-conscious philosopher (or rather, Sage). The Sage, therefore, is conscious of his finiteness and death; he looks it full in the face and abides with it. And this, surely, describes the experience of the soldier who sacrifices himself for the state.

Two additional remarks may be made about this passage. First, ontologically, Totality does not reveal itself to itself; rather, one of its finite parts does so and in so doing also reveals itself as finite. Metaphysically, therefore, the Being that reveals itself to itself is not God but Spirit, revealed Being, which implies the temporal (and temporary) revealer, Man. Human speech occurs 'over' time, first of all as the erroneous discourse that expresses the historical, negating actions of man, but eventually as the satisfactory discourse of the Sage that expresses his satisfaction with what is (and so the end of any further negativity). Second, since the satisfaction of the Sage implies full, complete, and perfect self-consciousness, he must be aware of his own finitude and death. Now death, as Hegel said, is a terrible thing; it does not make one happy or add to one's welfare. All it can do is satisfy one's pride, which is precisely the sort of satisfaction Hegel had in mind, since 'it is only by being and by sensing oneself as being mortal or finite, that is, by existing and sensing oneself to exist, in a universe without a beyond or without a God, that Man can affirm his freedom, his historicity, and his "unique in the world" individuality, and make himself recognized' (*IH* 551). If man were not mortal, he would not be free of the eternal and infinitely given, that is, he would not be free of God. Consciousness of this freedom, and it alone, can satisfy Man's infinite pride, that is, his unbounded desire for recognition.

Thus, according to Hegel, the immortality of the soul in any sense, whether mythical, philosophical, Christian, or anything else, is impossible. There is no real Beyond to which a posthumous being might repair (if, *per impossibile*, such a being existed). There exists only the quasi-immortality of biological generation and the prolongation of action, through education and traditions, into the next generation (*IH* 558–9). But in order to be meaningful, both of these ersatz immortalities presuppose, precisely, the utter and complete annihilation of the individual upon his or her death.

Let us summarize the argument so far: the true being of Man, Hegel several times repeated, is his action (*PhG* 236:193), which is the realization of Negativity manifest phenomenally, so far as man is concerned, in the conscious and voluntary acceptance of his own death. This consciousness is created when a being risks his given life solely for the vain desire for recognition, a desire not for anything given in any way at all, but rather for another's desire, for something that is *not*, for the presence of an absence of any given. This desire transcends the naturally given and, to the extent that it is realized in a result or product, will have proven itself superior to the naturally given by virtue of having negated it. It is perfectly true that the product that this desire achieves may simply be death. But that is not nothing; on the contrary, the disappearance of a being through negation while it is seeking recognition (and not obtaining it, since it disappeared) is an activity that is specifically human and in no way given, vital, or animal. But more to the point, the death of the proto-human, primordial animal desire that is not followed by his sheer disappearance creates the product Man. The risk of death, the willingness to die, through which activity Man gains the understanding that he is mortal and finite, allows death to endure as consciousness of death without resulting in the simple disappearance of human being along with animality.

Man appears, then, in the midst of the naturally given world, for the 'first' time when he risks his life in a murderous struggle for pure prestige. As Kojève said, rather grandly: 'To be a Man is, for Hegel, to be able and to know how to die' (*IH* 566). There are three possible outcomes to this primordial encounter. Each may die at the hands of the other, in which case both return to given-Being as they putrefy back to nature.

Ego may kill Other, in which case Ego is subjectively confirmed in his subjective certainty of self, but lacking the conscious mediation of Other, who is now dead, nothing has changed, and Other is, and appears to him, say, as meat. This outcome, Hegel called abstract negation, as distinct from that negation or supercession (*Aufhebung*) that preserves and maintains what is superseded and so survives its negation (cf *Logic* section 96). The third outcome leaves both alive but unequal: one of the self-consciousnesses shows himself to be attached to life. This one learns that life is as important as pure self-consciousness, sheer being for-itself. Something new has been introduced: two subjectively certain and identical self-consciousnesses have turned into two unequal and opposed forms of consciousness. 'The one is independent [consciousness], whose essential nature is being for-itself, the other is dependent, whose essential nature is living or being for-another; the former is *Master*, the other is *Slave*' (*PhG* 146:115). Each, we shall see, is initially incomplete, unhappy, or not (yet) satisfied. Both, nevertheless, are human.[19]

Mastery

Consider first the master: What has he done? What is the consequence of this act? How does the consequence accord with his intention?

In its most simple form, the Master has exercised 'the possibility of negating Nature, and his own nature, whatever it may be. He can [and did] negate his own empirical animal nature, he can [and did] *wish* his own death and risk his life' (*IH* 52). Since the negation of Nature or given-Being is also a manifestation of freedom, and since the risk of one's life, which was the whole of his biological, animal reality, was in favour of something non-existent, the act of the Master was an assertion of independence and autonomy from the cares of life (*IH* 497:225). The risk of his life, since it was voluntary (he could have refused to be provoked, or run away, or opted for slavery), is in this respect equivalent to suicide. But it is clear that while suicide may *manifest* freedom with respect to biological life, it cannot *realize* freedom because it ends in death and non-existence. Yet when one looks at the consequences of the fight as they exist for the Master, he appears to be, in a sense, already dead.

The life of a Master consists no longer in co-operative grazing with nothing between himself and his food; now his Slave comes between him and his food, which, moreover, the Slave prepares for him. In Hegelian terminology, the Master's animal existence is mediated by the Slave and, with this mediation, is humanized. Several changes are herewith introduced: the Master is related to things by way of the Slave insofar as it is his *Slave* who serves things up to him, but also he is related to the Slave by way of things insofar as *things* are what he is served up. That is, the Master is Master only by the appearance of the Slave. In Kojève's words, 'the "truth" of the Master is the Slave; and his Labour. In fact, others recognize the master as Master only because he has a Slave' (*IH* 26:20).[20]

So far as the Master is concerned, this is unsatisfactory. It is true that the Master seems to have achieved the sought-for recognition in that the Slave set aside his own desires to gratify the desires of the Master. But the Master has extorted that recognition through Terror. It has not been given freely, whereas in order for the pure Concept of Recognition to be actualized it is necessary 'that what the Master does to the Other he also must do to himself, and what the Slave does to himself he also must do to the Other' (*PhG* 147:116). In fact, however, Masters do not recognize each other as free and autonomous individuals but as owners of Slaves. Thus, recognition is also mediated by Slaves, and in a sense the Slaves, not the Masters, are recognized as having value. To be sure, they are seen to be (valued) Slaves and not free and autonomous individuals, but for the Master this is no compensation at all. And as for the immediate recognition the Slave gives the Master, this too is unsatisfactory precisely because it is a Slave, that is, one who in the Master's eyes is no more than an animate instrument, and not an individual human being, who accords him immediate recognition. Thus, recognition is 'one-sided and unequal' (*PhG* 147:116) and does not conform to its Concept, as described by the Sage.

Similarly, it is true that the Master seems to have achieved the satisfaction of the original desire of consciousness in that his independence of things is constantly confirmed through the interposition of the Slave between him and given-Being. Since the Master need never deal with the independence of given-Being but can appropriate to himself its dependent aspect, he may be said to live a life of enjoyment. But brute enjoyment or the exquisite life of a voluptuary cannot be termed satisfaction: at most it results in a reconfirmation by satiation of the subjective certainty already experienced as animal sentiment. The leisured consumption of a Master satisfies 'natural' or animal desires. But these were the very things he denied at the risk of his life.[21]

The intention of the Master was that he be confirmed in his autonomy by being recognized by a worthy Other. As Gadamer remarked in connection with a duel, the point is not revenge but, precisely, satisfaction, a restoration of honour that has been offended. 'He who is ready to fight with the other, he who does another the honour of being willing to fight with him, demonstrates thereby that he did not intend to place the latter beneath him. And, conversely, he who demands satisfaction, demonstrates for his part, that he cannot bear the humiliation he has suffered unless the other, by declaring himself ready to fight, nullifies it.'[22] The absoluteness of freedom and the absoluteness of death are connected in the consciousness of the Master, but the result is not yet free self-consciousness, Wisdom, or universal recognition. Instead, the Master has simply gained the unworthy, dishonourable, pseudo-recognition of his Slave, a 'thing.' He has achieved the valueless mediated recognition of other Masters who recognize not his own individual value but the value of his Slaves. He leads a life of enjoyment and does nothing. This was not what he risked his life for, so that the 'revealed reality' of the Master's struggle for recognition was an error. Even worse, it is an error he is fated to repeat again and again, for nothing essential changes in a life-and-death struggle with a change of weapons: an unguided stone missile has the same human meaning as an electronically guided one.[23] Hence, the Master's first act is also his last. Henceforth, he never changes. Now, what is unchanging, what remains identical to itself, is as good as dead, which is to say that the risk of one's life is not only intentionally equivalent to suicide, it is a kind of postponed suicide: 'One could say as well that the Master is in effect humanly dead in the struggle: he no longer *acts*, properly speaking, since he remains idle; therefore he lives as if he were dead: ... his existence is a simple "afterlife" (limited in time) or a "deferred death"' (*IH* 518 n1:248 n34). In short, as Kojève said several times, the attitude of the Master leads to an existential impasse in the sense that he can never be satisfied. He is fated ever to be confronted by a dependent consciousness and therefore can never be certain of the truth of himself as being for itself. Just the opposite: his truth is the Slave, the inessential consciousness and its inessential activity. This result, as Gadamer pointed out, is comic, at least for the Sage.[24]

Slavery

If the way of the Master leads to an inevitable and comic impasse, the way to genuine humanity must be Slavery. Just as the essential being of the Master turned out to be the opposite of what he intended, so too will the complete development of slavery reverse what the Slave initially is. We know already that the Slave is forced to serve the Master, but we have so far looked upon his service from the Master's perspective and now we will consider servile self-consciousness from within. Just as the Slave's appearance sustained the Master *qua* Master, so too is the Master the 'truth' or 'revealed reality' of the Slave. The Slave sees, esteems, and 'idealizes' the autonomy of the Master's existence, which he himself lacks. In principle, then, what the Slave must do is overcome the Master and thereby cease being a Slave, but in such a way that he does not become a Master himself. However that may be, it is true that the Slave, unlike the Master, is able, and indeed eager, to change. In the first place, it now appears clear to him that he did not initially wish to fight, but was provoked. Whereas the Master cared so little about death that he was indifferent to the continuation of his own life, the Slave knew, or rather learned, that he did not wish to die. The first and last act of the Master was pedagogical. His willingness to die or kill terrified the Slave who turned out to be unwilling to die and who had been unwillingly placed in a situation where he was faced with the unsatisfactory options of having to kill gratuitously for prestige, or serve another.

The experience of Terror taught the Slave (though he did not know it at the time) that he did not wish to be a Master, and remain evermore identical to himself, 'dead.' The Slave wished to live (though not as a Slave). Hegel described the Slave's experience as follows: servile consciousness 'was not anxious or afraid of this or that particular thing, nor for this or that moment of time, but it feared for its entire essential being, it underwent the fear of death, the fear of the absolute Master. By this [experience of Terror], it melted internally, it shuddered deeply in every fibre, and everything fixed and stable was shaken to its foundations. This pure universal movement, this absolute liquefaction of all that is steadfast, is however, the simple essential being of self-consciousness, absolute negativity, *pure being-for-self* that, accordingly, exists *in* this self-consciousness' (*PhG* 148:117). The Master cannot be changed: he can only continue repeating his one and only act or he can die, because the truth is not in him. And the truth is that the Master's steadfastness or stubbornness is not final. The Slave knows what autonomy is, since he can see it objectively appear in the Master, and he knows it is not (yet) his. This is why he had every reason to change. Moreover, Terror is absolute. Like Hobbes's notion of violent death at the hands of another, its meaning can be neither avoided nor distorted. There is no ambiguity, and no rationalization is possible. Consequently, the change the Slave desires is truly revolutionary (*IH* 33:29). He wants to change the world, the whole 'nature of things.'

Surprisingly enough, he can. The 'natures of things' are given realities, given-being (*Sein*), but the Slave who has experienced the absolute instability of Terror knows (albeit unselfconsciously) that nothing is stable and steadfast, that there is, in effect, no genuine 'nature of things.' Because it consists in labour, that is, in the transformation of the given World, Slavish life confirms objectively, in the world, the lesson first taught (also unselfconsciously) by the Master. No doubt, servile labour is frustrating. The Slave does not enjoy serving his Master's pleasure, preparing delicacies that he himself never tastes. But his frustration has its compensation. In the original struggle, the self-conscious desire who emerged as Slave subordinated himself to Nature, to the biological instinct for self-preservation. As a labouring Slave he does so no longer. Being forced to labour, the Slave is forced to repress his natural desires and instincts; he wants to eat, for example, the fine meal he has just prepared rather than serve it to another, but he must not. More generally, the forced labour of the Slave changes Nature, including his own 'natural' instincts, by educating and sublimating them (*IH* 30:24). Unlike the Master, he does not simply or immediately negate his biological life but transforms it. To be more exact, he transforms the world by preparing things for the idle Master to consume without a trace left behind. Now a thing prepared but not yet consumed is just as objectively real as a natural thing, and in addition it bears the 'imprint' of the Slave who prepared it. The Slave, moreover, can recognize his own work in the world as specifically human, artificial, and unnatural. In general one may say that the Slave's labour forms or creates a human world, a world in the proper sense of the term.

To impose form on a naturally given but chaotic, random reality is to endow it with the stability of an object. For a Slave to do so and see his own imprint upon things is to move from the absolute instability of a terrorized consciousness to the relative stability of action that creates a product within a nevertheless changing world. The Slave has begun to recognize the world, including its changes, as his own work; he has begun to overcome terror by changing the terrible world. In this way he has indirectly changed himself by changing the conditions of his life. Perhaps some day he will change the world so that there is no room for the Master's terror. In any event, it seems clear that, on the one hand, the Master does not change himself in any way; to the extent that anything about him changes – new weapons, for example – it results from the inventive Slave's labour. In this sense he is the utmost in petrified stability. But at the same time the satisfaction that comes when Desire is sated in pleasure is the most fleeting possible. In contrast, the Slave's labour is both desire interrupted and fleetingness staved off. Even a Slave can take pride in his products.

Kojève several times explained the role of Master and Slave by analogy with a chemical reaction (IH 30:25; 502:230); the Slave and his labours constitute the real elements that change from one compound to another, and the Master is a catalyst. Both are necessary to the reaction, but the catalyst is not altered by it. Both fear and the shaping labours of service are necessary to create a human world from nature. Without service, fear remains pure and mute and does not extend itself to the world of actual existence; without fear, the service of shaping a world is not serious but merely self-centred, empty, and playful. In the absence of either, consciousness reverts to nature and shows itself not to have been thoroughly purged of given-Being.

Both Master and Slave have been humanized by having been placed in the presence of their own death: the Master through a voluntary risk, the Slave through the involuntary dread imposed upon him by the murderous Master. Now, life in the presence of death is the life of the Spirit (IH 572). Alone of all the things of the World, Man knows he must die. He may, therefore, be specified as consciousness of death, or as a (temporarily postponed) death conscious of itself. Or again, because man's very being is finite, the opportunity for complete self-understanding exists. Thus, 'the full (discursive) comprehension of the meaning of death constitutes Hegelian Wisdom; which completes History by gaining Satisfaction for Man' (IH 572). The importance of the dialectic of Master and Slave, therefore, can hardly be overestimated.[25] Prior to the risk of life by the (eventual) Master and the submission by the (eventual) Slave, there was no history, no negativity, no Spirit, and no beings that were specifically human.

Stoicism and Scepticism

The earlier discussion of the cognitive elements in human existence ended in the puzzle of analytic thought and the dialectic of the inverted world. Leaving aside the active elements for a moment, consciousness has, first of all, recognized that it is itself a part of the World it grasps by Understanding; but second, with the immediacy of sense-certainty irretrievably gone, consciousness (or, rather, self-consciousness) understands itself as cut off from the world. Two attitudes are possible now: either the world is repudiated and reflective self-conscious freedom is exalted, or reflective self-conscious freedom is repudiated as mere subjectivity and the world is likewise dismissed as meaningless.

When the first attitude appeared 'as a conscious manifestation in the history of Spirit' it was called Stoicism (*PhG* 152:121). The principle of Stoicism is that consciousness is a thinking being, so that what makes a thing important is that consciousness thinks it to be so, and not the thing as given. Accordingly, for a Stoic who happens to be born a Master, the truth lies not in the actual, worldly ownership of Slaves; for a Stoic who happens to be born a Slave, the truth lies not in his actual, worldly service to the Master. 'Whether on the throne or in chains, he is equally free so it matters little what one is in the world or the State' (*IH* 61). The Stoic accepts his own death and thereby shows his superiority to the ordinary Slave, but the cost is that he is indifferent to the world and to other men. His freedom, therefore, is 'negative,' 'abstract,' 'unmediated.' He opposes the world but ends up withdrawing into his own thoughts; he does not fight against the world or against the Master, and, indeed, is 'free only in thought, more exactly, in *his own* thought' (*IH* 62). The Stoic has, it is true, achieved independence of nature, including his own, but he has not used his independence to reappropriate nature. Freedom of thought turns into freedom *as* thought. In this way it voids itself of any actual, worldly, determinate contents. The thought of the Stoic found no resistance and so no reality in the world. Hegel called his generalities uplifting, but added that they soon became tedious (*PhG* 154:122). Boredom, then, transformed the Stoic into the second alternative (*IH* 180:53).

The second alternative is the realization, Hegel said, of that for which Stoicism was merely the thought. Now consciousness seeks to overcome its boredom by denying the world, including itself and its thoughts, and becomes what Hegel called a Sceptic (*PhG* 155:123) and Kojève called a Solipsist or a Nihilist (*IH* 62, 181:54). Whereas the Stoic thought that the contingencies of the world did not count (and only his lofty but empty thoughts did), the Sceptic knows, precisely because they were the thoughts of somebody who was a part of the world, that the Stoic's thoughts are indeed empty (as are the Sceptic's own thoughts). This is a kind of recapitulation of the dialectic of inverted world, since the appropriate attitude to 'the vertigo of a perpetually self-induced disorder' (*PhG* 157:125), which is Scepticism, is, surely, the attitude of the Stoic, which holds that the disorders of the world do not matter. In short, Stoicism leads to Scepticism and Scepticism to Stoicism.[26] Every empty Stoic thought can be immediately negated by the Sceptic, which means that the Sceptic 'has itself the doubly contradictory consciousness of steadfastness and sameness, and of complete contingency and non-identity with itself' (PhG 157–8:125). The talk of the Sceptic is the quarrelsome squabble of self-willed children who contradict one another for the sheer joy of it.

Neither Stoic nor Sceptic acted, in the strong sense of the term, though their joint mental activity replicated the dialectic of Master and Slave. The Stoic's ideal, in the end, was that of the Master insofar as he had suicidal tendencies – but he did not really *risk* his life, he was subjectively indifferent to it. The Sceptic, like the Slave, engaged in negation; he negated the whole being of the external, natural world – but only mentally. In this way he achieved abstractly the Stoic's (equally abstract) ideal, freedom. The Stoic's principle, that I am free because I think so, necessarily took the things of the world seriously in order to be indifferent to them; the Sceptic built upon the implications of that principle by denying it. Either way the consequence was self-defeating. Both tried to attain a *state* of consciousness that thereafter could remain as it was, without further change. But it is impossible, both Hobbes and Hegel agreed, to remain alive and immobile: only the dead achieve a state that does not change further, and it is not a conscious one. As Kojève put it, 'freedom is not a property but an act. Man is not free once for all. Man is a dialectical, absolute dis-quiet (*Un-ruhe*)' (IH 66; cf PhG 156:124) and so could never be satisfied by any given *state* of consciousness. The Sceptic, therefore, must do something. But what? Alone with his thoughts, he discovered he was free. 'He wishes to think Negativity within his isolation.' If he does so alone, 'Negativity ends up in Nothingness, because Negativity does not exist outside of Totality: isolated from Identity (= Man outside the World), Negativity is pure nothingness, death. Results: suicide (without a purpose)' or, 'if he continues to exist, his continuation is inconsistent' (IH 66). Why? Because he has denied everything, all contents, including himself. The Sceptic is a human being so he must do something, but his consciousness seeks negativity, and it does so alone. In order to actualize negativity alone the Sceptic does the only thing available to him: he disappears.

A consistent and suicidal Sceptic is as boring for us as a Stoic is for himself. Accordingly, only the Sceptic who remained alive and became conscious of himself as Sceptic (whereas before he merely *was* a Sceptic, which was equivalent to being a self-conscious Stoic) could be an agent of historical change. 'In general, it is becoming conscious of a *contradiction* that is the motor of human, historical evolution. To become conscious of a contradiction is necessarily to want to be rid of it' (IH 181:54).

And, as Hegel said, 'in Scepticism consciousness experiences itself in truth as an internally contradicted consciousness' (*PhG* 158:126). Just as the dialectic of the inverted world led consciousness to self-consciousness, so too Scepticism learns of its own self-contradictory nature and with that knowledge gains the threshold of history. Consciousness has a new form, which Hegel called the unhappy consciousness.

The unhappy consciousness

Where the Stoic was the immediate freedom of thought and the Sceptic the negation of the Stoic, the unhappy consciousness is an internal duplication of the dialect of Stoic and Sceptic (or, with regard to the active elements, of Master and Slave). This new form of consciousness, Hegel said, knows that it is an internal contradiction, a dirempted single consciousness that appears as a duality. There are several versions of the unhappy consciousness, as Wahl pointed out, which range from non-pagan Judaism to the pagan dialectic of Stoic and Sceptic, to Christianity, and indeed to Hegel's contemporaries, the Romantics. None of these versions is wise. All are simply 'existential versions of the logical moments of position and negation, which undergo unstable resolutions within the deeper unity of the negation of the negation.'[27] The unhappy consciousness is simply the immediate unity of the self-identical and unchangeable with the self-bewildering and protean. Accordingly, consciousness takes the two as opposites, one of which, namely the Unchangeable, is considered as essential, whereas the Changeable is viewed as inessential. Aware of the estrangement of the Unchangeable and the Changeable, the unhappy consciousness identifies itself with the latter. Yet being itself *conscious* of the Unchangeable it cannot simply be preoccupied with what it takes itself to be: 'It cannot be itself an indifference towards the Unchangeable' (*PhG* 159:127). But the more the unhappy consciousness strives toward unity with the Unchangeable, the more aware it grows of the gap between itself and its goal (human existence remains absolute disquiet). The most it can do is bridge the gap by hope, which means that it can never reach its goal 'since between the hope and its fulfilment there stands precisely the absolute contingency or unmoveable indifference that lies in the very assumption of definite form, which is where the ground of hope lies' (*PhG* 161–2:129). Consciousness, internally dirempted, can hope for unity only in a Beyond.

Estrangement from the Unchangeable has the consequence that consciousness understands itself as a radically contingent particular. This is clearly an advance over Stoicism, which turned its back on particularity. It also moves beyond the unsettled particularity of Scepticism. The unhappy consciousness knows itself as a thinking particular, but it does not know that its object, the Unchangeable, 'is *its own Self*, is itself the individuality of consciousness' (*PhG* 163:131). The ignorance of consciousness concerning the nature of the Unchanging as a projection of itself appears as the activities of prayer, devotion, and 'good works,' an enactment of hope and faith in a Beyond, not the pure or explicit thought of the Concept. In principle, this attitude is not confined to Christianity, though Hegel's account is full of allusions to Christian prayer, orders, sacraments, the empty tomb of Christ, and so on. Catholic good works can turn into the Protestant 'work ethic' and this in turn into the 'revolutionary works' of our contemporaries, but nothing significant is altered thereby. The reconciliation of the dirempted unhappy consciousness, which is the point of all this work, is still in a Beyond. Even so, these several works are something *done*, though the meaning of them is not properly grasped. All that is required for a complete reconciliation of consciousness is for it to be purged of faith and hope in any Beyond whatsoever. But this, as we shall see, takes time. Indeed, it takes history itself.

Christianity

The unhappy consciousness was a Sceptic who learned to be something else and avoided suicide. He *did* something. What he did does not much matter so long as he believed it was truly meaningful. It is legitimate, then, to return to the active elements of existence and trace the movement from Stoicism to the unhappy consciousness as they are reflected in the dialectic of Master and Slave. Like Hegel we shall deal explicitly with Christianity, but the argument can be extended, as indicated earlier, to any number of spiritual movements toward a better world in a transfigured Beyond. The Beyond itself, of course, can be imagined as historically possible or as utterly transcendent.

But, to return to the dialectic of Master and Slave: the significance of the contradiction between the ideal of freedom as it appears to the Slave in the person of the Master and the reality of his own servility is no longer denied (as in Stoicism) and is not a cause of suicidal despair (as in Scepticism). Rather it is affirmed and accepted as the truth of existence. Life in this vale of tears is bound to be unhappy. It is but a perilous pilgrim's progress, a lengthy route toward the City of God, the labours of a post-pagan Sisyphus. The unhappy consciousness is truly in this world a Slave. But this is acceptable since, really, all men are Slaves, including the so-called Masters. 'Thus, he becomes a Slave to God' (IH 66) and follows the Master of all mankind, the Lord of All.

The religious attitude moves beyond both Stoic and Sceptic because the religious man could live with the unhappy truth that he was a contradiction of two selves. 'The religious man is Master and Slave at once; Master to the extent he is Slave, Slave to the extent he is Master: Master of the world – Slave of God' (IH 67). Faced with the choice between these two selves, the Christian chose his conpensatory, transcendent self because his worldly self was mortal (as Slave, he was still afraid of death) and unrecognized. The Christian, unlike the Stoic or Sceptic, conceived freedom as real, not ideal, but it was real in the Beyond. There was no need to be free in the world, this vanity of vanities, for the Christian knew the truth of Scepticism: the world qua world was valueless. There was no need to fight the merely human Masters, for the Christian also knew the truth of Stoicism: he was already equal to his earthly Master, in the Beyond, the only 'world' that counted. Moreover, the Christian avoided both the boredom of the Stoic and the suicide of the Sceptic because there was something to do: 'One changes and one must change, one must always go beyond oneself in order to raise oneself above oneself as a datum within the real empirical World, in order to reach the transcendent World, the Beyond that remains inaccessible' (IH 182:55). The Christian, then, had realized the Slave's ideal, equality with the Master, and he had done so without a fight, the one thing he truly dreaded. Alas, the good news was too good to be true.

What made the Slave a Slave was his real fear of death, expressed in his refusal to fight the Master at the risk of his life. As long as he was afraid and maintained his refusal, so long would he remain servile. 'A liberation without a bloody Struggle is therefore metaphysically impossible' (IH 182:56). The impossibility was revealed within Christianity itself, for in accepting the possibility of death in this world the Christian compensated himself by gaining life in the next; in freeing himself from fear of a human Master, he enslaved himself to an absolute Master, God. 'In the final analysis, Christianity is born from the anxiety of the Slave before Nothingness, his own nothingness; that is, for Hegel, from the impossibility of abiding the necessary condition of existence for Man – the condition of death and finitude' (IH 183:56). Thus, the only way to overcome the unhappiness of Christianity was to become free of the absolute but imaginary Master in the Beyond. One must become an atheist in order to realize the 'ideal' of Christianity. In this way as well one over-comes the story of human unhappiness, which is history. In the next chapter we shall begin to consider how this came about.

Man is self-consciousness. This summary of the outline of Kojève's answer to the dilemma of the end of history expresses the Slave's achieve-ment in overcoming his slavery. In the end the primordial Desire who became a Slave has mastered nature by transforming or 'humanizing' the world, 'this' world, in such a way that it would conform to his ideal, which was also the intention of the primordial Desire who became a Master. Man is, if you like, a synthesis of Master and Slave. 'Man is neither purely vital nor completely independent of life: he transcends his given existence within and by way of his life itself.' This means he does not transcend his life by death or an after-life. 'Man negates an after-life: the *Wahrheit* [truth, revealed reality] of man disappears with the dis-appearance of his animal existence. But it is only by negating this exis-tence that he is human' (*IH* 53). Human being is wholly and completely immanent and finite. Man, of course, is mortal, really mortal, with no after-life in a beyond: 'He is *death* incarnate; he *is* his own death' (*IH* 570). And he knows it. As Master, he denied death by a suicidal risk of life, and as Slave he laboured to overcome the effects of his terror of death. The fights and labours of Masters and Slaves are the occasions for the appearance of death; the realization of that appearance can come only with a reflective account of those appearances. But the fights and labours of Masters and Slaves are the substance of history. Consequently, the sought-for account will be an account of history. It will be also an account of man, the one whose being is historical. But then self-con-sciousness becomes self-knowledge or Wisdom. To a wise man, a Sage, nothing is foreign, nothing is alien. Consequently, he is satisfied; he is even self-satisfied. And Desire is extinguished (*IH* 551).

Conceptual history

So far in this chapter only Kojève's or Hegel's conceptual argument has been presented. The argument was not simply an attempt to construct an elegant conceptual system, however. It was, as Wahl said, a philosophy of the concrete and was intended to account for history. A philosophy of the concrete was a repudiation of abstract thought (philosophical form without concrete content) on the one hand, and common sense (concrete content without philosophical form) on the other. Now, concrete things change into other things, both through natural evolution and as a result of human agency. Accordingly, a philosophy of the concrete, at least so far as change was a human affair, must be a 'conceptual history.' Insofar as it is history, one must be concerned with the temporal order of succession; insofar as it is conceptual, the sequence must be logical and rational. True, correct, appropriate, etc., periodization was a logical order of categories of succession such that phenomena could be organized into the discursive whole of Science. This meant that the content of Reason was the same as the content of History insofar as they eventually had an identical conceptual form. The argument in detail is presented in the following chapters. At the outset one may anticipate that any commonsensical objections could be met with as little interpretative ingenuity as it took Hegel to place Islam within the Christian-Germanic world.

According to Kojève, the pure theory of recognition was the paradigm in terms of which all historical phenomena were ordered. There resulted three historical epochs. During the first, when the Master dominated the Slave, the meaning of History was revealed only through Mastery. But since History was a dialectic of *both* elements, the era of the Master must be followed by one when Slavery determined the essential reality of human existence. And lastly, if the end of History was a synthesis of the two, the epoch of Slavery must be followed by a third and final era when human existence was revealed to itself through the active realization of its own possibilities, including full and complete understanding. This was the era of the Citizen-Sage (*IH* 173:45).

This neat and unilinear development was complicated somewhat by the apparent repetition and recapitulation in modern experience of equivalent experiences from the ancient world. Bourgeois man submitted to the laws of economics in an experientially equivalent way, for example, to the submission by the pagan to the laws of the polis, or by the primitive to the laws of nature (*IH* 129). Twice, Hegel said, the world had sunk into boredom, *Langeweile*. The first time, in the wake of the Roman destruction of the societies of the ancient world, the 'infinite pain' of the epoch was redeemed by the resacralization of humanity through the suffering of Christ. Now Protestantism had destroyed that sacrality, but it had not redeemed the World. That task belonged to a 'new philosophy' (*Dok* 318–23). Kojève elaborated a similar problem, the succession of religious experiences: first there was God without man (natural religion), then there was man without God (comic atheism), then God became man (Christianity), and lastly man became God (Hegelian atheism) (*IH* 255). These echoes of ancient history in modern history – and doubtless others could be found – may bring to mind Toynbee's image of the chariot: the wheels turned, seeming to repeat themselves, but by their repetition the chariot moved, leaving a single track behind. The most accessible version of this recapitulative periodization, to which we now briefly turn, was *Philosophie der Weltgeschichte*.

The Philosophy of History, to use the abbreviated title of the abbreviated English version, was in many ways an exoteric presentation of the historical events of *Phenomenology*. Kojève said next to nothing about this text of Hegel. A Kojèvian account can be made of it, however. Likewise we shall see below that a similar reading can be made of *Philosophy of Right*, about which Kojève was also silent. The persuasiveness of these interpretations, to my mind, enhances the persuasiveness of Kojève's general interpretative strategy regarding the entire System of Science. In the Introduction to *Philosophy of History*, for example, Hegel allowed that, for history, the conception that Reason governed the World appeared to be a mere hypothesis. There were however, three reasons why this was not so. First, it would be absurd to believe that in world history, which included Reason and its genesis, anything occurred by chance; second, no historian could avoid thinking about the data he wrote up, so that the whole purpose of a historian's activity was to use his own rational faculty to grasp the rationality of History; and third, that there was reason in History 'is a *result* that happens to be known to me because I am already acquainted with the whole [of human History]' (*VPG* 22:10). In general, moreover, one must be reasonable in order to see the rationality of the World and of World-history: 'To him who looks at the world rationally, the world in turn appears rational' (*VPG* 23:11).

The constituent elements of Hegel's conception that Reason governed History were provided, not unexpectedly, by pagan philosophy and biblical religion. In particular Hegel pointed to Anaxagoras, who, he said, found in the natural order of the cosmos the first version of Hegel's own principle. But Anaxagoras did not apply his insight to the details of concrete nature, prompting the young Socrates to reject as insufficient his abstract and naturalist rationality (cf *Phaedo* 97–8). In religious representation another version of this conviction may be found. But religious convictions were based upon feelings, not cognitions, or, when cognition came into play at all, it was as a particularist revelation that cleared up some perplexity for an isolated person. Hegel's version combined the two: like that of Anaxagoras and Socrates, it was founded upon cognition not feeling; unlike theirs, but like the biblical version, it apprehended Reason in human and spiritual, and not merely natural, events. But unlike biblical religion, Hegel's Reason dealt with collectivities, states, and not merely 'inspired' or 'prophetic' individuals. His, he said, was the true theodicy because it combined a consciousness of the final purpose of the world with the fact that purpose has been actualized in the World (*VPG* 28:15–16).

The synthesis of pagan and biblical convictions considered two questions: What was the essential reality of Reason? and What was the ultimate purpose of World history?, as aspects of the same topic. The actualization of the essential reality of Reason was, in fact, the ultimate purpose of World history. The substance of History, we have already shown, was Spirit, not Nature. Thus Hegel was content merely to provide an abstract definition. Spirit, he said, was Being whose meaning was contained within itself. 'But this, precisely, is Freedom. For if I am dependent, I refer my being to something else, which I am not; I cannot exist independently of something external. I am free, on the other hand, when my being is contained within myself' (*VPG* 30:17).[28] Necessarily, therefore, Freedom was self-conscious; or, alternatively, the ultimate purpose of the history of the World was the self-conscious Freedom of Spirit.

The concrete means by which Spirit built itself up was, of course, phenomenal History, a melancholy tableau of passions, violence, and corruption, a slaughter-bench. All of this was but the appearance, on a collective scale, of that negativity without which nothing at all could occur. Only the clash of whole societies, because the State itself was at risk, which put into contention the entire moral order, provided a subject-matter sufficiently comprehensive to engage the principles of conceptual History. Under ordinary circumstances, the 'blank pages of history,' there was nothing problematic or difficult to understand: duties were clear and life went on. But with the disintegration of the State or civilization all meaning seemed to have fled, at least to those who suffered such a fate. Yet, World history, the World-Spirit, continued on its course, gaining an increasingly comprehensive self-consciousness. The great destroyers, the World-historical Individuals, Hegel said, enacted (perhaps without understanding) the purposes of History and showed by their success that the time was ripe for the appearance of their Truth. They were the temporary syntheses of Particularity (they had their own passions and motives) and Universality (they translated these finitudes into permanent acquisitions of the World-Spirit); the process of their creation and destruction Hegel called the cunning of Reason.[29]

The goal to be actually attained by Spirit, which cunningly used the World-historical Individuals for its own rational purposes, was the State and, eventually, the universal and homogeneous State. The State was a synthesis of subjective (but World-historical) volition and passion, with the substantive life of Reason, a moral whole or Universal within which the Particular, the individual, could enjoy his freedom. Actual freedom was not, therefore, mere volition but rather was mutual recognition mediated by the law and morality of the State, the actual manifest Universal. The State, in Hegel's words, 'is the Idea of Spirit as the external manifestation of human Will and Freedom' (*VPG* 66:47). Thus, historical change necessarily was bound to the State, and the development of the Idea appeared within the State as the succession of political principles. The final, fully developed State was, then, the embodiment of rational freedom, and its genesis, so far as World history was concerned, was the only object of consideration.

In other words, only those collectives and peoples that formed more or less adequate embodiments of the State were worthy of notice by World history since only as a State was human, spiritual, essential-reality – Reason – actually existent. In the absence of a State there were but 'animal feelings and crude instincts.' A collectivity or people, *ein Volk*, being primarily a spiritual entity, was manifest, as were all such entities, as action. Thus, the actualization of the World Spirit proceeded by way of the action of successive World-historical peoples. Each of these, from the perspective of (conceptual) World history, had a determinate and particular Spirit and so may be treated as an individual. To the human beings who comprised these peoples, however, their own Spirit, their *Volksgeist*, appeared as Universality. This shift in levels or perspectives had the obvious result that World history, Universal history properly speaking, was the manifestation of the absolute process of the highest forms of Spirit. And *Philosophie der Geschichte* was likewise exalted, as is shown below.

The pre-Germanic World

The developmental course of History proceeded in three stages of differentiation corresponding to one set of divisions of *Phenomenology*. Initially Spirit was enfolded within Nature (the animal cycle of 'contemplation' and desire); then Spirit distinguished itself from Nature (consciousness and Particularity); finally Spirit reflected upon itself (self-consciousness and Universality).

Hegel used the image of the sun to suggest 'the great day's labour of Spirit.' Rising in the East, the pure splendour and flaming glory of the ascending sun imparted self-forgetfulness and a feeling of complete wonder and astonishment. As it rose in the sky this feeling passed; objects appeared as discriminate entities, and the perceiving subject was distinguished from them. Ceasing to be absorbed in the spectacle of undifferentiated nature or of its separated parts, conscious activity had begun. By the end of the day 'man has built a construction from his own internal sun, and at evening, when he contemplates it, he finds it more valuable than the original external sun' (*VPG* 134:103). Thus, Hegel added, 'World-History moves from East to West, for Europe is plainly the end of World-History as Asia is its beginning' (*VPG* 134:103).[30] The movement of World history was also an illustration of the ordering of natural will, its subordination to the universal principle of rational freedom. Consequently, as the great day unfolded, there was a concomitant growth in freedom: in the East, only one was free; in the Mediterranean civilizations of Greece and Rome, only some were free; and in the Germanic world of northern Europe, all were free. The historical political forms changed from despotism to aristocracy and democracy, and ended with monarchy.

In the beginning was unreflected consciousness, rationality without subjectivity, obedience organized around a single moral and substantive centre outside which was only sheer caprice, banditry, and nomadic hordes. Within the Oriental empires all was stable 'unhistorical History': outside, all was strife, destruction, and majestic ruin. Individuality first appeared in Greece but remained mixed with materiality and so took the form of a charming but perishable beauty. The Oriental separation of individuality and substantive social order was here overcome, but only in an unmediated way. One finds, therefore, that the contradictory injunctions of Justice and Law that, demanding an unreflecting, habitual, and customary obedience, led to the eclipse of the beautiful freedom of Hellas. With Rome mankind entered upon a third phase: the state was now mediated to itself and based upon reflection. But it was an abstract entity, a Universal that subordinated individuality to its own purposes in return for which it granted an equally abstract recognition, legal right. National individualities and their spiritual expression were alike absorbed into Roman ecumenism and the Roman Pantheon.

At this point the abstraction of Roman universality proved its inadequacy. Retaining the lifeless formalities of the old constitution, concrete individual volition triumphed in the shape of imperial despotism. It made little difference whether the emperors were individually praiseworthy or vile, the essential feature of government was unchanged: it was simply the emperor's will. Spirit had been driven from the actual world; one could cope with this fate either by returning to sensuousness and animality, or by following Spirit internally into the Beyond and by adopting an attitude of hostility and contestation toward spiritless actuality. The Roman response to the pain and alienation of its own spiritlessness was either to ignore it (Stoicism) or to negate everything (Scepticism). Thus, if there were to be relief, it must come from without, that is, from the Orient.

In providing the needed relief, according to Hegel, may be found the World-historical importance of the Jews. The representational story of the fall that resulted from the quest for knowledge was chiefly an expression of the inadequacy of 'natural' (i.e. innocent) man. Conscious man had, if not yet knowledge of good and evil, at least an awareness of them because, *qua* consciousness he was distinct from good (and therefore, with respect to it as a simple unity, he must have been evil and 'fallen'). But now the question of reconciliation arose, for the Jewish consciousness, being Oriental, was founded upon a sense of the unity of the whole, that is, upon the identity of subjectivity and God. Thus the Oriental light and dark, which originally expressed the natural 'miracle' of sunrise, were transferred from Nature to Spirit and became sin and redemption. Both sin and redemption were elements in a single process whereby Spirit alienated itself from itself in order to become reconciled with itself.

The fourth phase of World history, the Germanic, began with the promise of reconciliation presented by Christianity. But Christianity had to undergo an institutional development, to become more than a Jewish sect within the Roman Empire, before it could reconcile anything in the world to itself. The initial phase, expressed 'with unrestrained energy' in the Gospels, established Christianity as a religion when, following Pentecost, the Spiritual world was elevated to a Beyond above the political. Second came the foundation of a society based upon that principle, the apostolic community, separated from the Roman State. The apostolic community was, in addition, an evangelical body whose worldly purpose consisted in spreading the good news concerning the redemption of the world. That is to say, Christianity was obliged to establish its own understanding of Truth and in meeting this obligation formalized its doctrines. The third phase dealt with the Church.

The Church involved both the relation of apostolic Christian community to the actual political world and the question of the truth of its doctrines. The Christian community was the Kingdom of Christ, a Spiritual actuality endowed, necessarily, with a phenomenal existence alongside other institutions. It therefore was organized into a hierarchy distinguished from the general community by its explicit spirituality, which was authoritative in matters of truth so far as the community was concerned. In this first phase, the contrast between the Spirituality of the Church and the violent, capricious secular world was reflected in the insistence that the barbarian kingdoms recognize the higher representative purposes of the Church.

Insofar as the Church was simply a human organization, however, its being a spiritual kingdom, geistige Reich, took the form of a sacral, geistlicher, one (VPG 402:333). An inevitable development characterized the second phase of Church history: the Church henceforth appeared as a privileged, property-holding, aristocratic corporate body. Thus did the sacral body degrade itself into the secular. 'Spirit is once more driven back upon itself; it produces its product, Werk, in the form of Thought and becomes capable of realizing Rationality from the principle of secularism alone ... The antithesis of State and Church vanishes; Spirit finds itself in the secular and builds it up as an organic, empirically existing entity on its own' (VPG 140–1:109). There was not, however, any question of returning to the pre-Christian communities of 'natural' tribes or quasi-natural poleis. Man had finally abandoned natural consciousness and volition in favour of History and Spirit.

Christianity had gained two important results that were in no way altered by the post-Christian secular state. First, slavery was henceforth impossible in principle. In Christianity, each person was loved by God and was equally important in the achievement of God's purposes. The infinite worth of the simple quality of man qua man necessarily meant that the worth of distinctions of ability, or birth, or sex, or native land paled into insignificance. Second, the infinite subjectivity of the human Spirit destroyed forever the authority of fortune. The Divine Spirit was to be found henceforth only in an equally spiritual subjectivity: oracles, auspices, astrology, and so on would have no authority. So far as finite existence was concerned, man alone was responsible. What Christianity could not find in itself, and ancient Rome could not supply, was the principle of accord between the inner spiritual life and the actual World. Without the principle of secular freedom, Christianity could not 'find the grounds upon which it might become actual and develop in the form of an Empire, Reich' (VPG 406:336). The final World-historical people, the Germanic, had as its vocation the reconciliation of the Spiritual and Secular in accord with the principle of Freedom and, therefore, of Reason as well. And this, Hegel said, 'is the final purpose of World-History, das Ziel der Weltgeschichte' (VPG 141:110).

The Germanic World

The aim and purpose of the Germanic Spirit, and so of the entirety of World history, was nothing less than the realization of Truth as self-making Freedom, a purpose identical, Hegel said, with the actualization of Christianity. Where the World Spirit assigned to Mediterranean civilization the task of creating an adequate religious representation of Freedom, the Germanic heirs to Rome had to actualize freedom spontaneously from their subjective self-consciousness.

This final historical epoch was unlike any that preceded it. First and most obviously, since the Germanic World was final it was unique in having no successor. Thus, in dividing the internal development of the Germanic World, no guidance could be gained from the historian's 'retrospective anticipation' of future developments: the Germanic World was how the story turned out, and it foreshadowed nothing new. Even so, the impact of its superseded predecessor, Mediterranean civilization, could be traced. Unlike the Greeks and Romans, who attained Spiritual maturity before embarking upon ecumenical adventures, the Germans were conquerors before they were civilized. According to Hegel, it was 'extremely important' that Germanic history was in this respect different from Greek and Roman.

There were two reasons to stress the significance of the external and indeed alien source of Germanic *Bildung*. First, the Germanic peoples fell heir to a religion of vastly greater spiritual depth than their own indigenous religions. They were attracted to what was already an alien Spirit, so that the internally destructive moment of self-alienation, which in the Roman World ended in the spiritual dead-end of the dialectic of Stoicism and Scepticism, was avoided. All the Germanic peoples need experience was the moment of return; they proceeded to take up, and overcome, these foreign elements in order to integrate them into the fabric of their own *Volksgeist*.

But second, and more important than the formal relation, often repeated, of the primitive conqueror to the sophisticated vanquished, the Germanic world appropriated the substantive contents of the Mediterranean Spirit in its completed and perfected form. Now, the Christian World, Hegel said, was the world of completion or perfection, *die Welt der Vollendung*. As a result, the principle of World history, namely Reason, had been fulfilled: 'The end of days is completely arrived,' and there was no point at which Spirit was not satisfied (*VPG* 414:342). The elements that comprised the completeness of the Mediterranean, Christian Spirit were the familiar constituents of Western civilization: Christianity itself, the philosophy of Greece and Rome applied to it as 'a perfected dogmatic system,' the hierarchic organization of the Church, the Latin language, and ecumenic Roman political symbols.

Since Christian spirituality was complete (even if not yet actual), there was no absolute outside, nothing was genuinely alien to it, nothing enjoyed World-historical existence beyond the Christian World. On the contrary, all nominally non-Christian Spirit was only relatively legitimate and 'is already implicitly vanquished' so that the actual conquest of the World by the Christian Spirit was a merely external operational detail. 'It follows from this that reference to external factors no longer applies to the determination of epochs in the modern World' (*VPG* 414:342). A new principle to divide the periods of modern History must be found. It was clear why. Heretofore the division of World history had been marked by the clash of World-historical peoples, each of which successively embodied in its own *Volksgeist* the universal *Weltgeist*. Thus it was possible to refer by way of geography, that is, by way of Space, to the historical movement of the World Spirit from East to West. But now, with the whole *ecumene* 'implicitly vanquished' by the Germanic perfection of the *Weltgeist*, it was no longer possible to divide Time, that is, Historical succession, according to criteria reflecting the conquest of Space. With the implicit conquest of the World by the Christian Spirit, it was obvious that a new division, reflecting the new Spirit by which the World was to be redeemed, was required. The old Spirit, the Spirit of pagan antiquity, was quite dead, as was the Spirit of Wotan, Thor, the Druids, and so forth.

The new Spirit, we recall, was Subjectivity, absolute self-willing or self-making, *Eigensinn*, that is, Freedom. Standing over against it, the result of this activity, its product or content, *Inhalt*, appeared equally absolute. The distinction that came from this principle was, Hegel said, between Church and State. On the one side, the Church was the self-conscious embodiment of Truth and the mediator between the individual and Truth; on the other, the State embodied secular consciousness and the actuality of recognition, confidence, and subjectivity. The History of this final phase reflected the common growth of each, their separation, and finally their reconciliation.

The first period, which extended from the Migrations, *die Völkerwanderungen*, to the empire of Charlemagne, was one of barbarous simplicity and consequently was without much interest. 'Then the Christian World is simply Christendom, a single mass where the spiritual and the secular are but different aspects of the same thing' (VPG 415:343).

The second period, from the death of Charlemagne to the mid-sixteenth century, was much more interesting. The sacrum imperium, which reached its perfection under Charlemagne, was bound to disintegrate insofar as it was held together not by any Volksgeist, but 'by the power and greatness of the noble soul of this one individual' (VPG 444:368). The first reaction, then, took the form of particular, national Spirits appearing in opposition to Universality, which now appeared as mere Frankish hegemony. Second, without the imposition of authority from above, the order of law disappeared and a substitute had to be reconstituted from below in the form of personal relations. 'Thus, all Right, Recht, disappeared in the face of particularist power: equality before the law, and the rationality of legal order, where the purpose of the whole, the State, exists, was no where to be found' (VPG 449:373).

In response to the disorder of an absence of Universality and as an expression of extreme isolation and a sense of nothingness, there arose twin irrationalities: debauchery contended with continuous penance. Here lay the more obviously spiritual side of the disintegration of Christendom, namely the abandonment of the principle of mediation, and its replacement by the principle of separation. All sorts of abuses and outrages followed from the separation of laity from clergy, from the adoration of the bones of dead persons to the worship of pieces of bread. In the absence of an internal spiritual mediation, which expressed the reality of Christian freedom and subjectivity, mediation took the form of ritual and external manipulation, and religious feelings were liberated to wander off in whatever direction pious whim commanded.

Not only were religious feelings distinguished from the secular realm, but they also positively opposed social morality, Hegel said, in three most important ways. As concerned love, marriage was degraded compared to celibacy; pauperism and inaction were regarded as more worthy than activity; and obedience to the arbitrary will of the Church was seen as more pleasing to God than freedom. Yet far from maintaining the spirituality of the Church, the vows of chastity, poverty, and obedience turned into an ecclesiastical power, an ordained group with lots of property. These and several additional contradictions[31] formed 'the most loathsome, and outrageous spectacle that ever was beheld, and only philosophy can grasp it conceptually and in that way justify it' (VPG 460:382–3). And that comprehension, as Hegel explained in the next sentence, was that medieval consciousness only expressed the truth of Spirit in itself. Consequently, it could not know the truth of Spirit, which is to say, it was not self-conscious, and for that reason was so much more alien to its own internal truth. 'But only from this alienation can come its own true reconciliation.'

Disappointed in its attempt to find God in the sensuous presence of things, Spirit once again was forced to rely on itself. This time it either created a sphere where it could exercise its proper function – in monastic and chivalric orders, in scholastic theology, in art – or turned toward the actual world and undertook the rational and morally justified tasks involved with the transition, mentioned above, from feudalism to monarchy, from external relations of force, caprice, and particularist submission to internal order founded upon the universal recognition of law. Also included among worldly activities were the recovery of ancient learning, its diffusion throughout Europe by way of printing, and the wider diffusion of the Germanic Spirit across the globe following the discovery of America and the passage to India and China by way of the Cape. These events, Hegel said, may be considered the rosy-fingered dawn of Spirit and Universality, which brought to an end the terrible night of the Middle Ages (*VPG* 491:411).

Modernity

The new age, *die neue Zeit*, the final period of the Germanic World, the Universal spiritual day itself, had three divisions: the Reformation, its political implications, and, dating from the French Revolution, Modernity itself, *die neuern Zeiten*.

The cause of the Reformation, we have already seen, was the corruption of the Church, its vain attempt to capture the Infinite in sensuous form. And the attempt was vain precisely because the World Spirit had, through its practical and active side, transcended the position where Spirit could appear as sensuous material. The practical world was, indeed, devoted to the finite, external, and sensuous; it was, after all, embarked upon the conquest of the globe. But it did not mistake its actions for the infinite, subjective, and spiritual. The Church, clinging to an obsolete spirituality, did, even going so far as to sell in the most grossly superficial and trivial way that spiritual satisfaction that the soul most desired, remission of sins and peace with God. Here Luther, a simple monk, expressed the heart's longing for spiritual reconciliation.

Luther's teaching may be summarized as faith and spiritual joy, both of which denied the significance of external activity and superstitious ritual and insisted upon an unmediated relation to Christ in Spirit. No longer was the external division between priest and layman valid; the internal, the heart, was the sensorium of Truth common to all mankind, which all must labour to receive. In this way Subjectivity made the doctrine of the Church its own and thereby actualized Christian freedom. Indeed, Hegel said, the essential content and product of the Reformation was the acknowledgment that 'mankind is through its very self destined to be free' (VPG 497:417).

Since Luther's day, History has had no other task than to make objective and explicit the reconciliation attained in principle by Lutheran free spirituality. The final work of *Bildung* was inherently political, for 'States and Laws are nothing other than the manifestation of Religion in the relations of actuality' (VPG 497:417). Once having gained consciousness of its freedom through the process of mediation between man and God, Spirit learned that the secular realm was also the abode of Truth, that morality and justice in the State were also commanded by God. Thus celibacy was no longer seen as more holy than marriage, the repudiation of work no longer a mark of sanctity, or blind obedience preferable to free obedience to the laws of the State. The laws were the rational embodiment of human will and action, so that 'henceforth Reason is also divine command' (VPG 504:423). In short, religious conscience no longer contradicted what is rational.

The harmonization, however, was only immediate. There had not yet appeared any manifestation, from the side of the State, of the absolute principle of Right in terms of the constitution of the State, the system of law and jurisprudence, the regulation of morality, and so on. The development of Universality and the recognition of the rational laws of freedom gradually transformed feudalism into monarchy. Three elements were especially significant. First, the realm became State property and no longer was the private domain of a paramount lord. Second, the private and particularist rights of several lesser lords became official state positions. And third, following the struggle of the Protestant church for political visibility (the round of conflicts beginning with the Thirty Years War and ending with the Seven Years War), a strictly political, rather than religious settlement formalized the external relations of European powers in terms of a system of States (VPG 508ff: 427ff).

Protestantism had affirmed the principle of subjectivity as the means by which harmony and recognition, *Befreiung* and *Befriedegung*, would be attained. But it still maintained a belief that the secular was inferior to a sacred 'Beyond.' The dogmatic quarrels of the seventeenth century, however, were cleared up by the Enlightenment of the eighteenth. Being the product of a reasonable God's design and initiative, the World was believed to embody Reason. Spirit had gained the level of Thought and so demanded that the external World be as reasonable as the thinking Subject. Belief in miracles gave way to experimental science and technology, and right and morality were no longer understood as founded on God's command but rather resulted from man's will, actual practice, and universalist political interests.

With Luther the principle was established that the achievement of man's purposes was his own affair. The contents of those purposes were, for him, revealed by religion. With the Enlightenment, however, the principle was established that the contents of human purposes must be capable of analysis and demonstration, with the result that all speculation upon human and divine things was done away with, an unsatisfactory state of affairs for the living Spirit and the concrete person. Here, Hegel said, we have come upon 'the last stage of History, our own World, our own days' (*VPG* 524:442). He immediately described it as secular: 'Secularity is the spiritual realm in empirical existence, the realm of Will brought forth into positive existence.' Henceforth freedom of the Will was to be the principle and basis of all Right. It could have no limitation and could will nothing external to itself – else it would not be free.

The formal details were worked out in German philosophy, and the practical implementation was left to the French. This was followed by the supersession of German philosophy in Hegelian Wisdom, the object of which was the comprehension of History, which in turn culminated in the supersession of the French Revolution in the Napoleonic Empire. The reason for this initial division of labour, Hegel said, was that in Germany the Enlightenment was undertaken in service to Protestant theology, which had already been unburdened of the most obnoxious medieval moral contradictions and constraints: vows of poverty coupled to great institutional wealth, and so forth. 'To this extent was the principle of Thought conciliated already; in addition the Protestant World had within it the consciousness that in the harmonization that had been evolved previously [i.e. in the realm of religion], there was present the principle that would result in a further development of Right' (*VPG* 527:445). In neither respect was this true for France.

The abstract understanding that French consciousness attained with respect to the formal, individual Will was sufficient to dissolve religion into superstition (whereas, for non-abstract religious consciousness, it was absolute Truth). Individual Will was held to be the basis of the State, and Right was its product. For the first time, Hegel said, a principle of Thought, *ein Gedankenprinzip*, was put forward as the basis of the State, namely the principle of certainty, *Gewissheit*, which was an identity with self-consciousness – though it was not an identity with Truth. However that may be, philosophy served as the basis for politics. It was, however, abstract philosophy. Thus, freedom of Will, as a philosophical principle, confronted actually existing Right, the *ancien régime*. The gap between actual but unreasonable Right and abstract Reason made 'the whole political system appear as a mass of injustice, *Ungerechtigkeit*' (*VPG* 528:446). Slow change proved impossible since only the government could undertake it, and it was least likely or willing to do so. Thus, 'Thought, the Concept of Right, suddenly asserted itself and the old framework of injustice, *Unrecht*, could offer no resistance to it' (*VPG* 529:447). In place of the *Unrecht* of the *ancien régime* a new constitution was built in conformity with the Thought of Right.

Hegel's emotional description of the Revolution and its aftermath made plain its significance: 'As long as the sun stands in the firmament and the planets revolve around it, has it not happened that man stood on his head, that is, on Thought, and built up actuality in conformity to it. Anaxagoras was the first to say that Nous governs the World; but only now has man come to the insight that Thought should govern spiritual actuality. This was, consequently, a glorious sunrise. All thinking beings shared in celebrating the epoch. Sublime emotions ruled the day; an enthusiasm of Spirit ran through the World as if the reconciliation of the divine with the World was only now actually accomplished' (*VPG* 529: 447). The reconciliation, however, was only imperfectly accomplished in actuality – it was accomplished only in principle.

In the next few pages Hegel traced the course of the Revolution, its triumphs and the reason for its failure. Napoleon restored France to the status of a major military power, made himself head of state in accord with the principle of Monarchy, settled French internal affairs, and then turned his attention abroad. 'No greater victories were ever won, no campaigns displaying greater genius were ever undertaken; but also never was the powerlessness of victory shown in as clear a light. Popular sentiment, that is, their religious and nationalist feelings eventually brought this colossus down' (*VPG* 533:451). In short, a narrow, particularist nationalism and an obsolete Catholicism prevented the French and their allies from keeping and maintaining the genuinely rational Napoleonic State, the foundations of which they had so gloriously laid.

The Catholic principle involved was that it considered its religious aims and truths higher than those of the State and, indeed, essentially alien to it. The Catholic still cherished truth in a Beyond, devaluing thereby all that was Worldly. According to Hegel, however, 'although religion and the State are different they are at bottom one, and the constitution finds its highest confirmation in Religion.' Consequently, one must speak plainly: 'With the Catholic Religion no rational constitution is possible' (VPG 531:449). As a result, the Restoration of the Bourbons was 'a fifteen-year farce.' The upheavals of 1830 showed only that the principle of Catholicism had not been fully extirpated.

However much of an improvement the July Monarchy was over the Restoration, it still had not resolved, as Napoleon temporarily had, the question of subjective Will. The problem turned upon the foolish belief that the Universal Will was an empirical Universal, a general agreement. It was not enough, Hegel said, that the State should establish rational laws, maintain individual liberties, and operate an efficient and honest public administration. In addition, the State was to reflect the formal and abstract aspect of Freedom, namely individual volition and whim. The result was the dreary operation known as liberalism. Any State act could be opposed as being merely the arbitrary result of a particular, not universal Will. The Will of the majority could get rid of the Government, which resulted in the former Opposition taking over only to meet with the same fate. 'History is presently concerned with this collision, this knot, this problem; it will have to deal with it in the future' (VPG 535:452).

The significance of the French Revolution was greater than its empirical aftermath, Liberalism. Its World-historical significance lay in the establishment, in principle, of a rational political order. Hegel ended his lectures with a brief survey of how the Revolution became World-historical, how the end of History became the standard by which all politics was henceforth to be measured.

The wider significance of the Revolution lay in the diffusion of its principles, whether by conquest or by emulation, and not in the creation of the formalities of Government and Opposition. Those principles were expressed equally in Hegel's formula, that World history was the development of the Idea of Freedom, as in the popular slogan of the Revolutionaries themselves: Liberté, égalité, fraternité. But the diffusion was initially merely outward, and the actual results were indifferent. Like the parable of the sower and the seed, some fell by the wayside, some fell upon stony ground, some fell among thorns. So far as the Latin peoples were concerned, Liberalism was introduced on the points of Imperial bayonets. 'The abstraction of Liberalism was imposed by France upon the Latin World, but that world was bound by religious Slavery into political unfreedom. For it is a false principle that the bonds of Right and Freedom can be broken without the liberation of conscience, that there can be a Revolution without a Reformation' (VPG 535:453). Here even the formalities of Liberalism did not take root, and these countries reverted to Mediterranean mediocrity.

Elsewhere, and especially among the Protestant nations, the effects of the Revolution were quite different. Austria remained a traditional Empire, a vast ramshackle assemblage of peoples and political organizations untouched by the Idea of Freedom (VPG 536:453). And farther to the east, Hegel had earlier remarked, the Slavs remained on the margin of Western Reason, in no way constituting a constituent element of the appearance of Reason in the World (VPG 422:350). With great effort, England maintained its old constitution, a complicated skein of particularist rights and privileges impervious to the truth of universalist principles. Its sole redeeming feature (apart from its secularism and commercial spirit) was that its corruption was consistent: electoral bribery allowed for the recruitment of experienced political men into Parliament. Thus the perfection of English Particularity contained implicitly a Universalist element. In Hegel's words, 'the sense, Sinn, of Particularity also acknowledges the universal Particularity of knowledge, experience, and skill that the aristocracy, standing outside their fellow-citizens, and devoting themselves to the interests [of knowledge, etc] exclusively possess' (VPG 538:455). In his discussion, written a year or so later, of the English Reform Bill Hegel was rather less generous in his opinion of British constitutionalism (HPW 295ff).

Finally, there was Germany. It had been conquered by the French and subsequently liberated itself along with the medieval fiction of the Empire.[32] The imposition of Napoleonic order by way of the Confederation of the Rhine and the reorganization of Prussia abolished feudalism and secured the recognition of freedom of property and person as fundamental political principles. 'Every citizen who meets the necessary conditions of ability and usefulness has access to the offices of the State' (VPG 539:456). The government, at least in Prussia, was officially a monarchy though hardly an arbitrary one: the strength of the State lay in the embodiment of Reason in its established laws not in the small area of discretion left to the actual king. Minor states had their borders guaranteed by their larger neighbours and so were not, properly speaking, independent. Besides, Hegel reiterated, 'a share in the government is open to everyone who has the knowledge, skill and moral will required' (*VPG* 539:456). And finally, the reconciliation between religion and Right had been attained: 'There is no sacred, no religious conscience that is hostile to, or even separated from, secular Right' (*VPG* 539:456). In other words, the end of History had been most perfectly actualized in Germany, the heart of the Germanic World.

History, according to Hegel, was the process by which the principle of freedom actualized itself. Once the regime where all were free had been, in principle, established, no further historical action was possible. Moreover, since 'Philosophy deals only with the glory of the Idea as it reflects itself in World-History' (*VPG* 540:457), the end of history is also the end of philosophy. In Hegel's terms, it is Wisdom.

In the Introduction to *Philosophy of History*, Hegel declared his intention to be to account for his belief that 'what was intended by eternal Wisdom was accomplished in the actual World and in active Spirit as well as in the domain of Nature. Our approach is in this respect a Theodicy, a justification of God's ways ... so that the evil, *Übel*, of the World will be grasped conceptually, and thinking Spirit reconciled to badness, *Böse*' (*VPG* 28:15). Hegel's concluding remarks affirmed that his intentions had been fulfilled. 'The true Theodicy, the justification of God in History,' he said, could be only the insight that World History was, indeed, the process by which the Idea of Freedom had developed itself. 'Only this insight can reconcile Spirit with World-History and actuality, that is, that what has occurred and daily still takes place is not only not without God, but rather is essentially the work of God himself' (*VPG* 540:457). The following chapters we examine in detail the architectonics of God's work; the guiding model is the pure theory of recognition, paradigmatically expressed in the dialectic of Master and Slave. The result was the universal and homogeneous State – the post-historical regime that overcame the contradictions of Master and Slave, that actualized on earth the 'ideal' of Christianity, which had been projected into a Beyond as compensation for not being present here below. Having overcome the dualism of Nature and Spirit man gained the final satisfaction for which he had been searching historically.

4

Apolitical and political attitudes

The dialectic of Master and Slave, which is the first 'impure' version of the pure Concept of Recognition, was also a paradigmatic account of the actual course of history. It served as the basis for selecting empirical historical evidence, which in turn was intended to persuade readers of the truth of the paradigm. But it also served, if one achieved a literalist-allegorical mood, as a myth of genesis for actual history. Here one might make a comparison with a fundamentalist belief in the literal truth of the myth of creation in Genesis. The mythic status of the original struggle can, moreover, be justified on Hegelian or Kojèvian grounds: before there was human being, there was proto-human Desire; hence, there was no logos, no discourse, properly speaking. Speech, if it existed at all, was a sort of instinctive murmur about food and biological urges. Thus, because there was no genuine speech by, there was no accounting discursively for, pre-historical proto-man, but only a hypothetico-deductive story of what 'must have been' *in illo tempore*. The pre-discursive account of the beginning of history was completed by the totally discursive account of the end, which in turn, because it was total, necessarily verified the truth of the beginning. In Hegelian or Kojèvian terms, myth is of the form of religion not philosophy. Hence there could be no conceptual account of the origin. Philosophy began with the first philosophical speech and so may be said to have no origin but itself. One could account for myth, however, which is, obviously, contrary to believing in it. This is the difference between mythopoesis and mythology. This question will be considered in chapter 5 in connection with the phenomenology of religious consciousness. For the present it is enough to recognize that the impossibility of giving a discursive account of the origin before one has reached the end is in no way a fatal objection. The discursive silence of the myth simply makes religious expression possible.

However that may be, according to Kojève *Phenomenology* reconstructed the real historical evolution of humanity in its essentially human characteristics and did so by an a priori deduction from anthropogenetic Desire directed at another Desire, which issued in a self-realizing action that accomplished the negation of given-Being. 'But once more this "a priori" construction can only be carried through after the fact' (*IH* 441–2:166). Alternatively, one could say equally that the mythical 'in the beginning' gave form to the whole story, and that the total discourse of the end was mythical from the beginning. We shall return to this possibility below. First, however, we must present the 'attitudes' between beginning and end that are said to exhaust fully and completely the range of human possibility.

Our presentation will follow Hegel's, which was more or less Kojève's. In the first part of *Phenomenology* Hegel studied the cognitive, emotional, and active elements found in varying proportions in each and every human being, but he did so without giving any consideration to the relation of these human beings to their historical societies. In the second half of his book, he dealt with concrete human attitudes, beginning with that of the person who is, or pretends to be, detached from his historically concrete society. The first part of *Phenomenology* dealt abstractly with concrete human beings, and the first topic of the second part dealt concretely with human beings whose existence claimed to be abstract. Specifically, these included the scientist, the moralist or man of enjoyment, and the man of letters, all of whom Kojève described as apolitical. The second topic of the second part was political attitudes. According to Kojève, Hegel divided his treatment of political attitudes into two sections, roughly corresponding to the vulgar Marxist categories of base and superstructure or, in Kojève's terms, the dialectic of historical reality and the dialectic of ideology. The first was divided topically into the antique pagan world, the medieval and modern bourgeois-Christian world, and the contemporary world of German philosophy and the Napoleonic Empire; the second considered the ideology that antedated the primordial historical fight, the ideology of warrior societies, and the ideology of successor societies dominated by labour. Finally, the post-historical and post-political attitude of the Sage is presented. In this chapter we consider briefly first the apolitical attitudes, before turning to the political attitude *par excellence*, that of the polis-dwelling pagan.

Lastly we examine the evolution and culmination of the bourgeois-Christian world.

Observant reason

In chapter 3, it was argued that the unhappy consciousness eventually became reasonable and satisfied. Nothing was said of how this came about. According to Hegel, the transition from the unhappy consciousness to Reason came by way of the Church. The Church was not, of course, a genuine or reasonable State and the community of believers did not constitute a genuine or reasonable Society because it was held together not by Reason but by faith (and, hence, by the unhappy consciousness). The priest was neither Slave nor Citizen, but a Servant (of God and of other humans); he was the mediation between transcendent perfection and immanent imperfection. But precisely because there existed a contradiction between the actuality of the world, the Earthly City, and the proper vocation of one's immortal soul, to be a pilgrim and seek the City of God, there could be no authentic recognition between priest and layman. The deeds of the layman were vain, though the priest may absolve him, if penitent, of sin; but since the deeds *were* the sin, absolution amounted to annihilation of the deed as well as the sin. What was not the work of sinful man, which, as sinful, was to be absolved and annihilated, was, for the believer, the work of God.

For the Sage, however, that is, from the 'perspective' of the wise man, 'God plays for the religious person the role that in reality is played by Society' (*IH* 72). It was true, then, that the religious person really acted in the world, but he did not (yet) know it: 'He thinks only upon his nullity and his death. He does not know that the world in which he lives is *his own* world, that it is the result of *his own* action; he thinks it is the work of God and that he remains sinful and unhappy' (*IH* 72). But then 'one fine day' it came to pass that the ideal representation or image of Reason appeared to consciousness, *ist ihm die Vorstellung der Vernunft geworden*, and consciousness saw 'that its (imaginary) God is in reality itself' (*IH* 72; *PhG* 171:138). When human beings recognized themselves in God, their unhappiness evaporated and they became 'reasonable.' The brevity of Hegel's account of the 'conversion' of human beings from theism to atheism was, according to Kojève, intentional: there was no necessity involved, and a person could remain unhappy and even rejoice in his religiosity long after Reason and Spirit had made their appearance and gained their proper form. In commonsensical language, this meant sim-ply that even the post-Hegelian, post-historical, atheistic world may harbour Christians (and, indeed, Jews, pagans, and adherents of the 'religion of light') in its midst. All alike were unreasonable and unhappy and could stay that way indefinitely.

And yet, if consciousness were to attain self-knowledge (as it did with Hegel) and if man were to become a Sage (and Hegel was the first instance of such a one) then the unhappy consciousness must be super-seded and consciousness must eventually achieve a satisfactory self-understanding, namely that human existence is free, historical, and mortal. And this meant that the idea of a Beyond must be abandoned. Consciousness 'must recognize that its genuine and unique reality is its own action freely effected here below for the here below; it must under-stand there is nothing outside of its own active existence in the World where it is born, lives, and dies, and where it can attain its own perfec-tion' (IH 75–6). When one does this one has transformed oneself from a religious person to a person of Reason who has no religion. The first 'man of Reason' who tried to live independently of Nature and the his-torical State was, according to Kojève, the bourgeois Intellectual.

The ideal of Reason, Hegel said, was the truth of self-certainty. It was the ideal 'of the certainty that, in its particularity, consciousness is abso-lute in itself, or is all reality' (PhG 171:138). This 'ideal' could become real only when the consciousness that envisioned the ideal actually revealed all reality, which revelation could occur only at the term of History. The error of ideal-ism, in this regard, was to treat the ideal of Reason as the concrete reality. That is, the 'idealist' simply declared his Ego to be the reasonable revelation of reality but did not account for the genesis of his attitude of Reason. In the absence of such an account, the reality revealed by Reason would be a pure abstraction.

There were other errors as well. The transformation of Self-Conscious-ness into Reason, of the unhappy religious person into the reasonable one, removed all dualisms: there was no more 'Beyond' as distinct from a 'here below' – at least not in principle. But in fact, the idealists (Kant and Fichte, according to Kojève), while they identified the World and Ego, understood the Ego in an abstract way, as an entity opposed to the World. But it was impossible to identify Ego and World by thought; this could be done only by action that transformed the World so that it con-formed to (reasonable) Ego. Furthermore, while the idealist Ego thought itself in such a way that 'it is as though the World had only just now come into being for it' (PhG 176:140) – because Reason named or revealed the things of the World to itself – this thinking was purely individual. The action that transformed the world, however, was collective. In short, the error of idealism was that it retained an essentially religious Ego, isolated, unjustifiable, and searching for an epistemological Beyond where Reason could be certain of itself.

Yet something had been gained: man no longer fled the World in search of meaning. Now he accepted the world, was interested in it, observed it, and might even enjoy it. But he did not yet act in the proper sense of the term and he forgot about the action taken earlier, within the Church, when he was merely Self-Consciousness and not yet Reason. The meaning of the World was no longer vanishing into a Beyond; it was permanent, the abode where man might find himself and his truth (*IH* 81).

Hegel's discussion of observant Reason, which dealt with physics, biology, cosmology, psychology, physiology, and phrenology, need not detain us. In general, 'Reason wants to find itself and to have itself as an existing object, as an actual sensuously present mode.' Consciousness that observed in this way sought not itself but the essence of things and, indeed, it did come to know what things were. 'But we come to know what consciousness *itself* is' (*PhG* 184–5:146–7). By implication, as Kojève pointed out, observant consciousness did not understand itself (*IH* 83). This isolated scientific consciousness was active to the extent that it asked questions of the world; but it was not activist in that it did not transform the world by technique.

Following the analysis of the isolated observer of nature was the analysis of the existential attitude of the reasonable man who was isolated from Society and indifferent to the State. This person was the 'existential idealist' or 'bourgeois Intellectual' properly speaking. He sought to be recognized, but without extending recognition; that is, he sought simply to be celebrated or famous. Accordingly, he lived in society as if he were the only individual in the world. On the one hand, his consciousness imaginatively existed in a world that eventually succeeded his own pre-revolutionary Society. In this way he may think of himself as living in isolated opposition to the customs and laws of that Society. But, on the other hand, he was actually, not imaginatively, prior to that State where he could find satisfaction as Citizen. The double contradiction between the imaginative world and the real one, and between his lack of satisfaction and his desire for it, motivated the dialectical transformations of his 'individualist' Reason.

This liberal, bourgeois self-consciousness was at 'the beginning of its ethical experience of the world' (*PhG* 260:215) but was in no way satisfied or even happy. It was like a Slave without a Master, a religious person without God, who gave himself up to the immediate satisfaction of his basic instincts, including 'sublimated instincts' and ideological fancy (*IH* 85). With the creation of ideologies, which Hegel said was quite familiar to his contemporaries, there came into being a conscious split between what was actually given and the end to be realized through the supersession, *Aufhebung*, of that given actuality (*PhG* 261:216). The project of an End to supersede the present unsatisfactory and unhappy actuality taught self-consciousness the value of sacrifice, even of complete sacrifice. Thus did the 'law of the heart' (Rousseau) become 'virtue' (Robespierre). 'The experience that virtue undergoes can be no other than this, that its End is already attained in itself, that immediate happiness is found in action itself, and that action is itself the good' (*PhG* 261:217). Thus ideology led consciousness to sacrifice itself for a good cause, which was an experience of action, which in turn was the actualization of the ideology.

But we look too far ahead. First Hegel described the dialectic of 'individualism' in terms of the forms self-consciousness takes: pleasure, sentimentality, and reform.

Bourgeois individualism

Pleasure was akin to proto-human Desire in that it was bestial and sought immediate satisfaction. But the man of pleasure was faced with possessions and not simply things. Hence, he purchased what he wanted within a legally regulated market society and did not simply take them. His was the attitude of a pseudo-Master. He enjoyed things, as a Master, but only after gaining the consent, perhaps only the tacit consent, of others. He did not kill or fight in any way. He was driven to consume by his passions, and ended up in bondage to them, which bondage was experienced as necessity, and hence as universal. The last moment of this dialectic arrived when the man of pleasure accepted this necessity, formulated an ideology in which he explained to himself that 'man is an animal.' Thus he believed implicitly that his acceptance of necessity was his own doing and not a consequence of the hostile natural world (*IH* 87). This, of course, may be read as Hegel's commentary on Hobbes.

Because he was still an 'individualist' but also because he was aware of an immediate necessity or universality within himself, the man of pleasure was followed by the sentimentalist who formulated a universal and necessary law, but one of the heart. For the first time we find a bourgeois critique of Society and hence a kind of action or negation. The relation of the sentimentalist to society, however, was one of complicity: he sought to become famous through criticizing society, but he must preserve it, through criticism, if he was to have anything to criticize and anyone to applaud his anguish and his wit. He did not wish to act in the full sense of the term. But he did like to talk.

Unlike the man of pleasure, this man's compassionate and tender heart would not stand, or stand for, the brutalization of cruel necessity. In addition, his verbal opposition, lead him to invent a counter-society, a utopia that he neither desired nor intended to realize. In his relation to society, then, he could be either criminal or crazy, but never revolutionary. Since he would not live out his ideal in public action (because this would transform his utopia into something other than the regime of the law of the heart and himself into something other than a moralist) but since he lived within, and depended on, an actual unsatisfactory society replete with oppression and suffering that contradicted the law of the heart, his existence was one of radical internal diremption. He took what was unreal, his utopia, to be real; he took what was real, the society he criticized, to be unreal. His 'heart-throb for the welfare of mankind' allowed him to think himself better than the whole world and turned him into a raving and fanatical bore. Who is not reminded here of Rousseau or of his enlightened colleagues? Their life's work consisted in denouncing the world as an utter perversion of the law of the heart and of the heart's happiness, 'a perversion invented by fanatical priests, riotous gluttonous despots and their flunkies who seek compensation for their own degradation by degrading and oppressing others, a perversion that caused the nameless misery of a deluded mankind' (*PhG* 271–2:226). Who is not reminded of their enlightened and noisy successors?

In fact, however, the sentimental moralist was no less perverted than the despots and priests he so gleefully criticized, and his tender heart no less unreal than the unreality of the actual world it was used to criticize. The transition to the man of virtue consisted in the realization that the 'solution' of the law of the heart was part of the problem. While the tyranny of despots and priests was a scandal to a Voltaire, Voltaire himself, by his merely verbal denunciations, showed that he was not a serious man, that he too clung in his heart to perversion. When consciousness became aware of its own attitude and understood it, it thereby superseded it. Then it knew that sheer individuality as such was the source of the perversion of society, since it was the common ground of the perverted men of pleasure as well as the sentimentalists (*PhG* 273–4:

228). Immediate individuality must, therefore, be sacrificed. In this way the sentimentalist became the man of virtue, familiar with the way of the world. He continued to criticize the order of things, but not as an 'individualist.' Now he joined with other critics and established a conspiratorial party: '"Virtue" is a party: a non-realized ideal, a phantom society. But nevertheless a society. Thus: progress as compared to the "tender heart"' (IH 88). Seeking the suppression of individuality, the party of Virtue united against the sybarites to effect social and/or moral reform. 'No struggle. No revolution, except in words' (IH 88). Nothing actually happened, but Rousseau's soul was purged.

The man of virtue sought to suppress 'individualism,' but he did so by seeking the reform of individuals: he wished to develop their moral capacities through personal sacrifice and educative ascesis. But this was to accept the essential aspect of society, its 'individualism,' and negate only its perverted details. The 'true ascesis,' Hegel said, 'is entirely the sacrifice of the whole personality as proof that in fact there are no individual particularities to be asserted. In this sacrifice, individuality as it is found in the way of the world is also annihilated, since individuality is the simple moment they have in common' (PhG 274–5:228–9). This sacrifice, a genuine supersession of 'individualism,' was, according to Kojève, the risk of death in a victorious revolutionary struggle (IH 89). In the absence of struggle and risk, the Slavish elements would not be overcome; in the absence of success the would-be revolutionary was a mere criminal. The sacrifice of virtue, however, was not so serious.

Virtue believed in its own goodness and in the goodness of human nature, once it had been 'clarified' to itself. Faith in goodness gave the man of virtue a purpose, namely triumph over the rotten ways of the world. But this meant that virtue really existed only in opposition to the way of the world and not in its own right. In this opposition, virtue and its enemy appeared to have the same 'gifts, capacities, and powers' so that the outcome at first appeared doubtful, and the fight appeared to be serious. But it was not. Virtue always had in reserve its belief in its own superiority; 'in the end' goodness won out. Hence, the only thing tested in the fight was the capacity of our white knight to act as the vessel and instrument of goodness. But capacities were not at issue; if the fight were serious, goodness itself would be at risk. The self-righteousness of virtue and the sincerity of its beliefs turned out to be proof against the very possibility of admitting of a real defeat. A serious risk and a genuine fight were therefore again impossible. A serious fight would be beyond good and evil.

As for the enemy of virtue, he was content perpetually to win an 'apparent' victory and so indefinitely postpone the 'inevitable' triumph of virtue. Yet the victory of this man of the world, an unreconstructed Master, was not a genuine victory precisely because he did not have a genuine opponent. There was no satisfaction gained in winning against 'this pompous talk about what is best for mankind, about the oppression of humanity, about making sacrifices for the sake of the good, and about the misuse of talents' (PhG 280:234). No satisfaction could ever come from deflating a bag of hot air, then or now. On the contrary, the spectacle of fatuous ideologues bloated with their own conceit was also rather a bore.

Now bored with its own chatter, virtue took stock of itself and its opponent and abandoned its faith in the principle of a faith in goodness that never gained actuality. The way of the world, the unreconstructed Master, was the 'actuality of the Universal,' so nothing could possibly be gained by further sacrifice (PhG 281:235). It no longer made sense to complain that the world perverted the high ideals of virtue, since what made them so exalted was precisely their otherworldiness. And then again, the virtuous one said to himself, half a loaf is better than none. He became a 'progressive,' and declared that virtue, even if 'perverted' in an ideal and so otherworldly sense, nevertheless had moved from the void of abstraction to the plenitude of actuality. And this was not nothing. Indeed, it eventually would amount to a change in the way of the world – but not yet, since truly to change the world meant to overcome the unreconstructed Master and engage in a genuine revolutionary fight. This the bored and self-righteous progressive bourgeois Intellectual reformer was not yet ready to do. And his contemporary successors are not yet ready, either. Individuality had one further trick up its sleeve before being forced into action: it could take itself to be real and profess an interest in itself.

Worldly individualism

Forced into a compromise with the world, individuality had learned that its activity was its own end, an act of self-expression. The party of virtue had been disbanded and consciousness reverted to individualism once again, only now it was a worldly individualism. The supercelestial pseudo-society of virtue had fallen to earth and smashed into countless pieces. When the pieces came together again, both individualism and otherworldliness would be superseded. But first the dialectic of worldly individualism had to work itself out.

The action of the worldly individualist, the Intellectual, 'changes nothing and goes against nothing' (PhG 284:237). Such action, Kojève said, was 'turned against itself, expressing itself: literary activity' (*IH* 90). Its objectives were similar to those of religious consciousness in being transcendent, but the transcendence was horizontal, not vertical. In principle, the perfection of a work, namely beauty, truth, etc., was attainable in the world even though any particular work need not embody or fully express those universal principles. The particular work, in fact, need only display itself as the incarnation of consciousness. That is why the activity that created the work changed nothing. All the intellectual did was speak his piece.

In terms of the self-understanding of the Intellectual, even this formulation was too activist. It would be better to say that the work was the occasion for display of a talent with which he, the Intellectual, happened to be gifted. He appeared to himself as an 'intelligent animal' who displayed his innate nature by way of his works.

Now, since action was the negation of nature, whether external or innate, the activity of the Intellectual was not action properly speaking. This is why the first part of the title of this section of *Phenomenology* was 'The Spiritual Bestiary,' *Das geistige Tierreich*: on the one hand it was human and so spiritual, but on the other it was animal and so a bestiary. Animals do not produce works, only humans do; yet humans can understand the production of their work as the appearance of a talent that is innate and so not really a consequence of their own action. Such a self-understanding was not properly human but rather was akin to what animal understanding would be if animals were able to understand (and not just sense) themselves. As Hegel said, consciousness as talent seemed unable to determine its own purpose before it set about its activity; yet before it acted it must know what it was going to do. But if it did, it would act on its own (*PhG* 288:240). As a contemporary Intellectual put it, 'A craftsman knows in advance what the finished result will be, while the artist knows only what it will be when he had finished it.' In other words, the Intellectual 'is' (his) talent actualizing itself in (his) work. Yet, since the work was a thing independent of its author, the author must be able, without destroying it, to transcend the work (having created it) even while the work remained an expression of his 'nature.'

One way for the Intellectual to do this was to create another work, since he was not simply a nature or a talent, but a human being, a free, historical, mortal individual. His work, however, was simply an artefact, a thing he could compare with other things, albeit in terms of the different natures expressed therein (*PhG* 289:241). What the Intellectual as 'critic' must not do, however, was judge the works as good or bad, since this would reflect upon the natures and talents that produced them. It would assign responsibility to the individual (who is free, historical, and mortal) and not to the talent (which simply is what it is – like Yahweh). This is why critics who are not neutral and disinterested and who make 'moral' judgments about literary works are held by Intellectual men of letters (even today) to be displaying bad taste and a mean temper. In other words, in order for Intellectual consciousness to transcend (its) work without destroying it (and itself) it must cease to be Intellectual and, like observant consciousness discussed earlier, give up the enjoyment of itself.

But it was not yet ready to do so. Instead, it produced artefacts, sending them into the world as actualizations of itself. Others did so too, and consciousness now acknowledged in the form of result what it earlier had acknowledged in the form of beginning, namely the difference between acting, which is spirit, and its product, mere given-Being. But the Intellectual consciousness again forgot about Spirit, since it was shot through with contingency, and cleaved only to the 'real intent' of the 'thing itself,' namely the famous and aforementioned eternal verities, truth, beauty, etc., which it pretended were objective, so as to pretend as well that it was disinterested. This, Hegel said, was called 'honesty.' But it was really an imposture: in fact, the Intellectual 'is interested only in himself, in his isolated particularity' (IH 93). The pretended disinterestedness of consciousness was expressed as a judgment on the work of others. But to judge was to betray an interest. The Intellectual could not 'let it be' even though he pretended the real intent of the work, including his own, was to let the eternal verities 'be.' Only the Sage would truly look on.

Indeed, deceit was inherent in the consciousness of a bourgeois Intellectual. On the one hand, he claimed to be concerned only with the eternal verities expressed through (his) talent or nature, and not in the mere contingency that these verities happened to get expressed thanks to him who was talented, or of an artistic, intellectual, etc., nature. But when he stepped into public view and 'showed' what he 'is' he did not sacrifice his egotistic interests for the eternal verities but rather made his contingent self a common property. And by doing this he showed that he craved applause and success, a place in the unchanged (hence 'natural') world. Thus we see the appropriateness of the second half of the title of this section: the spiritual bestiary was intimately linked with imposture, Betrug, and the 'thing itself,' that is, eternal verities, die Sache selbst.

How, then, to move beyond the spiritual bestiary, which Kojève identified with the Republic of Letters, a world of Intellectual boulevardiers?
Eventually it must be by transforming the Intellectual's narcissistic but
cowardly desire for recognition into a serious fight for recognition; consciousness must cease to be content with being celebrated and well
known and give up thought for action. But first the Intellectual must
think that his thought is universally valid and not simply the actualization of (his) nature. The speech of the chattering, self-advertising Intellectual thus turned into the legal, and so universalist, speech of the
moralizing Intellectual. This one presumed to speak in his own name,
and not, as the self-deceiving conduit of eternal verities, to the rest of
mankind in order to dictate morality to it. But still he would not act.

According to Kojève, Hegel began this section from the 'perspective'
of the Sage. The topic was the naturally loyal member of pre-revolutionary Society. This Society was not homogeneous but divided into 'masses,'
each of which had its own distinct customs and laws. These laws were
neither questioned nor justified, but simply accepted by different social
categories as 'natural' ways. Sound, commonsensical Reason, die gesunde
Vernunft, knew intuitively, in an unmediated way, what the law was and
likewise said so in a direct and straightforward fashion: 'This is good' or
'That is bad' (PhG 302:253). But once the loyal member of Society began
to reflect on what justified this particular law, or what made it, when
applied to this particular 'mass' or social category, 'good,' then he ceased
to be loyally in support of this Society. Now he sought to determine, in
thought, what was abstractly good and bad. The answer was problematic. His thoughts may turn out to be subversive.

Such an attitude gave rise first to the naïve moralist, who declared,
quite simply, that everybody should speak the truth. He was followed in
turn by the romantic advocate of the Golden Rule, and finally by the
astringent, but empty and formal, reflective or philosophical moralism of
Kant and Fichte. Here we have reached something like Kelsen's pure
theory of law, 'a mere standard for deciding whether a content is capable
of being a law or not, that is, whether the content is or is not self-contradictory' (PhG 306:256). Reason had ceased to be the giver of laws or even
a naïve justifier of this or that particular law; it had become the formal
critic of legal structures, apparently indifferent to their actual content.
This was the last form of intellectual consciousness, the last apolitical
attitude. As Kojève remarked, this 'rationalist' Intellectual was a caricature of the Sage.

The pure legal theorist-critic searched for non-contradictory laws, moral judgments, and modes of behaviour. And, in the abstract, he found several high-sounding and non-contradictory tautologies. In concrete reality, however, there remained all sorts of contradictions. In response, this last 'rationalist' avoided the contradictory concrete in favour of the more acceptable pseudo-world of abstraction. By so doing he showed himself still to be seeking after 'eternal verities.' No longer were the good, the true, and the beautiful conceived as criteria of truth. Sheer non-contradiction would be enough.

That this Intellectual was a caricature of the Sage may be suggested by the following consideration. Whereas Hegel claimed to have tested concrete particular instances in terms of the universal concept or 'authoritative substance,' the 'rationalist' compared the particular content only with itself to see if it conformed to formal tautological criteria (PhG 306:257). Hegel, that is, claimed to judge in light of a final and universal criterion, namely his comprehension of the final regime, the universal and homogeneous State, which in principle was a concrete historical actuality, whereas the 'rationalist' employed a mere formality that was indifferent to actual truth and untruth alike. For example, when one applied the criterion of non-contradiction to a practical question – for instance: Should there be property? – it turned out that it 'fits all cases equally well and so is in fact no criterion at all' (PhG 308:259). The futility of formal criticism, no less than the futility of law-giving moralism, showed that, taken in isolation, they were merely moments eventually to be integrated in a stable 'ethical consciousness,' namely Wisdom. But then Reason would have had to abandon the formality of non-contradiction and learn that contradictions were opportunities to be realized – it would have to give up thought for action and turn to politics.

Taken concretely but in isolation, the moralizing Intellectual was an insolent tyrant since his laws, like all laws, were contingent. In this instance, the contingency was whatever happened to be the contents of his moral consciousness. Similarly, the critic claimed for himself a kind of immunity from the contents of laws that was no less insolent because it treated all laws as contradictory and capricious. He was not a tyrant but an antinomian or anarchist. Both have effectively denied the authority of nature, though they had no idea what was implied by their negation. The one said that since there were no limits in nature we can legislate our own will; the other replied that since there were no limits in law we can express our own will. Both, moreover, were anti-political. Now, no one disputes that anarchy cannot properly be considered a political attitude; and tyranny, which isolated individuals from each other and the tyrant from them all, which has so often been condemned as inherently corrupt and perverted, equally violated the minimum criterion for politics, common action. The only ones who disputed the contention that tyranny and anarchy were inherently apolitical were those same nauseating Intellectuals who moralize and criticize but who think that they are acting politically. Even so, something had been gained by this caricature. Their attitudes were *always* wrong. Thus, if only the emptiness of the moralist received a content, if only the relativism of the critic were overcome, then would they cease to be Intellectuals and become Sages. But this would mean that the loyal citizen of the pre-revolutionary regime, whose very loyalty spawned both moralism and criticism, would have to have become the reflective citizen of the post-revolutionary regime. We shall see shortly where the loyal citizen came from. For the moment it is enough to know that, from the 'perspective' of the Sage, the apolitical attitudes had run their course to exhaustion.

Pagan existence in the polis

We mentioned above that, according to Kojève, *Phenomenology* was divided into two parts. One dealt abstractly with the constituent elements of human existence: first, sensation, perception, and understanding; next, desire, struggle for recognition, and labour for another; and finally, reason that enabled one to reflect upon oneself and the world. The second part dealt with 'real' man. This historical human being lived in Society and created through his collective action a State that was successively transformed until it attained perfection. The story of the genesis of the State was '*real* universal History' and was told in chapter 6 of Hegel's *Phenomenology*. Now, when man created History he revealed himself to himself by way of his creation. The story of the genesis of this revelation was '*ideal* universal History' and was told in chapter 7 (*IH* 97).

According to Kojève, chapters 6 and 7 of *Phenomenology* were not entirely parallel in their topical structure. Specifically, Hegel did not consider any political order prior to the Greek polis, whereas he did consider pre-Hellenic 'primitive religion.' This is because the polis was 'properly speaking the *first* State, the first human *Society* in the strong sense of the term.'[1] It was the first expression of the relationship between the particular person and the State, which, in contrast, claimed to represent not particularity but universality. Religion, the topic of chapter 7, 'reflects not only the relation of Man with the *State*, with the *social* World, but also his relations with the *natural* World, with Nature; that is, with the milieu within which man lives *before* the construction of the State properly so called' (*IH* 196–7). One should, perhaps, emphasize that the priority of the polis was logical rather than historical; it owed its place in the argument to the universalist implications of Hegel's use of the term 'State.' Just as the universalist Master defeated the particularist Slave, so too, as we shall see, the universalist polis crushed the appearance of particularity in the family.

There was but a sketchy account of the genesis of the polis. Nevertheless, its 'essential characteristic ... is determined by the fact that it is a State, a Society of *Masters*' (*IH* 184:57). But these Masters were real Masters, not paradigmatic ones. They were, of course, Masters of Slaves, but also Citizens of an aristocratic State and members of a family. Perhaps, like Cadmean *Spartoi*, they evolved naturally from the primordial herd of Masters. Or, as Kojève suggested, perhaps the first polis was created 'by the will of a Tyrant who "knows" and realizes the will of all ("general will") the People' (*IH* 98). His will was universal not because the others were his Slaves but because they were loyal and obedient, because their actions realized his will. The Tyrant was less their master than their god, the incarnation of their several particular wills. But tyranny must pass. On the side of the Tyrant, the instability of bodily human generation ensured the impossibility of producing worthy tyrannical heirs. On the other side, the loyal Citizen had accepted tyranny without a struggle; hence, eventually, it would turn into despotism. The despot did not 'know' the will of all, and the loyal Citizens refused to fight for his biological person. This spelled the end of the ancient world.

But even before Roman times, to which Kojève was rather fancifully alluding, tyranny had become obsolete. Once the State was established, the need for a tyrannical *nomothete* had passed: henceforth, the polis would be dominated by the *nomoi* he had given them. The law, Pindar said (frag 152), is King. The laws were now loyally and unthinkingly accepted by the Citizens. 'For the loyal Citizen, the laws *are*, and that is all' (*IH* 98). They are seen to be divine and unchanging and this, as we shall see, was the cause of their decay.

The polis, then, recognized only Masters, who were its warrior-citizens; or better, the warrior-citizens were the polis. Labour was done by Slaves, non-citizens (*metoikoi, perioikoi*, etc.), or citizens whose poverty effectively deprived them of citizenship. Labour, in effect, was excluded from the public realm. It followed, according to Hegel, that only the universal element of existence was recognized, while particularity was ignored, kept in the darkness of the household, or left on the fringes of Society. In other words, consciousness was divided (*PhG* 318:267). This division was 'fundamental' because 'Mastery corresponds to Universality and Servitude to Particularity' (*IH* 184:58). Accordingly, the conceptual dialectic of Universal and Particular complemented the paradigmatic or mythic dialectic of Master and Slave.

The Masters, the Citizen-warriors, achieved their humanness fighting for the polis, but the appearance of their humanity was anonymous. What counted was the polis, the universal, and the actual people who fought for it, that is, for themselves as a State, did not fight as individuals. Even the leaders were simply functions of the State: hence the exemplary character of Cincinnatus. The Slave, in contrast, gained his humanity in a purely personal and particular sense according to changing circumstances. He, unlike the Master, developed a 'personality,' but it was not recognized by the impersonal Master who, at best, acknowledged only the products of his labour, which he then 'consumed' as food or art: hence the relative obscurity of men such as Polygnotus of Thasos or Zeuxis of Heraclea. Now, we know from the dialectic of Master and Slave that so long as their respective activities were not synthesized in a single person, there could be no human satisfaction. Of necessity, then, the polis and pagan society expressed a contradiction and were essentially unsatisfactory.

The contradiction was most easily seen as it existed between the State and the family. Because the male members of the family fought, it was a human not an animal group. They did not, however, fight within the family, so that logically no human value could be realized or recognized there. The family recognized the value of biological or animal life, realized in the 'natural' biological 'action' of the father, namely, his potency and fecundity, the ability to 'produce' a family. The female 'action' of creative fertility was given only religious representation. However that may be, the father was recognized for what he is, not what he does; this recognition was called 'love,' and, since it did not depend on action, it could not be ended by inaction, even by the absolute inaction of death. 'Thus, death can change nothing in the Love, in the value attributed within, and by way of, the Family. And that is why Love and the cult of the dead have their place at the heart of the pagan *Family*' (*IH* :61). The cult of the dead, which gave value to, and recognized, one's unique-in-the-world particularity, was governed by rites, prayers, and rituals, that is, by divine laws and ordinances. These were the means by which the Particularity of the dead Citizen (who is also a member of a family) was rescued from an utterly anonymous annihilation implied by the swallowing of his (male) material body by the (female) earth, nature. In death, followed by an appropriate funeral, then, the ancient Citizen attained the sought-for synthesis of Particularity and Universality. A posthumous synthesis did not, however, give him any satisfaction (though the family may have believed they had given peace to his shade). So long as they lived, the male members of the family were governed by human laws, and these laws demanded that Citizen-warriors risk their lives for the polis, that is, for its laws. Thus, for the universalist Citizen-warrior, 'death is the perfection and highest labour that the individual undertakes on behalf of the polis' (PhG 322:270). Here, then, was one appearance of the contradiction: 'The Family is the reservoir of State forces whose proper activity, War, negates the Family because it kills off its members' (IH 100). The contradiction also appeared in terms of the incompatible demands of human and divine laws.

There were three possible sets of significant relations within the family: father-mother, parent(s)-child(ren), brother-sister. We shall see below why relations between children of the same sex were not important. The first set was not human but biological, natural, or animal, and was humanized only by the second, the common (and servile) labour of educating children. But this was insufficient since, although it may fill a father's heart with pride to see his son grow up, it could hardly satisfy him fully and completely. In any event, the son must leave in order to fulfil his vocation as a Citizen-warrior.[2] Two brothers did so equally, leaving the privacy of the family for the Universality of public life; two sisters remained equally in the family and did not change with respect to one another.

The relationship of brother and sister, however, was inherently asymmetric. They were of the same blood and loved one another, but there was no natural, sexual desire between them – or, if there was, it was overcome, thereby making it human, not animal. They were, Hegel said, 'free individualities with respect to each other' (PhG 325:274). The sister was not yet fully burdened with the natural demands of motherhood so could attain the highest, most ideal sense of moral consciousness: 'she represents the summit of familial existence, and her attitude is the least "natural" of all.' The sister was concerned wholly with the (inactive) being of her brother and not at all with what he did: 'That is why the death of the brother changes nothing for her' (IH 101). When the brother, who was, of course, also a son, left the family, the result for the sister was much more significant than it was for the father, who was simply proud of 'his' young warrior, or the mother, who was simply resigned to her loss, or perhaps had other sons to look after. The sister's unencumbered care for her brother and her heightened moral consciousness of familial values were concentrated in the life of her brother. And because there was no natural desire present, the brother was, for the sister, a similar being. Accordingly, 'the constituent-element of recognizing and being recognized, one of the *individual Self*, can here maintain its authority, *darf hier sein Recht behaupten*' (*PhG* 326:275). The brother's death, for the sister, was thus her greatest loss. But as Citizen, he was devoted, precisely, to giving up his life.

Action and Fate

We have seen that the Master who died fighting and was suitably buried achieved a posthumous synthesis of Universality and Particularity but was not thereby satisfied, being dead. If he did not die fighting he also did not receive satisfaction because the victorious Citizen simply did his duty and was loyal. To be loyal was to reconfirm what already existed and in no way constituted a negation or *action* in the strong sense of the term. To act, to negate, one must therefore be a criminal, either against the laws of the State or against the 'divine laws' of the family. Pagan Society was *inherently* criminal. Correspondingly, 'ordinary' criminals could redeem their transgressions by fighting and dying for the city.[3]

We said above that the citizens of the polis were loyal and unreflective because the polis was constituted by Masters who, in turn, were articulate only defending and speaking its laws. Masters did their duty without question and, as Leonidas and the Spartiates, died obedient. The only alternative was to disobey the laws: it mattered not whether one's motives were courageous or cowardly, disobedience was criminal Particularity because it was a manifest denial and negation of the very being of the polis whose public purpose was to uphold the Universality of the laws. This meant that the pagan warrior could never be a revolutionary. He could not place himself imaginatively outside the polis, since he was the polis. Or, what amounts to the same thing, once outside the polis he was a nothing, a dead ancestor. Accordingly, the State punished the criminal traitor not by killing him, since as Master, we know, he was indifferent to death and in a sense was already dead, but by depriving him of his individuality. The polis punished criminal traitors by prohibiting their funeral and depriving them of burial: 'no *universal* recognition (in funerary rites) of the *particularity* of death. Consequently, what is punishment for the State is a crime for the Family' (*IH* 103). The conflict of the laws was essential, not accidental. The fulfilment of one law by way of an actual deed transgressed the other and turned the same deed into a violation that demanded revenge or retribution (*PhG* 335: 283). Whichever set of laws he obeyed, the pagan Master was a criminal in terms of the other. Since he could obey only one set at a time, his situation was tragic (*IH* 102). The tragic conflict was not, however, a conflict of duties or a conflict between duty and passion. It was between two levels of existence, the Particular and the Universal or the private and the public, one of which was seen to be valid by the actor, but not by the others. These others may be divine or human, and, naturally, they take vengeance. 'The agent, the tragic actor, will not be conscious of having acted as a criminal; being punished, he will have the impression of submitting to a "destiny," which is absolutely unjustifiable but to which he submits without rebellion, "without seeking to understand"' (*IH* 102). When, nevertheless, the criminal actor did somehow understand his own criminality, he took vengeance on himself – Oedipus, for example (*IH* 104). In Hegel's terms, only by the submission of both sides equally could absolute right be achieved. When this occurred, Fate or Destiny, the negative but omnipotent power that engulfed them both, has appeared (*PhG* 337:285).[4]

We can see now why the asymmetric relation of brother and sister was so important. Only a Master could violate the laws of the polis; only to the sister of such a criminal brother would his act mean nothing and his given-Being ('He *is* my brother') everything. We can also see once again that the Master could not change: he was ready to die, to submit himself to Destiny either as a loyal citizen, if he succeeded, or as a traitorous criminal, if he failed.

The conflicts of *Antigone* and the *Oresteia* reflected the contradictions inherent in the absolute separation of the sexes, which in turn was a special instance of the separation of fighting and labouring, of Masters and Slaves. Now, the basis of the polis was the 'natural' ethnic unity of the people; so too was its internal contradiction, the 'natural' division of the sexes and its political manifestation, the contingency of two brothers with equal claims upon the community. In the conflict between the Universal and Particular, as between Master and Slave, the first round goes to the Universal even though by crushing the Particular it destroyed its own foundation. This was the tragic meaning of *Antigone*: Creon was a criminal ruler who violated the divine Law regarding funerals and for his pains achieved civil war (Eteocles vs Polynices) and the suicide of his family (Haemon and Eurydice take their own lives). More importantly, the divine law had not been annihilated but only wronged. Its power still ruled the underworld. Moreover, since the polis had the basis or root of its power in the underworld, *der offenbare Geist hat die Wurzel seiner Kraft in der Unterwelt*, the violation of the divine by the human law cut the former off from the latter (hence civil war, family suicides, etc.) and inspired other poleis, the sanctuaries and altars of which dogs and ravens had defiled with the carrion of the unburied one, to rise up in hostility and destroy the polis that had dishonoured the piety of the family (*PhG* 339:287).

The dialectic of divine and human laws has appeared so far only as the pathos of a tragedy involving single persons. The conflict of Particulariy and Universality, in this form, was also the historical transition from polis to *imperium*. The polis, we saw, attained actuality by dissolving the Particularity of the private in the Universality of public action, and it did so by suppressing womankind in general, creating thereby an enemy within. If the pure Universality of war, the activity of Masters, was to be altered, it must be by feminine particularity, by Woman, the natural labourer *par excellence*. Women, however, did not act, properly speaking, so it was necessary to turn war from the masculine, universalist purpose of prestige to essentially feminine ones, namely, to realize Particularity. The purpose of ostracism was to prevent just this happening (*IH* 243). Homeric and other heroes may have fought *for* women; subverted heroes must fight *as* women, that is, as feminized (though hardly effeminate) warriors.

Appropriately, Woman effected this change by intrigue, a counterfeit of genuine action. She undermined the education of her son, when he was still part of the family and under her care. She turned him away from the grave wisdom of maturity, which exalted only what was universal, namely the risk of life, and directed him toward the expansive joys of life and youth. The true worth of a son, his mother told him, lay in his being lord and Master of the mother who bore him, in his being a brother in whom a sister could recognize one equal to herself, in his being a young man by whom a daughter could obtain the dignity and joy of wifehood, freed from dependence within her own mother's household (*PhG* 341:288). On the one hand, the polis could preserve itself only by suppressing such subversive principles. On the other hand, suppression was self-defeating. Accordingly, the polis was bound to disappear because it existed as a separate polis only by admitting of the importance of Particularity, that is, it maintained its own external particularity only by seeking internally to suppress Particularity as something hostile; and because it could not merely suppress the Particularity of the family because it depended on its young men to fight, precisely, for that external Particularity that made the polis what it was, namely *this* particular polis. And so the raw and intrepid youthful warrior, this 'suppressed principle of subversion' in whom women found their pleasure now 'has his day and prevails' (*PhG* 341:289). He 'turns war into a means of realizing his *particular* (that is, familial) ambitions' (*IH* 105). These wars were themselves criminal, since loyalty to the polis had no place in them. There was, of course, much plunder and a kind of calculative allegiance to victorious generals – so long as they were victorious and able to reward their followers with booty.

The feminization of war and the end of loyalty to the polis alike expressed the 'natural' decline or decay of pagan consciousness. In no way was this change revolutionary. Because he was young and brave, the physical strength of the young hero with perverted particularist goals enabled him to triumph over fortune. But when political order depended on good luck it had already perished internally. More generally, since the laws of war favoured the big battalions, the strongest State slowly swallowed all the others and became an Empire (*IH* 188:62). As for the brave intrepid youth at the head of those batallions, he became 'a despotic chief of state, a Particular who wished to submit the State (the Universal) to his own Particularity: perversion of the existing "*Sittlichkeit*," of the customary (universalist), pagan, antique, morality, the morality of Masters (Alcibiades, Alexander the Great)' (*IH* 105).[5] Alexander's empire absorbed the Particularist political order of the polis into a Universal community 'whose sheer, *einfache*, Universality is spiritless and dead, and whose living activity exists only in the Particular individual *qua* Particular' (*PhG* 342:289). During the period of transition from one form of Spirit to another, once again there were political upheavals. The fatal weakness of the Alexandrian transitional empire was that it depended upon the biological existence of the conqueror. Universality could be immediately tied to Particularity only so long as the determinate single person lived; when he died, the life of the political order died with him. The result had to be either a reversion to a pre-Alexandrine political organization (the Hellenistic kingdoms) or change to a formal

Universality, the political manifestation of which would not depend upon the determinate Particularity of a single existence. This new form of Spirit appeared as the legal order of the Roman Empire.

The decline of the pagan world

The hidden divine law of the polis, we saw, was swallowed in the sheer necessity of Fate or Destiny. But, Hegel said, this Destiny 'is nothing other than the Ego of self-consciousness' (*PhG* 343:290), which is to say that actual Roman self-consciousness was equivalent to that obtained imaginatively by the tragic Greek. Consciousness had moved historically from the inwardness of an individuality that existed only in the un-worldly shape of a shade whose memory was preserved in the family, that is, as selfless and un-actual Spirit, to the outwardness of an individuality that existed actually but abstractly, that is, as a legal person. The Roman Empire was not, therefore, a 'spiritless community' based upon the 'natural' bonds of ethnicity and family. It was a conscious community. In principle, therefore, all human beings were potential or actual 'persons.' Thus, for example, when adult individuals could be made a part of a family, what counted was not their blood relationship but the deliberate, conscious law of adoption.

The abstract actuality of law and the legal person corresponded to the imaginary or abstract independence of the world attained by the Stoic. Stoicism, Hegel said, was 'nothing other than the consciousness that brings an abstract form to the principle of legal status, a Spiritless independence' (*PhG* 343:291). The legal person was likewise tied to neither wealth, nor strength, nor even human corporeality (Suetonius's story of Caligula and Incitatus, however apocryphal, has a modern equivalent in the business corporation). The legal person was, however, tied to property, a formal category without any substantive contents whatsoever; private property, 'this little world that is my own creation and that escapes all relativism' (*IH* 106), was an actual historical recapitulation of the *solus ipse* who eventually became the paradigmatic nihilist Sceptic. Just as with Stoicism and Scepticism, law and property reinforced one another. The absolute majesty of legal rights indicated the independence of law, but the equally absolute emptiness of legal rights indicated the contingency of its contents.

The Roman Empire was not, properly speaking, a State but rather a legal fiction. While divided into a multitude of atomistic 'persons' it was at the same time gathered together in the single person of the emperor whose property was the entire realm. He, or rather the office of emperor, the Lord of the World, was the absolute legal person (*PhG* 345:292), the conscious unity of the Whole. As absolute, he was 'the person for whom no greater Spirit exists' (*PhG* 345:292); as the conscious centre of actual political power, he first thought himself a living god, but as a purely formal person he was unable to direct or control these actualities. Hence he, like all other Romans, fell back upon his private life. Unlike them however, he lived out the dark and private world of dreams and excesses as debauchery. Eventually, he pondered the significance of his impotent frenzy and discovered that the 'natural' Greek ethical or political substance was gone and that his own ecumenic power organization had set Rome adrift upon an open sea of sheer potentiality, the most apparent manifestation of which was nothing but his own desires and whims. The world as a whole was alien to these masters of the *ecumene* precisely because anything could serve as the contents for the Roman personality. It had no 'natural' contents of its own. Nevertheless, the self-indulgence of the emperor and the existence of his imperial subjects taught him and them that he was, in fact, completely supreme. Accordingly, when the subjects, and eventually the emperor, adopted Christianity, they became equal to one another (as they already were as abstract persons) in the eyes of a God fashioned after the actual model of legal supremacy they saw before them in the shape of the emperor (*IH* 106).

So far as the Citizen-warriors were concerned, once the empire was established and the victorious polis had become an imperial capital, they no longer need fight. First of all, there were too few of them to defend the empire; but second, they were no longer interested in fighting and preferred to enjoy the spoils of war, namely vulgar or sophisticated bread and circuses. Consequently, the emperor had to resort to mercenaries in order to defend and extend the empire. Citizen-warriors were replaced by several varieties of police, and eventually, by ceasing entirely to fight, they grew content to watch gladiators. They were unable to resist the imperial particular, who thereupon overcame them as citizens and transformed them into private persons, ensuring, incidentally, the victory of the family, now expanded to the 'family' of mankind, and its divine law. 'In sum,' Kojève said, 'the ancient citizens become *slaves* of the sovereign. And they become such because they already *are*. In effect, to be a Master is to fight, to risk one's life. Citizens who no longer make war therefore cease to be Masters, and that is why they become Slaves of the Roman Emperor. And that is also why they accept the *ideology* of their slaves' (*IH* 188–9:63), namely Christianity.

We have reached, then, the bourgeois, legalist, property-holding, Christian world. The legal person was meant to be absolute but the emptiness of his personality, which appeared in the form of debauchery, etc., prompted self-consciousness, 'this universally acknowledged authority' (*PhG* 346:293), to ponder its own absolute inessentiality and perversion. Unlike the harmonious ethical world of the Greek whose individual self was posthumously and therefore not actually achieved, the Roman 'person' actually achieved selfhood, but it was alienated, *aber sich entfremdet auf* (*PhG* 346:294). In principle, the historical period of domination by the Master had ended, and the second period, characterized by alienation, determined by the Slave and his ideologies, and destined to endure until the French Revolution, had begun.

Self-alienation and culture

According to Kojève, part B of chapter 6 of Hegel's *Phenomenology* described the development of the former pagan citizen of the ancient world who, having accepted the religion of his slaves, became a Roman bourgeois, created the Christian world, and developed various religious and atheist ideologies to interpret his creation to himself. Specifically, it was a phenomenological analysis of France, the 'land of culture' (*PhG* 350:296), as France changed from feudalism to the Napoleonic Empire. Christianity had overcome the pagan split between Universal and Particular at the cost of projecting the ideal synthesis into a Beyond. Corresponding to the paradigmatic unhappy consciousness discussed earlier is the historically alienated consciousness, the present topic. Christian consciousness was split between the actuality of 'this' world and its meaning: 'What is present means merely objective *actuality*, the consciousness of which is in a Beyond; each single constituent-element *qua essential-reality* receives this [i.e. its meaning], and therewith actuality, from the other [order], and insofar as it is actual, its essential-reality is other than its own actuality' (*PhG* 348–9:295). As a result, the Christian world was 'dirempted.' It was a world full of pre-revolutionary bourgeois malcontents who talked a lot about the split between the actual world and their ideal but non-existent one. Indeed, precisely because they were malcontents did they speak up: they spoke about Nature because it made them suffer and die; they spoke about the State because they found it oppressive; they did political economy because society did not satisfy them as it was. In short, they were critics; they constituted a world of unhappy and alienated spirits some of whose apolitical aspects we have already encountered. But Hegel called them self-alienated, which implied not simply a split between the actuality of the world and its meaning, but that the origin of the split lay in the consciousness of it, in Faith understood as a flight from actuality into an imaginary world, constructed by consciousness, and called the Beyond (*PhG* 350:297). Being self-alienated, the Christian world contained within itself the means necessary to move beyond its present discontents.

The Spirit of the Christian world, Hegel said, was an essential reality permeated by self-consciousness that knew itself immediately as a Particular (*PhG* 350–1:297; cf *IH* 119–20). According to Kojève, the spirit of this world was the Christian God and its essential reality was the social collectivity. The permeation of the essential reality by self-consciousness meant first that one knew (or believed) the meaning of life, namely the ideal in the Beyond; second, the Christian believed he could realize himself immediately without having to act by way of others (or, in theological language, that he was directly related to God without the mediation of human society or its institutions); and third, self-consciousness knew itself only as Particular and not as Universal, which meant that the political shape of the Spirit of this world was an absolute monarchy. But, Hegel continued in this same lengthy sentence, self-consciousness knew essential reality as an actuality to which it was opposed or over against which it existed. The Christian was a stranger in the social world and, since he believed his real home was in the Beyond, could never fully be relied upon. They were pilgrims en route to the Heavenly City, holding dual citizenship, in the *civitas terrena*, here below, and in the *civitas dei*, up above.

As Wahl pointed out in his study, the unhappy Christian consciousness had alienated its own personality from the things of the world. The Christian would stay 'from the things of *this* world,' which statement, for a Hegelian, was evidence of his alienation. The self-conscious process of alienation created, precisely, the Christian world as distinct from, and opposed to, the pagan. The empirical existence of the Christian world and Christian self-consciousness could be maintained so long as that process was uninterrupted. And yet the Christian could not avoid being aware of the impossibility of his position: even while knowing that it lived in a Christian and not a pagan world, and that this world was, therefore, *its own* world, the Christian consciousness was still a stranger and still must take hold of, *bemächtigen, s'emparer*, its own world and become its master. The Christian world, Kojève said, was a long revolution by which the Christian sought to establish himself in the here below that originally he fled.

But, Hegel said a second time, the alienation of its being-for-self was itself the production of the actuality of the specifically Christian world. The Christian must *do* something if he were to live a Christian life, namely, make the effort of self-alienation. Christian self-alienation, to repeat, is a process not a state. Pagans were born pagan; Christians were reborn pagans, born-again pagans, which is to say they were made, or rather, self-made. Christian equality, therefore, was not immediate but abstract equality in the eyes of the law, but rather existed only through the mediation of the universal ascesis of self-alienation. It was undiluted by 'nature,' but was a genuine spiritual universality that had become itself and so gained self-conscious actuality. This effort Hegel called Culture, *Bildung*. The title of part B, 'Self-Alienated Spirit: Culture,' may be then explained as follows. First, the world appeared to self-consciousness as something from which it was immediately alienated even though self-consciousness was at the time certain that in principle the world was its own. Thus it could undertake to make it so. Its power over the world was gained by way of Culture. From the side of self-consciousness, however, Culture appeared as the process by which self-consciousness conformed to actuality. But from the 'perspective' of Hegelian Wisdom, the actualization of the power of self-consciousness over the world, achieved through a self-emptying, *Entausserung*, that eventually lead to a conformity with the essential reality of the world, was the development of the actuality of the world, that is, History (*PhG* 352–3:299).

Bildung, therefore, referred to the formation of the world. It was the result of an education that was a self-education, an education that was first of all unconscious, which is why self-consciousness felt itself a stranger. The world, after all, belonged to God (or later, to the Emperor, the King, the feudal Lords, and lastly, to capital). This division into opposites stirred the two extremes into contrary motion since each, being alienated from the other, gave meaning and existence to its opposite. The process that overcame this alienation, or, rather, that overcame this alienation that alienated itself, would return the contents from the separated extremes to the single and ultimate Concept that underlay their separation. But that final reconciliation was still distant.

Contradiction and dialectic

The Christian wanted to be saved, but what he did was create a world. The difference between his intentions and the results of his actions was a measure of his lack of self-knowledge, a gap that his *Bildung* would eventually have to overcome. Even though he was unconsciously realizing a world, the Christian was at the same time quite conscious of the contradictions of the world. There were three areas of conflict: between good and bad, between the public power of the State and private capital or wealth, and between the status-groups of nobleman and commoner.

Christian goodness replaced pagan perfection just as sin replaced pagan shame. In both changes there was a kind of conceptual unfreezing. Perfection was an ontological category; it simply *is*. Goodness was a moral category, a 'value'; it *must* be, which is to say, it becomes. Shame, in contrast to sin, could not be redeemed. It was fatal, in both senses of the word. Yet the two were related. The great pagan imperfection was pride. In addition, however, 'Pride goeth before destruction and a haughty spirit before a fall' (Proverbs XVI 18). The fatal imperfection was easily turned into a moral fault, a sin. Now the sin of pride was the result of the Slave's depreciation of the Master's desire for glory, which the Slave correctly called vanity. When this desire was no longer vain, sin would cease to be considered sin, and the Master's glory would be superseded by the recognized dignity of the Citizen (*IH* 123). Meanwhile, however, good was immediate and so not created by the Christian (bad was novelty); good was immutable and always identical with itself (bad was changing); good was universal and common to all (bad was particular and individual). But they were also complimentary, which meant that the one could not be realized without the other (*PhG* 353:299). The one could not be destroyed without destroying the other. The only solution that would destroy conflict, which was a bad thing whose destruction would be a good thing, would also destroy the Christian world, which was a good thing whose destruction would be a bad thing. This was not a tragic dilemma, a result of Fate. Rather, it was comic: there was a solution, but the Christian *qua* Christian did not know what it was. He was content to live out the 'human comedy,' unwilling to commit the impiety and crime of destroying the Christian world yet aware that the world was still the wicked world.

Christian thoughts of goodness and badness were reflected socially in the identical but this time actual conflict between the State and the Economy. Wealth, private property, or capital was the basis of the Christian world, but it was also the contradiction of evangelical poverty. The State was the guardian of the private property of a Particular, just as the Christian God was God for *me*, a Particular. But the State was created by Particulars for Particulars and so stood over against them (*PhG* 355:301). In short, the State tried to suppress the economy that supported it just as the economy tried to suppress the State that defended it. Once again, everything was both good and bad, and the Christian was ambivalent or indifferent to the world, seeking to choose only goodness, which could not be chosen here below.

The ambivalence of the Christian in society led to the third conflict. It did not matter to the Christian *qua* Christian whether he was rich or poor, citizen or non-citizen, circumcised or uncircumcised: what counted was the choice he directed toward the Beyond. What happened here below in consequence of his choice did not really matter. Accordingly, he could be either a conformist or a non-conformist. But the ambivalence of the world rendered his choice meaningless. 'First of all the Good is this: to accept the World as is because one believes it possible to realize one's personal values without transforming the World. Bad is, under these circumstances, therefore non-conformism. But this World is wicked. Therefore non-conformism is the Good' (*IH* 124). The Christian judged everything in terms of his own personal goal, the salvation of his soul, which meant he must not be concerned with 'lower' matters such as politics and economics. But from the 'perspective' of the Sage, *all* Christian decisions were both conformist and non-conformist (cf *PhG* 358–9: 305), which is to say Christian judgment necessarily reflected the diremption of the Christian world.

Considered on their own terms, two modes of consciousness reflecting two sorts of Christians now may be said to exist. On the one side were Noblemen, conformist and bourgeois former Masters; on the other were Commoners, non-conformist and bourgeois former Slaves. Both were property-holders, and both were riddled with anxiety. The Nobleman fought without risking his life because he believed his soul was immortal, and, in that respect, the essential respect, he was the equal of the Commoner. On his part, the Commoner laboured, but he was not for that reason a Slave, since there were no more Masters properly speaking. '*Laborare est orare*,' said the Benedictines; their founder himself had said '*qui orat et laborat cor levat ad Deus cum manibus*,' and raising one's heart toward God was the highest purpose of life. What, then, did it matter that one's lot was toil?

The historical Christian remained unhappy; his contradictions remained. For the Sage, therefore, the dialectic of the Christian and bourgeois world consisted in the elimination of the remnants of the pagan world as found in the opposition of Nobility and Commons. Both must be swallowed into bourgeois equality. So long as the Christian world lasted there would continue the opposition between the Universal (the State, God, and the pseudo-Masters) and the Particular (private property, the world here below, and the pseudo-Slaves). The first historical shape of this opposition was found in feudalism.

Decline of the Bourgeois-Christian World

The activity of the feudal Lord seemed to consist, at first glance, in service, the virtue that involved the sacrifice of particular interests to the Universal. Like the Slave, the Lord served an other; but unlike the Slave, his labour was to fight. By this self-cultivation, *Bildung*, the Lord gained attention for himself and was attended to by others (*PhG* 360:306). According to Kojève, therefore, the Lord's negation of his Particularity in service to a Universal made him the first Functionary, the first genuine synthesis of Particular and Universal (*IH* 125). But since attention, *Achtung*, is not recognition, there could be no genuine satisfaction. This was because the Lord did not serve, properly speaking, a self-conscious Other to whom recognition could be accorded and received. Rather, he served an authoritative principle, *Gesetz*, that had no particular will of its own. Thus, the Lord did not really sacrifice his Particularity; he only gave up his life, his given-being. Moreover, he did so not because he had decided to do so as a particular individual, but because he was born a Lord, and that was what Lords did. It was their 'way.'

The insufficiency of the feudal State can be seen in two additional ways. First, although the Lord served the State, he was also independent of it. Because it was not self-conscious, the same authoritative principle that bid him serve also specified the conditions and terms and enabled the Lord to retire to his own lands. Even worse, when the Lord returned from war, he was a danger to the State, since he thought only of his service to the State during war and not also of peaceful service. He would die for the State, but not live for it. He was a 'functionary of death' (*IH* 125), who in peacetime would as likely as not be willing to engage in civil war.

In addition to the problem posed by veterans who served mere authoritative principles, a second insufficiency was revealed by the kind of speech the Lords uttered. Of course, Lords preferred simply to do what the authoritative principles decreed and keep silent. But if asked to speak up, their speech took the form of counsel, that is, official technical advice that did not commit their whole personality but only their role as a loyal servant. The purpose of this counsel was ostensibly to advise on the general good. But since the State was authoritative rather than self-conscious, it had no way of distinguishing sound from stupid counsel. Thus, Hegel said, 'it is not yet Government, *Regierung*, and so not yet in truth actual state power' (*PhG* 361:307). Lacking an arbiter, the Lord's counsel was not transformed into speech about the general good but remained simply the articulation of his own self-interest. Eventually, the Lord grew content merely to chatter about the general good, the Universal, and not to serve it by fighting, even while the contents of his chatter served his own Particularity. This means that, in fact, he had claimed the right of opposing his private opinion and will to that of the State. In this respect, his service was self-cancelling and he was indistinguishable from the non-conformist Commoner.

Even though the speech of the feudal Lord may be no more than chatter, *Geschwätz*, it was nevertheless a discourse, *Sprache*, of sorts. In principle, discourse synthesized Particular and Universal: the Ego who spoke was universally understood by all others in their Particularity (*PhG* 362–3:308–9). In general, according to Hegel, speech revealed and then reconciled subjectively or verbally an actual contradiction. In the case of the feudal Lord, his speech revealed the contradiction between the universality of his military service and the particularity of his interest, which was based on his landed property. Likewise the State was both a Particular, a King, *primus inter pares*, and a Universal, a military unit. The King, therefore, also spoke: '*L'État, c'est moi.*' Having given up their swords for canes, which is to say, having sacrificed honour and nobility in exchange for survival and a badge of honour, the Lords became Courtiers and responded to the royal speech with flattery; the non-conformists at court responded with whispers, those outside, with pamphlets. We have, therefore a perfect linguistic or verbal synthesis of Particular and Universal in Absolute Monarchy (*IH* 127). The name of King distinguished him from all others and actualized state power in his person because the nobles continually told him, who sat on the throne, what he was (*PhG* 365:311). Everybody talked; nobody acted.

But, as the Psalmist said, 'They do but flatter with their lips, and dissemble in their double heart' (Psalm 12:2). Let us, then, examine a few of the contradictions of the *ancien régime*. Louis XIV may have been told by his courtiers that he was universally recognized. In fact he was recognized only by the tiny coterie at Versailles. Even there he was simply *called* a universal Master: in fact everyone tried to get away and live independently of him. The Sun King was absolute, therefore, only within the 'ornamental setting' (*PhG* 365:311) of the court. His Universality depended upon the verbal recognition or flattery of a series of Particulars, just as the Master, in the end, depended on his Slaves. To utter the famous words '*L'État, c'est moi*,' was an error, since no State is egotistical. All States seek as many citizens as possible. In any event, the whole collection of King and Courtiers depended on wealth, and wealth, for the Christian, was a bad thing. Moreover, it 'rejects those who wish to possess it and diminishes the number of those who do possess it. Wealth, in spite of appearances, is therefore hostile to the Particular. But it can have only the Particular as its goal.' Wealth, therefore, eventually must suppress itself (*IH* 129). The State, that is, the Monarch, depended for recognition on a particular group, even while Particularity was concerned with, and was expressed by, wealth or capital. Thus, the State too was in a process of turning into its opposite. It was becoming just another big business, which meant it was relinquishing political power (*PhG* 366: 312). Eventually this meant that wealth would gain universal recognition. It also meant that the particular self who underwent the debasement of monarchial splendour, Louis XV, learned that his was an empty name. Absolute monarchy had become constitutional or parliamentary monarchy, that is, a bourgeois State. Whether wearing a crown, a coronet, or a cloth cap, all bourgeois sought wealth, all were capitalists. The original anthropogenic desire for recognition had transformed itself into a desire for material abundance. This is, of course, what the original Master *got* as a result of his risk of life but it was not what he had *sought*. Now, with the modern pseudo-Masters, bodily rather than spiritual satisfaction was sought for its own sake. It, too, would be sought in vain.

Because wealth was sought by all, it appeared as an elusive and anonymous Universality even though the bourgeois thought it was compatible with his own Particularity. It is true, of course, that the bourgeois sought wealth in order to gain independence and thereby confirmation of his Particularity, but the universalist laws of economics, which governed the production and distribution of wealth or capital, ensured that the number who sought wealth was always greater than the number who possessed it. The formal contradiction of wealth, its being both the object of the activity of the Particular and intrinsically hostile to Particularity, meant that wealth appeared to bourgeois self-consciousness as having an objective, actual being of its own. Instead of being superseded, it developed its own essential reality and a spirit of its own (*PhG* 367:313). Accordingly, the dialectic of bourgeois society consisted in the elimination of the spirit of wealth, which was the spirit of capital or even the spirit of capitalism, as alien.

Initially, the Courtier accepted the gifts of the King with gratitude, failing to understand that the King depended upon his flattery. Now, when wealth was *the* goal and purpose of life, he who dispensed patronage and place also disposed of the recipient's own essential reality. Moreover, when consciousness reflected on the reciprocal dependence of the King, or upon the nature of wealth as the recipient's own product, the actual patron appeared as undeserving; that *this* Particular dispensed *my* wealth to *me* was a mere accident, a caprice. Thus, 'the spirit of its thankfulness is also the sentiment of deepest humiliation and rebellion' (*PhG* 368:314).[6] The bourgeois looked upon a world of his own making, namely wealth, that was at the same time completely alien and without any value whatsoever. 'When the pure Ego sees itself externalized and dirempted in this way, then all that had continuity and universality, all that was called an authoritative principle, *Gesetz*, good, and right, is thereby torn apart and falls to pieces; all coherence is gone and the utmost incoherence, the absolute non-essential-reality of absolute essentiality, and the utter externalization of being-for-self, is at hand; the pure Ego itself is absolutely dirempted' (*PhG* 368:314). This dialectic of the 'poor Bourgeois,' Kojève said, characterized the properly Christian State and in some respects was similar to the dialectic of the pagan world.

The poor bourgeois progressively transformed himself into an Intellectual who ideally suppressed servility and so was analogous to the Stoic. The difference, however, was this: the bourgeois was the Slave not of a Master but of himself, in the form of his ideological product, God, or his material product, wealth. He may someday rid himself of God but wealth, capital, was a *Gegenstand*, a worldly reality, to whose laws, willy-nilly, he must submit. An attitude of indifference toward capital was impossible subjectively as well because it was his own product, 'the conscious and voluntary foundation of his own *Selbst*' (*IH* 129). Yet he was alienated from it and grew increasingly dissatisfied: 'All moral values appear false to him' (*IH* 129), and he became an analogue to the Sceptic or Nihilist. Accordingly, 'even though this consciousness receives from Wealth the objectivity of its separate and independent being, and supersedes itself [as dependent on another's patronage] ... it has not yet attained its concept and is conscious of being unsatisfied' (*PhG* 368:314). The catalyst for change was money, or rather, the lack of money. No one was exempt from poverty, not even the comparatively rich bourgeois who, having riches, des richesses, necessarily lacked wealth itself, la Richesse (IH 130). Money linked Particular to Universal the way family war did earlier. The poor bourgeois, the client, the proletarian, realized the Christian 'ideal' of 'evangelical poverty.' He and he alone revealed the nothingness that was implied by the Christian status of 'creature.' He and he alone found the language appropriate to this final revelation of Christian truth, which amounted to the self-suppression of Christianity.

The corruption of the Courtier, a corrupted feudal Lord, resulted not in satisfaction or even contentment but in further alienation, unhappiness, and diremption. Accordingly, it destroyed itself, an sich aufgehoben. The mechanism was found in the dialectic of the rich bourgeois, who gave, and the poor bourgeois, who received. The attitude of the client, whether he be a Courtier receiving the favours of a King or a beggar receiving a penny from a passer-by, was, as we have seen, one of gratitude and rebellion. The arbitrariness of wealth was not less known to the rich. With them rebelliousness was replaced by arrogance. But arrogance did not dispel the patron's inner uncertainty. He took the easy way and simply, perhaps gratefully, accepted the sheer contingency of his own Wealth. For that reason the patron was superficial and not very interesting. Only the client, like the paradigmatic Slave, reflected on his condition and articulated the Spirit of this historical World. What he said, therefore, would describe the actuality of the Christian world and, qua reflection, necessarily would pass beyond it.

The language that reflected the meaning of wealth to itself was called by Hegel 'base flattery.' Those who spoke it were 'Bohemians.' Their speech was flattery because it gave wealth significance, but it was base because what it said to be true it also knew to be untrue. Yet the language of diremption was the perfect language for a dirempted world. What the contrary Bohemian revealed was that neither the actuality of power and wealth, nor the conception of them as good or bad, nor the consciousness of good and bad, that is, the noble consciousness and the base consciousness, possessed any truth whatsoever (PhG 371:316). The Bohemians, whether in garrets or in the Hall of Mirrors, enjoyed themselves by exercising their wits and cleverly telling how everything could be shown to be its opposite. The only thing that mattered was how one said whatever one said, not what one said. Such an emphasis on wit, Hegel said, was the absolute perversion of consciousness – nihilism. It would seem, therefore, that self-consciousness must pass through the dark night of utter senselessness and a kind of self-inflicted folly before it could attain self-knowledge or Wisdom.

At this stage of its education, the shameless embrace of deception was the greatest truth. The 'honest' man, who appeared as the eponymous literary persona of Diderot's *Rameau's Nephew*, was frank and sincere, and the truth he told was that everything was a lie. But this speech was obviously self-cancelling as well, and the nihilistic and dirempted consciousness that uttered it was well aware it made no sense. If he spoke at all it was only to say 'No' – which was no discourse at all – or else he merely confirmed the Intellectual's clichés: 'In spite of evil, good yet exists,' and so forth. The speech of the honest man was, therefore, indistinguishable from the lies of Intellectuals; if he tried to isolate himself from the perverted world, he was reminded that his isolation depended on the world; if he looked forward to a return to nature, he was informed of his own utopianism (*PhG* 374:319). Nevertheless, in his discontent with the bourgeois-Christian World and his realization that there was no escaping it, the Intellectual had already gone beyond it, though he was yet unaware of having done so. In short, the universality of discourse, even when it amounted to a denunciation of discourse, expressed a truth. Willy-nilly, by revealing the bourgeois-Christian World and its culture, this nihilist and dirempted but nevertheless discursive consciousness had already 'gained a still higher consciousness' (*PhG* 374:319). Consciousness did not, however, know what it had already become. Its speech, which revealed and derided corruption and confusion, also derided itself and so constituted the fading and decaying sound of the world it denounced (*PhG* 375:319–20).

The meaning of 'Culture and Its Realm of Actuality,' which was the title of this section of Hegel's *Phenomenology*, was, then, alienation. The awareness of alienation was the first act in superseding it, the first moment of the return of Spirit to itself. Before undertaking the creative revolutionary action of transforming the world, however, consciousness fled it once again into a Beyond where it sought to actualize in a positive way its having overcome the alienation of Culture.

Belief and Insight

The section 'Fideism and Rationalism' described the development of a 'pure' consciousness that had fled the alienation of actual culture. Thus it may be said to be an abstracted or 'pure' account of the development of alienated consciousness. In this respect, it served as a prelude to the account of the actual dialectic of the pre-Revolutionary World, the Enlightenment.

In the shape of belief, *Glaube*, and pure (Cartesian) Insight, this consciousness thought it had risen above the actual world of nihilism and alienation. But since there was, for Hegel, no other World, no Beyond, this consciousness had not overcome the alienation it fled. Instead, there occurred a split, characteristic of modern subjectivity, between the knower and the known. On the one side, in the form of Belief, consciousness abased itself in the externality of its object, and on the other, consciousness in the form of Insight turned everything into an object of itself. For Hegel, both were aspects of the same development. They were described first as they were complete in themselves, then as opposed to the actuality they had fled, and lastly as opposed to each other.

Turning to Belief, Hegel first described the result of the infusion of the cultural contents of the Middle Ages into the empty subjectivity of the paradigmatic unhappy consciousness. This historical development of Belief resulted in Trinitarian theology, 'the real World raised into the Universality of pure consciousness' (*PhG* 380:324–5) with no internal diremption. Second, he described the return of these 'ultimate realities' to the actual world where they were only partly at home: 'in opposition to its restful realm of its thought, stands the actuality of the real World as a spiritless existent, *als ein geistloses Dasein*, that, because it is spiritless, must be suppressed in an external manner' (*PhG* 381:326). The sheer suppression of externality was not, however, its supersession, so that criticism of actuality by Belief was always remote, isolated, and otherworldly. The Believer retired into religious isolation and impotence. The historical believer ended up dead to the world.

Turning to Insight, Hegel made the following comparison: whereas Belief actually was the undisturbed and tranquil consciousness of Spirit as essential reality, Insight actually was the self-consciousness of Spirit as essential reality. The first understood Spirit as unchanging, essential, etc.; the second understood Spirit not as essential reality but as itself. Hence it was not restful but sought to abolish anything independent of itself and transform it into its own categories, the categories of its reason, which is to say, the constructs of consciousness (*PhG* 382:326). Now, Belief proclaimed its absolute, inviolable objectivity and utter impenetrability by pure Insight. The religiously isolated believer was mysterious and proclaimed the mystery of things by his isolation and silence. For its part, Insight now declared Belief to be just another object for itself. In this imperious Universalism it found its superiority. Speech, even if it were just the pure discourse of Cartesian rationalism, which thought its conceptions constituted the world, was superior to the silence of the mysterious or even mystical and mystifying isolated believer.

Because Insight was pure, it met no resistance in objects. Specifically, it suppressed the cherished idea of Belief that man had a 'nature,' in this case, a 'sinful' nature. But equally, it eliminated determinateness resulting from judgments of good and bad. The variant textures of the world were therefore exposed to the mutual violence of genius, talent, and capacity. The spiritual bestiary seemed to have been restored. In more theoretical language, if the world depended for its meaning on the constitutions of consciousness, and not on 'nature,' that is, on fundamental and given differences, whatever differences existed in the world were a result of the contingencies of the isolated Particularity who *was* that presumptively Universal constituting consciousness. But this meant that there must be as many worlds as there were consciousnesses to constitute them, which hardly seems an improvement over cultural nihilism. Yet it was, Hegel said, because even though the actual shape of the World may be determined by will or strength and not Wisdom, nevertheless by making the World, including Belief and even itself, its own object, pure Insight showed that it understood, however imperfectly or tacitly, that consciousness was its own contents. By intention, therefore, this Particularist consciousness was also Universal; hence the sought-for Synthesis appeared as Hegel's exhortation that closed this section: '*Be for yourselves what you all are in yourselves, – rational*' (PhG 383:328). The response to that exhortation was the Enlightenment, a generalized suppression of determinativeness that enabled man, having understood himself as a being that was not determinate and was without a 'nature' (IH 134), to act in the strong sense of the term.

Dialectic of the pre-Revolutionary World

There were two ways of fleeing the actual world, to go 'up' into a Beyond that could be representationally apprehended only in Belief, or to go 'ahead' into a utopian Ideal that was supposed to be worldly but was not or not yet. This second kind of flight, which also involved a kind of belief, was undertaken by the activist Intellectuals of the Enlightenment. The 'activist reason' of the Enlightment may be contrasted with the 'observant reason' of the pre-Enlightment moralist and the 'contemplative reason' of Hegelian Wisdom. As worldly, it may be contrasted with Christianity, but, insofar as it rejected the given world, it shared a common attitude. Nevertheless, the world to which the man of the Enlightment repaired was, in principle, an earthly one, and for this reason his discourse was eventually revolutionary.

The flight to a secular or future world was possible because the historical evolution of the bourgeois-Christian World had fulfilled three important conditions. First, the bourgeois was personally secure. He lived a peaceful world with no threat of immediate violent death. Thus he was able to overcome his natural fear of death as such and give up his belief in immortality and the Beyond. Second, because he lived in a city, where Nature was humanized as parklands, pastures, and carefully prepared food, it no longer appeared as dangerous or hostile. Thus, he abandoned all those fears the origins of which lay in the remnants of natural religions. And third, he was not a Slave but a Citizen. He took part in politics, as Slaves did not, and he was recognized for it. Thus, he had no need to imagine a better world in the Beyond (*IH* 135). If there were to be a better world – and the man of the Enlightment had no doubt there would be – it would be on earth. The new heaven of the enlightened citizen was, therefore, worldly. It would not be won without a fight, however. Enlightened critical speech therefore was an anticipation, a preparation for its real, empirical actualization by means of Revolution.

Simply from its position in *Phenomenology*, we know already that Enlightenment would amount to a negation of the particularist nihilism expressed in *Rameau's Nephew*. What it negated, however, was not nihilism but Particularity. Comparing Diderot, the author, to Rameau's nephew, his creation, Kojève noted that Diderot could say nothing new because Rameau's nephew was perfectly self-conscious, the apogee of individualism. All the author did was transcribe the words of Rameau's nephew and make them available universally by producing a book. 'Rameau's nephew is at the extreme point of individualism: he is untroubled by others; Diderot, on the other hand, suffered and wished that everybody would pay attention to him. Thus, if *everybody* spoke as Rameau's nephew, the world would be changed by that [i.e. by discourse]. A *universalized* Rameau's nephew – that is what the *Aufklärung* is' (*IH* 135). Enlightment meant propaganda for the ideas of Rameau's nephew and against the ideas of fideism and the World it implied. But Rameau's nephew, for all his self-confidence and self-consciousness, had no ideas, properly speaking. He was against a great deal – but only verbally. He was, Kojève said, an 'agitator' as well as a propagandist. His business was agitprop.

The first stage of Enlightenment was essentially subversive. Insight knew that Belief was, in general, opposed to reason and truth. Moreover, it could see the results, a veritable 'realm of error' (*PhG* 385:330). At its base were the credulous people; above them the crafty priests, claiming a monopoly on insight, who played on the naïveté of the people and conspired with unenlightened despots. These in turn used both the clever clerks and the submissive people for their own purposes. Enlightenment bent its efforts first to reforming naïve belief. It sought to change the believers' feelings and not to destroy the corrupters directly. The result was the insinuation of a new spirit. In attempting to purify religion of superstition, Belief necessarily used Insight as its purgative. But this could only destroy the naïveté of Belief and confirm the claims of Insight. The result was that Belief shrivelled into idolatry: 'If the infection has overcome all the organs of spiritual life, then one fine day, a day whose noon is not red with blood, there will be merely the memory of an old and enigmatic story, the dead form of Spirit in an earlier shape' (PhG 388:332). There would be no struggle, the noonday would not be red with blood. Instead, the old belief, which was sustained by a Spirit of confidence, would turn into a defensive argument. But when belief must argue its case it has already been converted by the spirit of its critics. Thus, religion collapsed into an old and enigmatic story.

Religion was clearly a scandal to an Enlightened man. Just as clearly, it must be crushed. But since, according to Hegel, Enlightenment amounted to the principle that knowledge and its object were the same (PhG 389: 333), if the principle were truly universal it must also apply to religion. In fact, religion existed; but, in theory, it was irrational. Thus, when the subversion had run its course and consciousness surveyed the ruins it had made, a great uproar occurred: how could such a thing as religion be? For Hegel, the Sage, Enlightenment and Superstition, even in their (verbal) struggle, simply expressed two aspects of a same (and still alienated) consciousness. On his own terms, however, the Enlightened man thought himself above the stupidities he surveyed. He did not consider that his calumnies of Belief and the 'realm of error' in fact simply bound him to what he denounced. For its part, Belief rejected the calumnies of Enlightened insight: the object of Belief was not its sheer appearance, as if the significance of the host were found in its being an unusual sort of bread; the grounds for Belief were not in the evidence of history, as if the biblical narrative were an unusual sort of newspaper; the meaning of charity and worship was not their utility, as if renunciation and prayer were an unusual sort of compulsion.

In other words, the criticism of Enlightenment seemed to have achieved no more than a restatement of the disparity between the Beyond and the here-below. If it was superstitious to see infinite significance in the finite, perhaps one could see the infinite directly. That claim, which was equally a matter of belief or superstition, constituted the positive content of Enlightened propaganda. According to Enlightened Insight, the significance of the objects of Belief was attributed to their determinative characteristics – as, for example, odd bread, weird newspapers, strange compulsions – whereas the truth of the matter was that absolute Being was indeterminate and without imaginary transcendental meaning: bread is bread. Thus, the most fundamental cognitive element, sense-certainty, was reintroduced, but now as full and complete truth, since consciousness had purged itself, through Insight, of all alternatives. And things were related to consciousness not in terms of any intrinsic significance, for all such predicates had been banished to the void of non-sense, but in terms of usefulness: one asks not whether a thing is good or even what it *is*, but what it is good *for*. It is what it is for another.

We come, then, to the synthesis, the interaction of Enlightenment and Superstition, the result of this war of propaganda. For Belief, the calumnies of Enlightenment were an abomination, its positive doctrine a sterile platitude. Indeed, 'to discredit society is in fact to be attached to it. Thus, the Revolutionary is a liar' (*IH* 136). By calumniating Society, the propaganda of the Enlightened 'honest man' was the self-calumnation of Society. Society was deceitful and knew itself to be; the 'honest man' was turned thereby into an agent of Society's self-understanding and therefore also a liar. On the other side, the offence of Enlightenment against Belief, according to Belief, was an offence against divine law or right, *göttlich Recht*; the authority of Enlightenment, in turn, was granted by human law or right, *menschlich Recht*. The contrast of divine and human rights reminds one of a similar pagan conflict: 'In Paganism, the one is the Rights of the dead (of the Family), the other – the Right of the living (of the State). The one – the right of being decently buried; the other – the right of the living to bury the dead; – or rather, and quite exactly, the right of the dead to bury their own dead. For, when Belief is dead, the Aufklärung is no less so: it dies burying Belief, for it lived only by criticizing it' (*IH* 139). The victory of the human and living over the divine and dead, of Action, *Tun*, over given-Being, *Sein*, was assured by the fact that the Believers were human, alive and conscious. They were, therefore, unable to deny the human and finite truth of the Enlightenment, even though they took offence at (but did not refute) its calumnies.

In short, when Belief became articulate it turned into a kind of Enlightenment, an 'unhappy Enlightenment' one might say. If it still sought to preserve itself, it could be only as a silent sentiment, a nostalgia for a past forever gone, or an empty longing for relief in a Beyond that could not even be named. On its side, Enlightenment thought itself satisfied, but its satisfaction was purely subjective. It had gained a bloodless victory over Belief, which is to say, over itself. Yet in so doing it had created 'the stain of an unsatisfied longing' (PhG 407:349) within itself, an essential ignorance at its own heart, namely Belief itself. This could be overcome only by moving from interpretation to action; the Enlightened Intellectual must abandon the Ideal that he believed in and plunge into the Revolutionary action that would actualize it.

Since the ground of permanence, the unreality of Belief in the Beyond, appeared to Enlightenment to have been destroyed, consciousness now could return to the essential reality of the World and act upon it. 'It can do with the World what it wishes. Distinctions internal to the World are no longer accepted as given; rather, human activity voluntarily and consciously introduces such distinctions into the World – and, equally, destroys them' (IH 139–40). Consciousness could and did so act, but it did not yet reflect upon what it had done and so was not yet self-consciously Revolutionary.

The victory of Enlightenment over Superstition was followed shortly by the schism of the victorious party. Both, from the 'perspective' of the Sage, were essentially the same, and their apparent differences resulted merely from their having forgotten their common root. Consequently they maintained different recollections of their prior struggles. If they pushed their thoughts further they would have seen that they coincided. But they did not and instead fell apart into the hostile pair, agnostic Deism and atheistic Materialism (PhG 409:352). The one, Deism, took the Christian notion of transcendence to an extreme: the 'Supreme Being' was so far removed from 'here below' as to have nothing to do with it. Materialism or sensualism appeared, therefore, as nothing but a necessary complement. The initial truth of the Enlightment, then, was simply a recapitulation of Christian dualism in the form of an 'irreducible' opposition between Idealism and Materialism. When the 'Supreme Being' was forgotten entirely, the result was Utilitarianism: everything was for Man who, accordingly, was the 'measure of all things.' Materialism had to exempt the materialist from being swallowed into unconscious matter just as Idealism had to negate something material in order to transcend that thing as an 'ideal.' Both, therefore, had to forsake the empty unity of their abstract formulations and appear in the world as useful activity. What was useful was a thing, a piece of matter; but at the same time, it was useful only for a consciousness. Thus, the two moments of Enlightenment appeared together again as Utility. In Kojève's words, 'thought has value only if it is put to work – this shows that *Nützlichkeit* [Utility] is dear to "enlightened" Reason' (*IH* 140). Henceforth everything could be considered useful to man, including man himself; the highest human purpose was to become a useful member of a useful gang, *Trupp* (*PhG* 399:342). Consciousness could not yet answer Lessing's question, 'What is the use of use?' The truth of utilitarianism, then, was not absolutely true. Man still thought of utility only with respect to what already existed. Utility was not yet infused with active negativity. 'The idea that one makes oneself from oneself does not yet impinge upon social reality; this reality still has the form of a *Gegenstand*. Man lives always within a World not his own (a pre-revolutionary World). In addition he wants to use what is, and not to *create* (by the action of Struggle and Labour) what is useful to him' (*IH* 140). Soon enough the Enlightened one would act.

Nevertheless, Utility did appear to satisfy Desire because it allowed consciousness to enjoy the world of material things. This was, once again, the easy road. The ultimate justification of utilitarian (liberal, capitalist, democratic-socialist, socialist, technological, etc.) society, which clearly has not yet lost its charm or effectiveness, was that it delivered the goods. Alas! it too had its own contradiction. The good news was once again too good to be true: even though each Desire sought to gratify itself at the expense of the World, which included all others, it must, as a practical matter, accommodate itself to the desires of others. 'One hand washes the other' (*PhG* 400:343). But as has been argued in connection with Hobbes's account of this peace based upon social contract, the primordial belligerence of Desire had not been transformed but only suppressed, and then only in theory. Or rather, the theory of the social contract expressed the truth of Utility, that politics was simply a matter of will and the clash of wills. Every limitation was therefore purely conventional, a merely pragmatic compromise. Every institution was a contingent reflection of predominant Desires and triumphant Will and had no significance on its own account. Utilitarianism was already implicitly Revolutionary. Hobbes's new political science was therefore also implicitly Revolutionary. But it was only *implicitly* so.

Dialectic of the Revolutionary World

Utility appeared to have overcome the great dualism that began with the first stirrings of consciousness in the primordial fight. The Beyond had been abolished and the here-below existed only insofar as it was penetrated by (utilitarian) consciousness. In Hegel's words, which concluded the section on the truth of Enlightenment, truth was united with actuality, 'both Worlds are reconciled, and Heaven is transplanted to the Earth here below' (PhG 413:355). The earth, however, did not know it until the attempt to realize the Christian 'ideal' was made during the Revolution (IH 141). Consequently, the first words of the next section declared: 'Consciousness has found its Concept in Utility.' But, he added, Utility was still partly an object and a goal to be attained (PhG 414:355). It was, therefore, a limit or restriction. Or, what amounted to the same thing, self-consciousness had not found its Concept. Accordingly, satisfaction was still lacking. Even as Utility, consciousness still thought it must conform to an object. As was noted above, consciousness did not yet know that it alone would decide what was useful. Now, satisfaction could be achieved only when all objects were transformed, that is, destroyed as independent objects, and consciousness gained the knowledge that it had been responsible for their transformation. When Utility reflected upon itself and made explicit its own implicit revolutionary form, it would understand itself as absolute freedom. The logic of this transformation was clear enough: if all things were conventional, consciousness could reconstruct what was merely existing along whatever lines it wished.

Hegel said very little about the course of 'the actual revolution in the actual world' (PhG 414:356) because there was nothing of significance in the fall of the ancien régime. In a sense it was already dead, killed off by the propaganda of Enlightened Intellectuals, so that the Revolution itself was simply a burial detail. After all, if political institutions, including the alliance of throne and altar, were to be sustained and justified in terms of their utility, everyone would agree that they must be removed when they are no longer useful. In Hegel's words, the ancien régime died of infection (PhG 392:331) and not as the result of a bloody battle. Like the antique pagan world, it died a natural death, in bed, with its boots off. But now, with the corpse safely disposed of, what was there left to do?

The pre-Revolutionary World, with all its traditions and givenness, had disappeared as an actual, worldly entity, and was now present only as memory. There was no conformity since there was nothing, neither community nor State, to conform to. Wordsworth's sentiment, 'Bliss was in that dawn to be alive / But to be young was very heaven,' suggested again the experience of sheer potentiality. Nothing stood between man and his satisfaction – yet it remained as far away as ever. 'There was liberation with respect to the given, which no longer existed, but there was not yet *creation* of a new *real* World' (*IH* 141). Sheer potentiality amounted to complete emptiness: this was the meaning of 'absolute freedom.' There were no status-groups to mediate the Particularity of the individual and the Universality of the State. But that did not mean that the dialectic of Particularity and Universality had been played out. On the contrary, each Particularity conceived itself as Universal. Social order contracted into the idea – any idea – that anybody might have of it, into 'constitutional plans' that were neither criminal nor mad. Indeed, anyone could say anything, including '*L'état, c'est moi,*'' because there was nothing given or stable to contradict one's words. This first revolutionary phase of freedom and anarchy consisted simply in the process by which consciousness internalized Universality in any Particular will. It was pure liberation; accordingly, it achieved nothing permanent or 'positive.' Indeed, Hegel said that the work of absolute freedom was '*negative action*: it is only the fury of destruction' (*PhG* 418:359). Terror, implicit in the first moment, now surfaced in the open.

When each and every consciousness could say '*L'état, c'est moi,*' each claimed to be, literally, a dictator. But this meant also that none of the claims could be redeemed in actuality. Each consciousness was absolutely impenetrable to every other. Now, since all were potential dictators, all opposed one another mutually; but all they had in common was their biological existence. Thus, they began to exterminate one another, and, eventually, the victorious dictator committed suicide: the Revolution devoured its own children. The sole accomplishment of absolute freedom, then, was to introduce death, absolute nothingness. Moreover, it was a particularly meaningless sort of death, 'with no more significance than slicing off a head of cabbage or gulping a draught of water' (*PhG* 419:360).

The transplantation of Heaven to Earth amounted to the introduction of nothingness, death. This is hardly surprising if Heaven is conceived of as the consequence of a flight from actuality, as a void. In any case, the action that actually buried the *ancien régime*, from the meeting of the Estates-General in 1789 to the execution of Louis XVI in January 1793, involved no genuine risk of death. Thus, the revolutionary bourgeois who disposed of the bourgeois king remained themselves essentially bourgeois. To supersede bourgeois consciousness, its servile element had to be purged. Now, we know that, properly speaking, the bourgeois had no Master, but had enslaved himself to an artificial Master, wealth or capital. So long as he remained innocent of the experience of death, which could be attained only at the risk of life in a bloody Fight or

Struggle, that long would he remain unsatisfied. But how to 'kill' the artificial, pseudo-Master capital? How actually to purge the bourgeois of his pseudo-slavery? It would be appropriate to stage a pseudo- or artificial fight, but one that at the same time met the 'metaphysical' necessity of a genuine risk. The Terror directed by the Jacobins clearly met the second condition; it met the first one as well, at least in one crucial respect, in that it was in no way needed to overthrow the *ancien régime*, and in this respect was 'useless' or superfluous.

The dialectical meaning of the Terror for the Sage was not, of course, the 'expressionless syllable' of the actual Terror as it appeared to itself. The Jacobins embodied the Universal will insofar as they were the government; but they were also a 'club,' an exclusive, private, and Particular will. As Particular will, they were necessarily opposed to the Universal will and so had to act as a 'faction' even while they claimed to act as the Whole. Their claim gained verisimilitude only because they happened to be victorious. The gap between its professed intentions of Universality and its actual factional behaviour turned the reign of Virtue by the Incorruptible into rank hypocrisy. Under these circumstances, all action would be guilty action, and all justification would be in terms of 'mere intention.' Consequently, suspicion of one's intentions was equivalent to guilt. Deeds would always give the lie to whatever words were uttered, since all consequences could not be forseen. Since nothing could possibly be gained by attending to the words that expressed the intentions of the faction, the fitting and appropriate external action was the simple and cold-blooded destruction of those Particulars from whom nothing else could be taken but mere given-Being (*PhG* 419:360). There must be a 'useless' slaughter of the innocents.

The rage and fury that were expressed in the destruction of factions during the Terror were not, however, utterly futile. Absolute freedom appeared to consciousness as Terror. It became an object to itself and saw itself for what it was, an abstract self-consciousness that destroyed indiscriminately all distinctions by reducing them to sheer biological existence, which it then proceeded to annul. 'It is objective to itself as follows: the *Terror* of death is the immediate apprehension, *Anschauung*, of the negative essential-reality of freedom' (*PhG* 419:361). Bourgeois consciousness was shocked and became 'conservative.' This was not what it had sought or intended; the actuality of Terror did not correspond to bourgeois self-understanding. Yet, absolutely free self-consciousness is Terror and the bourgeois finally learned that his intentions no longer mattered. Or, more generally, he learned that the separation of intentions and consequences, the employment of good intentions as an alibi for disastrous consequences, and the ultimate justification for the separation of the two, namely the Christian dualism of a corruptible body and an incorruptible soul, led only to the Terror of Robespierre, the 'absolute transposition' of rule by Virtue, by the Incorruptible himself, into the sheer destruction of material bodies.

If self-consciousness no longer distinguished between intentions and consequences or between soul and body (in the sense that the one refers to a 'real' Beyond and the other lives out a 'merely' contingent existence here below), several consequences followed. By means of Terror, it learned that absolute freedom was abstract: to desire absolute freedom was to desire the absolute abstraction, death. Consciousness was thus re-formed: no longer did it think its own Particularity to be the immediate embodiment of Universality, but, having sensed the fear of death, 'the absolute Master, they again submit themselves to negation and distinction, and arrange themselves in various status-groups, and return to their limited and restricted activities, but also to their substantive actuality' (*PhG* 420:361). The Terror of death was the aforementioned 'metaphysically necessary' melting of consciousness and liquefaction of all stability (cf *PhG* 148:117) that purged bourgeois consciousness of its servile constituent elements. Henceforth, consciousness would seek satisfaction here below, as Citizen. Henceforth the reformed consciousnesses of the bourgeois were 'disposed to admit of a State where they could realize themselves in a divided and limited way, but where, however, they were truly and really free' (*IH* 144).

There could be no going back to any prior form of consciousness or to any prior social and political organization, because the post-Revolution State was essentially different than any prior one. The Revolution was not an action in pursuit of an Ideal or a goal to be achieved: it was a 'useless' negation, pure and simple. As sheer destruction of all appearances of given-Being in political institutions, religious beliefs, and even the biological constitution of human beings, the Revolution was the moment of utter nothingness out of which could emerge the new creation. 'All these determinate phenomena [political institutions, religious beliefs, etc] have disappeared in the loss that overtakes the Self in Absolute Freedom; its negation is meaningless death, the pure Terror of the Negative that has within it nothing Positive, nothing that gives it contents' (*PhG* 421:362). Unlike the biblical *creatio ex nihilo*, this new world was the self-conscious creation of man. Terror was, therefore, the last act in the *Bildung* of Man. What made the post-Revolutionary State unique was that it presupposed as its basis, which was now superseded, precisely that absolute freedom toward which all other States had been striving. The French Revolution, then, constituted the completion and destruction of the bourgeois-Christian world.

The State that followed from this work of absolute Negativity would be the dialectical reversal of it, namely 'absolute Positivity' (*PhG* 421:362). We will consider the political implications of this Positivity below, along with the 'other realm' (*PhG* 422:363) to which self-consciousness now repaired, namely German philosophy. First, however, we must consider the historical dialectic of social ideologies.

5

The dialectic of historical ideologies

Hegel's religious views

The text of Hegel's *Phenomenology* that is considered in this chapter dealt primarily with 'Religion' and was described by Kojève as being concerned with the dialectic of historical ideologies. This approach deviates from Hegel's presentation (as well as Kojève's commentary), so a brief explanation is in order. We begin indirectly.

At the close of *Republic*, Plato returned to a topic he had discussed earlier, Homeric poetry. Speaking very broadly, one might say that the earlier discussion was concerned with the use of stories by philosophers for the benefit of non-philosophers. For example, it was useful for victory that young warriors emulate in battle the fierce Achilles. In book X, however, Homeric poetry was considered not in terms of its usefulness but in terms of its truth. Indeed, Socrates earlier remarked (377a 2–5) that taken 'as a whole' *mythoi* were false. Indeed, it was because they were formally unconcerned with truth that they were useful in its service. But when poets, even great ones, claimed to be more than helpers to philosophers they were claiming to tell the truth about things. Now, as a man must not be honoured above truth (595b 8–10), so poets must be measured not by their technical qualities but as truth-tellers. In this light, poetry was shown to be an imitation of an imitation and so, 'as a whole,' false. That is, 'as a whole' poetry was subordinate to something beyond itself. In Plato's earlier discussion it was subordinate to the philosopher; in existing Homeric poems and stories, it was subordinate to the action of heroes. Earlier in *Republic* Socrates criticized the injustice of heroic action; in book X he criticized the poet for claiming more than a subordinate role. From the philosopher's vantage-point the great defect of poetry was that the poet, Homer, did not account for his own speeches. As with the hapless rhapsode, Ion, who celebrated Homer, Homer's celebration of heroism was silent about his own significance. While Plato's account of the difference between poetry and philosophy was, of course, more complex than the preceding paragraph would suggest, it may serve as a first approximation. More to the point, Hegel's criticism of religion followed closely the surface meaning of Plato's. Religion was, 'as a whole,' the production of representations, Plato's images and imitations. These imitations presented to Consciousness an ever more comprehensive assimilation of Nature, but Consciousness, so long as it remained religious, did not grasp the meaning of that assimilation. This interpretation of Hegel's 'philosophy of religion' has not been universally accepted.[1] It was, however, forcefully argued by Kojève (following Koyré) and certainly expressed the meaning that religion had and has for most modern human beings.

Much of the continuing controversy over Hegel's meaning depends upon the global interpretative strategy one has adopted in coming to terms with *Phenomenology*. There are, of course, several explications of the structure of Hegel's argument. To see how Kojève's interpretation of Hegel's philosophy of religion is consistent with what has already been presented in this essay, a brief and perhaps exaggerated recapitulation is required. Two aspects have been emphasized: In chapter 3 was summarized Hegel's description of human existence considered in abstraction, that is, without reference to actual historical contingencies. In the next chapter I presented Hegel's version of the inner course of Western history, from the Greek polis to the French Revolution. The section of chapter 6 of *Phenomenology* that followed the analysis of the French Revolution dealt with the fortunes of Spirit in that 'other realm,' German philosophy, which in turn was followed by chapter 7 on religion. Following Hegel, one might simplify the argument at this point into the distinction between form and content. German speculative philosophy was the true form of Spirit; but the contents were found in religion. Religion, as we shall see, had its own history. According to Kojève, however, German speculative philosophy was in principle post-historical. Following him, then, one ought to present the historical development of religion before considering how it, and the historical worlds it reflected, were superseded by, and into, Hegelian Science and the universal and homogeneous State.

Hegel used the term 'religion' in a very broad sense. In *Philosophy of History*, for example, Hegel said that religion was the sphere where a people endowed itself with a definition of its own truth; the representation of God held by a people was the very fundament of a people (*VPG* 100–1:50). For Hegel the term included the topics 'primitive religion' such as is studied by social anthropologists, Egyptian monuments, Greek and Roman art, and medieval liturgy and presumably could also include French architecture of the Second Empire, Afrikaner poetry, Chinese newspaper writing, Canadian cinema, Burmese theatre, Polish radio, Moroccan dancing, or Italian television. In short, it included all those phenomena we might ordinarily indicate when speaking about the spirit of antiquity or of suburbia, of Paris or of Calcutta, of Spanish Catholicism or of Scotch Presbyterianism (cf *IH* 200).

Bearing in mind this broad sense of religion, it is apparent that the contents of chapters 6 and 7 of *Phenomenology* overlapped. The three sections of chapter 6 dealt with the world of pagan antiquity, the bourgeois-Christian world, and the post-Revolutionary world of German philosophy; the three sections of chapter 7 dealt with 'primitive' religions logically prior to the world of pagan antiquity, the religion of pagan antiquity, and Christianity. Thus, sections 1 and 2 of chapter 6 corresponded to sections 2 and 3 of chapter 7. But there was nothing in chapter 6 that corresponded to 'natural religion,' the first part of chapter 7, and nothing in chapter 7 corresponded to the third part of chapter 6, on German philosophy. This apparent asymmetry was reconciled in chapter 8 of *Phenomenology*. The reason for it was that whereas chapter 6 dealt with the social and political side of human existence, and so began with a consideration of the first State properly speaking, chapter 7, in addition to social and political existence, was also concerned with the relationship between human beings and nature, that is, with a logically pre-political condition. Now, since religion reflected that dimension of existence, it was possible to consider a 'natural religion' whereas a 'natural State' was a self-contradiction (*IH* 197).

Even so, as Hegel explained in the opening paragraph, religion understood as consciousness of absolute essential reality had already appeared, so why must a special chapter be devoted to the topic? This same sentence continued: religion had appeared *vom Standpunkte des Bewusstseins aus*, only from the perspective of externalizing Consciousness (to follow Kojève's rendering). Accordingly, the essential reality so grasped was not in and for itself; it was not, therefore, the self-consciousness of Spirit that appeared in these concrete forms (*PhG* 473:410; *IH* 197). Now, the perspective of externalizing Consciousness distinguished between Ego and non-Ego, subject and object, knower and known, Citizen and State, etc., but most important in the present context, between the autonomous and independent World and Ego. Because this World was autonomous and independent, man appeared to depend upon it; he had the sentiment of insufficiency and the World appeared divine. In the first six chapters of *Phenomenology*, then, the topic of religion appeared mediated by the attitude taken by historical human beings toward the divine, which was itself conceived as other.

In chapter 7, this same topic was considered from the point of view of Self-consciousness. The question 'How does Spirit understand itself?' replaced 'How does the individual understand Spirit?' According to Hegel this self-comprehension of Spirit, which he called *Volksgeist*, folk-spirit, or Spirit of a people, appeared as Religion. Accordingly, chapter 7 dealt with the accounts of the gods, the theologies, that human beings created to interpret this understanding of Spirit (which, from the 'perspective' of the Sage, was themselves) to themselves. As Shklar observed, *Phenomenology* was 'a call to rethink ourselves now that we know that we ourselves, and not God, created mankind.'[2] These religious accounts were not, however, philosophies because, in Hegel's words, 'in Religion, self-knowing Spirit is, in an immediate way, *unmittelbar*, its own pure Self-consciousness' (*PhG* 474:411). As immediate, it existed as it was in itself or for the Sage, but not for itself, that is, for them who believed on it: the theologian believed in the gods about whom he spoke; the Sage, however, knew that his speech and his gods were concerned with the human, not the divine, Spirit. Consequently, the sense that Hegel found in religion was not theistic.

We know from the earlier chapters of *Phenomenology* that to seek other-wordly goals was to flee this world. In the end, therefore, the servile element of historical consciousness was responsible for the desire to flee the actual world in search of an ideal beyond it. This servile refusal of the World accounted for all dualisms, and its objectification in theologies would last so long as any dualism persisted. In addition to existing in thought or discourse as the disjunction between the ideal man had of himself and his actual Self, religious belief also imparted a genuine dualism to the world. 'Religion never includes the *totality* of human existence: there is never any genuine *theo*-cracy. Religious existence takes place *alongside* properly human existence [*Dasein*], which is life in the concrete World, and the Religious person is *always* more or less a monk, cut off from "the world" or "the age"' (*IH* 212). As a dualism, religion contained within itself the basis of its own destruction, namely contradiction. Thus, religion was bound to disappear eventually. In discussing religions as they existed for themselves, therefore, Hegel could not possibly give an account of them that was faithful to the several religious self-understandings. The reason for this is obvious enough: religion is a matter of belief whereas giving an account of it is a matter of discourse. Just as giving an account of a myth transfigured it from an immediately experienced reality into a reality mediated by speech (from myth to mythology), so too Hegel argued that religious representations or pictures, *Vorstellungen*, must be transfigured into the realm of discourse where they may be grasped conceptually.

A complex interweaving of logical and temporal sequences in the first six chapters of *Phenomenology* explained the position of chapter 7 in the structure of Hegel's argument (*PhG* 477–8:412–13), from which Kojève drew three conclusions. 1 / Religion logically presupposed social reality, the fights and labours of historical persons that eventually contrived the universal and homogeneous State. Even though logically subordinate, religion was nevertheless the means by which human beings became conscious of what they had done insofar as it reflected an all-encompassing picture to them. As a picture or representation, religion was not a historical reality properly speaking. Rather, it was an 'ideal superstructure' founded upon the 'real infrastructure' of historical actions. Nevertheless, this same superstructure raised the activities of mankind from the level of social animality to genuine humanity. The evolution of historical reality was, therefore, duplicated in the evolution of religions that re-presented that reality to itself. 2 / Each particular religion would, accordingly, accentuate one or another aspect or constituent element of human existence. 3 / Insofar as religion was immediate, *unmittelbar*, but also all-encompassing or absolute, it was a positive or unconscious form of Hegelian Wisdom.

On the basis of these points, three corollaries may be drawn. 1 / The entire double process would come to an end only with that supression of dualism that realized (i.e. made real) religion. 2 / The integration of all constituent elements of existence would at the same time be the self-consciousness of all partial actualizations of those elements in different religions. 3 / The mediation of religion by speech or discourse raised it to the form of the Concept, which is to say, transformed it from belief to knowledge. When, therefore, religion was realized, all dualism disappeared, and with it disappeared religion as a distinct phenomenon. Henceforth, it would be a constituent element of Wisdom, the complete but discursive revelation of the World by the System of Science.

Hegel's transformation

The concluding paragraph of the introduction to chapter 7 of *Phenomenology* justified Hegel's division of religion into three successive categories, natural religion, religion of art, *Kunstreligion*, and absolute religion. 'The first actualization of Spirit in religion is in the pure Concept of religion itself, that is as immediate and thus natural religion' (*PhG* 480:416). Here Spirit knew itself as a thing. The second actualization arose when the Ego transformed the given natural thing into a work. This was a genuine supersession in that materiality was preserved even while it was re-formed after the image of the artist who constructed it. Finally, the third actualization superseded the first two by retaining the immediacy of consciousness of the first along with the mediation of consciousness (or the self-consciousness) of the second. This third actualization, in the form or shape of Being-in-and-for-itself, was revealed religion. Yet it too must be superseded because it was not absolutely compelling and did not command the assent of all persons. Even a revelation must be seen to be believed.

It was true, Hegel said, that Spirit had attained its true shape as revelation, but to the extent that it appeared as any sort of shape at all, to the extent that even revealed religion was a representation and not a discourse, it could not account for itself and so had not acceded to the realm of the Concept. Theologies of revelation were still myths, incomplete accounts; as discourses, they had the appropriate form, but as discourses about gods they were unself-conscious *anthropo*logies. When, however, theological discourse was completed, and the aspect of representation was shed, it would become self-conscious anthropology. But then the form of actuality would also be changed, since it would then be a discourse, and not representation. Revealed religion, we know, must be superseded in Absolute Knowledge, which was set forth in chapter 8 of *Phenomenology*. There Spirit understood itself in the way that, to this point, only 'we' Hegelian Sages have done, namely as Concept or comprehensive account. The form or shape of this Spirit, to the extent that it was a comprehensive account, was itself Spirit. Spirit that knew itself as Spirit was its own form and content. The empirical existence, *Dasein*, of this form of Spirit that also was its own content, was G.W.F. Hegel himself (*IH* 223–4), the author of the book that described the genesis and completion of Spirit.

Hegel enlarged on this remarkable claim in the introduction to the section 'Natural Religion' (*PhG* 481–3:416–18). The attitude of religion was one of Consciousness, of a subject that knew an object; but in this instance the object known was Consciousness itself, apprehended as a given-Being, a nature that remained identical with itself even when it was known. In order for this Consciousness of self to be true, Man must really be an object for himself; it has already been argued that all objectification was the result of activity, of an actual negation of given-Being, and that the results of this activity constituted History – the technical and political World. This World was just as real and objective as the given-Being of Nature; indeed, it was argued that man knew the given-Being of Nature only because he negated it as given and appropriated it for his human World. Since, therefore, man was his action, human being was self-actualizing being. Man 'does not *exist* outside his works. And *that* is why he cannot become conscious of himself except by relating to himself as an object, by relating to his *works*, the *product* of his action' (*IH* 227). By becoming conscious of their works, human beings became conscious of themselves, since they were what they did.

Such action, which was objectified in works and conscious of itself, was itself Spirit. Thus, 'the Spirit that knows Spirit' was Man, namely the Spirit that knew that it was Action, that was conscious of itself in and by its works (*PhG* 481:416; *IH* 227). This first phrase of the section 'Natural Religion,' then, referred to Hegel whose work was *Phenomenology*, the result of which was Knowledge, Absolute Knowledge, of Spirit. In other words, before Hegel (or before the coming of Hegelian man) Man was only Consciousness of the World; he did not (yet) know that 'Consciousness-of-the-World' was, in fact, Self-consciousness, because he did not (yet) know that the World of which he was conscious was his own work, his own action, and, therefore, that the World was himself. Consequently, he believed (wrongly) that the World was something fixed, stable, and independent of him, and he recognized himself in the World as determinateness of form or shape, *Bestimmtheit der Gestalt*. And it was in this form that man understood himself in religion. Only the religious take seriously the notion of 'human nature.'

Even if religious self-understanding conceived of Man as a given-Being related in a fixed and immutable way to another given-Being, God, neither being was purely natural. Even while remaining extra-human, both remained spiritual given-Beings. Thus, Hegel continued, 'the difference between external-Consciousness and Self-consciousness falls at the same time within the latter' (*PhG* 481:417). In other words, the religious person really found the opposition of Particular and Universal within himself and not, for example, between himself and Nature. The Universal Spirit within (or partly within) the religious person was God. Thus, he distinguished within his own Self-consciousness what, for him, was his own Self-consciousness, namely his being connected to the Universal, God. Because the two were connected, neither was radically non-human, but, as just noted, both were Spirit; but because they were opposed, even as connected, Spirit was conceived as given-Being, as a determinate form, *bestimmte Gestalt*. The several religions considered by Hegel were distinguished, precisely, by the particular form taken by Spirit when it was conceived as God.

At the same time, however, they were no more than variations of a single religion inasmuch as religious consciousness was consciousness of the whole, concrete human being, which implied all the constituent elements of existence. In this respect, the determinate forms by which the several religions were distinguished were reflections of the accent that each religion placed upon one element alone, with the result that the remaining elements more or less dropped from sight. Since, moreover, each specific religion corresponded to the element of existence realized in a specific historical World, there was an evolution or development of religion, as such. The stages were marked by specific religions.

The goal and term of this evolution were the supersession of the difference between external-consciousness and Self-consciousness (*PhG* 481–2:417), which is to say, the suppression of transcendence and the understanding of Spirit simply as human, not divine (*IH* 235). To attain this end, man must understand that he had created God and not vice versa. The process by which this understanding was obtained consisted in conceiving God in such a way that he increasingly resembled the idea that man had of himself. The history of religion, or rather the phenomenology of Spirit in its religious appearance, was, therefore, the story of the successive anthropomorphizations of God. For the succession also to appear as a success, the inferior or imperfect determinations, which constituted a series of false gods created by men, must be destroyed in the name of the true God in whom the religious person believed. The truth of any particular religion appeared, Hegel said, in the fact that the actual Spirit – the actual people who believed in any specific religion – was constituted in the same form as was their conception of God. Thus, for example, the incarnation of God as found in certain pre-Christian Eastern religions had no truth because its actual Spirit, Eastern societies, did not reconcile Particularity and Universality, which was the meaning or idea of the Incarnation.

Applying this procedure to Christianity, it was clear that Christianity became a truth only with the actualization of the idea of the Incarnation. But when it was actualized, it ceased to be an idea. In other words, while the limit of anthropomorphization of God was found in the idea of Christ, the final result of the history of religion, understood phenomenologically, came with the understanding that this idea too was a product of the human Spirit. Then man ceased to use theological languages because he no longer projected his ideas into a Beyond. The realization of Christianity, then, was likewise its destruction; having become a truth, it had equally become Hegel's atheist anthropology.

In chapter 2 of this essay Kojève's understanding of ideology was reported. According to him an ideology was a partial account of things that took itself to be total and complete. We have just argued how Hegel's transformative procedures led to the consequence that, on its own, religion in general was ideological. With Hegel, critical destruction of error was invariably followed by an incorporating restoration of truth. Such was the very meaning of supersession, of *Aufhebung*. The final restorative moment of interpretation was, once again, formed on the claim to have undertaken successfully a complete discourse. Once again as well, we accept this claim, *ex hypothesi*, and turn to Hegel's direct treatment of religious phenomena. One final preliminary observation: since ideologies in Kojève's sense were essentially interpretations of reality, the empirical end of history in the Napoleonic Empire did not necessarily mean the end of religion. One could irrationally choose to be irrational. One could remain unhappy. One could undervalue self-consciousness. In short, a minimum of interpretative ingenuity is required to find contemporary examples of any religious attitude at all. We shall, indulgently, refer to some.

Natural religion

The first religion, studied in *Phenomenology* under the heading 'Licht-wesen,' religion of light, referred to the social ideologies of primitive gatherer-societies. The constituent element of existence emphasized at this level of religion, where man was immediately conscious of the given-Being of nature and of himself as pure Ego, was Sensation and Desire. His immediate self-consciousness, then, contained implicitly the form of the Master before the primordial Fight. But there were no Slaves. 'It is a Society where one goes hungry and where one wants to make love [and is satisfied by] feasts and sexual orgies' (*IH* 239). This giveness and this immediacy were stabilized in the 'shape of shapelessness' and symbolized to itself as light and darkness, which expressed the plentitude of Nature and the emptiness of Desire. The interaction of the two aspects appeared to consciousness as life-giving 'torrents of light' (only given-Being, i.e. food and other bodies, can satisfy Desire) and as all-devouring 'streams of fire' (Desire destroys the given) (*PhG* 484:419). The essential contents of this religion, its sublimity, grandeur, and majesty, would be preserved in a superseded form until religion as such disappeared. Under contemporary conditions, this religious attitude could be recaptured either by deliberately rigorous traditional ascesis or, more easily, by drugs. The first stage of its disappearance consisted in the dispersal of its immediacy into the determinate shapes of sacrificial totems from which individuals drew substance and sustenance.

Totemism referred to the social ideologies of societies of hunters and warriors; here the constituent element of existence that was emphasized was not Sensation and Desire, but Perception and Fighting. From an innocent perceptual division of nature into several plant spirits, each of which was an immobile object that could enfold or absorb consciousness in Kojèvian 'contemplation,' the plurality of separateness became mobilized as distinctive and hostile animal spirits. The new religion 'has death within it' (*PhG* 485:420) and corresponds to the anthropogenetic Fight, though not to its result. Totem animals, that is, gods, were sacrificed; it was a religion of mutually hostile folk-spirits who hated one another and fought to the death with no intention of obtaining a victory beyond the destruction of the other. Their fighting did not result in the enslavement of one or another, but in annihilation of the defeated. Yet, in the fury of fighting, warriors became aware of themselves as determinate animal Spirits, which is to say totemic objects separated from other totemic objects. Now consciousness perceived these totemic objects as objects. Copies of them were built. In this way, as in the pure dialectic of Master and Slave, the Slavish artificer began to overcome the fighting Master, only this time within the medium of religion. Contemporary totemism is seldom as serious as primitive totemism, though occasionally the behaviour of fans at sports events takes the shape of ritual annihilation of the other. Mostly it takes the form of aggressive but not serious ritual, namely cheering and rioting.

We pass, then, to the third 'natural' religion, the religion of the artificer or artisan. This religion encompassed the social ideologies of labourers who worked 'naturally,' without the terror of Masters; here the constituent element emphasized was Understanding. Here too consciousness moved from vague and unidentified primitive religions to the religion of a high civilization, Egypt. Labour in Egypt, as with totemic fights, logically antedated the anthropogenetic fight; it was, therefore, merely forced and not servile. Egyptian labour was conditioned by necessity and not by Terror; one laboured for one's biological self, and not for a human Master. Because labour was not servile, there was very little education: a great deal of effort achieved modest and geometrically simple forms, pyramids and obelisks. The very simplicity of these abstract forms expressed an attempt to rationalize and measure the 'roundness' and formlessness of nature. Moreover, these products were useful: one gained life eternal by having one's corpse placed properly within a pyramid, the obelisk served as a sundial, and plants, no longer sacred objects of contemplation, could serve as decoration for the first genuine and monumental works of architecture, at Karnak.

The increased mediation between God and man pointed toward the absolute mediation of the Christian Incarnation. But this movement was also proceeding toward atheism, since each stage was equally characterized by increasing humanization, and consequently greater estrangement from God. One may go further: 'Man, with each progression, is superior to the god of the preceding stage' (IH 241). Hegel also mentioned or alluded to several intermediate forms: hieroglyphs, which combined human and animal forms, the so-called statue of Memnon,[3] which emitted a wailing sound when struck with the rays of the morning sun, the cube of the Kaaba. All these examples contained representatively the inner and outer expression of Spirit. Only with the Sphinx did the blending of natural and self-conscious form reach its perfection. Here the instinctive mode of labour ended; to this 'ambiguous being, a riddle even unto itself' (PhG 489:424), one could address prayers and questions – as one never would do to a pyramid. Moreover, one received answers that, even though they were difficult to understand, were recognizably spoken words, not the whistling of the wind. Henceforth, the artificer would confront in his own product a being that, in a yet inchoate way, contained Spirit, his own. Moreover, the world had been changed by the Egyptian's labours. He had begun to labour for others, in this case, gods, when he turned away from the necessities of a hydraulic civilization – keeping the dikes repaired and the ditches clear – to the realm of Spirit properly speaking, in this case, his own artefacts. He had also begun the movement away from the religion of the artificer, centred on production, to the religion of the artist, centred on consumption.

Artistic religion

Artistic religion was the religion of Greece. 'Man comes now to *speak of* gods: mythology; and he comes to *speak to* gods: prayers' (*IH* 241). Anthropomorphic gods signalled the end of natural religion, the victory of human form over natural material. Man had now become a spiritual labourer, *geistiger Arbeiter*; or, as Kojève said, an intellectual labourer (*PhG* 490:424; *IH* 241). Whatever an intellectual labourer might be, it was distinct from the labourer of Egypt. He could come into being only because, somewhere between Egypt and Hellas, perhaps Crete, but still within a basically agricultural society, a class of Masters emerged who lived, without labouring themselves, on the surplus produced by others. The division of labour ceased to be natural, in the sense of being imposed by nature – the flooding of the Nile, the difference between earth (peasants) and metal (blacksmiths), and so on – and became self-conscious and free. In terms of the pure Concept of Recognition, the conditions for the anthropogenetic fight had actually been fulfilled historically, and human beings, paradigmatic Masters and Slaves, rather than animals of the species *homo sapiens* had actually been created.

Section B of chapter 7, like section A, was divided into three parts. They dealt, as before, with Desire, Struggle, and Labour, only now the context was not man consciously living in the midst of 'eternal' Nature, but man living self-consciously within his own creation, the finite, temporary city. The antique world, we know, was dominated by the Master. He was distinguished from the Slave, who accorded him inauthentic recognition, by being leisured. On occasion he had to fight, but most of the time he did not have to do anything in particular. Indeed, one might say that he must not do anything in particular. Yet he had to do something; in Greek, the verb *scholazo*, which in English is rendered in the passive voice, 'I am leisured,' is active without being specific. His labours, therefore, were 'spiritual' or intellectual, in that he received the material products of the Slave's material labour and transfigured them spiritually. In short, he appreciated the beauty of a thing.

A beautiful thing is an object that gives pleasure without pain, the pain of production. 'Thus, his Religion will be a *Kunst*-religion, which divines *Sein* [given-Being] as Beauty (while forgetting that Beauty is a human *work*)' (*IH* 242). The Greeks, like the Egyptians, built temples. What mattered to the Greeks however, was not monumental geometric shape, but the effortless beauty of a well-proportioned world. Of course, the Master could also stupefy himself in a life of sensuous pleasure. Both the refined aesthete and the vulgar sot desired pleasure without effort; both found it in an illusory world. Both, therefore, from the 'perspective' of the Sage were simply variations of a single attitude.

In order for there to be a religion that did not simply express immediate desire, the Master must become dissatisfied with the World in which he lived and become aware of its insufficiencies. One side of this question appeared in tragedy and was discussed above. Now we must deal with the public religion, the Religion of Masters that expressed the religion of the State, and not the private, servile, family religion. The insufficiencies of a life of sensuous pleasure were obvious enough: the body wears out, orgiasts abused themselves, and died. The insufficiencies of spiritual pleasure were more subtle. The structural defect was that the joy experienced in the appreciation of beauty could not satisfy because the mediating labour had not been undertaken by the one who enjoyed it. Hence, it was not his work. All the aesthetic Master could achieve through appreciation was subjective certainty, not recognition. 'There lies his dissatisfaction. He laments the loss of his World; he is an "emigré," he is in mourning of his World. He flees it because he dares not change it so as to make it conform to his aesthetic "ideal"' (IH 244). This was why he aspired to a religion in the first place. A religion, to repeat, provided consolation, here below, for the dissatisfactions of life by promising compensation in a Beyond.

The religion of art unfolded once again in three stages, corresponding once again as well to Desire, the Fight, and Labour. The first example, the plastic arts, the products of which were the statuary and the temples that housed them, was abstract because it presented itself as pure objectivity and ignored entirely the spirit that created the objects. Its Apollonian purity reflected the silent, static material perfection of the body. The second example, the choral hymn, was abstract for precisely the opposite reason. Its Dionysian purity reflected the ec-static, spiritual perfection of the soul that was no less silent because it was the direct 'speech' of perfected gods to one another. Only with oracles did gods speak to humans. But because they were gods who spoke, the language was not yet human, but inspired, mysterious, baffling. Third was the symbolic mediation of body and soul, statue and choral hymn, in the religious cult. The action of the cult symbolically overcame the estrangement of gods and humans. By ensuring the real presence and participation of the gods, and hence the interaction of humans and gods, cultic action thereby also overcame human dissatisfaction – again symbolically. The cult itself developed from the ecstatic poetry of the choral hymn and proceeded by way of mysteries, which symbolized Desire, to sacrifice, which symbolized the primordial Fight, to the ritual construction of a temple, which was also useful for man, as a treasury, for example. Thus, the cultic work effectively reversed the movement toward externality, and a unity of divine and human was made visible.

The second stage of the religion of art, the living art-work, was the ideological representation of the victorious Master. There must be struggle, because it was to represent the *Master*, but there must be no genuine risk of life because it *represented* the Master. Here one ascended from the orgiastic mysteries of the inferior gods to the higher mysteries of the superior gods, the Olympic games, and the dithyrambic celebration of victory. The orgiastic mysteries synthesized the public cult of sacrifice with the mystic element, which reflected Desire and was found in all religions. But as with the choral hymn, orgies could not last very long; and one could not live always in a temple. The 'sports world,' in contrast, was genuinely human since there may emerge a 'world champion,' that is, one universally recognized in his particularity at the end of a struggle with other contenders. But it was not 'serious,' since his recognition was gained without committing a crime. One could not avoid the contradictions of polis-life, whether they be between male and female, public and private, living and dead, without committing a crime against one of the elements. Simply in terms of games, this had the form of a restriction: one must always play by the rules or suffer scorn as a cheat or spoilsport. Moreover, the athlete gained recognition only insofar as he was a victorious body, and not in his whole person. This was, and is, especially true of the world of boxing (or gladiators, etc.), whose first citizen was preeminently 'world champion.' But, being merely a champion body, the victor was silent. No one could take his words to be seriously meaningful . except, perhaps, as descriptions of the fine points of technique. The rest of the champ's amazing speech was merely amusing. Once again, therefore, Desire and the Fight were superseded by Labour, this time with the speech of the poet (Pindar) who sang the victory of the Olympic champion. Modern Pindaric publicists sing on television. In both instances, the champion depended on the labours of the poet to give sense and meaning to his glorious victory. And this meant that athletic victory could ever be fully satisfying. The classical ode, still deeply influenced by choral hymnody, served, therefore, as the transition from the artistic religion, whether in the form of the 'dead' art of statues or the 'living' art of athletics, to a literary one.

This third stage consisted of 'intellectual' or 'imaginative' labour within the struggle for recognition. As labour, it consisted in the construction of a non-natural world, but because it lacked physical effort, that world was fictional or literary. 'The pagan literary (religious) World was born with the Epic, lived in Tragedy, and died as Comedy' (*IH* 250). The community of the epic was a negative unity, a unity *against* (against Troy, for example), led by a single commander, *Oberbefehl*. It lacked governance by a single sovereign or governor properly speaking, *Oberherrschaft*. When a preeminent epic hero chanced upon the scene, he destroyed the peace of the alliance either by fighting and dying or by transforming the 'united nations' into a single empire. On his own, the epic hero mourned his anticipated early death and in this way became a tragic hero. But the tragic hero merely represented the Master's impasse by way of an actor. Accordingly, tragedy could not be serious either – actors did not really kill one another or themselves. Once again the way of the Master showed itself to be impossible, or, what amounts to the same thing, there existed either dead Masters or honorific ones, that is, Masters who 'play a tragic role,' who were, therefore, hypocrites (*PhG* 517:450). But hypocritical Masters were as comic as epic gods who acted humanly. Hence, the end of Aeschylus's *Oresteia*, which saw the taming of the Erinyes, was, from the 'perspective' of the Sage, equivalent to Aristophanes' *Peace*, which saw the son of Cleonymos, a notorious coward, welcomed into the house of the hero, Trygaios, and the son of Lamachus, who had attempted to sing warlike Homeric verses, thrown out. What this meant, according to Kojève, was that 'Aristophanes is already a Bourgeois who has a nostalgia for Mastery that is no more, and Aeschylus is yet a Master who longs for the Bourgeois that is about to arrive' (*IH* 254). In any event, the self-conscious tragic hero abandoned his mask and his role and stepped forth in the knowledge that his fate was that of the chorus and its gods. In other words, the Particular, lately a tragic hero, was at one with the Universal, the gods of the chorus. Their common, human finitude, however, turned out to be 'all too human.'

The youthful, comic bourgeois World, Kojève said, was homogeneous. Knowing his own fate was that of the gods, the former tragic hero knew there were no absolute conflicts, neither between men, nor between gods, nor between men and gods. Everyone could get on with life. There was no need to flee the world. Self-consciousness rejoiced in its absurd finitude. Why not? This brand of atheism was new, and it was necessary if comedy were to exist, but it was a self-indulgent make-believe atheism. To laugh at ridiculous gods (rather than be laughed at by them, as in tragedy) was still to believe in them, to think them worth laughing at, and, indeed, to believe unself-consciously in a God who was not to be taken so lightly and not to be laughed at. The comic bourgeois, then, remained religious, and the pagan gods who died happy, laughing at themselves, still retained enough vitality to reappear as Christianity, the unhappy religion of the crucified God.

The bourgeois did, however, wish to preserve his natural, biological being. His laughter also reflected his enjoyment of life. Accordingly, he had to destroy nature as the terrifying source of religion. Although comedy did not conquer nature through physical technique, it nevertheless used mental ingenuity to ridicule nature's independence by using it for decoration, feasting on sacrificial offerings, or exaggerating in a purely physical way the significance of genitalia. Likewise, the young bourgeois was interested in thinking, or rather in a kind of analytic scrutiny of the maxims and thoughtless, traditional wisdom of the chorus. Bourgeois criticism cut apart the contingent shape of duty and right and reduced it to formlessness. What lost its shape spread, like water, and was raised, like clouds, to the abstract simplicities of the Beautiful and the Good whose contents could be anything at all. The comic bourgeois world, then, seemed to be without terror: nothing human was foreign to it. But this soft happiness was gained only by forgetting the harshness of Mastery, by retreating from public life into the quiet of the family. The flaw of the young bourgeois world was that it sought to realize Particularity as Particularity without at the same time considering the Universal. Old comedy merely suppressed the Universal that had appeared in tragedy. It did not, therefore, supersede it. In theological language, the gods did not go away when they were laughed at, they just blushed and hid. To make them truly go away they must be murdered. But first they must be manifest, *offenbare*; thus happy but unconscious atheism was followed by unhappy but self-conscious theism.

Religion based upon labour

With the religion of art, knowledge of Spirit moved from the form of substance, where it was apprehended by way of real statues, beautiful temples, etc., to that of subject, where it was apprehended as the self-revealing speech of the comedian. Spirit had, in effect, reversed the experience of the religion of light, where the self was simply a predicate of the infinite, by reducing the infinite to the finite, the Universal to the Particular. Now there occurred a further reversal, but one that preserved the insight of comedy, namely the conscious attribution of meaning. The new religion would give priority to God, as a natural religion, but it would do so self-consciously, as in the religion of art. Thus do we find two self-consciousnesses, two selves, confronting one another, and not one human self confronting a divine given-Being, *Sein*. The result 'for us' who are Hegelian Sages was the knowledge that 'the divine Nature is itself what the human is, and it is thus unity that is intuitively grasped [by man]' (*PhG* 529:460).

The actual historical phenomena involved were the religious movements of the Roman Empire, especially Christianity. Judaism, one may note in passing, was not, for Hegel, a revealed religion. Negatively, Judaism was speechless, so there was nothing for speech to reveal: Yahweh was both unreasonable and absent. On its own or positively, it was a religion of Nature, a 'paradoxical' synthesis of 'mana' and totemism (*PhG* 502:435; *IH* 248). However that may be, when the comic bourgeois reflected upon his own finitude and absurdity his joyful certainty broke, his confident trust deserted him. When 'the self is absolute essential-reality' (*PhG* 521:453) and also self-consciously finite, it appeared to itself as emptied of Spirit. Consciousness could endure this condition for a time (Stoicism and so on). Eventually nostalgia for the vanished Universality, which appeared historically as the ethical life of the polis, transformed consciousness into the Unhappy Consciousness that we have already considered phenomenologically as an attitude.

The cultural mania of comedy had become the cultural depression of unhappiness. The attempt to reduce the Universal to the Particular ended with the emptying of all substance and with the utter loss of self. Consciousness found itself within a cruel monism of pain, able only to lament the death of God (*PhG* 523:455). In his longing after the dead god, the bourgeois was still unable to appropriate the Universal and so could not yet claim that he had murdered God. This was why he constructed a religion. The religion he constructed, however, must take into account the wreckage and spiritual rubble of the ancient world. Confidence in the law of the gods was gone; no one trusted oracles; statues were lifeless copies of Greek originals; even the desperation of Julian, the bull-killer, was testimony to the atrophy of the pagan Spirit: late antiquity was no more than a collection of antiques. Like art, it externalized Spirit; but the Spirit it externalized was dead. For the Hegelian Sage, to internalize the Spirit of antiquity was to internalize death. But it was also, as an internalization, to give birth to Spirit conscious of itself as Spirit, and so no longer conscious of itself as art (*PhG* 525:456). As Kojève remarked, the development of Christianity was the development of atheism, which was nothing other than Spirit conscious of itself as Spirit (*IH* 256).

Hegel's 'theology of kenosis' completed the process of interpenetration of subject and substance. On the one side, substance emptied itself of itself and became self-conscious; on the other, self-consciousness emptied itself of itself and made itself Universal or gave itself 'thingness' (*PhG* 525:457). Kojève interpreted this 'theology' in terms of a synthesis of prior religious experience. The primitive, Judaic, naturalism of 'mana,' which was the first Universalism, combined with comic bourgeois atheism, which was the first Particularism, to produce a Universal God whose Universalism resulted from his incarnation in a particular person, Jesus. This Man-God was a self, an Individual, a concrete realization of the abstract person of Roman Law. Individuality was not, for the Christian, an ideal to be realized since it already existed, in the Beyond, in the person of the resurrected Christ (*IH* 256–7; cf *PhG* 525:457). Accordingly, to use the language of natural generation, this Spirit may be said to have an actual mother, *eine wirkliche Mutter*, but *einen ansichseieden Vater*, a father whose essence is not actual but implicit, transcendent, and so yet to be realized (*PhG* 526:457; *IH* 257). The non-actual, non-existent essence of the father was the project of History, realized by the action of fighting and labouring.

The first result of the kenosis was that Spirit grasped only its second aspect. Self-consciousness had made itself substance so that "all existence is spiritual essential-reality only from the standpoint of Consciousness and not as it is in itself' (*PhG* 526:457). On the one hand this gave rise to the fantastic subjectivism of the mystery religions, but on the other to the perfected paganism of Plotinus. The antitheses of vulgar subjectivism and astringent esotericism were reconciled in the actual appearance of God in Jesus, where 'the believing Consciousness sees, feels, and hears this divinity.' The Incarnation was the 'simple content of the Absolute Religion' (*PhG* 527–8:458–9), which was appealing to the former votaries of Mithras and Isis. But at the same time the appearance of Christ Jesus was not simply immediate ecstacy: he appeared to others who thought about what they saw. And the God they saw revealed in the man Jesus was the Jewish God understood in terms of pagan perfection, which was very appealing to the former neo-Platonic philosophers.

So long as Jesus lived, the contents of absolute religion were manifestations of his consciousness of himself as Spirit. But as a man, Jesus died, and with him the immediacy of his revelation. Henceforth God could not be immediately present: where formerly God rose before consciousness as a sensuous being, now he had arisen in Spirit (*PhG* 531:462). The death of Jesus was the moment of negation of the immediate existence of absolute essential reality. Henceforth this essential reality would be mediated by Self-consciousness (the deliberate remembrance of Jesus' words, and so on), and made immediately actual as the community of believers. This was possible, as we noted earlier, because from the 'perspective' of the sage, the divine and human natures were the same. That is, in the Church were combined the Universality of spiritual communion with the Particularity of the sensuous presence of the believer. It was, therefore, a real World where human beings could live.

So long as the rituals and remembrances of the Church were taken to exhaust its Universality, it remained imperfect, akin to the mystery religions and unable completely to account for itself. All that had occurred was a movement from sense experience to pictorial representation, *Vorstellung*. So long as Spirit was self-conscious as a specific religious community, as a Church, so long would Spirit be unable to move beyond representation. Instead, there would persist a split between the Beyond and the here-below, as between the true contents, namely absolute Spirit, and a defective form, namely representation. Accordingly, consciousness must cease to portray the true content to itself and accede to a higher cultural level, *Bildung*, where 'its intuitive apprehension of absolute substance is raised to the level of the Concept, and equate for itself its consciousness with its self-consciousness just as has occurred for us [who are Hegelian Sages] or in itself' (*PhG* 532:463). The process by which absolute Spirit came to exist in its true form appeared as the theology of the Church, a discourse concerned with the God of the universal community.

Theology and philosophy

The god whose redemptive death reconciled the divine and human and who was remembered when two or three gathered together in his name and partook of his creatures, bread and wine, was for them a dispenser of holy mysteries. The recipients of those mysteries were members of the mystical body of Christ and heirs through hope of his everlasting kingdom.

The truth of Christianity for the Sage, however, was not to be found in the internal and mediative significance of mystery, hope, and ritual. And it was not in the externalization of this spirituality into doctrines, formulae, or rubrics such as those just paraphrased, but 'in becoming an actual Self, reflecting itself to itself, and being Subject' (*PhG* 532:463). The revealed reality of Christianity was the actual community of persons who recognized one another as members and who, as subject, knew that they had made the World in which they lived, that what made theirs a Christian World was themselves. Or again, 'this [i.e. the truth or revealed reality of Christianity], then, is the movement by which Spirit accomplishes its community; this is the life of the community' (*PhG* 532:463). A phenomenology of Christianity must, therefore, consider both the theological thought as it existed on its own or for itself, and what it meant from the 'perspective' of the Sage or 'in itself.' As a methodological postscript, Hegel remarked that one would not grasp what Christianity was in and for itself by historical archaeology: one could not gain access to the Concept by way of a quest for the historical Jesus, or by the posture of 'primitive Christianity,' or, one may say, by any reformation whatsoever, since it would invariably involve a return to the source of faith, the words and deeds of Jesus Christ, and these were bare externalities, a spiritless recollection of mere historical contingencies (*PhG* 532–3: 463).

There were again three stages to the analysis. The first considered the abstract theology of the Trinity, which, for the Sage, was a representation of the trinitarian structure of absolute Being, namely essential reality, consciousness of it, and the confirming recognition of the necessary relationship of the first two moments (*PhG* 534:465). The theological idiom by which this structure was expressed represented the first two conceptual moments by the wholly inappropriate natural relationship of father and son. In contrast, the Holy Spirit, which even Christians had to admit went beyond any relationship found in nature, was misconceived as a tradition.

Second, theological morality was likewise governed by representational form, namely the relationship between creator and creature. Because of the difference between God and the World, God must be killed before man could be at home in the World and be recognized properly speaking. Now, because Christians were still fully human, they sought recognition, just like everyone else. But they forbore killing God. The consequence of refusing to take this 'metaphysically necessary' mediating action was that they postulated an immediate or abstract morality of recognition that did not correspond to the actualities of the World. Specifically, Christian morality was one of loving one's neighbour as oneself (in addition, of course, to loving God). In this context, love was equivalent to recognition. Thus, the Christian counsel of love was, according to Kojève, a counsel of mutual recognition. But mutual recognition was predicated upon the primordial fight and could not be obtained directly or, therefore, without the mediation of that fight. Hegel indicated (and Kojève elaborated) several consequent deficiencies in Christian morality before turning to the true account of relations between God, man, and the World.

Love, or recognition, could exist only among or between equals. So long as History existed there was no equality but rather only various forms of inequality that resulted from struggle and labour. Until the advent of the universal and homogeneous State, therefore, there could be no mutual recognition or true love. There could, however, exist misbegotten, warped, and false varieties of love that might, for a time, appear as recognition. There was, for example, natural love, love for the person as given-Being. As we saw earlier, this developed within the family and found classic expression in *Antigone*. There was also Christian love, charity, which bid us love all others as 'human beings'; that is, it demanded that we ignore or overlook Particularity. But studiously to avoid considering Particularity or, in social terms, inequality, would be to assume the existence of inequality, which then may be transcended by making certain that one did not pay attention to it. But this would be a social fraud. Between genuine equals, then, charity was impossible. For Christians however, genuine equality was in the Beyond, which meant that inequality 'here below' was inessential, and charity a great virtue. Contempt for the things of the World was carried through to oneself as well, as the charitable person was also to be humble. Christian love, therefore, was insufficient and eventually unsatisfying because it maintained social differences in the World in order to ignore them in the Beyond. Yet it was an image or an ideal of mutual recognition. Like all ideals it could be realized historically. But this realization had nothing in common with charity as it existed for itself (*IH* 260; *PhG* 535–6:466–7). Indeed, the realization of the Christian ideal of charity was, in fact, the universal and homogeneous State.

For Hegel, the representational language of the creation of the world, Adam and Eve, the Garden of Eden, sin, Lucifer, and the overcoming of these by the Incarnation, death, and resurrection of Christ, expressed as a mythic temporal sequence what was really a logical account of absolute Being. As before, representational language was inadequate to convey the truth of its claims. The life of Christ, for example, was simply a symbolic representation, not a conceptual account, of human history: 'Christ sacrifices his Particularity (= Jesus) in order to realize the Universal (= Logos), and the Universal (= God) recognizes the Particularity (= Man) who is himself God (= Christ). Christ laboured; he was a carpenter. He sacrificed his life; here is [the Master's] Struggle and Risk. However, he did not, properly speaking, engage in a struggle since he remained a Slave (death on the cross). Even more, Christ revealed the final atheism, the death of God. He came to life again as a real Man, that is, as a Community, the Church (= Prototype of the Napoleonic Empire)' (*IH* 262). The conceptual inadequacy of the believer's symbolism was expressed, on the one hand, in the image of Christ's ascension to the Beyond and, on the other hand, in the division, within the Church, between the mystical body and the actual worldly organization. Once again the task of history consisted in overcoming the split between the ideal and reality. Hegel's task was to describe the process.

So far in this section we have considered two stages of Hegel's analysis. The first, the abstract theology of the Trinity, was both a representation of the structure of absolute Being and, in itself or from the 'perspective' of a Hegelian Sage, its first moment, essential reality. The second moment, Consciousness of essential reality, was expressed in theological morality, and likewise had a two-fold significance. On the one hand, it was a moment within the dialectic of post-apostolic Christianity, and, on the other, it had its own internal dialectic, with three moments, sin (given-Being), the conflict of good and evil or Jesus and Lucifer (Consciousness of given-Being), and the solution to the conflict, death and resurrection (the confirming Self-consciousness). We come now to consider the third moment of the dialectic of post-apostolic Christianity. Once again we find an internal dialectic with three moments. But because it was the concluding moment of the larger dialectic, its own final moment, namely Self-consciousness, raised the whole process to Self-knowledge and effectively ended all religious ideological speculation.

In representational language, the death and resurrection of Christ were followed by the revelation of the Holy Spirit. As Spirit, it existed within a community that was conscious of it, namely the Church. The adjective 'Holy,' therefore, was a linguistic indulgence, a remnant left over from Consciousness of nature and destined to be superseded as the implications of Spirit were eventually made plain. Henceforth the analysis proceeded not at the level of empirical actualities, of things and Consciousness of them, but of Self-consciousness, of the interpretation of Consciousness of things that Consciousness made to itself.

The representational language that spread the good news of the resurrection informed the early converts from paganism that the World would soon end. But it did not, which meant that Christian existence within an enduring Christian World would have to be justified. When the pagan became a Christian, he did not become what he had not been earlier, namely a sinner. That is, he did not gain a new nature. Rather, he became conscious of what he had always been, namely a sinner; always he learned of his 'true nature.' What was a fact or an event for Evangelical Theology, the Fall (Adam) and Redemption (Jesus), became for St Paul a matter of interpretation. Not the reality of sin but consciousness of sin was what mattered; likewise, not the empirical reality of Jesus but faith in the Saviour would ensure salvation. 'With Saint Paul there is, as it were, a second murder of Jesus' (*IH* 263). Pauline theology consisted in a dialectical identification of good and evil, which crystallized as the doctrine of *felix culpa*. By giving man the Law, God tempted his transgression of it so as to redeem mankind from that transgression. All that was needed to effect redemption was a 'dying to sin' (*PhG* 544:474), that is, a conversion.

But if all that were required was conversion and faith, the life, as distinct from the death and resurrection, of Jesus would not make any sense. The immediacy of Pauline theology was, therefore, its great flaw: if salvation came immediately from God, it was an act of grace, in which case a Christian life, as such, was senseless. But if it came immediately from the metanoia of human consciousness, then neither Adam's fall nor Jesus' salvation mattered. Faith must, therefore, be mediated by life, which is to say by good works and by the Church.

Topically, the second moment was the Eucharist. There the life and death of Jesus Christ were transfigured from the representational language of immediate fact to the symbolic language of Catholic doctrine. The life and actions of Christ were recapitulated in the Mass; the faithful Catholic was not simply a Pauline convert but also a faithful, that is, regular, communicant. The death and resurrection were no longer what happened to Jesus once upon a time, but were universalized in the community of the faithful on a daily basis (*PhG* 545:475). Only by communication, which implied the mediation of the universal Church and the real presence of the communicating partners, could the Christian be saved. Such was the Christian life in a Christian world. Because the Eucharist was not a simple memorial ceremony but rather a 'daily miracle' that maintained the Church as the institution that mediated God's way to men, it symbolized the reconciliation of Particularity and Universality. But it was only a symbol, a 'throwing together' that depended for its meaning not on the discursive account that Hegelian science gave, but on the miraculous nourishment of the body and blood of Christ. At a purely physical level, it depended upon bread and wine, not a book; that is, upon the immediacy of biological life and Desire, not the mediation of speech and Consciousness.

We are brought, then, to the third moment, which was the transition from religion to knowledge. Here we shall consider only the defects of the religious community, leaving for a later section the description of the everlasting regime that was, and is, without imperfection.

The religious community of the Church knew that it was maintained by communion, but it did not yet know that this communion was really a communication with itself. 'This community does not have a conscious awareness of what it is; it is spiritual Self-consciousness that is not an object to itself, as this self-consciousness, or that does not develop into a clear Consciousness of itself; rather, insofar as it is Consciousness, it has before it those representational thoughts, *Vorstellungen*, that we have considered' (*PhG* 547:477). The religious community was the perfect community but it did not (yet) know it. The language of miracle with respect to the absolute reconciliation of the Eucharist indicated that the satisfaction achieved was not understood by the community as being its own work. 'Its satisfaction thus remains burdened with a Beyond to which it is opposed' (*PhG* 548:478). Eucharistic reconciliation was always surrounded with a nostalgia for the past (and innocence) and with an anticipation of the future (and transfiguration). What was supposed to overcome this twin absence was, of course, love. But Christian love was merely sensed, *fuhlt*, and not grasped as an object before Consciousness. It remained an 'ought.' Instead, what was before Consciousness was both a representation of reconciliation in the Beyond and an actually present World in need, precisely, of transfiguration. Consciousness knew that love effected the reconciliation, but it did not know love. When it did, love became recognition, and absolute Consciousness became absolute Self-consciousness or Self-knowledge, Wisdom.

One may summarize Hegel's discussion of religion as follows. The first religion was natural religion, God without man. The first atheism was Comedy, man without God. Then came Christianity, and God made himself man. Lastly we have the second atheism, Hegelian Wisdom, where man made himself God (*IH* 255). We have dealt with religion not as the content of individual consciousness but as social ideology. The 'contents' of religion were 'true' in the sense that they revealed man's fear of nature and his overcoming of that fear. Modern, atheistic, mortal human beings lack reverence; nature contains no terror because (in principle) it has been comprehensively assimilated. In plain language, modern man has no awe of nature's sacredness. We may worry about the danger of environmental pollution as a result of our technical activity, for example, but we are not concerned with religious pollution, or the wrath of the gods, as a result of that activity.

The true contents of religion, however, have not gained true form, which is conceptual rather than representational. Now, the great defect of representation was that what was religiously represented remained other than the Consciousness that did the representing and therefore alien to it (*PhG* 482:417). Only with conceptualization and ultimately with Wisdom, because it was self-produced and understood itself conceptually, that is, as being self-produced, was the otherness of representative form overcome. In short, only 'philosophy' could give an account of things, including itself, whereas religion could not. For Hegel this was true not simply for his own philosophy but for all philosophy, starting with the Greeks. Philosophy as a self-productive activity was recognized, however, only by modern, German speculative philosophy, an ideology that existed in historical continuity with religion. Accordingly, one may summarize the history of religions as follows. Initially political religions expressed or represented the mythic 'natural' social order prior to the anthropogenetic fight. Next, the religion of political society expressed the fight for recognition, which in turn was followed by the religious ideology of post-political society, the society whose dominant spirit expressed labour after the primordial fight but before the final Revolution. The next topic, to which we now turn, is the ideology, or rather, ideologies, of post-Revolutionary society. After considering the origins of the form of Science, we shall deal with the post-historical attitude properly speaking, namely the attitude of the Sage, Hegel, and the reality that his speech reveals, namely the universal and homogeneous State. One should, perhaps, again make the point that, because ideologies were essentially interpretations, the appearance of the final regime and the Sage did not mean that historical regimes, religions, and philosophies were ended. Mistakes were always possible. But then, too, they could always be corrected. We turn, then, to Hegel's survey of historical but post-Revolutionary errors.

Kantian morality

In section A of chapter 6 of *Phenomenology*, Hegel discussed customary morality, *Sittlichkeit*. There he described the pagan Master's unreflective and unquestioning obedience to collective, inviolable divine ordinances.

Section C, which is to be discussed presently, was given the sub-title *Die Moralität*, Reflective Morality. Here one knew that one had invented and promulgated the moral teaching in question, that it was one's own even if one also thought it Universal. Specifically this section dealt with German philosophical or speculative morality as it developed from Kant to Hegel himself.

Section C concluded Hegel's discussion of Spirit and, appropriately enough, included within itself all that preceded it. As with customary morality, reflective morality was immediate; the self knew and did its duty. But unlike customary morality, it did so not because of a noble character or nature. On the contrary, duty was at the same time mediated, as with belief and culture, by a reflective understanding as to why this duty was to be done. That is, there existed an identity of knowledge and its object. The substance of a self was no longer alien or even external but existed within consciousness as *reine Pflicht*, pure duty. The very purity of duty, however, suggested already its limitation.

One further preliminary remark is necessary. The title of this subsection was *Die moralische Weltanschauung*. Hegel was not, therefore, concerned focally with the systematic metaphysics of his predecessor so much as with the implications of Kant's argument for a 'moral view of the world.' Recalling the title of this entire section, Spirit that is certain of itself, the emphasis centred upon the spirituality of this moral consciousness and the reasons why it was, for itself, certain of itself. In so doing Hegel also showed why 'for us,' who adopt the attitude of Hegelian Sages, the moral view of the World was self-destructive.

'Self-consciousness knows duty as absolute essential-reality' (*PhG* 424: 365). What was outside Self-consciousness, namely nature as described by Newtonian physics, was of absolutely no significance for duty. The independence of nature from human action in Kant's teaching led him to ignore the significance of labour, which transformed the World. Moreover, this dualism, as all modern dualisms, was evidence of its author's attachment to pagan and Christian cosmology (*IH* 149). Once separated, the great problem for Kant was to get morality (or Consciousness or Spirit) back together with nature.

Kant's elegant and appealing argument may be briefly summarized. Moral consciousness sought only to do its duty (treat every individual as an end, never as a means, and so on). But this counsel of duty depended for its moral appeal on the existence of a wicked world where men acted not dutifully but naturally and in accord with their *sinnlichen Willens*, their sensuous will, which is to say, unjustly. Since nature was indifferent to duty, this Self-consciousness was free to postulate 'the harmony of morality and nature' (*PhG* 426:367). Now, to postulate, Hegel said, was to demand that something that was not actual or existent be so. But in this instance it was not a mere wish, but the very content of duty. Or, to put it more plainly, the duty of a moral person consisted in overcoming his 'natural' inclinations, such as treating persons as a means. It was, therefore, a struggle. Even more, it was an endless struggle since, if victory ever were achieved and there actually existed the sought-for unity of duty and nature, morality, which presupposed freedom (and freedom did not exist in nature), would disappear. Thus, a second postulate: the harmony of duty and nature was achieved 'at' infinity, which is to say that moral progress, the actions by which nature is harmonized with duty, was an infinite (or at least indefinite) task. The act of faith that supported this postulate was Kant's belief in the immortality of the soul.

There was thus a third postulate that reconciled the first, namely the final purpose of the World as the harmony of nature and morality, with the second, namely the final purpose of Self-consciousness as the harmony of 'natural' inclination or sensuous will with duty. This third postulate was the existence of another Consciousness who must be represented as the divine moral legislator of the World who, so to speak, guaranteed the ultimate eventual harmony between duty and happiness. Thus, one would receive one's reward in heaven for virtuous actions performed here below.

The actual Consciousness of an individual, however, was not divine; and it was not heavenly; it could not consider the relationship between duty and happiness as necessary. Indeed, its experience was just the opposite. When the two did coincide, then, it was a gift of divine grace, in no way merited. Now, when all significance adhered to moral activity, but when this activity could take place only in the indifferent natural World, all activity would equally appear moral and immoral, depending on the actual, concrete projection of the conscience, *Gewissen*, involved. Such subjectivity was, in the end, what made such a Consciousness certain, *gewisse*. In other words, while it was absolutely true that justice and happiness ought to go together, yet since there actually were no just men, there was no reason to expect happiness this side of the Beyond. Yet the projection of pure duty as the essential reality of this Self-consciousness meant that its actual imperfection remained untouched by merely natural imperfections.

Man sought perfection insofar as he was imperfect; because he was imperfect, perfection lay elsewhere. This implication of the Kantian split between noumenal and phenomenal, a more complicated version of the dialectic of the inverted world, was overcome, Hegel said, by pretence, *Verstellung*. If one's actual, finite, worldly act was, in comparison to one's true purposes in the Beyond, insignificant, if what really counted was conscience and doing one's duty (whatever that entailed in the wicked world of nature), then whatever so-called morality existed in the world was merely provisional. The succession of such 'moralities' would not bring conscience any closer to moral perfection. The fitting response to the gracious gift of happiness was an imaginative leap. 'In this way the first proposition, that there exists a moral Self-consciousness is re-established, but it is bound up with the second, that there is none, which is to say, there is one, but only as representation; or, in other words, there is indeed none, but all the same one Consciousness is allowed to count as moral by another Consciousness' (*PhG* 434:373–4). In other words, since complete moral Self-consciousness was merely pure, there could be no actual moral perfection. But there could be an ideal, a representation, and it could be treated by another moral Consciousness as if it were perfection. Kantian morality was therefore indistinguishable from moralism. That is, it was not serious.

Hegel discussed with relish the shifts back and forth between the dual perspectives of moral conscience and non-moral activity as well as the moral 'shiftiness,' *Verstellung*, involved in this movement. The self-destruction of Kantian moralism may be summarized as follows: if duty were the sole goal of morality, and if its actualization were indeed an infinite task, and then if we were to take seriously infinity, any finite moral progress must be equivalent to zero (as any finitude divided by infinity is zero). But if however, we thought of moral progress as akin to the relation of a curve to its asymptote, then as we got closer to moral perfection, as our sensuous will conformed increasingly to duty, will would provide less resistance and so less scope for duty, and one would become less moral. Thus, progress in morality must either be zero, or it turned itself into progress in non-morality. To postulate a transcendent guarantor only made things worse, since this 'purely moral being' would be completely devoid of sensuous will and therefore would have no duty and so would be purely immoral.

Why, then, was this a step toward Wisdom? Because, Hegel said, here Consciousness had produced its own object, pure duty, even if it represented it to itself and gave this object imaginary attributes. The contradictions of the moral view of the World finally would drive Consciousness to the knowledge of its own pretence. The imperfections of morality, on its own terms, meant either that all so-called moral activities were mere conventions and that really everything was permitted, or that morality must be completed within the 'natural' and sensuous World. The second and Hegelian alternative entailed the abandonment of God, of the dualism of nature and duty, and, consequently, of the hypocritical purity of the *moralische Weltanschauung*. Consciousness could still, however, flee the World, even the two-tiered and unsatisfactory World of morality. It could not flee into a Beyond, since the Beyond was now just the upper floor of the World. But it could abandon the World as sheer externality, making the number of tiers to its structure a matter of indifference, and retreat into itself. This was its last retreat.

The Consciousness that scorned the World, and with it a *moralische Weltanschauung*, was called by Hegel pure Conscience, *reines Gewissen*. 'It is in itself the simple self-certain, *gewisse*, Spirit that proceeds conscientiously, *gewissenhaft*, without the mediation of any representations and in this immediacy possesses its truth' (*PhG* 444:383). The retreat of Consciousness into Conscience, Hegel said, was simply self-conscious moralism, a higher hypocrisy expressing itself in the denunciation of hypocrisy. The World was a nasty place, this Consciousness said to itself, and nastiness was a thing to avoid, especially for such an exquisite and delicate Conscience as my own.

Romanticism

The opposition of pure duty and natural sensuous reality that was found in Kant's moral view of the world led, on the one side, to a view of the self as a self-making – one must will one's pure duty if one is to be moral – but a self-making whose ultimate locale was the Beyond – no actual dutiful act was unequivocally moral. The theoretical paralysis of Kantian inaction would be superseded, in effect, by the actual requirements of life. If we looked to the moment of concrete action, the distinction between the here-below and the Beyond would be eclipsed by the appearance of a concrete moral Spirit that, 'in an unmediated unity, is a self-making moral essential-reality, *verwirklichendes moralisches Wesen*, and the act is an unmediated concrete moral form, *Gestalt*' (*PhG* 446–7: 385). This form of Spirit, 'immediately certain of itself as absolute truth and given-Being' (*PhG* 445:384), had overcome the division between the purity of duty and the impurity of sensuous nature. In any case where moral action was called for, this Consciousness knew immediately what to do, namely follow the voice of Conscience, its own Conscience.

The Romantic, as Kojève remarked, was a Kantian who had understood himself. There was no more talk about good intentions having come to nought, or complaints about good men who fared badly (*PhG* 450–1:388). The Romantic knew there were no transcendent guarantees and that he could not honestly speak to or of God. He was, therefore, an atheist even if he had not worked out all the details. Instead, the Romantic said that the perfect man 'lives in conformity to himself.' To be sure, this morality considered what Kant's did not, namely the immediate and personal element of moral Consciousness; but its immediacy, which allowed it to supersede Kant, also was its limitation. The Romantic transcended given-Being by elevating his soul, but he did not realize his negation by transformative action, by fighting and labouring (*IH* 149–50). The 'actions' of his Conscience were, therefore, imaginary. Or, what amounts to the same thing, romantic Consciousness vainly tried to turn reality directly into a product of will.

For Conscience, *Gewissen*, the self knew itself as absolute. There was no standard beyond Conscience to which Consciousness might appeal for guidance. The essential reality of Conscience was, therefore, personal conviction. By avoiding the diremption of postulating pre-existent duties and concentrating only upon the fact that it was Consciousness itself that postulated these duties, *Gewissen* simply denied the alterity of any situation whatsoever. Thus, 'action as realization is in this way the pure form of will' (*PhG* 447:385). It was at the same time sheer arbitrariness, *Willkür*. For Conscience, truth lay in its own self-certainty, its 'sincerity.' The contents of that truth therefore depended upon the actual moral action that appeared in the process of creative self-making. The result was not the self-creation of a moral superman but the demand that one's convictions be shared by everybody. That is, the man of conscience mistook the sincerity with which he held his convictions for their universality. But since his sincerity was inherently internal and subjective, purely a matter of conscience, nothing was actually recognized.

Recognition could be gained only if one were willing to fight for one's convictions, to impose them on others, and make them objectively Universal. The Romantic, however, did not wish to fight; he lacked the courage of his convictions. The Romantic, one might say, believed in his own complete self-actualization only insofar as it was distinct from something that was not self-actualization. In terms of his equation of will and reality, one would say that the Romantic was shrewd enough to suspect his own arbitrariness. In short, the celebration of will was constantly plagued by a guilty conscience, and the Romantic was forced to admit of the emptiness of his sincerity. When he saw that others did not recognize his convictions as truth he contented himself with the knowledge that at least they were truly his own, and covered up his failure of will with the platitude of tolerance.

The Romantic was, in short, just another Intellectual. Unlike those of the spiritual bestiary, however, he had seen the results of the Revolution. According to Kojève, he merely accepted the result and not the bloody fights and painful labours that led up to it; in this he was just another sybarite, feasting on the efforts of others. The duplicity of a good Conscience was, and is, the ideology of political and economic liberalism. 'Romantics *chatter* about the *public* good while businessmen *act* on the basis of their *private* interests.' It was actually post-Revolutionary but essentially pre-Revolutionary, combining extreme Particularism and atheism. Whereas the principle of the pseudo-society presided over by the Church was 'each for himself and God for all,' in the absence of God this had been changed to 'each for himself in real life, and Romantic chatter for all' (*IH* 150–1). The essentially unserious Romantic self-making was incarnate by the equally unserious self-made man.

For the man of Conscience, duty had no authority because it came from another. In any actual, concrete situation, therefore, Conscience, which meant the subject, must decide what to do. But what it decided to do might appear to others, including other men of Conscience, as different from what was intended. Aggressive violence may appear as justifiable self-assertion, praiseworthy self-making; alternatively, moderation and prudence may appear as cowardice. The contents of Conscience were inherently arbitrary insofar as they bore the 'stain of determinativeness' (*PhG* 454:392). Moreover, it was contrary to Conscience to allow factors constitutive of what Max Weber called an ethics of responsibility to enter into consideration. As Hegel said, 'it is Spirit certain of itself, certain of having the truth within itself, in its self, in its knowledge, which is a knowledge of its duty' (*PhG* 455–6:393). This meant that, with respect to any particular so-called duty, Conscience was absolutely free: what made Conscience do its duty was its own self-determination and not any alleged demands of duty.

The pure self-identity and self-sufficiency of one Conscience existed for other similar Consciences. These conscientious actors observed and judged by their own lights the conscientious acts of the others. But because these others were equally self-determining, it was not at all certain that they would acknowledge the conscientiousness of the other. They might, as in the above example, see conscientious moderation as cowardice. Indeed, Hegel said, not only could one Conscience not know the conscientiousness of another, it must suspect it not only because it knew of its own 'shiftiness' with respect to the demands of duty, but because, if it were to maintain its own self, it must see in the other's Conscience nothing more than his taste or preference. Yet, in principle, all could be men of Conscience and all actions could (and for Conscience should) be conscientious. But precisely this possibility expressed the non-actuality of Universal conscientiousness. In short, because his conscientious actions merely should be (but are not) recognized, the man of Conscience remained, and remains, unsatisfied.

Once again Consciousness has been faced with the possibility of acting, that is, of seriously demanding recognition for what it had done. Once again, however, Consciousness did not make that demand but clung to itself as Conscience and, in effect, made up excuses. That is, Conscience began speaking; it 'expresses its conviction; this conviction and it alone is the action of duty; it is, as well, valid as duty only through the conviction being expressed' (*PhG* 459:396). What counted, what was recognized, was not, therefore, what had been done, but what had been said. Indeed, what had been done was a matter of indifference since all universality was a consequence of speech. Accordingly, the formal universality of speech was acknowledged as actual: 'the self is actual, as such, in language, declares itself to be the truth, and by so doing recognizes all other selves and is recognized by them' (*PhG* 460:397). The Romantic could say anything he pleased; all his words excused his deeds or lack of them because he was 'interesting.' He should certainly be tolerated. Perhaps he should even be encouraged. Or so he thinks.

The sublime Conscience of the Romantic expressed the belief that satisfaction could come from having others accept his lofty words. He lived in a literary world, especially a world of the novel, *der Roman, le roman*. His acceptance by the literate public was seen by him as recognition and was the source of great satisfaction. His genius was both moral and original because he knew, in his heart, that he spoke with divine authority and for this reason deserved to be the legislator of mankind. Thus, in Kojève's words, he was a thought thinking itself, an Aristotelian god. 'Thus there is already an anthropotheism; but one is contented with so little, with mere identification with a pagan god (Hegel wishes to be Christ).' It is true that, unlike the Aristotelian god, these divine Romantics did create a world from nothing for the sole purpose of being recognized in their works, and in this they were akin to the Christian God, but it is also true that their world unfortunately was not real. It was just fiction, merely a lot of books (*IH* 152). Worse, these gods were not widely acknowledged divinities. They tended to huddle together in a sect or chapel. 'The Spirit and substance of their association are thus the reciprocal assurance of their conscientiousness and good intentions, the rejoicing over this mutual purity, and the refreshing of themselves in the gloriousness of the knowledge, and the expression of fostering and cherishing such an admirable state of affairs' (*PhG* 461:398). This mutual admiration society, ensconced in a fine ivory tower, was, Hegel said, absolute untruth, *die absolute Unwahrheit*, the extremity of Self-consciousness submerging Consciousness within it – in other words, pure fiction. Self-consciousness without an object was the curious spectacle of the divine Romantic proclaiming the non-reality of gods, an unhappy Christian consciousness that mislaid God (*IH* 152). For a Sage, it was amusing.

What could the Romantic possibly do? His absolute certainty of self had nothing to be certain of; it was like an echo without an initiating noise. 'It lacks the strength of externalization, the strength to make itself into a thing and to endure given-Being. It lives in dread of staining the purity of its inwardness by action and existence.' Retreating from the actual world it had produced a hollow where Consciousness of things once was; it filled this hollow, therefore, with the Consciousness of emptiness, *Bewusstsein der Leerheit*. Its only activity was a yearning that ended up as madness or suicide, 'an object with no essential-reality, lost.' The light flickered within the transparent purity of this unhappy and beautiful soul, 'and it vanishes as a shapeless vapour dissolving into thin air' (*PhG* 462–3:399–400). Thus did the Romantic eventually find his beautiful death – beautiful, yes, but also 'a final and definite defeat' (*IH* 152), the 'spiritless unity of given-Being' (*PhG* 470:407), death.

Hegel's justification of Napoleon

Hegel's consideration of Kant showed that doing one's duty was an infinite task, an action that, of itself, was finite, but the significance of which, as guaranteed by Kant' several postulates, was nevertheless registered within the infinite economy of posthumous salvation. The Kantian moral view of the World self-destructed into hypocrisy, which in turn became self-conscious as pure Conscience. This Self-consciousness was sure of itself, but it did nothing and cared for nothing; it was sincere but empty, and so in its way just as hypocritical as that of the moralist. In the third part of this sub-section of *Phenomenology*, the finite activity of duty was dialectically combined with the infinite self-certainty of the beautiful soul.

Virtually every commentator on these passages, including Kojève, has remarked on their ambiguity. The ambiguity can hardly be denied though for our purposes it can be ignored. The title of this sub-sub-section is *'Das Böse und seine Verzeihung,'* evil and its justification or pardon. Two obvious questions are come to mind. Is it evil in general or some particular evil? Who does the pardoning or forgiving or justifying? Kojève's answer – one could hardly say *the* answer – was that evil is the French Revolution as realized in the Napoleonic Empire and its justification was accomplished by Hegel in his *Phenomenology (IH* 152). Let us try to justify this interpretation with reference to Hegel's text.

At the conclusion of part B of chapter 6, which dealt with the dialectic of the Revolutionary World, I quoted Hegel's rather obscure words that absolute freedom took leave of its self-destructive actuality in the Terror of the Revolution and moved *outre-Rhin* to the land of the Self-conscious Spirit where freedom was not actual, though it was accepted as truth. In the thought of this truth, which would be actualized as freedom, Spirit was edified and refreshed. The actual refreshment that Spirit enjoyed was the knowledge that thought enclosed within itself, as Self-consciousness, complete and perfected essential reality. Hegel concluded with the observation that the new form of the moral Spirit had come forth (*PhG* 422:363).

On 29 April 1814, Hegel wrote a letter to his friend, Niethammer, where he explained that 'absolute freedom' referred to his earlier description of the abstract formal freedom of the French Republic as it emerged from the Enlightenment, and that the land he had in mind was really a country, Germany. Moreover, in *Phenomenology* in 1806 he had said that this new form of the moral Spirit *'ist ... entstanden,'* has come forth or emerged; in his letter of 1814 he said it *'ist ... vorhanden,'* is present. In other words, the truth of abstract freedom and terror may be grasped by Spirit when Spirit was in the form of thought, and thought, we know, was a constituent element of Science. Historically, this thought was German; it emerged prior to 1806 and in 1814 was fully at hand. Now, one does not wish to make overmuch of a change in words; *entstehen* makes as much sense grammatically as *vorhanden*. Perhaps Hegel was quoting from memory and his memory slipped – though this was unlikely since in his letter he referred to a specific page. Perhaps any number of things. One thing at least is clear, the absolute but empty self-consciousness of the beautiful soul must gain a conscious content. What could be more appropriate than the actualization of the French Revolution?[4]

Assuming, then, that Hegel was talking about the French Revolution and the Napoleonic Empire, we must deal with both elements of the *Geist*, namely evil and its justification.[5] Both began from the internal certainty of conscience. Consider first evil, concretely, Napoleon, or, in Hegel's language, 'Conscience ... considered as acting' (*PhG* 463:400). The mutual recognition of the mutual admiration society broke apart when its members stopped chattering and actually did something. Acting Conscience was a self-actualizing or self-making; but it was also absolute, which is to say that it sought to have its non-verbal self-actualization universally acknowledged. Yet it remained an individual self-making. Hence there arose opposition, and therefore suffering and evil, between individual self-makings. In addition there existed a contradiction between any one individual and the absoluteness he claimed and proclaimed. The actualization of the conflict between individual self-makings, what we may call post-historical pseudo-politics, will be considered below. Here we consider only the second conflict, the penultimate appearance of the dialectic of Particularity and Universality.

Conscience knew it was free from the authority of duty. But it was also a specific action, and so filled its freedom, its moral emptiness, with its own specific content. As self-actualization it made its own content, its self, 'as a natural Individuality.' When this Conscience spoke, it may well have spoken of its own Conscientiousness, but at the same time it could not remain unaware that its action concerned an actual purpose or goal, *Zweck*, undertaken as a particular individual. It was therefore 'conscious of the opposition between what it is for itself and what it is for others, the opposition between Universality or duty and its own [actions] being reflected outside of Universality and duty' (*PhG* 464:400–1). Acting conscience knew what it was doing *qua* self-actualization but also that any specific or particular action contradicted its self-proclaimed Universality. Hence, it ran into opposition. Or, what amounts to the same thing, its self-proclaimed Universality necessarily appeared as Particularity until it was acknowledged by others, until one self-making was recognized by all others, at least in principle. Then opposition to any one particular self-making would have been superseded. Moreover, it would have been genuinely superseded and not simply overcome or crushed: loyalty would have become self-conscious. Or, in Hegel's language, the evil of political action, with its attendant sufferings, would have been forgiven or justified. So far as the active conscience was concerned, the attainment of recognition was anticipated as the expectation of judgment.

No man, not even Napoleon, could act as his own judge. Accordingly, Hegel turned first to the judgment of Kant and then to that of the Romantics, thereby recapitulating the previous accounts. Romantic internal self-making Particularity contrasted with Kantian consciousness of Universal duty. For Kant, Napoleon was evil because his internal subjective life did not correspond to the Universal. But since Napoleon had proclaimed his actions to be Universal and in accord with his conscientious duty, he was held by the Romantic to be a hypocrite (*PhG* 464:401).

The first step in Hegel's discourse was to show that acting Conscience, Napoleon, *was* evil. It was not difficult to admit that the Emperor did treat other men as a means to his own ends, that in Hegel's language, he used being in itself as mere being for another, implying thereby his contempt for that person (*PhG* 465:402). According to Kant this made him evil. According to Conscience, however, Kant had no authority in such matters. Napoleon simply let his Conscience be his guide. In other words, if the Kantian judgment were correct the Romantic accusation would evaporate. According to the Romantics, Napoleon betrayed the Revolution. But this was an empty condemnation of Napoleon's Conscience since, by its own claim to judge, Conscience set itself up as its own particular law, which, as Particularity, could be superior to no other. When Beethoven rescinded the dedication of *Eroica* to Napoleon, he merely trivialized his art by attempting to have his exalted sensitivity make a way in the world as action. Yet it was precisely that sensitivity (and not physical cowardice) that necessitated his hiding in a cellar during the bombarding of Vienna by the French artillery. But is not such inaction parading itself as action evidence of the very hypocrisy it claimed to denounce?

Indeed, Hegel generalized the Romantic condemnation of Napoleon by quoting Napoleon himself, that no man was a hero to his valet. And he added, quoting Goethe, that this was because a valet dealt not with the individual as hero, but as a person who eats, drinks, desires clean underwear, and so on. The Romantic Conscience that judged 'illuminates action only in the light of Particularity and pettiness' (*PhG* 467: 404) and so acted the role of a moralizing valet. Thus the Romantic looked to the motives of Napoleon and denounced vanity and ambition, forgetting that by the same token all action was vain, whether it succeeded or not. In this the Romantic was akin to Kantian preachers of duty, who did nothing but talk, as if duty existed in the absence of action (*PhG* 466:403). In short, all that the several judgments of Napoleon achieved was to bring to light the meanness of those who presumed to judge, as well as their hypocrisy.

Even so, the man of action, Napoleon, was intensely interested in the opinions of others, whether favourable or not. He saw the justice of their words because he understood them as coming from another self. Sensing an identity with his critic, the man of action admitted that his deeds were evil. He made this admission, *Geständnis*, to another whom he regarded as equal to himself and expected this other to return in words of understanding the equality he, the man of action, had just expressed through his admission: 'he expects that a condition of mutual recognition will exist' (*PhG* 468:405). This admission on the part of the man of action was not an abasement or humiliation, *Erniedrigung*; it was given not as a confession to a priest but as the expression of his having seen revealed in the other an equality with himself. It was spoken because language 'is the existence of Spirit as an un-mediated self' (*PhG* 468:405). Speeches of admission and judgment were, therefore, reciprocal tokens of mutual recognition.

The Romantic moralist, however, did not reciprocate. He rejected any community with the man of action and became a 'hard heart' persisting in the enjoyment of its moralism. But the man of action now understood that it was he who had been wronged by the moralist. The moralist was like a child; he wanted things both ways. He contrasted the inert beauty of his own soul with the acknowledged evil of action but refused to admit that action (and therefore evil) were what distinguished human from non-human being. If 'only a stone is innocent' it would appear that the moralist wished to become a stone, but one that somehow knew itself in its inert innocence. The uncommunicative moralist renounced Spirit itself in his refusal to form a community with the man of action. Consequently, 'it does not know that Spirit in the absolute certainty of itself is master [*Meister*, not *Herr*] over every act and actuality, and can cast them aside and make them as if they never had been' (*PhG* 469:406). Spirit, indeed, was the ground or being of all that was properly speaking human. Lacking both in Spirit and in the power of externalization (having shut itself up in the inertness and beauty of its stone-hard heart), the Romantic would be left to die beautifully, like Novalis, of consumption. In short, the adversaries of Napoleon 'are pure inactivity, that is, a *Sein* [given-being], a Nothingness: – if Germany (German philosophy, that is) refuses to "recognize" Napoleon, it will disappear as *Volk*; the Nations (*Besonderheit*) [Particularity] wishing to oppose the universal Empire (*Allgemeinheit*) [Universality] will be annihilated' (*IH* 153). Hegel would avoid this dead-end and, incidentally, thereby save Germany.

The true equality of the two sides of self-certain Spirit, which is to say, their self-conscious and existent equality, was implicitly present in the acknowledgment of action and its subsequent deeds of annihilation, 'the breaking of the hard heart and raising it to Universality' (*PhG* 470:407).

Accordingly, both the evil inherent in Napoleon's action and the forgiveness or justification of it by Hegel were manifestations of Spirit, the one showing the power of Spirit over actuality, the other showing the power of Spirit over its determinate Concept.

For his part, Hegel renounced hard-heartedness because he had in fact recognized himself in Napoleon's action. In this way he turned his back on his own immediate actuality, renounced himself as a particular consciousness, and showed himself to be superseded Particularity. Or, in other words, Hegel had, in recognizing Napoleon, also transformed himself into a moment of Spirit, the conceptual moment, as it happened. 'He turns from his external actuality back into his own essential-reality; thus does the universal Consciousness [Napoleon's] know itself there [i.e. in its essential-reality, Hegel's conceptual account]' (PhG 471:470). In Kojève's words, Hegel revealed Napoleon to Germany by recognizing him in this way. 'He believed he could save Germany (by way of the *Phenomenology*), and preserve it in a superseded form (*aufgehoben*) within the midst of the Napoleonic Empire' (IH 153). When Hegel extended his justification, *Verzeihung*, to Napoleon, he put aside his own self as of no account, which was only proper since Hegel had now identified himself with the actual action, *wirkliches Handeln*, of Napoleon. This meant that what was thought to be evil, namely action, was now recognized as good. Or rather, Hegel abandoned private moralizing judgments altogether in the same way as Napoleon abandoned private action. Napoleon was revealed by Hegel to be beyond good and evil in that his actions were not his own only, but were also universal actions, manifestations of the power of Spirit over actuality.

Hegel described this remarkable achievement as follows: 'The word of reconciliation is the empirically existent Spirit, *der daseiende Geist*, which recognizes the pure knowledge of itself as universal essential-reality in its opposite, in the pure knowledge of itself as absolute and self-contained Individuality, – a mutual recognition that is absolute Spirit' (PhG 471: 408). In translation, Hegel's *Phenomenology* was the actualization of Spirit speaking its word of reconciliation and thereby justifying Napoleon's actions or, to use religious representational language, forgiving his sins. It did so by recognizing Napoleon's significance, namely universal essential reality, self-contained Individuality, or, in religious language, his perfectedness. But this universality and so on were also Hegel's insofar as he was also the manifestation of the power of Spirit over its determinate Concept.

The actualization of absolute Spirit occurred, Hegel continued, only when its pure knowledge of itself was also an opposition, *Gegensatz*, between absolute Individuality or Napoleonic existence[6] and absolute knowledge of itself as essential reality or Wisdom. Both manifestations were necessary and both were Spirit certain of itself, its purpose, and its own reality and empirical existence. They were, therefore, different not simply as the distinct persons, Hegel and Napoleon, but absolutely, since the elaboration of their difference was undertaken conceptually. Yet it was precisely because of their opposition that reconciliation was possible – if there were no opposition, there would be nothing to reconcile. Each self-certain manifestation of the power of Spirit was, in itself, Universal even though it was determinate and so Particular with respect to the other. Together 'they fill out the whole range of the self' as the inner and outer aspects of absolute Spirit even while remaining for one another as absolute opposition. More precisely, what was completely inner, namely the genesis of Spirit that had been philosophy and now was manifest as Wisdom, came into empirical existence by being opposed to what was completely outer, namely the genesis of Spirit that had been the fights and labours of History and now was manifest as Individuality. Because Hegel and Napoleon were opposed as individuals bearing the two significations of Spirit indicated in the preceding sentence, their opposition took the form of Consciousness. When, however, Knowledge of externality had returned to itself, that is, when Hegel had justified Napoleon, when Wisdom had accounted for Individuality, when Man had become fully and completely understood – all these phrases being rigorously equivalent – then knowledge would return to itself and the form of Consciousness would be superseded as Self-Consciousness or, rather, Self-knowledge. In justifying Napoleon, Hegel had relinquished his distinctive selfhood and gained 'universal knowledge of himself in his absolute opposite.' This reconciling 'yes,' which justified Napoleon and through him all History, was, Hegel said, 'the empirical existence of the Ego that has expanded into a duality, *Zweiheit*; this Ego remains there [i.e. as *Zweiheit*] identical with itself and, in its complete externalization, *Entausserung*, and alterity, *Gegenteile*, possesses certainty of itself; – it is the manifest God in the midst of those who know themselves as pure knowing' (*PhG* 472:409). Hegel's empirical existence had expanded, through his identification with, or justification of, Napoleon, into a *Zweiheit*, a two-in-one. Because of who Napoleon was, namely the realizer of the French Revolution, the actualization of the end of History, etc., Hegel's justification was the manifestation of God to the Sage. Or, as Kojève indicated earlier, Hegel had become Christ inasmuch as what was meant by 'God' was Wisdom, and what 'those who know themselves as pure knowing' actually knew was, precisely, Wisdom. Thus 'God' knew himself as Wisdom in the thought of the Sage, Hegel.

According to Kojève's lectures of 1936–7 (*IH* 153–4), the Hegel-Napoleon pair was, in fact, a dualism. On the one side was the universal action of Napoleon, on the other the absolute knowledge or Wisdom of Hegel.

There is *Bewusstsein* [Consciousness] on the one side and on the other *Selbstbewusstsein* [Self-consciousness]. Napoleon is turned towards the external (social and natural) World: he understands it since he is successful in his action. But he does not understand himself (he does not know he *is* God). Hegel is turned towards Napoleon: but Napoleon is a Man, that is, the 'perfect' Man in virtue of his total integration of History; to understand him is to understand Man, to understand oneself. By understanding (= justifying) Napoleon, Hegel thereby completes (*parachève*) his own *Self*-consciousness. In this way he becomes a Sage, a 'completed' (*accompli*) philo-sopher. If Napoleon is the revealed God (*der erscheinende Gott*), it is nevertheless Hegel who reveals him. Absolute Spirit = plenitude of *Bewusstsein* and of *Selbstbewusstsein*, that is, the real (natural) World that implies the universal and homogeneous State, realized by Napoleon and revealed by Hegel.

However: Hegel and Napoleon are two different men; *Bewusstsein* and *Selbstbewusstsein* are therefore still separated. Now, Hegel does not like dualism. Is not this final dyad to be suppressed?

This could have happened (and yet!) if Napoleon 'recognized' Hegel as Hegel 'recognized' Napoleon. Was Hegel waiting (1806) to be called to Paris by Napoleon in order to become the Philosopher (the Sage) of the universal and homogeneous State, whose duty would be to explain (justify) – and perhaps direct – Napoleon's activities?

Ever since Plato the great philosophers have been tempted in this way. But the text of the Phenomenology dealing with this point is (deliberately?) obscure.

In any case, History is ended.

There were several difficulties with Kojève's interpretation. First there was the letter to Niethammer, quoted earlier, where Hegel prided himself on having predicted the whole upheaval. Likewise, in an earlier letter, 11 April 1814, he said that the greatest tragedy there was was to watch the immense spectacle of an enormous genius destroying himself. It may be objected that these were written in 1814, not 1806, and that in 1806 Hegel may well have expected to be called to Paris. Perhaps.

Second, in terms of the dialectic of absolute Spirit, which we have just traced, the man of action had already effectively recognized the power of Spirit over its determinate Concept in his acknowledgment that action involved evil. Only when this gesture of comity was refused by the Romantic moralist was it necessary to break his hard heart. Hegel's task in this connection was merely to explain what Napoleon already sensed, that Universalist morality was empty and that, in effect, Napoleon was indeed beyond good and evil.

Third, one can point to Hegel's lectures on the history of philosophy for evidence that he did not share Plato's 'temptation.' There he remarked that the particular individual could not realize his ideal for a state and that Plato was essentially a utopian who made an especially inept choice in Dionysius.

Whatever the weight of these objections – and one cannot insist that they are unanswerable – it seems clear that certain ambiguities are here present. Kojève's tentativeness was enough evidence for that. Two years later, in his lectures for the academic year 1938–9, this evident problem had been cleared away, as we shall see in the next chapter.[7]

The argument of this chapter presented a rather contentious line of interpretation of Hegel's texts. The reasons for the controversy and its political significance are apparent to any but the dullest observers. It is equally apparent that, ex hypothesi, I have accepted Kojève's interpretation. In terms of the interpretative strategy outlined in chapter 1 of this book, it ought be clear that the accuracy of Kojève's contention that Hegel was an atheist, that, in effect, to be a Sage one must be an atheist, hardly makes much difference. What Hegel 'really' believed is a matter of biographical contingency, a relatively trivial historical fact. Of great significance, however, is the place of atheism in the modern post-historical world. In this regard, the argument of the chapter has endeavoured to account for the origin, growth, and transformation of religion and philosophical ideologies that were tied to religion. In Hegelian or Kojèvian terms, it was a conceptual presentation the purpose of which was to demonstrate concretely that the alterity of religious re-presentation has been left behind for good.

This was true first of all for the texts and writers Hegel examined. 'The Romantic poets, Schelling, Jacobi, Kant himself, in fact divinized man. For them, man is the supreme value, is absolutely autonomous, etc.: they are, in fact, atheists. In the same way, the Protestant theology of a

Schleiermacher is also already an atheism: God, for Schleiermacher, has a meaning and a reality only to the extent he is revealed in and by man; religion is reduced to religious *psychology*; etc.' (*IH* 211). The moral discourse of German philosophy was very close to Hegelian Wisdom. It was, if you like, unconscious Wisdom. The German philosophers and poets and theologians were speaking about real, conscious mankind alive in the World, though they thought they were talking about some ideal or other in terms of which 'this' world might be judged.

The different judgments of Hegel and the rest simply served to delay the process by which Spirit came to know itself by finally and definitively superseding the last dualism. Unlike the preceding dialectics however, the development of Spirit now was absolute. Once the absoluteness appeared to Consciousness there were no more alibis available, no more heavens to flee toward, no more transcendent excuses. The World, or more precisely, that part of the World that counted historically, namely Revolutionary France, was to be understood, not judged. To the moralizing Romantic (or any of his predecessors), *tout comprendre, c'est tout pardonner*; to Hegel, however, the pardon was merely its moral appearance: what counted was the understanding and the conceptual account of it. When Spirit had become absolute, the conceptual form it took was absolute knowledge, the contents of which were found in chapter 8 of *Phenomenology*, to which we now turn.

6

The post-historical attitude

The final chapter of Hegel's *Phenomenology*, a mere fifteen pages, was titled 'Absolute Knowledge,' *das absolute Wissen*. Formally it was a retrospective summary of the account of the appearance of Spirit contained in the preceding five hundred or so pages. It was to serve as an introduction to the second part of the System of Science, *Logic*, and was written, as were the preface and several interlarded 'notes,' from the 'perspective' of the Sage. Moreover, it was, in addition to being a formal retrospective, an account of absolute knowledge. The topic, then, was no longer what had been done historically or what philosophers had made of this doing but rather what the Sage made of the philosophers. Of course, this had been brought up intermittently in the various 'notes' that described to 'us' Hegelian Sages what something or other signified 'in itself.' Now, however, the topic was simply truth, knowledge, etc., in itself, that is, as it is from the 'perspective' of the Sage, not as it had appeared to historical consciousness.

There exists a great deal of scholarly controversy centred upon the relationship of *Phenomenology* to the System.[1] In part this stemmed from certain ambiguities and inconsistencies in Hegel's own descriptions. But in part as well it came from the nature of the claim, made in the preface to *Phenomenology*, that its author sought to abandon philosophy as love of Wisdom that it might become actual Wisdom (*PhG* 12:3). In chapter 8 that Wisdom was set forth, and it was intended to be distinct from mere love of Wisdom. In other words, Hegel promised in the preface to transform a Philosopher into a Sage; and in the last chapter he set out to describe the attitude of the Sage. Kojève's contribution to this controversy consisted of six lectures – one-half of the course offering of the 1938–9 academic year – devoted to two topics, first, Philosophy and Wisdom, and, second, Eternity, Time, and the Concept. We shall not consider his discussion of these questions in detail because their theoretical significance was primarily a defence of Kojève's hermeneutic, the soundness of which we have been assuming. We would, however, look at the results.

The Philosopher and the Sage

'All philosophers,' according to Kojève, were agreed on the definition of a Sage even if they were not agreed on the question of whether a Sage could exist actually in the World. A Sage, then, was 'the man capable of answering in a comprehensible, that is, satisfactory way all questions that may be asked of him on the subject of his own acts, and answering in such a manner that the entirety of his answers forms a coherent discourse. Or again, what amounts to the same thing, the Sage is the fully and perfectly self-concious man' (IH 271:75–6). The Sage, in short, could answer, at least in principle, all questions. They might concern God, death, evil, the nature of the soul, or angels, or any other metaphysical or theological topic; or they might concern the construction of the DEW line, the chemistry of DNA, the value of the Swiss franc, the song of the humpback whale, or any other historical or technical or scientific topic. To be able to answer all questions would be to have, in the full sense of the term, an encyclopaedic or universal Knowledge. This Knowledge would include oneself, which was why the Sage must be perfectly or fully self-conscious. Kojève provided a witty elaboration of this definition, the practical import of which was the observation, obvious to anyone who ever opened Phenomenology, that it was not written for just anyone. In other words, Hegel's promise, to transform a Philosopher into a Sage, might well be indifferently received by those who have no concern for philosophy. Or, in still other words, it might well be true that the Sage is perfectly self-conscious; it might even be true that Hegel (or Kojève, or anyone else) was a Sage; but it was also true that some (or many, or perhaps most) people could not care less. Eventually, as we shall see, these indifferent ones would be made to care. For the moment we need observe only that Phenomenology was addressed to those who, for one reason or another, happened to desire full and perfect Self-consciousness. These people were, according to Kojève, philosophers.

Philosophers may be distinguished from Sages in three ways. First, 'if Wisdom is the art of answering every question that can be asked on the subject of human existence, Philosophy is the art of asking them' (IH, 280:86). A corollary is that eventually the Philosopher would ask a question that he could not answer coherently, or in a manner consistent with the rest of his discourse. Second, if the Sage was satisfied by that of which he became conscious in himself, namely (his) Wisdom, the Philosopher was dis-satisfied by that of which he became conscious in himself, namely (his) lack of Wisdom. The corollary here was that the Sage, being satisfied by what he was, did not desire to change what he was, whereas the Philosopher consciously wanted to be other than he was because he did not know what it was to be satisfied by what is. Furthermore, since self-consciousness was expressed as discourse, and since the kind of discourse that instigated change by posing questions was called dialectic, every Philosopher was a dialectician. A Sage, in contrast, was not. He was, according to Kojève, a phenomenologist and perhaps, eventually, a logician. Third, the Sage was the model or paradigm for himself, being fully and perfectly self-conscious, and also the model for the Philosopher, being what the Philosopher desired but was not, whereas the Philosopher was a negative model for both, one who 'reveals his existence only to show the necessity of not being as he is, to show that man wishes not to be a Philosopher but a Sage' (*IH* 281:87).

The conclusion to be drawn from this set of distinctions was that philosophical discourse was dialectical in that it expressed the Philosopher's movement or progress toward Wisdom. The Philosopher, in short, knew what he ought not to be, namely what he was, a dissatisfied un-wise man; and he knew what he ought to be or what he desired to become, namely a Sage. If somebody picked up *Phenomenology* and read it, Kojève said, he showed he was interested in philosophy; if he understood it, and learned more of himself, that is, if his Self-consciousness increased, he showed he was a philosopher, that is a person who wished to be a Sage, perfectly self-conscious and satisfied, a model for all Philosophers.

The whole question, then, was to know whether it was utter foolishness on the Philosopher's part to think he may become, actually, a Sage. Hegel, we know, claimed he was a Sage; following Plato, other Philosophers claimed that this was impossible. As a practical matter, the question, from Hegel's 'perspective' at least, was a matter of fact. Even so, there did exist an argument between the two. According to Kojève, two questions were involved. First, what did it mean to accept the ideal of Wisdom but deny it could be actualized? Second, what did Hegel mean by saying he was a Sage?

Granting the proposition that 'all philosophers' were agreed on the definition of a Sage, if nevertheless some philosophers denied that any person could actually be a Sage, this could mean only two things. Either these people, wanting to be what they knew they could not ever be, were crazy, or they were mistaken. Granting that the 'divine madness' of the philosopher, which appeared as the most stern sobriety, was different from the frenzied madness of chasing rainbows, we must conclude that the Philosophers may simply have been in error. Errors, however, may be corrected. Or, in other words, what once was a truthful statement may become incorrect, and then this error may be made right. For example, in 1930 it was true to say that one could not go from New York to London in six hours. It is not true today even if it may be true a century hence. That is, to repeat the true statement of 1930 today would be to make a mistake, which may be corrected (cf *IH* 464:188). This is a trivial example, one may object. Travel between New York and London depends upon new physical techniques and inventions, and these have nothing to do with the metaphysical topic under discussion. Kojève (and Hegel) insisted, however, that the question of the wrong opinion of some philosophers concerning the actualization of Wisdom was formally identical with this trivial example.

In the first place, these philosophers who were in error did not simply deny the reality of Wisdom, they denied that it could be realized by man, living and dying 'in' time. But they immediately added that another sort of being that neither lived nor died as humans did and who was, therefore, 'outside' time may quite well be wise. Indeed, most of these philosophers insisted that this being, God, was wise. 'Outside' time, God was what he was, without change, identical with himself. 'In' time, the philosopher (and the World) changed. Now, if truth was what was unchanging, one might say that the discourse of these philosophers aimed at revealing God, the unchanging one. Accordingly, Wisdom would not be self-knowledge but knowledge of God, which meant that the opposition between philosophers of a Platonic tenor and those of a Hegelian tenor did not really occur within Philosophy but as between Philosophy and Theology. The analogy with travel between New York and London was quite clear: it had been at one time true that man could not be wise, but it was no longer true. To repeat an absolete statement would be an error, but one that could be corrected by human action, just as human action between 1930 and the present was needed to make true the proposition about travel.

The opposition between Philosophy and Theology or, more precisely, between Wisdom and Religion was described in several ways. For the Philosopher the attainment of Wisdom, which was knowledge of himself, was a lengthy and continuous process of dialectical pedagogy and

Bildung. For the Theologian, the attainment of Wisdom, which was Knowledge of God, was sudden and abrupt and was conditioned in part at least from an external element revealing itself. For the Philosopher, the totality of Knowledge was a discourse that excluded nothing. For the Theologian, the totality of Knowledge was not such a discourse because it necessarily excluded giving an account of God and had to rely on representation, myth, ritual, etc to articulate or, more precisely, to represent the divine presence. Not only was the method of gaining Wisdom and the expression of it once gained different for the two types, but their relationship to the world was also distinct. For the Philosopher, the discourse of Wisdom revealed only man and his world. When the Philosopher transformed himself into a Sage his discourse would reveal a reality and not an ideal. This was possible only after all ideals had been transformed into worldly realities. Or, to use Kojève's shorthand symbolism, the historical, actual, worldly reality that transformed the universal, total, and circular Knowledge of the Sage into a homogenous truth, that is, a truth revealed, in principle, to everybody, was the universal and homogeneous State, which came into existence at the end of history. For the religious person, there was revealed not simply the truth of man and world but also of divine presence, which, incidentally, made the world God's not man's. Consequently, for the religious person, the universal reality that transformed his Knowledge (or rather, his faith in God's Knowledge) into a homogeneous truth also revealed, in principle, to everybody, was God. And since God did not come into actual existence 'at' any time, he was free to reveal himself at any time, anywhere, to anybody. Likewise the religious person could express his faith in God's absolute Knowledge anywhere at any time (*IH* 284–5:89–91).

It did not follow from this presentation of differences that the Philosopher could refute the Theologian (or the Sage refute the religious person). He could show that the religious person was unhappy, but the religious person could reply that life was a vale of tears, etc. The religious person could remain 'satisfied' by unhappiness for the following reason: the appeal (or request or demand) by the Sage that the religious person extend his own Knowledge further, become more fully self-conscious, and in this way understand and begin to overcome his unhappiness, may easily appear to him as the ultimate impiety, deicide.

The author of *Phenomenology* was addressing only those persons who happened to wish to become self-conscious, to know themselves, to know what they were. Moreover, the book was about that person, how he tended increasingly to approximate full and complete Self-conscious ness, which was Self-knowledge, Wisdom. As did all Philosophers, he began by asking the question, 'What am I?' But he eventually answered not 'I am a Philosopher' but 'I am a Sage.' Now, since he gave that answer on the basis of reading Hegel's book, the proof that Wisdom could be actual and Worldly must be found in his answering 'I am a Sage.' The actual existence of the Sage, then, was the living proof that Philosopher-Theologians of the Platonic kind were, at present, wrong (even though they were once correct). Thus, for Hegel and for Hegelians, the discourse given in and by *Phenomenology* constituted a factual refutation of the Platonic Philosopher-Theologian.

The danger involved in such refutation was that it seemed indistinguishable from what Hegel called modern subjectivity. Like the unreconstructed Masters, the refutation of recalcitrant Philosopher-Theologians may end up being left to the guillotine. Possibly in anticipation of some such objection, in 1937–8 Kojève reformulated his commentary on *Phenomenology* in terms of a series of premises. 'There is no human existence without consciousness nor without self-consciousness, that is, without the revelation of Being by speech or without the Desire that reveals and creates the Ego. That is why, inside the *PhG*, ... in the elementary possibility of the *revelation* of given-Being by speech (implied in [the attitude of] 'Sensual Certainty') on the one hand, and on the other, Action (which is born from and by way of Desire) destroying or negating given-Being, are two irreducible givens that the *PhG* presupposes as premises' (*IH* 167–8:39). The premise of immediate concern was that speech reveals given-Being, for upon it depended the notion of Wisdom as complete speech revealing the whole of Being (or, simply, the Whole).

Hegel described his premise as follows: 'In my opinion, which can be justified only through the exposition of the System itself, everything depends on this, that one expresses and understands the True not just as Substance but also and equally as Subject' (*PhG* 19:9–10). By implication, all pre-Hegelian philosophy exclusively identified the True with Substance, the unchanging object of discourse, while forgetting that the subject who articulated the discourse was equally primordial. In contrast, Hegel argued that not only was philosophy a truth, that is, a true description, or a revelation of Being and Reality through Discourse, but it was also a description of the True, that is, Being-revealed-through-Discourse, or revealed-Being, which implied an account of the revelation of Being through Discourse. If the Sage was to describe totality, then, he must speak not only of what was given, namely Substance, but also of himself as he was speaking of given-Being or Substance and insofar as he was speaking of himself, a subject (who is speaking of Substance). As Kojève remarked, philosophy must explain how and why Being was realized not simply as Nature, Substance, given-Being, but also as History and Subject. It must be just as much anthropology as natural philosophy (*IH* 529–30). The Sage, Hegel himself, served as an icon of Wisdom. Like any guide who ushered neophytes into the presence of the True, Hegel must have already made the journey. But had he? Was it a fact that Hegel was Wise? Or, to put the matter less abruptly, how could one know that Hegel's discourse was, literally, encyclopaedic?

Criteria for Wisdom

In the preceding section it was argued that to accept the ideal of Wisdom by denying the possibility of actualizing it meant that, in the end, one was a Theologian rather than a Philosopher. Now we turn to the second question: What does it mean to say that Hegel was a Sage? It is assumed at the outset that 'all Philosophers,' in the Kojèvian sense indicated above, were agreed that Wisdom was complete discourse, the total answer to all possible questions. What they were not agreed upon were the criteria by which one could know that a total answer had been given and no further questions were conceivable. Hegel provided these criteria, and, according to Kojève, this exhausted his originality. 'Hegel is, I believe, the first to have found *an* answer (I do not say *the* answer) to the question of knowing if the understanding one has of *oneself* and consequently one's understanding in *general* is or is not *total, unsurpassable* and *unable to be modified*, that is, *universally* and *definitively* valuable or *absolutely* true. This answer is given, according to him, by the circularity of understanding or knowledge. The "absolute Knowledge" of the Sage is *circular* and *all* circular Knowledge (only one such Knowledge is possible anyhow) is the "absolute Knowledge" of the Sage' (*IH* 287:94). This was a surprising answer for two reasons. First, it simply made explicit what was already presupposed in the definition of the Sage. Second, it was circular, and one may assume that 'all philosophers' were familiar with the inadequacy of circular arguments, that is, arguments that proved as conclusions what they assumed as premises. Now, Hegel and Kojève knew of vicious circles and of consistent paranoia. But those kinds of circularity could be modified and surpassed by sane persons who asked questions, that is, by dialectical discourse. With consistent insanity, it was clear that the circular discourse of the mad person was not total or all-encompassing: it could, after all, be modified. The mad could become sane. (But also, the sane could go mad.)

Several things followed from the criterion of comprehensive circularity. First, unlike the arguments of deductive reason, there were no axioms or principles properly speaking. That is, the discourse itself was based upon no Knowledge outside itself. This meant that Hegelianism apparently avoided the arbitrariness of non-deducible axioms or principles. In Kojève's words, 'Absolute Philosophy [i.e. Wisdom] has, so to speak, no object; or rather, it is itself its own proper subject ... Absolute Philosophy has no object that might be external to itself' (IH 38). Now philosophy, the coherent speeches of the paradigmatic Slaves, we know, revealed the several worlds the Slaves had formed, including the attitudes of human beings to those worlds. If Phenomenology were indeed absolute, it would 'consider all possible philosophical attitudes as existential attitudes,' each of which was a true description and expression or genuine Weltanschauung of its own particular historical world, but none of which was the True. Each 'is true qua a "moment" of absolute Philosophy' (IH 39). Since there could be but one all-encompassing absolute circular discourse, which was Wisdom, there could be no modification of that discourse once it had been generated, though it could be repeated indefinitely (IH 480:206). Wisdom, in other words, was a singular discourse that included all historical philosophies as its own elements and co-ordinated them as the total revelation of Being.

The necessary circularity of the True could be seen as well by its double purpose. On the one hand, it described the origin of Discourse (i.e. Man, Subject) in the midst of Being (i.e. Nature, Substance) and its evolution to produce Man revealing the Totality of Being by means of Discourse; on the other hand, it was itself this Discourse revealing the Totality, which in turn implied the Discourse that revealed it and so as well the process by which this final Discourse became what it was. In other words, 'just as the Totality it describes, absolute philosophy [i.e. Wisdom], cannot be objectively realized except in and through its "development," that is, as the entirety of its circular discourse forming an indivisible whole that reproduces the closed dialectic of reality. This circularity of [absolute] philosophical discourse [i.e. Wisdom] guarantees its unsurpassable and immodifiable totality, and thus, its absolute truth' (IH 532).

The criteria for Wisdom as explained so far were purely formal. It would perhaps be more precise to say that they referred only to the individual existence of the Sage, Hegel. It may be that Hegel was wise, one might say, just as Jesus may well have been the Son of God. But it was also clear that nothing could be gained with a 'search for the historical Hegel.' That is, from the visible icon we are referred to the logical icon, to Hegel's book. The contingent biographical details of the author mattered far less than the truth of Spirit that his discourse revealed. But the Book, Hegel's *Phenomenology* was written to reveal what is, so that we are directed away from the logical icon and back to the World, specifically the post-historical World of the universal and homogeneous State.

The structure of the argument here was familiar. The ontological ground of a subject was Negativity that appeared as Action that realized a product. The Slave spoke of his own deeds, that is, his transformations of and within given-Being and formed ideas or ideals of what to do or become next. These speeches by self-conscious Slaves were philosophical to the extent they were coherent revelations of the World the Slaves had made. There have been a succession of philosophies just as there have been a succession of Worlds resulting from the Slave's transformations of given-Being. Or, more simply, the Slave's (philosophical) speech was a 'superstructure,' or *Weltanschauung*, or even ideology, and the World was a 'base.' Negativity split Being into Subject and Object, which appeared as Man opposed to Nature; but this same Negativity, which resulted in a product, realized by human activity in the midst of Nature, restored Subject and Object to unity insofar as Discourse was identical with the product it revealed. The True or revealed-Being was, therefore, a product, a result of a lengthy process that began with the opposition of Man and Nature. The progressive transformation of the World, which overcame the opposition between Man and Nature, was accompanied by a corresponding expansion of self-consciousness. Non-philosophers took their bearings in the world by the speeches of those who wished to understand it and themselves, while philosophers took their bearings by the ideal, as it then was, of complete, discursive, comprehensive knowledge, or Wisdom.

Wisdom re-established Unity, which existed initially as the contemplative 'absorption' of the Subject by Substance, by means of an adequate description of Totality. The author of this description, the Sage, ceased to oppose himself, as Subject, to Nature, as Substance. But since Totality implied human Being, which appeared as creative action, the final and adequate Unity of Being (Substance) and Discourse (Subject) could occur only when human Action, and therefore History, had ceased.

In other words, Wisdom, which Hegel claimed to have achieved, had as its concrete (and not definitional) criterion the individual existence of the Sage who could exist only at the end of History, that is, in the universal and homogeneous State. Bringing the definitional, abstract criterion together with the concrete one we get the following result: 'in the absolute Knowledge of the Sage, each question is its own answer; but it is so only by passing by way of the totality of questions-answers that form the entirety of the System. Similarly, in his existence, the Sage remains in identity with himself because he passes by way of the totality of others, and is enclosed within himself; but he remains in identity with himself because he passes by way of the totality of others and is enclosed within himself because he encloses the totality of others in himself' (*IH* 288: 94–5). Bringing these two criteria together meant, very simply, that only a Citizen of the universal and homogeneous State could be a Sage. Only in this non-expandable and non-transformable State could a single person exist through and for all others; only if a person did synthesize Universality and Particularity in that way could he actually reveal that Synthesis in his discourse.

Formally, therefore, Wisdom could be actualized only at the end of History, when there was nothing further to change or to be changed. Or, putting it the other way around, when everything was known, there was no further philosophical pedagogy to undertake, and so no change. Materially this could occur only when the universal and homogeneous State actually existed as the basis or infrastructure of Wisdom. In Kojève's words, 'the Citizen of this State actualizes as active Citizen the circularity he reveals, as a contemplative Sage, by his System' (*IH* 289:96). In *Phenomenology* Hegel described this state, and 'it is enough for the reader to observe historical reality to see that this State is real, or at least to convince himself of its imminent realization' (*IH* 289:96). The necessary circularity, in short, was shown by the argument of *Phenomenology* itself.

This result, however, was not altogether satisfactory. Supposing the reader did observe historical reality but did not see that this State was either real or likely? Did this not give him grounds to dismiss Hegel's claim to be a Sage as being simply impossible? Kojève had several theoretical replies to make to this objection. The practical implications will be discussed below.

First, he said, it was not necessary that the universal and homogeneous State be established as a kind of ecumenical government, actually realized 'in all its perfection.' Writing in 1806 and observing the Napoleonic Empire, Hegel did not assert anything more than 'that the germ of this State was present in the World and that the necessary and sufficient conditions were in existence.'

Second, even if we argued that Hegel's observations and assertions of 1806 were unsound and have not been confirmed since, that did not allow us to conclude that the universal and homogeneous State was impossible in principle. And if it were possible of actualization, so too was Wisdom. At the very least, therefore, if Wisdom were possible, we know with the utmost certainty that there was no reason to abandon efforts to search for it and endeavour to actualize it. That is, there was no reason to abandon atheistic philosophy for religion.

Third, supposing that the universal and homogeneous State were not actualized, even as a germ, that Hegel's atheist anthropology were not a truth since it did not reveal a reality, this did not mean that his entire enterprise was an error. It was impossible to prove, Kojève argued, that the State he had in mind and, with it, the actualization of Wisdom were utterly and completely impossible, because no assertion of this kind could ever be proved. 'Now what is neither an error nor a truth is an idea, or if one prefers, an ideal. This idea can be transformed into a truth only by negating action that, by destroying the World that does not correspond to the idea, will create, by this same destruction, the World conforming to the ideal.' The importance of historical evidence to support Hegel's claims therefore sank into insignificance, as Kojève readily admitted in the sentence following the one just quoted. One could accept Hegel's anthropology and the State and Wisdom it implied, Kojève said, even knowing the Sage did not (yet) exist, 'on condition of wishing to act with a view to the realization of the Hegelian State that is indispensable for the existence of this man: to act, or at least to accept and "justify" such an action, if it is done by somebody, somewhere' (*IH* 290–1:97–8). If one accepted Hegel's teaching, it was not on the basis of historical evidence, which Kojève admitted was, or may be seen to be, ambiguous. On the contrary, it would be accepted on the basis of its comprehensive circularity.

We may see this in another way. Suppose the reader did observe historical reality and saw the truth of the assertion that the Napoleonic Empire was the germ of the universal and homogeneous State. And suppose as well that the reader was of the opinion that such a State was a bad thing. What then? Such a reader would be asked for the grounds of his opinion and the basis for his objection to the advent of this State. If Hegel's System were comprehensive and circular, any conceivable objection would already have been contained and met within it. The logic of this reply, at least, was impeccable. And, in fact, the options Hegel presented were stark in their simplicity.

The introduction to 'Absolute Knowledge'

In chapter 8 of *Phenomenology* Hegel explained his criterion of circularity in some detail. This chapter followed immediately upon Hegel's discussion of Religion, which implied that there were but two options: absolute Knowledge was either Knowledge of self or Knowledge of God. In both cases the contents, being absolute, total, etc, were the same. The only difference was one of form. For the religious person, absolute Knowledge could come to him only by way of an absolute Other, God. For the Sage, everything that the religious person subordinated to God he related to himself really as a Citizen of the universal and homogeneous State and ideally as the possessor of absolute Knowledge. The third way, namely pagan philosophy, which affirmed truth to lie in nature, especially the circular motion of the heavens, had been rendered impossible or obsolete by the labours of the Slave that had transformed the autonomy of nature. The import of technical transformations, to repeat a point made earlier, was not that the existence of 'nature worship' had been made impossible but that it had been made senseless or irrational. But nothing prevented human beings from being irrational.

With the pagan way effectively closed, then, one must be either a Christian or a Hegelian. Kojève's formulation was a veritable parody of St Augustine: 'There is no possible transition since there is nothing between them. To be in the one [attitude] is to decide against the other; to reject the one is to establish oneself in the other. The decision is absolutely unique; and is as simple as possible: what is involved is to decide for one's self (that is, against God) or for God (that is, against oneself). And there is no "reason" for the decision other than decision itself' (*IH* 293). One should add that similar decisions arose at earlier stages in *Phenomenology*, but at no point could the existence of a decision be considered a defect in the argument or a criticism of it. Consciousness could expand no other way. At the end of chapter 4, for example, there was no 'reason' for the religious person to turn into an Intellectual, just as at the end of chapter 5 there was no 'reason' for the Intellectual to turn into a Citizen – none, that is, until he actually did become an Intellectual or a Citizen. The same process of self-choosing obtained, Kojève said, in the move from the religious attitude of chapter 7 to the attitude of the Sage in chapter 8. Moreover, this 'undeducibility,' this impossibility of foreseeing the necessity of the transformations of consciousness, had been present from the beginning. In the paradigmatic primordial fight, there was no way to deduce beforehand whether any one or which one of the self-certain proto-human animals would choose to submit to the Desire of the other.

According to Kojève, chapter 8 was divided into a short introduction and three sections. The introduction began by summarizing chapter 7: Christianity was the absolute religion and the Christian theologian the highest form of consciousness. 'All that now remains to be done is the supersession, *Aufheben*, of this mere form [of representation, *Vorstellung*]. Or rather, since this [form] belongs properly to Consciousness as such, the truth of this form must already have been present in the shapes that Consciousness has already assumed [in the course of *Phenomenology*]' (*PhG* 549:479). The meaning of the first sentence was clear enough: Christian Consciousness must be transformed into Hegelian Self-consciousness. The second sentence explained how. Consciousness had already appeared in a post-Christian form; specifically, at the end of chapter 6, Hegel described Napoleon, the Napoleonic Citizen, and himself as the revealed truth of theological discourse. At the same time he showed the utter emptiness of the idea of God that the theologian mistakenly considered to be revealed truth. Looking back, one could see both the actual truth of Christianity in its Hegelianized, scientific, and actual form as well as the fraudulent vacuity of ordinary so-called theology. This retrospective glance showed consciousness where, in fact, it had come to; what, in fact, it had become; and so what it truly was.

The second part of the introduction described the real, existential conditions of absolute knowledge. The process by which the objects of Consciousness had been overcome, *diese Überwindung des Gegenstandes des Bewusstseins*, throughout *Phenomenology* was not, Hegel said, a subjectivism of any kind. Rather the object had become manifest to consciousness as 'a vanishing presentation,' *als verschwindend darstellte*. It had been overcome dialectically and had been preserved even while vanishing. Christian theology, for example, was the theology of the dead God, considered as a God. It was, therefore, a symbolic or unconscious atheism. Wisdom, therefore, must involve the self-suppression of Christianity but in such a way that the death of God was preserved, namely in the self-conscious atheism of Hegel. A similar procedure was required for the natural and social worlds. In general one may say that Wisdom presupposed the total success of the negating action of men. Socially this implied the universal and homogeneous State where no person was external to any other and that consequently there was no social opposition left to be negated. With regard to nature, this meant that nature had been tamed by the labour of human beings so that it no longer was opposed to him. Nature and nature's gods (or God) were no longer a source of terror; the natural terror of death was likewise superseded as consciousness of one's mortality. In short, the Sage could legitimately affirm that there was an identity between Being as such and the being he was because he had experienced the supersession of all conflicts between himself and the World (*IH* 301). In short, the Sage understood reality rationally.

Even more important than his Consciousness of the supersession of negativity was the rational understanding that man was indeed the labouring, fighting Citizen of the universal and homogeneous State. 'It is not enough any longer to be the integral Man. It is still necessary to reason about this integral man who one is' (*IH* 302). The purpose of the historical fights and labours that created the post-historical World without negativity was to enable man, in the person of the Sage, to understand it and write a book containing absolute Knowledge. History and the State were necessary for the genesis of Wisdom; but Wisdom was what justified History and the State. 'The State must be homogeneous and universal with a view to the homogeneity and universality of the Knowledge that is developed in it. And the Sage knows it' (*IH* 303). And there must be a State in the first place (and not, for example, a 'permanent Revolution') because Man was a Totality, Synthesis, etc and not *just* Negativity (cf *IH* 504 n1:233 n27).

In the first part of the introduction Hegel spoke about the difference between the religious person and his theological knowledge and the Sage and his anthropological knowledge; in the second part, he spoke of the conditions for absolute Knowledge 'or, if one wishes, of the Sage in his relationship to Wisdom' (*IH* 303). In the third part, which also served as an introduction to the first part of the chapter, Hegel dealt with the relationship of the Sage to the Philosopher, that is, with the development of Wisdom from philosophical knowing.

The dialectic of the Sage and his World described in the first part of the introduction contained, Hegel said, 'the totality of the constituent-elements of Consciousness' (*PhG* 550:479). The Sage, therefore, must integrate within his existence all human existential possibilities. This could be done only when History had been completed; and History was completed only with the appearance of the Sage who integrated the totality of possibilities. So much is obvious. In addition, however, Consciousness must relate itself to the totality of the possibilities of the World by way of the standpoint of these possibilities. This meant that every Citizen of the universal and homogeneous State must be a Sage, at least virtually. Only a philosophically inclined Citizen would be an actual Sage, but every

Citizen would have integrated in himself the totality of History, every Citizen would be post-historical. That the Sage integrated all existential possibilities guaranteed the universality of (his) Wisdom; that all Citizens had, in their actual concrete existence, integrated in themselves the whole of History (even if not in a conceptually articulate scientific form) guaranteed the homogeneity of (his) Wisdom. In other words, anyone could, in principle, become a Sage; anyone who had become a Sage was both loyal and reflective. Wisdom was, therefore, also the highest form of patriotism.

The Sage, we know, was both a self-conscious Citizen and a successful Philosopher. As Citizen, the story of his genesis was found in the fights and labours that constituted History; as Philosopher, it was found in the history of philosophy. To be self-conscious meant to be aware of this double genesis – or, rather, of this single evolution with two complementary aspects. So far in the text of *Phenomenology* it has been the anthropological or existential aspect, not the philosophical one, that has been in focus. The philosophical aspect obviously has not been ignored, but it has been treated implicitly.

But since the Sage, a successful or satisfied Philosopher, had integrated History and the totality of existential possibilities, his philosophical treatment of History necessarily presupposed the existential. Having set forth at great length the existential aspect, we now may summarize the relationship of Consciousness to the totality of determinate possibilities as possibilities of the self, the self who eventually became a Sage. This, Kojève said, meant reading *Phenomenology* under its 'metaphysical' aspect (*IH* 305).

The road to Wisdom

The first section of chapter 8, following the short introduction, dealt with the Philosopher, the second with the Sage, and the third with Wisdom or Science. This first section, therefore, dealt with the road to Wisdom. In the discussion of the introduction to chapter 8, just presented, Hegel summarily described the first seven chapters as dealing with Consciousness. This is rather surprising since the term Self-consciousness appeared as early as chapter 4 of *Phenomenology*. By characterizing all seven chapters as an analysis of Consciousness, Hegel wished to emphasize that, throughout the evolution described there, there had always been present two different, though complementary, aspects. The first was Being understood as Man-in-the-World; the second was Being understood as the

World-wherein-Man-lived. When one read the first seven chapters of *Phenomenology* under the first aspect, that is, as describing how Man understood himself, that is, as a description of human Self-consciousness, one ended up with the anthropological reading as given by Kojève. When one read these same chapters under the second aspect, that is, as ways that Man understood the World or Being in general, as a description of Consciousness, then one obtained a 'metaphysical' interpretation. This is, properly speaking, the topic of *Encyclopaedia* even while it was the goal and purpose of *Phenomenology* to introduce it and bring it to light. In any event, Hegel provided a reprise of the first seven chapters, now considered 'metaphysically' and not phenomenologically.

Considered 'metaphysically,' then, Wisdom revealed both Man and the World, both Self-Consciousness and Consciousness. Phenomenological Consciousness of the World must coincide with phenomenological Consciousness of Self because 'metaphysically' Man implied World, and vice versa. This did not, of course, mean that there could not be a World without man, but that there is not.[2] The coincidence of Consciousness and Self-consciousness meant, Kojève said, that 'one could as well say that it is the World that is revealed by the Sage as say that it is the Sage that is revealed by the World (or more exactly – by his revelation of the World). But it is more correct to say that it is the totality of real Being that is itself revealed to itself and by itself as the absolute "System of Science"' (*IH* 310). To be fully Conscious of the World was to be fully Self-Conscious since the Self was a worldly being. And the Self was a worldly being, we know, from the phenomenological analyses of the first seven chapters.

The 'metaphysical' problem was to account for the coincidence of Consciousness and Self-Consciousness. Before examining Hegel's account, I would indicate what was implied by this coincidence. First, the moment of negation implied by the separation of consciousness and thing, that is, human action, will have to have come to an end. Thus, all possible actions must have been accounted for in the first seven chapters. Second, the Self-consciousness of the Sage must exist within the post-historical regime of the universal and homogeneous State where such negativity as has appeared in human action had no place. Here the Sage could know, in the full sense, what he was because he was all that Man could be (*IH* 309). Third, this coincidence could occur only when Consciousness and Self-consciousness had become total, since if one (and, therefore, the other) were partial, it would be simply a perspective that revealed an aspect or a part of reality. Of course, one would believe that one's perspective or ideology was a total theory or Science but, as Philosopher, one would inevitably betray one's awareness that it was not by eventually speaking of a Being that was other than oneself. In other words, any theory of the World that did not imply all possible theories was *eo ipso* ideological. And ideology in general could be overcome only by integrating all ideologies. But before all ideologies could be integrated they must be described, and this was what Hegel said he had done in the first seven chapters.

If, therefore, one had written those seven chapters, if, indeed, one had read them and understood them in the way they were meant to be understood, then one would have achieved this integration by one's consciousness of what had been said. This assumes, once again, a reader willing to be convinced not only by Hegel's argument but also by Kojève's elaboration of it. We turn, then, to the 'metaphysical' question itself.

An object, *Gegenstand*, Hegel said, is revealed by consciousness. And Consciousness had three aspects: Sensation, Perception, and Understanding. Likewise the object had three corresponding aspects. Corresponding to Sensation was the sheer 'somethingness,' the here-and-now-ness of Being. But Sensation was always integrated within Perception, and Perception was always of something, of a determinate object, not 'objectness.' There was always a relationship between the 'thingness' of a thing and its qualities. In addition, there was a relationship between or among these qualities. Corresponding to Perception, then, was the determinateness of the Being of a thing. But real Consciousness was, in addition to Sensation and Perception, also Understanding. To perceive a table, for example, was not to *perceive* a table but to understand that what one perceived was an actualization of 'the table,' which was understood verbally or conceptually. Now this conceptual table was not confined to the here-and-now, even though the actual word 'table,' which corresponded to the conceptual table, was sensed and perceived in the here-and-now. 'The word-concept is as are things; it too is part of Being. That means that real Being is also, in one of its aspects, – Concept' (*IH* 314). In addition to being what one is here-and-now, in addition to what one is in a specific determination, 'to be' meant to be universal.

There was, therefore, a dialectic among the constituent elements of real existence. Every Consciousness was a Whole formed by the sensation of a Particular, the perception of a Specific, and the understanding of a Universal. The dialectical movement of this Whole may move either by integrating particular sensations by specifying them in perceptions that universalize understanding, or by an insight into universal understanding specified by perception in sensuous particularity.

In abstract isolation, that is, one could conceive of going from the here-and-now sensation to the concept 'table' or vice versa. In reality one must say that Consciousness was the reality that revealed real Being, which was to say that real Being was the Whole formed by this dialectical movement. Granted, then, that Consciousness revealed these three aspects of Being, it also appears that we have just revealed three aspects of Consciousness. That is, Consciousness must understand that it was itself the same Being as its object. In Hegel's words, 'Consciousness must know the object as itself' (PhG 550:480). To do this, one need only discover the integrating unity of the object and see that it coincided with the integrating unity of the three aspects of Consciousness. Consciousness then would know that it was its object in each of its aspects and so, through the dialectic of their interrelationship, that it was their totality or the Whole.

Lest one think Hegel is being completely preposterous, one should recall that Phenomenology was not concerned with the totality of Being, or even with its natural aspect. It was concerned only with Man qua Man, which was a more restricted topic than, for example, the conscious reality of Man discussed in that part of Encyclopaedia entitled 'Philosophy of Spirit.' When, therefore, Consciousness believed it was opposed to an object, Hegel wanted us to understand that, in fact, it was really only opposed to itself as a real Subject. Once Consciousness learned this, the object qua object was superseded. The statement of Hegel quoted in the last paragraph therefore meant that the object that Consciousness was to know as itself was itself. Accordingly, when the self recollected the stages it had already traversed in experience it would understand both that being, in its restricted human aspect, had resolved itself into the self and, conversely, that the self had become one with Being. The self, that is, has become all that Man qua Man could be, and it knows it.

Formally, Hegel's procedure was quite straightforward. If one were to consider the first seven chapters as dealing with Consciousness, all one need do was take the constituent elements of existence as described phenomenologically in part A of the book and see how, beginning in part AA, a specific aspect of Being was revealed. Thus Hegel considered the immediate Being of observant reason, utility, and morality as characteristics of Being. Now, just as the stages of the development of Consciousness contained the prior stages as dialectically overcome or superseded elements within itself, the same was true with regard to the aspects of

Being. With morality, we already know that Consciousness had become certain of itself. Just as Understanding, which concluded part A, served as the integrating unity of the constituent elements of existence, now *Gewissen*, Morality, or Spirit certain of itself, which concluded part BB, became the integrating unity of Self-consciousness as it has been described phenomenologically. Considered 'metaphysically,' then, *Gewissen* was the certainty of Being. In addition, the expression of *Gewissen* was found in discourse (and not ritual, music, etc.), the 'element' of the Concept. That is, Knowledge or Wisdom was nothing if not a discourse that was certain. Consider again the résumé of chapter 8 regarding the phenomenon of religion: whereas the formal 'forgiveness' by Hegel of Napoleon's 'sins,' carried out at the end of chapter 6, was present to Consciousness only as representation, as God forgiving Man's sins, in the element of the Concept, the contents of religion had been grasped as human, not divine.

The last 'metaphysical' level, like the last phenomenological one, integrated all prior aspects of Being. Here, with Christianity, Being was a revealed Totality; but, as Consciousness, this revealed Totality was distinct from the revelation of it. 'Revealed Being is now total, but it is still opposed to the Being that revealed it. And this total Being, which is nevertheless opposed to something, is the transcendent God of Christian Theo-logy. This Theo-logy is by definition the last stage of "Reflection" *on* Spirit. To move beyond this to Science, which *is* revealed Being or Spirit, it is sufficient, therefore, to suppress this element of transcendence. What is involved is to identify oneself with the Christian God; one must know and be able to say that the total Being about which Christian Theology speaks is in reality Man himself speaking of himself' (*IH* 318). In Hegel's words, the contents of religion, which were represented as an other, were now to be understood as the act of the self. In short, Hegel and all competent readers of *Phenomenology* were to understand that the total and infinite Being about which Christian Theology used to speak and identified as God was really oneself.

How, one may ask, was such a thing possible? Because, Hegel said, the Concept integrated all things in such a way that its own content was the activity of the self, namely 'the knowledge of the fact that the action of the self, undertaken within itself, as entire essentially and entire empirical existence, the knowledge of this Subject as Substance and of Substance as this knowledge of the Subject's action' (*PhG* 556:485). This had been shown, Hegel said, in the contents of *Phenomenology* insofar as it collected together the separate constituent elements of Spirit. But it would not be convincing until it had become a discourse, just as the private emotional experience of religion only became convincing when cast in the form of a Theology. The discourse of Spirit, Hegel's *Logic*, could only arise after the collecting of *Phenomenology* had been done. The collecting of *Phenomenology*, however, was sufficient to actualize what had never before existed, the Sage.

The Sage

The 'metaphysical' summary of the first seven chapters had as its purpose the suppression of Philosophy insofar as Philosophy meant reflection on Being (and, in particular, human being) in the form of Consciousness. Henceforth, Knowledge was to be absolute, which is to say there could be no separation of subject and object. Being itself was to be revealed in and by (or as) knowledge or, as Hegel said, as Science. Science, in turn, was revealed within Being as the empirical existence, *Dasein*, of the Sage. One may distinguish, therefore, between Science and the actual person who possesses it. Indeed, the concluding words of the first part of chapter 8 distinguished between knowledge as Concept, *Begriff*, and knowledge as the form of Consciousness, *Gestalt des Bewusstsein* (*PhG* 556:485). Moreover, Hegel said that the form of Consciousness, the Sage, came into existence before the Concept, Science.

Phenomenologically, the Sage was the full realization of Self-consciousness, but 'metaphysically' he still had the form of Consciousness, which is to say that as Sage he was opposed to the world. To overcome this opposition he must undertake the 'metaphysical' summary; after he had done so, knowledge would exist as Science. Recalling the restricted anthropological scope of *Phenomenology*, one could say, 'what exists before this Summary, that is to say, before the *PhG* itself, is the man capable of writing the *PhG*, Hegel as author of the *PhG*; what exists after this Summary, that is to say, after the *PhG*, is the man capable of writing the *Logik*, or more precisely, the man writing this *Logik*, or better still, this *Logik* itself, that is to say, Science' (*IH* 322). The second part of chapter 8 dealt with the man who had written *Phenomenology* and was capable of writing *Logic*.

There were three tightly organized sections to this part of chapter 8. In the first Hegel defined the Concept of the Sage. The opening words of this section referred to the Sage as *diese ... Gestalt des Geistes*, a concrete form of Spirit, whereas the closing words of the previous section referred to a *Gestalt des Bewusstseins*, a form of Consciousness. The change in terminology was significant inasmuch as the activity of the Sage as a form of Consciousness transcended the given-Being of subject and object, which was implied by Consciousness, and produced a reality beyond the difference between subject and object, namely Science, which was objective and universal Being, revealed in its real Totality. 'Now, the Being-that-is-itself-revealed-to-itself-in-the-Totality-of-its-reality, that is to say, the self-conscious objective-Reality, or objectively-real Self-consciousness, – is *Geist*, Spirit.' Thus, even while being a real and ordinary human being, a form of Consciousness, 'the Sage is, as participant in Science, a *"Gestalt des Geistes"'* (IH 323). As *Gestalt*, the Sage was a self; but as the contents of that self were the revealed totality of Being, the Sage knew that his Knowledge was also the content of Spirit. Thus, one could say that Spirit knew itself as *Gestalt* in and by way of the Sage. This was why, in the preface to *Phenomenology*, Hegel went to some length, as was pointed out in discussing Kojève's 'corrections' of Hegel, to characterize himself as the agent of Spirit, a 'mere Particularity' of no particular importance. If, as Hegel said, it was in the nature of Truth to prevail when its time has come, then he who articulated that Truth was but the contingent agent of its development (*PhG* 58–9:44–5). Let us consider more closely the relationship of the Sage to Science.

The problem may be stated quite clearly: Science was *his* Knowledge but it was also Knowledge *per se*. The solution may be stated with equal clarity: Science was indeed the result of the Sage's efforts and the Sage was indeed a Consciousness. Now for every Consciousness there must be an object, a *Gegenstand*, and for the Sage this was the Concept, complete Discourse (*PhG* 556:485). Or to be more precise, this object was the empirical existence of that Discourse, which is to say, a book entitled *Phenomenology of Spirit*. 'This Book is produced by the Sage; and at the same time it appears to him as a *Gegen-stand*, as an Object, as an external thing. But the contents of this object – are the Sage himself' (IH 326). Now Spirit, we know, was self-produced and self-revealing Being; and empirically existing Spirit was Discourse, in this instance the Discourse set forth in *Phenomenology*. The Sage, the author of the Book, identified with this Discourse, Science, which revealed the Totality of Being. In his own self, therefore, he realized the conscious integration of Being, but he did so in the knowledge that it was his own work. In other words, the final definition of the Concept of the Sage was that he (or she) was a Synthesis of the Particular and Universal, not an annihilation but a supersession, *Aufhebung*. The Sage ceased to be a sheer Particularity because he became *himself* universal; but it was he (or she) who became universal, which means that his Particularity was conserved within the Totality. 'He remains a man, and he remains this man, G.W.F. Hegel. Of course, he is reduced to his Knowledge, and his Knowledge is universal; but it is nevertheless *his* Knowledge, which no one but he has been able to realize' (*IH* 327). There were, therefore, three distinct things: the Sage, his Book, and the real World that included them both.

In the second section of the second part of chapter 8 Hegel discussed the reality of the Sage as defined in the preceding paragraphs. His opening remarks concerned the actualization of the Sage, that is, how he could appear only as a Citizen of the universal and homogeneous State because it was only there that had been actualized the total reality which the Book containing Science revealed. Because Being was always a Totality, the possibility of Science existed elsewhere; but because one could understand conceptually only what existed for oneself, until the Totality of human reality has been revealed as oneself, Science had to remain merely a possibility and not a reality. Only the Citizen of the universal and homogeneous State had superseded the opposition of Universality and Particularity and so had the ability to reveal that totality.

In any political order other than the universal and homogeneous State, philosophical Self-consciousness would be correspondingly impoverished and would leave to religion the task of revealing the totality of human reality – albeit in a symbolic way. In the universal and homogeneous State, however, the supersession of the difference between Church and State, predicated upon the negation of divine reality, made possible the actualization of human reality in the full sense of the term. Human reality, recreated for Consciousness as Science, was an object unlike any religious object. It was not external, transcendent, or divine. It was utterly and completely immanent to knowledge, being consciously created by the Sage. That is, it was the Concept, a construction or co-ordination of the Totality of human reality that religion had revealed symbolically or representationally.

Granted, then, that the reconstruction of human reality undertaken in *Phenomenology* was necessarily the act of a Citizen of the universal and homogeneous State, it was also the means by which a Philosopher became a Sage. It was, as Hegel said, the ladder to Wisdom (*PhG* 25:14). Now Wisdom or absolute Truth, 'all philosophers' agreed, had always been held to be identical with itself, unchanging or eternal, even though revealed or discovered upon particular occasions. Accordingly, whenever one raised the problem of Truth, or even of partial truths, one necessarily raised the problem of time, 'or more particularly, the problem of the relationship between time and the eternal or between time and the intemporal' (*IH* 336:100). In Hegelian language, one must move from a concern with the actuality of the substance of human reality in the universal and homogeneous State (*PhG* 557–8:486–7) to the relation of the Concept, the coherent whole of discourse, to time.

Kojève provided an ingenious and often amusing three-lecture introductory 'Note,' the details of which need not concern us. The two texts upon which Kojève based his explication were nearly identical in phrasing and quite identical in meaning: the Concept is time (*PhG* 38, 558:27, 487). The purpose to be gained by identifying time and the Concept was to account for the free, historical, and mortal individual that Hegel sensed himself to be. The time Hegel was concerned with, then, was human time, the time that Man lived (or was) and the speeches he made about his living (or being). To say that time is Man in the World, with a real History, summarized the whole teaching of *Phenomenology*: 'Man is Desire directed towards another Desire; that is to say, Desire for Recognition; that is to say, negating-Action undertaken so as to satisfy this Desire for Recognition; that is to say, bloody Struggle for prestige; that is to say, relation between Master and Slave; that is to say, Labour; that is to say historical evolution that finally ends up in the universal and homogeneous State and absolute Knowledge that reveals the integral Man realized in and by that State' (*IH* 371:139). Metaphysically, it meant that the World was such that Man so understood may be realized, has been realized, within it.

We would emphasize one particular feature of this identity: if the Concept was time in the full sense of a future that would never become a present or a past, and if Man was the empirical worldly existence of the Concept, Man must also be the empirical, worldly existence of a future that would never be a present or a past. For Man, the only future that would never be his present was death. Man essentially was, to use Heidegger's later formula, a Being-towards-death. Since this future could be present as knowledge of one's death, if one were to be a Sage one must know one will die. One would not 'be-there' anymore, and obviously one would not be anywhere else either. Now, if the Concept was time and so, as we just argued, essentially finite, the Being revealed by it must also be finite. That Being, we know, was History. 'Thus History itself must be essentially finite, *finie*; collective Man (humanity) must die just as the individual human dies; universal History must have a definitive end, *fin*' (*IH* 380:148). For Hegel, this end of History was signalled by the appearance of the Sage who wrote the Book that revealed Science, the epitaph of History. The moment of completion was a moment for which there was no future; anything that happened 'later' would simply repeat what had already been said. Absolute knowledge was, then, eternal. Or better, it was Eternity. Yet it had been engendered by or 'in' time. Hegel explained how in the next page or so (PhG 558–9:487–8).

Pre-Hegelian philosophy opposed reality and the Concept (and, therefore, time) in various ways. This was not, in those far off pre-Hegelian days, an error. Before the end of History, reality and the Concept did not, indeed, coincide. Only by labour has Man been able to supersede the opposition between himself and nature, and only by struggle has he been able to supersede the opposition between Particular and Universal, public and private, family and political, etc. Thus, pre-Hegelian philosophy was not false until it had been superseded by Wisdom, which, in turn, could not come into being until human Desire had been fully and definitively satisfied, until there was no further negativity, no oppositions to be overcome. Now, since Desire and the negating actions to which it gave rise were the manifestations of human time, when Man has become reconciled with what is, with reality, he ceased to act and so ceased to be time.

The Concept and time coincide within, by way of, and for, the Sage. And, clearly, the Sage appeared in time even though by appearing he marked the end of time because his temporal activity, the creation of Science, was the creation of something timeless or eternal. More precisely, it was Eternity revealing itself to itself by way of a Discourse written down in an empirical, worldly, temporal Book. Spirit henceforth would have worldly existence as an inorganic reality; correspondingly, those organic realities that, historically, were human beings would henceforth be without Spirit (IH 388 n1). The political consequences of this implication will be considered below. For the present one need note only that the Book, being without negativity (since the last 'historical' act was Hegel's writing it) did not change either itself or the Being it revealed. Here is Hegel's summary of the relationship between the Sage and time: Spirit, having completed itself as World Spirit, could attain its completion as self-conscious Spirit (PhG 559:488). This, of course, meant not that nothing 'happened' after 1806 but rather that nothing has been added to Hegel's System of Science as a result of empirical events since his day (excepting, perhaps, Kojève's 'corrections' noted earlier). In other words, empirical events since 1806 have not introduced any logical novelty. This interpretation of recent events has not, of course, met with widespread acceptance. But it cannot, for that reason alone, be dismissed.

The first part of the second section of chapter 8 dealt with the relation of the Sage to the actuality of the universal and homogeneous State, the second part, with the relation between the Sage and time. Both were, in a sense, abstract inasmuch as actuality was temporal. In the third part of this section, to which we now turn, Hegel combined the previous two topics dialectically and considered the relation between the Sage and the actuality of time, namely History. 'The process,' Hegel said, 'of carrying forward this form of Self-knowledge is the labour it [i.e. Spirit] accomplishes as actual History, *wirkliche Geschichte'* (*PhG* 559:488). The labour of Spirit (i.e. of humanity) was the production of a knowledge, namely the knowledge that Spirit has gained of itself. Thus, in the final analysis, History was the history of philosophy and not, for example, of religion or art. Initially, philosophy was impoverished as compared to religion. During the course of history, however, religious meanings had been forced to give way to conceptual ones. Correspondingly, philosophic consciousness had more and more to reveal since the Particular (the individual philosopher) increasingly approached the Universal, namely Wisdom, by way of the conceptual knowledge that his particular philosophical speech articulated. Increasingly, that is, Man understood History as his own doings, and, correspondingly, there was a decrease in the area left for religion to reveal symbolically. In this way the substance or content of religion was superseded in and by the form of philosophy. In this synthesizing third part of the second section of chapter 8, then, the topics of the first two were treated as constituent elements of the reality of the Sage.

The historical labours of Spirit were fulfilled in Wisdom, Hegel said. Looked upon the other way around, the action and desire of Man, whose Being is time, which achieved the actuality of the universal and homogeneous State were but constituent elements of the now eternal Discourse that revealed the World and historical Man. 'Man properly speaking, Man who is truly real as Man is, therefore, the Philosopher. Natural Man or the animal of the species homo sapiens, on the one hand, and the Man-of-historical-Action, that is, the Man-of-Struggle-and-Labour, on the other, are but necessary conditions for a truly human reality, which is the philosophical existence of Man' (*IH* 397). The natural world was there so Man could subdue it to his own purposes; but Man laboured only so he could speak about what he had done, so he could become

Self-conscious, so he could become a Philosopher or, to be precise, so he could become a satisfied Philosopher, which is to say a Sage.

Kojève here raised an objection to Hegel's claim that the Philosopher was alone truly human. The basis for this claim was Hegel's assumption that Self-consciousness tended 'by nature' (as it were) to extend itself until it obtained complete satisfaction. Kojève said he doubted that Man was naturally a Philosopher (as this hypothesis seemed to imply). Moreover, this doubt led to another. According to Hegel, the schema of historical evolution was as follows: man acted and thereby transformed the given World; he lived in this 'new' World and so was himself transformed by it; being transformed he necessarily became aware of the transformation within himself; being in this way aware of himself, he learned he was once more not in harmony with the given, though now transformed, World, and so on until there existed the sought-for accord between Concept and World, at which point History was over and philosophy was Wisdom. Kojève said he doubted the validity of this argument because it held true only if the man of action were a philosopher. Now Hegel himself had referred in the introduction to *Phenomenology* (*PhG* 69:51-2) to those who were undisturbed by thought, that is, whose Consciousnesses did not, and probably never would, extend themselves but who remained, and probably always would remain, in a state of unthinking inertia, *gedankenloser Trägheit*. Were these, then, really not human? Was the opposite to them really not the Philosopher but the Blond Beast of Nietzsche? 'In short, the man of Action is by definition in no way a Philosopher' (*IH* 402). Hegel's view that the Philosopher was the representative Man, Kojève declared, was an 'occupational defect' (*IH* 404). Hegel's opinion had resulted from a professional bias in favour of philosophers. It was no more than nostalgia for his youth, before the time he became a Sage.

One undertakes to dispute Kojève's reading of Hegel with as much reluctance as Kojève showed in disagreeing with Hegel, Nevertheless, two short points of objection may be raised. First, concerning the hypothetical character of the proposition that Self-consciousness was 'naturally' self-extending, Kojève's objection was that it was undeducible and that Hegel was forced to rely on the fact that philosophers had become conscious of historical facts and the fact that he, Hegel, had become a Sage (*IH* 398:400). If, as Kojève argued, the transition from Philosopher to Sage was a decision, an act of freedom (cf *IH* 293), then it would be undeducible beforehand anyway. Accordingly, if one were a Sage, one could only appeal to this fact because the one who doubted it clearly was not a Sage, as had been made evident precisely by his doubting. This sort of argument would be valid, of course, only for the more comprehensive Self-consciousness, as Kojève agreed (*IH* 404). In any event, it certainly seems to be confirmed by experience that, as V.S. Naipaul once said, one cannot unlearn what one had learned.

Second, Kojève said that the man of action was in no way a Philosopher. In a straightforward sense this was true enough. However, as we saw earlier in this book, Hegel did find an equivalence between the actions of the Napoleonic armies and his own activities. In J. Hoffmeister's collection of *Dokumente zu Hegels Entwicklung*, the following remark may be found (314): 'Death alone is absolute labour as it supersedes determinate Particularity. Courage brings its absolute sacrifice to the State. The humiliation of not having died is the fate of those who do not perish in battle and still enjoy their Particularity. Accordingly, there is nothing left for them but speculative thought, the absolute knowledge of truth, as the form in which the single Consciousness of the infinite is possible without the determinateness of an independent Individuality.' One may conclude with Kojève that the man of action was not a Philosopher, but for Hegel, the Sage, comprehending the man of action, necessarily contains within himself a reality equivalent even to death in battle (cf *IH* 529ff).

Whatever the significance of Kojève's difference with Hegel, it was clear that in the end, for Hegel, History was the history of philosophy. Philosophy, as has been shown, aspired to total knowledge or, in Hegelian terms, to the synthesis of Consciousness and Self-consciousness. In the first seven chapters of *Phenomenology*, various philosophies appeared as representatives of Consciousness; after the 'metaphysical' summary of chapter 8, they appeared as unsuccessful attempts at synthesis. So long as History continued, that long would there exist contradiction between Man and World, and so negativity, action, etc. Every historical synthesis, therefore, would be proved false because eventually it would not accord with Reality. The negativity of historical action was found in the history of philosophy as well – indeed, without it, there would have been no *history* of philosophy. And the history of philosophy was simply 'the history of necessarily abortive attempts at realizing a Totality of thought before having realized the Totality of existence' (*IH* 406). These premature attempts were carried through successfully only by the Sage; that they could be carried through only at the end of History was shown by the fact that it was then that they were in fact carried through.

The history of philosophy, then, was concluded by the Sage. To say that he successfully carried through prior and unsuccessful attempts at synthesis was to define his activity. Now the Sage, like everybody else, was what he did, and what he did was speak in such a way that he showed he understood himself fully and completely. This meant that he understood his own genesis, the fights and labours of History, etc. In Hegel's words, the Sage was the 'dialectical movement or process, *Bewegung*, of the Self' (*PhG* 561:490). If we recall Hegel's definition given earlier of 'actual History,' namely the *Bewegung* of carrying forward Self-knowledge, it is clear that the self-revelation of Spirit as the process of the thought of the Sage was identical with the Sage's remembrance of History and its process in (or as) that same thought.

The knowledge of the Sage, Hegel said, consisted 'in this seeming inactivity, *scheinbaren Untätigkeit*, that merely contemplates the way in which differentiated entities are dialectically self-moved, *das Unterscheidne sich an ihm selbst bewegt*, and return to their own unity' (*PhG* 561:490). The Sage seemed inactive because he did not change anything (no negativity, etc) but only seemed that way because what he contemplated was action, the *Bewegung* of History that lead to the comprehension of Being, which was eternally itself. Thus, Kojève remarked, 'Science essentially presupposes Action. And that is why Science is itself, if you like, an Action in the sense that it is a perpetual circular movement. In other words, it is dialectical. But it is dialectical only because the Being it reveals is dialectical. And Being is dialectical because it in fact implied Man or Action and because Being that implies man is realized and revealed within and by way of Time, that is, within and by way of human, historical Action' (*IH* 410).

The actual activity of the Sage was expressed in a dictum of one of Hegel's spiritual successors, Mallarmé: 'all earthly existence exists in order to end up in a book.' And, indeed the Sage wrote a Book. It was not just any old book, however, but one that recapitulated conceptually the *Bewegung* of History. Henceforth, all dialectical movement existed within the Book and not within the World. On the one hand this occurred because the World, having been purged of contradiction and negativity, could not 'move.' It had nowhere to 'go.' It was 'dead' or 'past.' On the other hand, the Wisdom of the Sage was the knowledge of this 'dead' World, which is to say, how it had come to 'die,' to become eternally at one with itself. Thus, the only 'place' where there was 'room' for movement, for *Bewegung*, was in the story of how and why the World had come to be what it evermore would be. And this story was told in a Book – or to follow Kojève's conceit, in The Book.

Wisdom

The first part of chapter 8 of *Phenomenology* dealt with the road to Wisdom or Science; the second with the empirical existence, the *Dasein*, of Science in the Sage; the third and final part dealt with Science as such, Science considered apart from its historical genesis or incarnation. The advent of the Sage, as has been shown, was the last historical event. Henceforth there was no further opposition between Man and nature, no action, no desire but, on the contrary, complete satisfaction with what is. With the articulation of Science, the *Dasein* of Spirit in the World was clearly not the fights and labours of History or even the person of the Sage, but the Concept itself, the complete, final Discourse eternally identical with itself, circular, and 'incarnate' in The Book. In Hegel's words, having attained the Concept through the efforts of History and lately through the efforts of the Sage, Spirit developed its own *Dasein* and *Bewegung* within the Concept, 'the ether of its life,' and was Science (*PhG* 562:491).

There was a difference between Spirit in the form of History, Time, or Man, and Spirit in the form of The Book, Eternity, or Science. *Phenomenology* described the forms of Consciousness, Man, and the historical movements of Spirit. In Science, description involved distinct concepts, *bestimmte Begriffe*, and their self-grounded dialectical movement, and not Man at all. This movement was circular, eternal, internal to the Concept, etc. It was a logical movement of Discourse, which reproduced the movement of Being, namely time, History, etc. In no way was it itself a temporal movement of negation or action.

Yet it was related to temporal movement since what logically was eternally itself got that way by becoming itself. Rather like Heidegger's distinction between philosophical anthropology and fundamental ontology, Hegel's System hung together in two parts. In the first, *Phenomenology*, the temporal anthropological movement of History was described; in the second, *Logic*, the eternal, logical movement of the Concept. To understand Being as it became what it was, one must read and understand *Phenomenology*. Having done so, one was thereby introduced to the topic of *Logic*. Having now read *Logic*, one learned that Being was Idea, that is, Being was Being-revealed-to-itself of Spirit. And it was this because it had become so, which reintroduced the topic of *Phenomenology* (*IH* 421).

Within *Phenomenology*, a similar cycle returned us to the beginning. Science, Hegel said, contained within itself a necessity of externalizing itself out of the form of the pure Concept and, consequently, a passage,

Übergang, into the form of Consciousness because Spirit that knew itself as Concept (i.e. Science) was an immediate identity with itself (*PhG* 563:491). Being and the Concept were perfectly coincident within and by way of The Book. 'Being is entirely revealed by the Concept that develops the meaning of The Book, and the Concept is completely realized within Being by the existence of The Book' (*IH* 424). Yet there remained a difference or distinction, *Unterschied*, between the Sage, a human being, and The Book, a sensuous thing, which, Hegel said, returned us to sensuous experience, the topic of the first chapter of *Phenomenology*. Moreover, this return to sensuous Consciousness was 'the highest freedom and security of the Self-Knowledge' of the Sage (*PhG* 563:491), because it was only by way of sensuous experience that the Sage could write The Book that we, Hegelians and non-Hegelians alike, could read. In short, Wisdom could never transcend sensuous reality.

The circularity of the argument was, formally, proof for the completeness of *Phenomenology*. In addition, however, the return to sensuous experience was proof against any theological interpretation of the text. In Kojève's words, the being of Spirit as Science 'is the incarnate Logos. But it is not a God who was born and died, lives, eats and drinks in spite of his divinity but who could pass beyond such things. No, the being Hegel has in mind is Logos because he eats and drinks, is born, lives and dies, and dies for good, without any resurrection. His spiritual reality is the (discursive) revelation of his sensuous reality, and it cannot be detached from it' (*IH* 426).

Returning to *Phenomenology*, then, the entire work may be characterized as being concerned with the relationship between Consciousness and Self-consciousness, thought and reality, subject and object. We have seen how, from within the development of the subject, we are returned to the starting point. But this was insufficient, Hegel said. The object had not yet gained its 'full freedom' (*PhG* 563:492). Such an object was external to, and independent of, the subject and could in no way be deduced from the subject, from knowledge, etc. In short, Hegel's 'philosophy' was realist rather than idealist (as those terms are conventionally used).

Hegel's 'realism,' however, was of a most unusual kind. The primary fundamental reality was Spirit; but Spirit was a result, a synthesis of (objective) Being and (subjective) revelation of it, of space and time, of nature and history. Knowledge of Spirit, that is, Science, was the coincidence of the above oppositions, but this knowledge could not forget its own genesis in those oppositions. Now, the only way for the oppositions to be maintained was through realism – idealism would 'deduce' the object from the subject. The form that this realist genesis took, Hegel immediately added, was that of a 'free contingent happening.' In other words, no *a priori* 'realist' or 'idealist' deduction on the basis of either of the two terms of the opposition could ever result in knowledge of Spirit. One could only reconstruct the path of the becoming of Spirit. As for the becoming of Spirit itself, it was made up of the opposed elements indicated above, but now identified by Hegel as self or time, and given-Being, *Sein*, or space.

Given-Being, space, was nature, the 'natural World' outside time and, in Hegel's words, the 'eternal externalization' of Spirit. The movement of nature – geological and biological evolution – produced the proto-human animal who, once constituted as specifically human, confronted nature and began a wholly novel 'evolution,' namely the transformation of given-Being, History. Accordingly, the end of History was not a natural or cosmic disruption. Nature, being independent of time, necessarily would 'survive' it (*IH* 444–5:157–8).

The other side of the becoming of Spirit was History, time, self. Man was the negating action that preserved itself by annihilating and transforming nature, space. In contrast to nature, Man was in no way eternal: he was born and he would die (no 'afterlife'). The movement of History was a sluggish process, *eine träge Bewegung*, a rich gallery of images that Spirit has come to know as its own becoming. Each successive 'image,' each successive historical World, has been preserved as a re-collection, *Erinnerung*, that was also an internalization, *Er-innerung* (*PhG* 563:492).

The goal of the entire sluggish process, as has been shown, was the absolute Concept, Science. But the path to it, Hegel immediately added, was the internal recollection of historical spirits as they had existed in themselves. This involved on the one hand the preservation of their free, contingent appearance as historical narration, *Geschichte*, and on the other hand the preservation of their conceptual organization, *ihrer begriffnen Organisation*, as the Science of appearing knowledge or *Phenomenology*, the logos of phenomena. The two together, that is, *Geschichte* and *begriffnen Organisation*, constituted conceptual History, *begriffne Geschichte*, which 'forms the internal re-collection and the Golgotha of absolute Spirit, the actuality, truth, and subjective-certainty of its throne, without which it would be lifeless and alone' (*PhG* 564:493). This last sentence, Kojève added, provided the hermeneutical canon under which he had proceeded upon his entire interpretation. 'The *PhG* cannot be understood without a prior knowledge of real history, just as history cannot be truly understood without the *PhG*. Thus I was right to speak of Athens, Rome,

Louis XIV ... and Napoleon, in interpreting the *PhG*. So long as one does not see the historical facts to which this book refers, one will understand nothing of what is said in it' (*IH* 441:166). In addition, *Phenomenology* re-presented or reconstructed the basis of History in the essential characteristics of human existence as they first arose in the anthropogenic desire for recognition, which was the foundation 'myth' and paradigm of Kojève's interpretation of the whole text.

Finally we come to the mutilation of Schiller's lines from his poem 'Freundschaft.' Schiller wrote:

Fand das höchste Wesen shon kein Gleiches,
aus dem Kelch des ganzen Seelenreiches
Schäumt *ihm* – die Unendlichkeit.

Though the Supreme Being found no equal,
From the chalice of the whole realm of souls
Foams *to him* – infinity.

Hegel 'amended' this to read:

aus dem Kelche dieses Geisterreiches
schäumt ihm seine Unendlichkeit.

from the chalice of this realm of spirits
foams to it, its own infinity.

Hegel's three modifications had the same purpose. First, substituting the realm of spirits for realm of souls, Hegel indicated he was concerned with human history and not any Beyond where a Supreme Being might comfort 'souls.' Second, he said 'this' realm of spirits not 'the whole' realm of souls, which reinforced the first change. And third, where Schiller wrote 'die Unendlichkeit,' Hegel wrote 'seine Unendlichkeit,' once more denying the possibility of any infinity beyond Man. 'Eternal-infinite-revealed-Being, that is, absolute Spirit, is the infinite or eternal being of this same Being that has existed as universal History' (*IH* 422:167). Accordingly, the infinite involved was Man's infinite and the science that revealed it was a Science of Man, first because it was the end-product of History, which was human activity, and second because its contents dealt with Man as he became what he is.

In this chapter we discussed what Kojève identified as the post-historical attitude of the Sage. We distinguished between love of knowledge, philosophy, and actual knowledge, Wisdom, and how one progressed from one to the other. Finally we considered the existence of the Sage and 'his' Book, which was The Book, and what Wisdom is. This brings us to the end of *Phenomenology* and points us, as Kojève indicated, toward *Logic*. In the next chapter, however, we do not consider *Logic* and the 'metaphysical' question it dealt with. Rather, we consider in more detail the shape of the political order that made possible the advent of the Sage, namely the universal and homogeneous State, the post-historical regime.

7

The post-historical regime

In an earlier chapter I discussed the historical configurations leading to the establishment of the Napoleonic Empire and its aftermath, liberalism. In this chapter the focus is chiefly on the principles of the state, in Hegel's language, the idea of the state, compared to which any incarnation would initially seem imperfect. The main text to be considered is Hegel's *Philosophy of Right*[1]; it is followed by an account of Kojève's explication of the rules governing life both in the state and in civil society.

The private realm

Philosophy of Right has been characterized by scholars in several ways. Formally, however, it was a textbook, a compendium the subject-matter of which was 'the closed circle of a science' where 'content is bound up with form' (*RPhil* 3–4; 1–2). His method, Hegel said, was 'logical.' Philosophy of right was first of all a part of philosophy, 'the apprehension of the present and actual, not the construction of a beyond, supposed to exist, God knows where, or rather that exists, and we can perfectly well say where, namely in the error of a one-sided, empty ratiocination.' Since, moreover, 'what is rational is actual and what is actual is rational,'[2] a book on the science of the state had as its object the conceptualization of 'the state as something rational in itself. As a work of philosophy, it must be a long way from any attempt to construct a state as it ought to be' (14–15; 10–11). The account, in short, was to show how *the* state (not *a* state) was to be reasonably understood. In the language we have been using, it was a compendium of political principles appropriate to the post-revolutionary, post-historical epoch. The penultimate paragraph of the preface, one of Hegel's finest and most famous, made his concern with conceptual 'eternal' principle, not historical genesis, most clear. The concept, which was also the indubitable truth of history, he wrote there, demonstrated that only when actuality had attained its proper shape could it be truly grasped by thought; the green salad-days of action had given way to the grey sabbath of thought or, rather, of wisdom. 'The owl of Minerva spreads its wings only with the falling of the dusk.' Rational political principles of the state, Hegel's political wisdom, could be elaborated only with the end of history.

In *Philosophy of History* it was shown that history was the story of the actualization of freedom and therefore of rationality. Here Hegel began at the other side of the argument. The basis of right was spirit, he said. More specifically, its basis was the constituent element of spirit, namely will, that was free. Thus, freedom was the substance and goal of right, and 'the system of right is the actuality of the realm of freedom, the world-spirit brought forth out of itself as a second nature' (*RPhil* 4). The will was free, since on the one hand will without freedom was nothing and on the other hand freedom gained actuality only as a subject, that is, as will (*RPhil* 4A). Eventually, the idea of will would be actualized in its revealed reality as freedom willing freedom (*RPhil* 21A); in principle, then, the freedom of one eventually willed the freedom of all. In Kojève's language, this was the regime of mutual recognition of each by all.

Right, as the existent embodiment of free will or self-conscious freedom, was 'sacrosanct' and to be obeyed because it actualized and expressed the revealed reality of spirit, reason, the 'wisdom of the world.' The first shape in which freedom was manifest was as property, since property implied the subjection, by will, of given-being, nature, or external reality. The development of contract, which was formal right, provoked the creation of its opposite, subjectivity, which together served as abstract moments of the synthesizing process of ethical life, first of all as family life, then as civil society, and lastly as the universal and homogeneous state, 'the supreme and absolute revealed-reality of the world-spirit' (*RPhil* 33A).

A minimum of interpretative ingenuity may bring to light in this new context the familiar dialectic of master and slave and the pure theory of recognition: the first constituent element, abstract legal personality, corresponded to the primordial desire of *Phenomenology*: the struggle for recognition between desires was recapitulated in terms of a particularist insistence on formal rights, which was a mark of vulgarity, and a universalist appropriation of nature as property (*RPhil* 39).

Property relations were only implicitly mediated by reason in the shape of the mutual recognition of property-holders through contracts. But contracts have come into existence arbitrarily, as is made clear when they were violated. For the contract-abiding property-holder, property was sacrosanct; for the thief who would rob him it was simply based upon will. The conflict of thief and property-holder brought to light, therefore, the rationality of crime: crime was reasonable inasmuch as it showed the inadequacy of property-holding, or more precisely, of personality, as the basis of right. To move beyond the oscillation of property-holder versus robber one must move beyond the legal person to what Hegel called a subject, who combined in himself universality and particularity. For a subject, the law he obeyed was his own law. Criminality was no longer merely the alien name the propertied person inflicted upon the thief. Rather his own rationality informed the thief that in violating the law he also violated his own will. Thus, the conflict between law and criminality ceased to be external and became an internal conflict between what ought to be done and what was done. In Hegel's terminology, we have progressed to the realm of 'morality.'

Morality and immorality were based upon the subjectivity of will. As subjective, this will was opposed to, and contradicted by, an object. It was not, therefore, a synthesis or a revealed and stable reality. Hence, the interminable conflicts, the tiresome chatter about 'is' versus 'ought.' So long as one dealt with right merely as a question of morality, that long would the instability and incompleteness of the discourse continue. The conflict of the moral will developed from the contradiction between purposes and responsibilities. Crime charged internal purposes; responsibility, however, contained only the external decision as to whether one has or has not done a particular act. It did not follow that, because one was responsible, one intended the act. Indeed, the moral will could repudiate all consequences inconsistent with its purposes. It could not and did not repudiate the will to act, however, but attempted to resolve this contradiction by insisting upon the element of intention. But as in *Phenomenology*, the 'law of the heart' served only to make explicit the gap between the claim of the 'ought' to be absolute and its not actually being what it claimed (otherwise it would not be an 'ought' but an 'is'). The absolute end-point of the moral will was the good, a concrete determinate universality. But as it was determined by mere subjective certainty, the result was the conflict of consciences. Again, as in *Phenomenology*, this conflict was no sooner explicitly identified than it was implicitly resolved: the abstract universality of right as good contradicted the abstract particularity of will as conscience only because one first posited their mutual independence. Only by moving on to ethical experience could these two constituent elements be resolved into a subjective disposition that did not contradict an objective content.

Ethical life, *Sittlichkeit*, Hegel said, was the idea of freedom in the double sense that the good had become self-con-scious, and self-consciousness had its basis and purpose in the actualization of the good. The synthesis of subjective and objective constituent elements of moral will resulted in the totality of *Sittlichkeit* whose order depended on the subjectivity of individuals but whose subjectivity was understood by them to be both their own and a universal substance. When individuals identified themselves with *Sittlichkeit*, it appeared to them as a tradition or custom, *Sitte*, a 'second nature'; in fact, Hegel said, spirit had come alive and was substantively present in the world for the first time. The development of *Sittlichkeit*, of ethical substance, was the transformation of this 'second nature' into self-conscious spiritual activity.

The process unfolded in the familiar dialectical way. The immediate phase of substantive unity was the 'natural' unity of the biological family. What held the family together was love. It would be better to say that love *was* the unity of the family since the bond among the several members was experienced by them as more fundamental than their own individuality. The natural feeling of unity that grew from family love left no room for differences, and so right, properly speaking, found no place there. Indeed, Hegel said, the form of right appeared for the individual only upon the dissolution of the biological family and the substitution of law for love. In place of sheer and immediate natural generation was found the law of marriage, love made self-conscious and endowed with purposes beyond the particularist dispositions of lovers. In place of the acquisition of property by the imposition of individual will upon given-being, the family obtained estate, *Vermögen*, a possession that 'belonged' to several generations, the inheritance of which was again determined by law. The constituent element of legal marriage was the immediate form of the concept of the family, and estate was the external form mediated abstractly by time in the form of laws of succession. Children, upon whom the succession devolved, were the external, but also concrete and actual, form of the concept of family. And with them the family, both conceptually and naturally, was fulfilled and so began its dissolution. By law, children must be maintained physically and educated or socialized spiritually at the expense of the family estate; as they were potentially free, they were in no way parts of the estate. When the process of ethical

Bildung had been completed, the children would legally have come of age, could become property-holders, found their own families, and so forth.

The ethical dissolution of the family into legal adults and biological children, and the deaths of the parents, which was the natural dissolution that enabled the legal mechanisms of inheritance to operate, resulted in a plurality of families, 'each of which conducts itself as in principle a self-subsistent concrete person and therefore as related externally to its neighbours' (*RPhil* 181).[3] The constituent element of difference, unable to appear within the family, now appeared as between families. Natural unity and universality had become difference and particularity; the loving warmth of family had given way, for the individual, to the cool selfishness of civil society.

Civil society was the realm of the concrete particular person seeking to fulfil private ends, which nevertheless, being common to the particular as particular, were also in themselves or implicitly and inwardly universal.[4] In pursuing private ends people created a system of interdependence, a unity of necessity and need, not of freedom. Hence, the caprice of particular subjectivity must be constrained by legal universality, first of all by the laws of economics[5] that expressed the variety of human needs, the effort, *Arbeit*, that satisfied them, and the status-groups, *Stände*, that resulted from the division of labour. As to which status-group a person belonged, this was partly a result of natural capacity and partly of the natural accidents of birth and circumstance. The essential feature in either event was the individual's will. To him at least, whether he be a member of the immediate, substantive agricultural group, or of the calculative, formal commercial group, or of the *Aufhebung* of these, the universal group of civil servants, his position in life appeared as his own doing, which was what one commonly means by the term freedom.[6] Wherever he may be in this status hierarchy, he must needs be somewhere specific. The ethical frame of mind, therefore, Hegel said, 'is rectitude and *esprit de corps*, that is, the disposition to make oneself a member of one of the constituent-elements of civil society by one's own initiative, to maintain oneself in this position by one's own energy, industry, and skill, and to take care of oneself only through this process of self-mediation with the universal, thereby gaining recognition in one's own eyes and in the eyes of others' (*RPhil* 207). Even within the system of needs and the laws of economic social organization, then, was absolute universality implicitly contained. In principle, and within the context of mere utility, rectitude and recognition already have achieved the synthesis of particular and universal, master and slave – but only in itself or in principle, only abstractly, because the system of needs and economic laws expressed the rights of property, which in turn became actual, and so may be recognized, as the administration of justice.

The necessary regulation of the selfish utilitarian particularism of civil society by the laws of economics gained explicit expression and actuality through codified law, *Gesetz*, and courts of justice. Crimes against the legal person and its property were annulled in this way and the universality of society was maintained, though again only in itself or as a 'legal fiction.' Hegel mentioned two mediating agencies. The first, the public authorities, *Polizei*, maintained the safety of the person and his property. The contingent, subjective willing of evil, which was crime, must be prevented or, failing that, the criminal must be brought to justice. More importantly, the day-to-day affairs of society must be ordered and directed, public works constructed, social welfare measures undertaken, and so forth. In short, the *Polizei* took the form of an external organization charged with protecting the interests of civil society as an entity endowed with its own collective but nevertheless particular ends.[7] To give a common example: it is in everyone's interest that traffic be regulated even though it may be in my immediate particular interest to break the speed limit or run a stop-sign because I am in a hurry. The *Polizei*, then, were the first quasi-anonymous agency by which universality implicit in the interests of particularity was made to appear in civil society.

The second agency Hegel called the corporation.[8] The corporation was especially important as a mediating structure for the calculative status-group, the business or commercial men. Living in the midst of traditional family life, the agricultural group experienced the substantive universality of biological nature as its own basis and the group of civil servants had universality as its goal and purpose and was charged with consciously mediating the two. The middle group, however, was essentially occupied with the particular. By establishing standards of skill and performance, by recruiting members and providing them with a measure of protection and education, the corporation would appear to the individuals who belonged to it as a universal. And, indeed, it was, insofar as it was the same for all of them. But since its purposes were identical with the particular interests of the members, the universality of the corporation was restricted. It was, Hegel said, like a second family, though one whose membership conferred a general and public respect (*RPhil* 252–3). But respect resulting from one's social position was recognition of one's unique individuality.

However important the family and the corporation were for the organization of civil society (*RPhil* 255), they could not provide full satisfaction. As a whole, civil society constituted 'the middle term between the first phase, which is that of the struggle to death for recognition, and the last, which is that of the state conceived as the locus of reciprocal recognition, or the spirit of a people.'[9] The privacy of the family and its love excluded at least that satisfaction resulting from universal recognition; the restricted purposes of the corporation meant that its universality existed only for its own members and not for the whole. The externality of the *Polizei*, with the strict separation of administrative function and individuality, meant that the efficient performance of duty was an expectation in no way deserving of individual recognition. Absolute universality and absolute actuality were combined only in the state. There too was found absolute or, rather, universal recognition and satisfaction.

Internal public law

The state, Hegel said in the opening paragraph of part III, was the actuality of the ethical idea, *die Wirklichkeit der sittlichen Idee*, the ethical spirit revealed to itself, substantial will thinking itself, knowing itself, and achieving what it knew insofar as it knew it. The immediate or given existence of the state was in the form of tradition, custom, and a 'second nature' that was in no way self-conscious and so was politically invisible. The relation between the *political* individual and the state was much more complex. On the one hand, the existence of the state was mediated by the self-consciousness of political individuals and by their knowledge and activity, and on the other hand, the self-consciousness of political individuals was mediated by their disposition toward the state, which they understood to be their own essential reality, the purpose and product of their activity, and their own substantial freedom (*RPhil* 257). By way of this double mediation (of self-consciousness by the state, of the state by self-consciousness) the state actualized the substantial wills of political individuals; since these wills rationally willed freedom, the state was likewise rational. Consequently, the state, the substantial unity of self-consciousness, was an absolute end where freedom was fully actualized and came into its supreme right (as mutual recognition of self-consciousnesses); reciprocally, 'this final end has its own supreme right against the [political] individual, whose *supreme obligation* is to be a member of the state' (258). The non-political individuals, for whom the state existed immediately as tradition, etc, dropped from sight, as was perfectly correct, for their consciousness was not ethical, their activity and knowledge were not directed toward the actualization of substantive freedom, and they did not seriously seek universal recognition.[10] The non-political ones did not simply disappear, of course. They were not negated but superseded; as we shall see, they were in fact represented within the legislative element.

The idea of the state had three constituent elements. The first, to which Hegel devoted the greatest amount of space, was the immediate actuality of the individual state as an independent entity, as a constitutional structure, *Verfassung*, or internal public law, *inneres Staatsrecht*. Before giving details of its internal and external structure, Hegel again outlined its essential reality.

The state was the actuality of concrete freedom, he said, which meant that personal individuality and particularist interests not only obtained full development and recognition (which were also, though not universally, achieved in the family and within civil society) but also passed over into the realm of universalist interest. Here, knowing and willing the universal, the particular individual recognized the state as his own substantive spirit and in turn was recognized by the state, that is, by the mediation of all (*RPhil* 260). In this respect, there could be no greater contrast than between oriental despotism[11] and the modern state: whereas in the former there was no individual inner life that gained recognition, in the latter, subjective freedom was respected – for example, in choice of occupation (262, 262A) – and the state, the conjunction of public and private ends (265A) was the objective embodiment and guarantor of that inner life (261A). One must again emphasize, as the lengthy note to *RPhil* 270 indicated, that the 'inner life' about which Hegel was concerned was not religious: the inner life was the free self-actualization of the citizen, the political individual.

Hegel turned first to the internal organization of the state and the process by which its constituent elements were differentiated and co-ordinated into an empirical whole conforming to its concept (and so thereby achieving rationality). The three constituent elements of the internal constitution of the state were the legislature, which was the competence to determine and achieve the universal; the executive, which subsumed particular cases under the universal; and the crown, the subjective will that expressed the ultimate competence of constitutional monarchy and bound the other elements into a unified individual. The development of the state into the form of constitutional monarchy, Hegel said, was the achievement, *Werk*, of the modern world; the history of this deepening of the world spirit, this genuine formation of ethical life, was the real content of universal world history, *die Sache der allgemeinen Weltgeschichte* (273). Consequently, any state in the modern world that ignored the concept of that world, namely the rational freedom of the subject, would necessarily be inadequate (273A).[12] Not all Hegel's contemporaries were modern men nor did they deserve (or get) a modern state (274).

The first fundamental characteristic of the state was that it was an individual, a unity of particularity and universality capable of political action. The crown expressed this individuality most perfectly in principle; it actualized this individuality most perfectly in practice to the extent that its agents were qualified by neither birth nor wealth but rather by ability, skill, and character (277A). The theoretical unity of the crown and the actual universality of its functionaries constituted state sovereignty (278). After sovereign unity, the second fundamental characteristic of the state was that it existed as a self-certain subjectivity, an actual single individual, the monarch, whose will was the will of the state. Not that his will was capricious (on the contrary, the monarch followed precedent and abided by the actual, concrete advice of his counsellors; during times of stability, he did little more than sign bills into law), but that finality resided in human self-consciousness, in the monarch's pronunciation 'I will,' and not in nature, for example, not in the entrails of animals, the flight of birds, the mumble of an oracle, or the interpretation of a priest (279A). Yet sovereignty was based upon nature insofar as the monarchy was hereditary and the king ascended to his throne in virtue of his royal birth. Hegel dismissed the action of elective monarchy as expressing the irrational opinion that the constitution was no more than a contract (and so essentially an aspect of civil society) (281). At the same time he drew as sharp a distinction as possible between 'obsolete purely feudal monarchies,' where division of governmental authority was simply a result of power, and modern constitutional monarchy, where divisions were formal results of specific mutually conditioning constituent elements (286). In the former, freedom was eclipsed by the irrationality of whim; in the latter it was guaranteed by the rationality of the self-conscious monarchical will. In short, it was less the form of monarchical succession through an established, royal lineage that was important than that there exist a quasi-biological continuity of will.[13]

Distinct from the monarch's decisions were their execution, the upholding of prior decisions, laws, rules, and so on. The task of applying the universal will of the monarch to particular circumstances fell to the executive, especially the police and the judiciary who, as noted above, constituted the supervisory presence of universality within the particularist order of civil society. The concrete details of the tasks of executive civil servants have been defined beforehand by the functional requirements of administration. 'Between the individual person and his civil service function there is no immediate, natural link,' so that such people were appointed on the basis of neither birth nor personal endowment, but solely on account of their knowledge, *Erkenntnis*, and proven competence (291). In this way functionaries simply performed state functions. All citizens had an opportunity to gain membership in this status-group. The objective aspect of the civil service extended to their duties as well: they performed no discretionary services but fulfilled themselves only by the dutiful discharge of their public functions (294). In Eric Weil's words, 'the functionary is the genuine servant of the state – and its genuine master,' an observation that is amply documented in any number of studies of modern state-bureaucracies.[14] If the objective aspect of the civil service was tied to its competence and duty, the subjective side, at least as concerns the monarch's advisers, was a consequence of the disproportion between the indefinite plurality of candidates, whose relative merits could not be precisely ascertained, and the restricted number of places available. The actual incumbent, therefore, would in part be determined by his seriousness, the power of his own subjective will, as well as by the pleasure of the monarch (292).

The third constituent element, the legislature, was charged with the determination of universality through the enactment of statute laws to ensure the welfare of citizens and exact services from them. Considered as a totality, it included the other two constituent elements: the monarchical supplied the requirement of ultimate and authoritative will, and the executive a supervisory oversight. Considered abstractly, the legislative element articulated formal subjective freedom. It was the political expression of the status-groups of civil society, *hoi polloi*, an empirical universality of opinion (300–1). In this way the status-groups of civil society gained political visibility as public opinion; moreover, they deserved this visibility and recognition (317A) even though greatness in politics (or in science) could be achieved only when public opinion, in itself a mixture of truth and error, was ignored.[15] Public opinion did not sanction people's ability to say anything at all, and freedom was not the ability to do just as one pleased. On the contrary, by emerging into public and by being charged with considering the universalist topics of government, opinion became articulate and refined. In this respect the political status-groups mediated the totality of government (and so prevented the growth of arbitrary will on the part of the executive or monarch) and the particularist interests of civil society (and so prevented the creation of a mass public in opposition to the state). Likewise, within the totality of government the status-groups mediated the other two elements, as they each mediated between it and the third, which several mediations created, precisely, the totality. The details of function and structure – Hegel's account of the franchise, bicameral parliament, freedom of expression and so on – were simply the institutional consequences, visible everywhere in modern political life, of his rational political principles. The result was that the state was a unity incorporating the different constituent elements into a totality, an actual, sovereign individuality (321).[16]

Individuality, 'as exclusive being for itself, appears as a relationship to other states each of which is independent with respect to each other' (322). Thus a consideration of the internal aspect of sovereignty was followed by a consideration of its external aspect, the relation of several states to one another. Hegel's discussion presupposed the empirical existence of the European state-system, even to the extent of casting aspersions on those who wished to sacrifice the autonomy of Prussia for a larger political entity, to be called Germany.[17] The empirical configuration of political units, however, did not touch the principles of the universal and homogeneous State, the idea of the State, that Hegel was here discussing. The argument is logically impressive: 'history possesses a determinate meaning and direction in its orientation towards the realization of freedom-reason, towards the organization of a common life where each individual finds his satisfaction insofar as he is reasonable (by the suppression of all non-mediated and non-human relations with nature). What has been gained by this process remains an acquisition, and every attempt to reverse the process is, strictly speaking, unreasonable and, on that basis, immoral (even though, as one knows, attempts in this direction can be undertaken and, a priori, nothing stands in the way of their success – the sole consequence of which would be that history would have to undertake its travail over again).'[18] And, in any event, even if the universal and homogeneous State became an empirical ecumenic organization, which, as has been argued, was in no way necessary to the truth of the argument, it would still remain an individual unit with respect to the historical and post-historical states that preceded it. Indeed, the universal and homogeneous State attained its empirical existence when its principles informed the spirit of only one or of several independent or individual states.

The independence of any particular state, considered a universal in itself, implied a negative relation to other equally particular states. But from this negative relation, Hegel said, the absolute positivity of the state appeared. It was recognized by the citizen as his duty to defend the state even at the sacrifice of property, rights, and life itself (323–4). War, therefore, may be justified to citizens as the willed acceptance of mortality and transience (and not as an accident, the result of foul passions, or the displeasure of gods). Sacrifice in war was the duty of all citizens when the state was endangered, though in the normal course of foreign relations a specific group, the soldiers alone, vowed to fight in its defence. The courage of the citizen-soldier involved more than the personal virtue that expressed one's freedom from the cares of mortality and transience because, Hegel said, it served 'the principle of the modern world,' namely the sovereignty of the state and the integration of the particular with the whole (328).

External public law

Following his discussion of the first constituent element of the idea of the state, internal public law, *das innere Staatsrecht*, in terms of both its own internal constitution, *die innere Verfassung für sich*, and external sovereignty, *die Souveränetät gegen aussen*, Hegel considered the second one, external public law or international law, *das aussere Staatsrecht*. His analysis was very brief, a mere ten paragraphs, with four short additions.

International law was the creature of autonomous states. Analogy with the moral relation between persons arising from the social contract 'theory' cannot be pushed very far.[19] In the first place, private persons in civil society were under the higher jurisdiction of the *Polizei* who gave effect to what was in itself right, but no such higher authority existed for the autonomous totality of the state. And second, what existed for the state in international law was right in the form of 'ought' or non-actuality, which was the exact opposite to what existed in the state.[20]

A people formed into a state, Hegel said, were spirit in its substantial rationality and unmediated actuality (*RPhil* 331). The implications of substantial rationality, namely its self-mediation and internal articulation, we have already considered. The consequence of unmediated actuality, Hegel immediately added, was that it was the absolute power on earth (and since there was no beyond, it was the absolute power, period). Formally, all people who gained the form of the state were entitled to be recognized as sovereign; whether they actually received such recognition depended on the first constituent element discussed above, namely the internal constitution of any particular state and its relations with neighbouring states. Between sovereign states particular relations were formalized as contracts or compacts that, in principle, ought to be honoured. In practice sometimes they were honoured and sometimes not, depending on how the interest or welfare, *Wohl*, of the state would be served (332, 336). Disagreements, therefore, led to war (334), but wars, at least as between modern states, were not motivated by personal, particularist animosity or hatred. States maintained at least a tacit recognition of their enemy and followed specific rules regarding envoys, prisoners, noncombatants and so on (338–9). Nevertheless, modern states remained, with respect to each other, particularities. Hence, their relations reflected the instability of passion, contingency, and selfish interest, and necessarily so, for it was only as particularity that the *Völkergeister* existed as objective, actual, self-conscious entities. 'Their fate and actions in their mutual relations are the revealed dialectic of the finiteness of these spirits from which arises the *universal* spirit, the *spirit of the world*, unrestricted and self-produced, exercising its own right, which is the highest right, over these finite spirits in *world-history*, which is the *world's court of judgement*' (340). As Hegel said in the addition to the preceding paragraph, the only judge of states was the universal and absolute spirit, for which each state was a particularity, however absolute it may be for itself. And this judge was the selfsame world spirit whose genesis had been traced in *Philosophy of History*.

World history

The third and synthesizing constituent element of the state was world history, 'spiritual actuality in its whole compass of internality and externality.' It was a court of judgment because, being universality in and for itself, all other particularities (i.e. the penates, civil society, and the several actual *Völkergeister*) were for it finite and determinate, as the process, *Bewegung*, of spirit in the element of world history (i.e. its actual, empirical configuration when scientifically grasped) attested (341).

The remaining nineteen paragraphs amounted to a précis of *Philosophy of History*. World history was the process by which reason and the freedom of self-conscious spirit created itself through its own activity. Each of the particular actors in the development of the world spirit, whether they were states, peoples, or individuals, whether they knew it or not, whether from a moral standpoint they were good or bad, noble or base, guilty or innocent, weak or strong, was a necessary constituent element, and each, when its time had come, had its proper part to play, and play but once.[21] The chief actors were the *Völkergeister*. Now a *Volk* did not begin its existence as a state. It only gradually actualized its ethical, *sittliche*, substance in appropriate form and thereby gained objectivity for itself and for others. That is, a *Volk* gained recognition only as a state. Prior to attaining the form of a state, 'before the beginning of actual history, we find, on the one hand, dumb innocence that is of no interest at all and, on the other, the raw courage, *Tapferkeit*, of formal struggles for recognition, and revenge' (349).[22] The initial act by which a clan, horde, tribe, etc. was transformed into a state was always absolutely justified: the right of heroes to found states cannot be abrogated (350; cf 102).[23] How could it? It was the work of the world spirit, the act that initiated history for a particular people, the act, indeed, that created them as a people properly speaking, that is, as a unity capable of recognition.

By courtesy of the world spirit, or rather by the necessity of its own internal self-development, the prerogatives of heroic founders were extended to the relatively civilized as compared with the barbaric. Pastoral peoples may treat hunters as barbarians, agriculturalists may treat pastoralists in the same way, and in general, those who have less fully developed the substantive constituent elements of the state may properly be treated as barbarians, unequal in right with the civilized, and possessed of an autonomy that was no more than a formality (351). Formalities could surely be dispensed with, at least where civilized states were concerned, in order to bring rationality and freedom to the backward and barbarian peoples of the world. This transparently self-serving justification for European expansion was excused by the ends that European domination served. 'What gives a meaning for World-history to the wars and strife that arise under such circumstances,' Hegel added, 'is that they are constituent-elements of a struggle for recognition that is related to something of determinate worth,' namely, the idea of the state, the development of the universal and homogeneous state. If, in these wars and struggles, the barbarians triumphed over the civilized, all one can say is that such victories were meaningless for world history. Eventually, perhaps a sage would have to explain how barbaric victory was historically necessary, etc, but such possibilities did not concern Hegel.[24]

Finally, there were the criteria by which civilized could be distinguished from barbarian *Völkergeister*. They were provided by the world's court of judgment itself, and are quite familiar already, having been set out in some detail in the preceding chapter.

The *Völkergeister* found their revealed reality and fulfilment as constituent elements of the world spirit, the actualization of which in specific and concrete circumstances was testimony to the grandeur and glory of the absolute universality that appeared through them. The world spirit, as spirit, was nothing but the process of its own activity moving toward absolute self-knowing. In the course of freeing itself from the unmediated condition of natural existence and developing itself as self-consciousness, four world-historical realms, *welthistorische Reiche*, each with its own principle, have been created (352). Corresponding to the principle of unmediated appearance without internal division or individuality was the natural, patriarchic communities of the oriental realm. Corresponding to the principle of knowledge of the first principle, i.e. knowledge of substantive spirit, which is being for-itself, was the particularist, superstitious, slave-based Greek realm. Corresponding to the principle of abstract universality and spiritless objectivity, which is developed as the perfected differentiation of the second principle, was the Roman realm of private persons whose formal rights were bound together solely by imperial will. Corresponding to the principle of reconciliation by which the infinite separation of the third principle was overcome and substantiality restored was the Germanic realm, the final realm. 'The present epoch has gotten rid of its barbarity and unjust caprice, and truth has abandoned the beyond, with its arbitrary sanctions, so that true reconciliation has become objective and the *state* is shown to be the image and actuality of reason' (360). In the state, Hegel concluded with a flourish, self-consciousness found all it ever sought, the actuality of its substantive knowing and willing coherently developed. In religion, the feeling associated with this development and the imagery appropriate to it were set forth, while in science self-consciousness found the free conceptual knowledge of this entire revealed reality in the mutually coordinated manifestations of state, nature, and idea.

The criteria of civilization were, therefore, two-fold. First, there was the empirical existence of the Germanic realm, institutionalized as the modern state and described in principle as the idea of the state or as the universal and homogeneous state. All empirical communities may be measured by this idea, and, to the extent they fail to meet its standards, their independence may be viewed as a formality. Second, there was the criterion of science, which was the fullest conceptual development of the world spirit, the self-comprehension of this spirit and, therefore, if not the Praetor whose absence was so keenly felt by Hegel (cf *RPhil* 333), then the presiding magistrate of the *Weltgerichte*.

Barbarian conflicts

This reading of *Philosophy of Right* has been guided by the opinion that the idea of the State described by Hegel was indistinguishable from the universal and homogeneous State developed through Kojève's interpretation of *Phenomenology*. According to Kojève, the universal and homogeneous State, the post-historical regime, was not a locus of action in the strong sense of introducing novelty and negativity, because nature, especially nature in the shape of the absolute other, the absolute given-being, namely God, had been overcome and 'humanized.' Instead of the negativity of action, the movement that had historically introduced novelty into the world, henceforth there would be only the movement of concept, the repetitive quasi-action of the post-historical struggle for recognition, and the complacency of those who do not seek recognition. In chapter 6 I considered in some 'metaphysical' detail what the sage was and what his relation to (his) wisdom meant. The relationship of the sage to the state may be summarized very briefly. The importance of the sage as the one who truly grasped the course of world history could hardly be overemphasized.

Kojève's interpretation of *Phenomenology* indicated that Hegel's forgiveness of Napoleon's 'sin' was, in non-representational language, his justification of the revolution, which took the form of wisdom that explained the genesis and meaning of the post-revolutionary state. For that wisdom to be truly true, for it to be a coincidence of subjective certainty, *Gewissheit*, and objective truth, *Wahrheit*, the reality that the discourse of wisdom revealed in the book must be fully and totally completed, and therefore perfect and without further possibility of extension or change. 'This "total" and "definitive" reality is the Napoleonic Empire. For Hegel (1806) it is a *universal* and *homogeneous* state: it unites the entire totality of humanity (at least that which counts historically) and "suppresses" (*aufhebt*) within itself all "specific differences" (*Besonderheit*): nations, social classes, families. (Christianity itself being "suppressed," there is no further dualism between church and state.) Thus, wars and revolutions are henceforth impossible. That is to say that this state will no longer modify itself and will remain eternally identical with itself. Now, man is formed by the state where he lives and acts. Therefore, man will no longer change himself either. And nature (without negativity) is in every way "completed" forever. Consequently, the science that correctly and completely describes the Napoleonic world will remain completely valid forever. It will be absolute knowledge, the final end point of all philosophical research. This knowledge is self-certain spirit' (IH 145). There is, accordingly, a strict parallel between the total discourse of wisdom and the totality of the state it described.

On the one hand, wisdom could not have existed empirically until after the state had been actualized, that is, until the completion of history (IH 284:90). That the sage could become what he (or she) truly is, namely, absolute self-consciousness, only as a citizen of the absolute state (IH 297) was clearly implied in Hegel's image of the owl of Minerva, as was indicated earlier. On the other hand, 'the sage and his wisdom are the final justification of the state and of history. The state must be homogeneous and universal in view of the homogeneity and universality of the *knowledge* developed in it. And the sage knows it. He knows that in the end the "absolute" state is but a means to gain self-conscious satisfaction by a true and genuine identification with the totality of being in absolute knowledge' (IH 303). The fights and labours of history had the purpose of engendering the universal and homogeneous State; that State, in turn, had and yet has the purpose of engendering wisdom (IH 398).

Wisdom is speech rather than silence. All speech aims at perfection, that is, at the coincidence of particular words and universal meaning, but only the perfected speech of absolute knowledge could attain that goal. 'In the final analysis: the perfect (Napoleonic) state is understood by the perfect citizen (Hegel) speaking the perfect language (of the *Phenomenology* and the *Encyclopaedia*)' (IH 126). Or, to use Kojève's later formulation, the flesh and blood human being delivered a discourse in the form of an empirical book revealing the totality of Being. The sage identified himself with his science, his discourse, and so with the totality it revealed: 'His ego is a *universal* ego; he realizes the conscious *integration* of being within his personal existence. But the knowledge of the sage is *his* knowledge in a double sense: it is his work, and it reveals the being that he himself is. Also, even while remaining fully *universal*, the ego of the sage remains *his own* ego; he is a *Selbst*, a *personal* ego, the ego of a concrete man named Georg Wilhelm Friedrich Hegel' (*IH* 327). The perfection of the discourse of the sage, we saw in chapter 6, lay in its circularity, in the 'fact' that Hegel has spoken/written the complete Book. In distinguishing between the sage and the philosopher, Kojève made the point that, in principle, both are agreed on the definition of wisdom, namely complete speech. One may well expect disagreements between the sage and the philosophers concerning the validity of the claim (for so it appears to the philosophers), as distinct from the fact, of the sage's wisdom. This conflict is most apparent where silence, not speech, has been understood as wisdom.

To employ the terminology used by Kojève, the conflict is over whether human perfection is full, total, and complete self-consciousness or full, total, and complete unconsciousness. Here one may invoke 'Hindu thinkers who say that man approaches perfection-satisfaction in dreamless sleep, and that perfection-satisfaction is *realized* in the absolute night of the "fourth state" (turia) of the Brahmins or in Nirvana, in the extinction of all consciousness, of the Buddhists.' Generally speaking, the conflict reached its extreme when the non-Hegelian sought 'perfection-satisfaction in *absolute silence* that excludes even monologue or dialogue with God.' Finally Kojève added the examples of Nietzsche's 'Chinese' ideal of the person who had been animalized within and by way of the security of his well being,[25] and the person whose ideal of salvation was to be gained 'by (unconscious) erotic or aesthetic (e.g., musical) "ecstasy"' (*IH* 278:84). One could also add the philosopher-theologian who refused to murder God by giving a complete account of him and so necessarily took refuge in the silence of prayer and ritual and doctrinal belief, or in the quasi-speech of myth.

All these sorts of people are satisfied in the sense that they may well voluntarily remain identical with themselves until they die. Moreover, one could say that they were (or could be) morally perfect in that they were taken (or might be taken) as models of human existence. If they were taken universally as models of human existence then it would be entirely correct to speak of the perfect satisfaction of such people. 'Eh bien,' commented Kojève, 'these are *facts* that are here opposed to Hegel. And clearly, he can have nothing to reply. At best he can oppose the *fact* of the conscious sage to the *facts* of the unconscious "sages." And if this fact did not exist?' Kojève did not provide an answer to this rhetorical question. Presumably it was contained in a prior comment on Nietzsche: 'Nietzsche seriously envisaged the possibility that the ideal that he called "Chinese" might become *universal*. And that does not appear to be absurd: it is possible, if it is not opposed.' There would seem to be, therefore, an active, not to say aggressive, implication to Hegelian wisdom. It seems that a totally or partially silent sage cannot be refuted by speech: the unconscious sage could not speak and at the same time remain wise, the eroticist likewise could not enjoy his erotic ecstasy and at the same time discuss it, the believer could not worship a God that he could fully comprehend, and so on. 'So then he [the unconscious sage] can be refuted only as one "refutes" a fact, a thing, or an animal: by physically destroying it' (*IH* 279:84).[26] No longer, as in *Phenomenology*, could the dead be left to bury their dead (*PhG* 58:45). The quick must assist.

The death of the other was, of course, an integral part of the original conflict of desires that resulted in the dialectic of master and slave. Here it is recapitulated, only now Hegel appears as a synthesis of master and slave, the perfect citizen-sage. The element of mastery had not, for all that, disappeared.[27] If human self-consciousness arose from the conflict of human being-for-itself and being-for-another, as the entirety of *Phenomenology* as interpreted by Kojève has shown, when absolute self-consciousness had been attained and man has become wise, the difference between consciousness and self-consciousness had been finally and definitively overcome. Accordingly, any who were outside the circle of wisdom were, as compared with the sage, merely one-sided being-for-itself. If they were yet called human beings, the sage was clearly something more (*IH* 418). The sage was, to use representational language, a god;[28] he was both being-for-itself and for-another (who was himself). Accordingly, the non-sage and the silent 'sage' were completely inessential. To use the language of *Philosophy of Right*, they were barbarians whose independence, whose being-for-itself, may be treated by the sage as a mere formality.[29]

What is one to make of this purely formal negation of the non-sage by the sage? In a preliminary way, the following points may be made. So far as the sage is concerned, conflict between himself or herself and the others could only confirm (his or her) wisdom; the struggle was a pseudo-fight since he or she must be indifferent to the actual outcome in that it could not possibly bring about anything new. But what of the non-sage and the non-Hegelian? So far as the Hegelian non-sage was concerned, the highest Hegelian meaning this conflict could attain would be equivalent to the meaning of the original anthropogenic struggle. That is, it recapitulated the first genuine act on the way to self-education, a way that necessarily ended in wisdom. And as for the non-Hegelian, who was perforce not a sage, the conflict with the sage appeared to mean that an essential product of wisdom was death, by which is meant not a meditative act but the actual murder of non-sages, whether Hegelian or no. Common sense would anticipate that this exceedingly practical consequence would likely be resisted by those upon whom a formal death sentence had been passed. To the non-Hegelian, the supreme height of inaction, wisdom, is apparently indistinguishable from the most primitive negation of a thing, metabolism. Does this mean that the sage presides indifferently over a death-camp?[30] This question will be considered further in chapter 8. Now, however, we turn to the 'civilized' politics of citizens and sages within the universal and homogeneous state, where everyone knew and abided by the Hegelian rules.

Civilized conflicts

As in the relations between sage and non-sage, 'civilized' politics also recapitulated the historical dialectic of master and slave. Now, however, each participant was a citizen, a synthesis of the elements of mastery and slavery, 'a citizen who fights and labours, the soldier-worker of Napoleon's armies' (IH 91). Of course, the sage was also a citizen, as Kojève has often insisted; moreover, we have Hegel's testimony that the speculation that resulted in wisdom was equivalent to the death in battle of a Napoleonic soldier whose end helped actualize the universal and homogeneous state. Likewise one would have to conclude that the citizen was implicitly or in principle also a sage. In any case, whether speculative or pragmatic, the synthesis did not simply abolish the elements of mastery and slavery but also preserved them. They can, therefore, be seen to appear in new, though thoroughly recognizable, forms.[31] We shall consider first its true 'tragic' political form, then the correct or proper relationship between the leader and the sage, and in the next section the social 'comedy' of post-historical life.

In *Philosophy of Right* (93, 93A) Hegel argued that the violence of heroic founding was impermissible after the state had been established. Then it became crime or madness (cf IH 32:28). Kojève's interpretation of this piece of Hegelian jurisprudence, which he discussed in terms of Hegel's ethics, was that 'true ethical judgements are those that support the state (ethical = legal).' States, in turn, were judged by universal history, which, of course, made sense only because history had been concluded. 'Now, Napoleon and Hegel concluded history. That is why Hegel can judge states and individuals.' What counted as "good" was what had prepared the way for Napoleon and Hegel. But this preparation consisted in action, negation, and therefore was also evil, a sin. 'But sin can be pardoned. How? By its success. Success absolves crime because success means a new *existing* reality. But how to judge success? For this, history must be terminated. Then may be seen what maintains itself in existence: definitive reality' (*IH* 95). One might expect to end this train of reasoning with a typical 'right-Hegelian' interpretation concerning the inherent reasonableness of existing arrangements. Kojève's meaning was, in a sense, quite the opposite. Excluding the abstract possibility, no sooner raised than dismissed, and unknowable anyhow, that the 'definitive reality' was not the idea of the state but some unthinkable form of barbarism, the meaning of actual violence in the post-historical world could only be that it supported the state, that it was a necessary element in the process of its ever more complete actualization.[32] And, indeed, this was Kojève's interpretation.

The universal and homogeneous State was definitive reality because it provided full and complete satisfaction to its citizens. Consequently they had no desire, no reasonable desire, to change (i.e. negate) it. 'I am fully and definitively "satisfied" when my personality, which is exclusively my *own*, is "recognized" (in its reality and in its value, its "dignity") by *all*, on condition that I myself "recognize" the reality and value of those who are charged with the duty of "recognizing" me.' To be satisfied is to be both unique-in-the-world and yet also universally valuable, which was precisely the position of the citizen in the universal and homogeneous State. On the one hand, because it was universal, one would be recognized by *all* men (in more restricted form, by all who counted historically); on the other hand, because it was homogeneous, it would truly be oneself who was so recognized, and not merely the one, who happened to be oneself, but who was seen as a representative of a specific sex, an ancient family, a wealthy class, a powerful nation, and so on. In Kojève's words: 'The particular (I) is directly related to the universal (state) without having any screens formed by "specific differences" (*Besonderheit*: families, classes, nations). That is, in the post-revolutionary world, individuality is realized (for the first time).' And an individual, properly speaking, was one who was satisfied by what he or she was and had no desire to transcend his or her self or become other than what he or she had become. The self-understanding of an individual in this sense was 'to understand integral, definitive "perfect" man. This is what Hegel did in and by means of his System' (*IH* 145–6).

Power and wisdom

Prior to the creation of the system by Hegel there occurred the violent action that founded the 'germ' of the state whose idea the system described and justified. Prior to the labours of spirit in Hegelian form, there occurred the labours of spirit in Napoleonic form. Accordingly, 'only the leader of the universal and homogeneous state (Napoleon) is *really* "satisfied" (= recognized by all in his reality and personal value).' Thus only Napoleon had become truly free and unlimited by the *Besonderheit* of family, class, nation, etc. But, Kojève added, 'all citizens are here "satisfied" potentially, for each *one* can *become* this leader whose personal ("particular") action is at the same time universal (state) action, that is, the action of all (*Tun Aller und Jeder*).' There were, however, certain conditions involved. Hegel explained in *Philosophy of Right* that membership in the universal status-group was to be determined chiefly by personal talent but also by certain non-objective factors (292, 294). As Kojève remarked, heredity, a 'specific difference' (moreover one that is natural, pagan, and, properly speaking, unhuman), no longer would play any part in individual advancement and recognition. All would depend upon history, one's personal history: 'Thus, each can actualize his desire for recognition: on condition of accepting risk of death (element of mastery) that, in this state, implies competition (= political struggle; this risk guarantees the "seriousness" of the candidates), and on condition also of having previously taken part in the constructive activity of the society, in the collective labour that maintains the state in its actuality (element of servitude, of service that, moreover, guarantees the "competence" of the candidates)' (*IH* 146). The citizen who gained complete satisfaction was, therefore, indeed a synthesis of the master-warrior and the slave-labourer. Furthermore, all other citizens would, from time to time, be called upon to make war (cf *RPhil* 326) and to undertake social service. As for Hegel, he was content to understand the whole process, to reveal by his knowledge the reality incarnate in Napoleon, the monarchic 'I will' described in *Philosophy of Right*.[33]

Napoleon was recognized universally because he conformed to the requirements outlined earlier: his personal action was also the action of the state. 'Napoleon has made everyone recognize his "vanity" and the state is the revelation and realization of this "vanity"; thus, in Napoleon vanity is no longer "vain" and is no longer a sin,' having been 'forgiven' by success. Moreover, Napoleon was in accord with the state he had created. It was his work, and he knew it. 'Thus, there is an absolute coincidence between willing and knowing. Napoleon has *raised himself above Sein* [given-being], but he has not *fled* from it; he is "actually present" in the world (in the state).' Napoleon knew he was free because he had proven it to himself and to others through his actions. But, Kojève added, 'Napoleon does not know that in the end satisfaction comes from knowledge and not from action (even though knowledge presupposes action). Thus, it is Hegel who is absolutely satisfied' (*IH* 148). Satisfaction must come not from being the incarnation of the perfect state or even from founding it, but from revealing that perfection. This was why Hegel, not Napoleon, was called by Kojève the perfect citizen (*IH* 126). Moreover, just as satisfaction came from revealing perfection rather than being perfect, or from becoming a Platonic or Aristotelian god (which for a pagan was, of course, impossible), so too the meaning of post-historical life could be seen not from the recitation of a catalogue of events, however suggestive or persuasive, or even from the consciousness of such events as revealed by the self-interpretation of those who enacted them. The meaning of post-historical life could come only from self-conscious Hegelians, or at least from those who imaginatively had assumed the attitude of a self-conscious Hegelian, a sage.

In chapter 5 I discussed the relationship of Hegel to Napoleon by analogy with the relationship of consciousness to self-consciousness. The limitations to the analogy are obvious enough: consciousness could *become* self-consciousness. It is hard to see how Napoleon could become Hegel, even if Hegel could understand, justify, or 'forgive' Napoleon. In any event, the relationship of Hegel to Napoleon was, Kojève said, the model for the proper relationship between sage and leader. Even if it seemed unlikely that Hegel ever would rule, or act as an adviser to rulers, perhaps he would be the teacher of future rulers. Perhaps some day a Hegelian would rule. Perhaps serious and competent civil servants would become wise. Kojève later provided some more general reflections on the topic of the relationship between the leader and the sage in a review of a commentary by Leo Strauss on Xenophon's text, *Hiero, or Tyrannicus*, which text consisted in a dialogue between the poet Simonides and the tyrant Hiero.[34]

According to Kojève, Simonides was a typical intellectual who criticized the world on the basis of certain verbal ideals to which he unjustifiably granted eternal value and truth. 'In fact, Simonides presents his "ideal" in the form of a "utopia,"'' in the sense that 'starting from the utopia, one does not see how the given concrete reality must be transformed in the future to make it conform to the ideal in question' (*OT* 220:145). According to Strauss and Xenophon, an enlightened or popular or just tyranny is impossible. Simonides was therefore morally correct in giving useless and utopian advice. Kojève replied that, first, whereas Xenophon's discussion of tyranny was, in context, utopian, the advice he gave to Hiero concerning an 'ideal' tyranny was actually in the contemporary world 'an almost banal reality.' Simonides' advice amounted to 'distributing "prizes" of all sorts, especially honorific ones, so as to establish in his state a "stakhanovist" model in the fields of agriculture, industry, and commerce,' a sort of expanded Legion of Honour or Queen's Honours List. Second, the tyrant should replace a hired mercenary bodyguard with a 'state police.' 'A permanent armed force' would serve as the nucleus for an army created by the general mobilization of citizens who had already been partially trained through a program of compulsory military service. Third, he ought to turn his personal property into state property 'and construct public buildings rather than palaces.' In this way, he would gain the 'affection' of his subjects (*OT* 221–2:146–7). From this admittedly 'banal' list, Kojève concluded that modern 'tyrants'[35] (Kojève named Salazar) have in fact actualized Xenophon's utopia, proving, in effect, that it was not simply utopian, merely historically utopian, an 'ideal' at that time, but no longer.

Kojève's explanation of how the utopian advice of Simonides became actual unfolded, not unexpectedly, in three parts. In the first section he raised the question of whether modern tyrannies are philosophically justified by Xenophon's dialogue. His answer was a qualified 'no.' First, Simonides and Hiero argued from within the world of classical pagan masters for whom labour and the consequences of it were of no immediate importance. As a result, second, Hiero was forced to admit that he was unable to attain the honour, recognition, or authority that he truly desired. That is, Hiero experienced the master's 'existential impasse' described by Hegel. 'Thus does one understand why he listens to the counsel of the sage who promises him "satisfaction" by indicating to him the means of obtaining "recognition"' (*OT* 228:151). On closer analysis, however, it turned out that Hiero exaggerated his dissatisfaction when he complained of the necessity of ruling by terror. Rule by terror, as Hegel showed, was the absence of a state. But clearly, for Hiero, a state still existed. His complaint, then, was not that no one recognized his authority but that not everyone did. Xenophon and Hegel were therefore agreed that 'in the last analysis the leader of the state will be *fully* satisfied only when his state includes the whole entirety of mankind' (*OT* 232:154). No such state existed in Xenophon's day, and one does not exist today. Thus, a modern tyrant would have the same reasons as Hiero for listening to a modern Simonides. But in order not to have the same reasons as Hiero for rejecting his advice, a modern Simonides must not be a utopian. He must tender realistic advice.

The second question Kojève proposed to discuss was whether the modern tyrant had been able to realize Simonides's 'utopia' without relying on the advice of philosophers or, on the contrary, only because philosophers have from time to time advised tyrants (*OT* 223:147). Raising this topic immediately involved answering two preliminary questions: could philosophers have done anything else but talk of political ideals, and, if so, did they want to do anything else (235:156)? Kojève concluded: 'Contrary to a commonly accepted opinion, the philosopher is perfectly capable of taking power and governing or participating in government, for example, by giving political counsel to the tyrant' (238–9: 159). Accordingly, the only question was whether or not the philosopher wanted to take part in government. Like all questions having to do with will, it could not be definitively answered *a priori*, no more than one could give a full account of why one desire became a master and another a slave. As with all such questions, one could only look back and see what did in fact happen.

Taken on its own terms as it appeared to the philosopher in quest of wisdom, politics was a distraction or a threat. But, Kojève added, thinking this way was based upon an assumption concerning being and truth, namely that being 'is essentially immutable in itself and eternally identical to itself and that it is completely revealed for all eternity within and by way of an intelligence perfect from the outset' and that truth was 'this adequate revelation of the atemporal totality of being' (*OT* 241:160–1). Man, in this view, was related to being and truth in a way that did not depend on time or place. For this reason one lost nothing in staying 'aloof' from politics. But if one did not accept this traditional and 'theistic' view, if one were a radical Hegelian atheist, if one understood being as essentially a temporal, historical, and geographical process, then one must avoid solitude, the isolation of an aristocratic-pagan Epicurean garden or the restricted society of a bourgeois-Christian 'republic of letters.' Indeed, one must take part in history, since it was there and there alone that being created itself, and there only could one reveal it. But if that were so, there was no reason why the philosopher ought not to take an active part in government. Besides, there was a great danger that, isolated in their 'garden' or 'republic,' the philosophers would form schools, sects, and prejudices; they would grow out of touch with the changing reality around them, and their ideas, even if once upon a time true, would become false. Only these philosophers, having become sectarians, would fail to notice their own irrelevance (OT 247:165).

More importantly, however, even the philosopher desired recognition from those who were competent judges of his merits. According to Kojève, there was no reason to restrict the number of disciples of a philosopher more severely than the number of competent judges of a tyrant. The danger with imposing such restrictions, especially for philosophers, was that they may mistake agreement with their own opinions for competent judgment. In this way they would succumb to unphilosophic prejudice, a mild form of lunacy. The cure was to engage in discussion with other people whose number could no more be determined beforehand than could the topics of conversation. But, by engaging in conversation, philosophers would be recognized by their interlocutors for what they are. Not least of all, they would be recognized for their pedagogical talents and efforts. Now, the tyrant was also a pedagogue, and the state as a whole was a pedagogical institution. In principle, therefore, the philosopher was bound to be in competition with the state: willy-nilly, he was involved in politics. 'And if the philosopher does not wish to restrain artificially or unduly the extent of his pedagogical activity (and so court the risk of the prejudices of the "cloister"), he will necessarily have a marked tendency to take part in some way or other in government as a whole so that the state would be organized and governed in such a way that his philosophical pedagogy would be possible in that state and be effective' (OT 259:173). The problem, however, was that philosophers wanted it both ways: they wanted to be politically effective pedagogues (since this could not be avoided anyhow) and they wanted to be free of the 'distractions' of politics in order to pursue truth (which they may well think is timeless). The result was a compromise: philosophers offered verbal, utopian advice that tyrants quite rightly ignored, confirming thereby the prejudices of philosophers against politics in general.

What could be done? If the philosopher's advice were to be realistic, not utopian, he would have to make himself familiar with the details of concrete political problems. This would take a great deal of time. In fact, he must give up philosophy. If he would remain a philosopher he must give up political action because he lacked time to do both. Was this reasonable? Unfortunately, it is impossible to say in advance, which is why the discussion of the relationship between the philosopher and politics has been, historically, so interminable. The question could only be settled after the fact. In the end, it could be decided only by means of a post-historical phenomenology, what Kojève here called 'historical verification' (*OT* 265:178).

In the first part of his commentary, Kojève posed the question: Are modern tyrannies justified by Xenophon, an ancient philosopher? The second part discussed the question: What do philosophers do? The answer is: they talked and didn't do anything, which lead them into a political dilemma fully as serious as Hiero's. The third section of his commentary resolved the aporias of the first two. It was, then, an example of Hegelian dialectical exercise. Modern tyrannies could be justified by a certain kind of talk, not that of a philosopher but that of a sage. But the sage's talk was true only because an active, historical (and not just verbal) dialectic had already taken place, had come to its conclusion, and so had left the sage with nothing further to do except give a correct account of what had already happened. This account would resolve the problem of the relationship of wisdom and tyranny or of the sage and the leader.

At first sight, history appeared to confirm the vulgar opinion that tyrants have had nothing to do with philosophers and their empty ideas. But when one looked closely at the model tyrant, the one whom successive tyrants, including Napoleon, had imitated, namely Alexander the Great, one could see that he was a pupil of Aristotle, who was a pupil of Plato, who, like Xenophon, was a pupil of Socrates. The Socratic element in Alexander's conquests was found not so much in his desire to dissolve the ethnic particularism of Greek and barbarian (according to Kojève, this was properly Aristotelian) but in his desire to establish a universal dominion, 'the political expression of a *civilization*, the material actualization of a "logical" entity, universal and one, like the logos itself' (*OT* 271:182). Prior imperial organizations of the ancient world (Kojève mentioned Ikhnaton) were based not upon the universality of the logos but on the equality of all people before the one true god. Religious universalism led, however, not to a political empire but to a conception of social homogeneity (in a beyond, it is true). Now, 'the political goal that humanity presently is pursuing (or combating) is not only that of a politically *universal* state but equally that of a socially *homogeneous* state or "classless society"' (272:183). Once again, therefore, politics was a tributary of philosophy, only this time the philosophy in question was the negation or secularization of religion, whose notion of homogeneity it necessarily presupposed in order to negate. 'The tyrant who here inaugurated the *real* political movement consciously followed the instructions of the intellectual who, in order to apply it politically, willfully transformed the idea of the philosopher so that it ceased to be a "utopian" ideal ... and became a political theory on the basis of which one could give concrete counsel to tyrants that could be followed by them' (275:184). These two historical examples, Kojève concluded, showed that, when duly prepared or distorted by intellectuals and publicists, the political advice of philosophers had indirectly or in a mediated way been followed.

The correct Hegelian understanding of the relationship between the tyrant and the philosopher was, therefore, dialectical. The utopias of philosophers provided a perspective on political reality by introducing an alternative to what actually existed. Eventually someone, let us say a tyrant, acted on this now more or less distorted advice and more or less actualized the original utopia. The process continued: on the one side, philosophical progress toward wisdom, on the other, political progress toward the universal and homogeneous State. That is, if philosophers did not offer advice and create utopias, there would be no political progress and no history; if political men, and especially tyrants, did not act on that advice there would be no philosophical progress toward wisdom since there would be nothing new to understand.

Kojève's 'historical verification' showed all this to be quite reasonable: 1 / the tyrant was reasonable in that he did not try to apply utopian theory since he had no time to fill in the gap between utopia and actuality; 2 / philosophers were reasonable in refusing to fill in details, since it would leave them no time to philosophize, in which case they could not legitimately give philosophical advice; 3 / intellectuals were reasonable in trying to apply the philosophers' advice to actuality and in the process simplify and distort philosophical ideas; and 4 / the tyrant is reasonable in trying to follow the intellectual's distortion and not the philosopher's utopia. 'In short, everyone behaves in a *reasonable* way in historical *actuality*, and it is by behaving in a *reasonable* way that everyone eventually obtains, directly or indirectly, *actual* results' (OT 279:187). Conversely, it would be quite unreasonable if: 1 / tyrants denied the value of philosophy simply because it was inapplicable; 2 / philosophers condemned tyranny 'on principle' or on the basis of their utopian theories alone (because the philosopher is clearly incompetent in such matters – otherwise he would judge not on principle but within a concrete context, knowledge of which may only be slowly acquired, which would leave no time for philosophizing); 3 / intellectuals refused philosophers the right to judge the philosophical value of their opinions or if they refused political men and tyrants the right to select and distort their ideas (as they selected and distorted the ideas of the philosopher) with a view to actualizing those that admit of actualization. 'In a general way,' Kojève concluded, 'history itself is charged with "judging" (by "results" or "success") the acts that political men or tyrants undertake (consciously or not) as a result of the ideas of philosophers adapted for practice by intellectuals' (OT 280:188). An equally reasonable division of labour would place some of these intellectuals, the 'liberals' about whom Hegel spoke at the end of *Philosophy of History*, in university institutions, and others, political intellectuals, could serve the state in the executive branch, or even the 'fourth estate.'

Kojève's analysis of the relation of the sage to the leader was, on its own terms, identical to Hegel's. It was, therefore, an example of what Kojève took the task of the sage to be in the post-historical world – namely, to explain its inherent historical rationality. Moreover, this synthesis of power and truth, this actualized 'utopian' philosopher-king imitated both Hegel and Napoleon by choosing the career of the political intellectual, and so becoming a wise adviser to the leader, the formal monarchical 'I will,' a civil servant whose seriousness showed him to be a master still. One cannot resist the observation that, oddly enough, Kojève's account of the proper relationship between the political man and the philosopher read remarkably like an *apologia pro vita sua*.

Social life

Not everyone in a post-historical regime seeks universal recognition by way of political struggle. In *Philosophy of Right* Hegel discussed the recognition gained by one's 'inner life' in the form of actualizing one's subjective freedom in one's choice of occupation within civil society (262, 262A), to which one could add, for example, the freedom of adults to contract the marriage of their choice rather than have parents do so, and so on.[36] Civil society, in short, does provide a realm for restricted, though not universal, recognition. Presumably it can provide satisfaction for those who are less competent or less serious about gaining universal recognition. However that may be, the position of the state as the realm of universal recognition, of full and complete satisfaction, and its absolute singularity in this respect, cannot but alter the hitherto existing contours of limited recognition and satisfaction previously found within civil society. In other words, prior to the existence of the universal and homogeneous state, there were certain 'natural' limits, present even in civil society, that constrained that realm even more than it is inherently constrained. The potentiality for universal recognition that was opened by the idea of the state did not leave civil society untouched. It is to a consideration of those alterations that we now turn.

Perhaps the easiest way to see the changes to civil society brought about by the universal and homogeneous State would be to recapitulate Hegel's scheme of periodization (*IH* 173:45). The first period, tragic pagan antiquity, was dominated by the Master, given expression in philosophy, and characterized by the separation of private and public and of male and female. Indeed, this last separation brought about the decline of the pagan world: Oedipus and Antigone were *both* criminals (cf *IH* 104–5, 253). The second period, the comic, bourgeois, Roman, and medieval era, was dominated spiritually by the Slave and the celestial reconciliation of Christianity. The third period, the age of the Citizen, synthesized here below what had been for the Christian his pious hope: no philosophy and no religion, no Master and no Slave, no transcendent beyond, and no separation of the sexes. As Hegel said in *Philosophy of Right* (166), the family was a natural unity. Following the humanization of nature, a new unity that combined male and female in a properly human way emerged. Kojève discussed this new and comic androgyny under the headings of divinity and re-animalization.

In the biological realm, what united the particular and the universal was the species; in the historical human world it was the people, *Volk*. 'Now a people is something entirely different than a species,' it is an 'organic whole' that has a real unity; the *Volk* was a genuine middle term 'at once a simple individual and a universal: universal for its members, individual for humanity.' Because of this mediation human beings were historical. With plants and animals, one moved directly and without mediation from the universal to the particular; consequently, they have no history (*IH* 83–4). But history was finished, and the specific difference, the *Besonderheit* of the *Volk*, had been superseded by a genuine or absolute universality, for which there could be no negation. 'And man who no longer *negates* no longer has a genuine *future* (since he forever accepts the present as given). Thus, he is no longer Hegelian or historical ... There is no more history; the future there [in this state] is a past that has already been; life is therefore purely biological. Properly speaking, therefore, there is no longer man' (387). What took the place of 'man' was a curious sort of being. Kojève first described him or her by the two Aristotelian alternatives, a beast or a god. Later he changed his mind somewhat.

The sage, quite plainly, was an Aristotelian god. Since wisdom was the possession of truth, which was one and the same for Hegel and his readers, one sage could not differ from another. 'That is to say that he is not human in the same sense as *historical* man (no longer being *free* in the same sense since he no longer negates by his action): he is, rather, "divine" (but mortal). The sage is, however, an individual in this sense, that in his existential *particularity* he possesses *universal* science. In this sense he is still *human* (and therefore mortal)' (508 n1:238 n30). Fortunately, just as anyone could become leader, likewise there were no 'natural' limits to apotheosis: 'This integration [of history] or virtual wisdom, is found in each citizen of the absolute state' (*IH* 304), so all a citizen need do to become a god would be to become aware that he or she already had become one (cf *IH* 309).

If this result were not astonishing enough, it turns out that by becoming a god 'man' also became an animal. Kojève argued that human, historical time was not natural or cosmic time. Accordingly, the end of history was not the end of the cosmos. All that 'happened' was that there came into being a world without negativity. One way to characterize this condition, as indicated earlier, would be to say that nature had been 'humanized.' This 'humanization' and the resulting political 'humanism' were favourite expressions of Hegel's younger followers. One could equally say, as Marx did, that man had become 'naturalized.' In both cases the opposition between human and natural being, and the resulting negative relation between the two, had disappeared. Either way no cosmic catastrophe or, indeed, biological catastrophe was involved. Human being simply had lost its specifically human attributes but maintained its physical and biological ones. 'Man remains alive as an animal who is in *harmony* with nature or given-being.' To live in harmony with nature, as so many of our gentler contemporaries promise, meant 'the disappearance of bloody wars and revolutions.' Although contemporary advocates of natural harmony did not emphasize this (for reasons too obvious to mention), it also meant an end to philosophy because, since human being no longer essentially changed itself, 'there is no further reason to change the (true) principles that are the basis of his knowledge of the world and himself. But everything else can be maintained indefinitely: art, love, games, etc.; in short, everything that makes man *happy*' (434–5 n1:158–9 n6). No post-historical reader of *Whole Earth Catalogue* could possibly disagree with such sentiments.

Kojève had an opportunity for further comic reflections in a review that parodied the style of three very funny books by the editor of his lectures on Hegel, Raymond Queneau.[37] He was going to judge Queneau's work, Kojève said, from a Hegelian point of view 'because the three novels in question deal with wisdom. In them Queneau described three incarnations of the sage, that is, three of his aspects or "constituent-elements," different from one another but complementary.' Literary incarnations of the sage have usually not been very compelling portraits, but when Queneau showed us 'modern and normal persons, acceptable to all points of view and giving the impression of leading the life of sages, then, for a reader who has made a few philosophical studies, it is almost a duty to try to see more closely if we are not dealing with a case of authentic wisdom,' namely 'perfect satisfaction accompanied by a plenitude of self-consciousness' (388–9). Indeed, it is impossible to avoid being a Hegelian if one is going to philosophize at all in the present world. Yet non-Hegelian idioms existed, and with them non-Hegelian understandings of wisdom. These would have to be disposed of.

Kojève again mentioned Hindu *turia* as an option, but added that as soon as these so-called sages opened their mouths they destroyed their alleged wisdom, whatever their discipline and sincerity. 'No one with a grain of common sense could really take them seriously.' And, anyhow, most of the time they either leave one indifferent or else arouse indignation. One might just as well describe a state of drunkenness as satisfaction. Besides, sexual and nutritive emaciation leading to a kind of paralysis hardly looks like satisfaction. In contrast, the religious ideal of complete self-consciousness (but which was not followed by complete satisfaction) appeared to be an improvement. Complete satisfaction was held by the pious to be impossible because it was sinful and presumptuous to think that man could achieve self-perfection. God's grace was needed. The lay version of this pseudo-ideal, Kojève reiterated, had led to a host of well-known species inhabiting the 'spiritual bestiary' of the contemporary republic of letters. In all cases, whether it be that of a philosopher who did not turn into a sage, a poet, critic, psychologist, or professional existentialist, when these people were dissatisfied, as they inevitably proved themselves to be, they almost always wanted to change things to correspond to their judgments about how things 'ought' to be and almost never considered that their judgments were simply out of touch with reality. In short, they were tiresome moralists who also either leave one indifferent or arouse indignation.

However that may be, no one denied that wisdom was a human ideal. How, then, did Queneau's characters measure up? At first sight, the very question ought to provoke outrage: 'What is there in common, one says, between the daily grind of banal life led by these unemployed *"voyous"*[38] and the deep but as yet unpublished wisdom that perhaps one day will be the supreme reward for the studious life of philosophers?' Besides, they were vulgar and ungrammatical. But think further. It is true that they did not speak like our professional academic philosophers, but how do we know that Socrates, also an unemployed *voyou*, didn't speak more or less the same way as Queneau's characters? If the encrustations of philosophical jargon serve simply to hide rather than reveal reality, then surely a return to vulgarity would be the first step to the achievement of any real philosophical progress: one step back to take two steps forward. One may grant, then, that their language was revealing. But what did they in fact reveal. What did they talk about? 'Well! these heroes speak about everything and anything, by speaking, in the end only of themselves' (392). In short, they revealed their world phenomenologically. Were they then satisfied by what they revealed, that is, with themselves? Who could doubt it? Were they truly self-conscious? Of course. 'Of course, their banality could deceive us. But would that not simply be too bad for us?'

Kojève's interpretation, which might appear to normal readers as artificial or arbitrary, was saved by his personal knowledge that Queneau was 'full of Hegelian philosophy' and so was quite likely to have written such books. But this consideration raised another question: 'How, before history had been completed, can these three men have obtained wisdom, that is absolute or definitive, because total, knowledge?' (394). In the past, of course, counterfeit wisdom had been proclaimed in various Epicurean or Voltairean gardens; were not these three, a bored proletarian with aristocratic tastes, a poet who had published nothing, and the soldier who was professionally anti-military, just Epicurean pseudo-sages? No, not at all. Naturally, there would be rearguard actions and final touches to be put on certain works, but the eventual outcome was not in doubt. The final battle was done, hence the pacifist soldier; there was nothing new to be said, hence the unpublished poet; there was nothing more to do, hence the proletarian aristocrat. But were they not ridiculous? Ridicule, Kojève replied, only touched those who let it. 'And then, can one *reasonably* aspire to something other than peaceful happiness in perfect satisfaction that results in a oneself that one knows perfectly and who is attractive not only for the (divine or human) author who created them, but also for *all* those who run into him (in life or in a book) *without any prejudice*, that is, as philosophers?' (397). In summary, Kojève concluded, 'if the *new world* (and the last one, since it resulted from the last war) is to be the world of Queneau's novels, one could say, without irony I think, that it is brave. And one could say it even in English.' One may question Kojève's understanding of Huxley's dystopia without calling the rest of his commentary into question. In any event, even in this new world of lazy and vulgar sages, one piece of 'nature' still must be overcome, sexual differentiation.

Kojève's remarks on this topic were contained in a review of Françoise Sagan's first two novels.[39] A new world of dubious paternity, Kojève began, has been born in literature. The dubiousness involved was no doubt a result of having so many claimants for the role of father. There was, first of all, a German philosopher of genius who saw and understood the doings of a Great Corsican (even though many common-sensical people did not take seriously his account or the even more disturbing opinions of one of his apostles, Marx). In England, a contemporary (Brummel) seemed to have seen things the same way, though this 'peaceful genius' died a martyr, unknown for his sensational discovery that honour and virile heroism could henceforth be gained only in civilian life. And lastly, in France there was a marquis (de Sade) jailed by the tyrant but freed by the people who 'also understood that in this new free world everything could be committed, at least in private' (703); but he was taken for a libertine and the truth remained not widely known. 'To tell the truth, it is because I have wanted to reveal at last this mystery so carefully guarded by those who control it (assuming that they still exist) that I decided to write and even publish the few pages that follow, dedicating them to all who read them and certainly to Miss Sagan, who will no doubt receive them through the good offices of a vigilant Argus' (703).[40] Thanks to the travail of this girl, this veritable virgin-mother, the new world mentioned above had been born in literature. Before 1954, it seemed, no one had written about this aspect of post-historical life except to complain about it. Hemingway, for example, dealt with the world his father had castrated and chased about the globe looking for a real man, eventually settling upon an ancient Caribbean gent whose battles were waged against heroic and very powerful fish. 'But this quite recent natural history of a modern Anglo-Saxon will remain entirely too esoteric as compared with the already venerable German apocalypse of universal history' (704). Thus was it left to a very young French girl to reveal what it meant to live in a world where all glory had been harvested – though her revelations were somewhat naïve or unconscious.

Her world, the same brave new world of Queneau, was a world without real men, as seen through the eyes of a girl. It was a world where men presented themselves, more or less in the nude, to women. In the past it took a great deal of effort to get a man out of his armour, or even to get his riding boots off (at least in literature). Now, at best, her men, her boys, wear pajamas: 'The simple and comfortable pajama of effeminate India has conquered the western and free world, thanks to the British conquerors of the servile east' (705). In literature, up to now, pajamas had been restricted to clowns. It would be hard to imagine pajamas figuring in the literary life of a hero in the Spanish Civil War whose pure and virile initiation into love-making would have taken place on blood-drenched soil with a woman who had previously been raped by troops of fascists. In our new literary world, however, girls did not have to be raped to become competent at love-making; moreover, they could affect a very masculine, Amazonian indifference to the male bodies, the hunks, they watched parading along beach and boardwalk.

That all of this was very humiliating for those who have chanced to be born with (or into?) male anatomy is undeniable; courage was required, then, not to deny or oppose or complain about it, like Hemingway, but to admit of its reality and adjust. For thousands of years, men 'took' girls; later, it was the style for women to 'give' themselves. 'But is it the girls' fault if, in a new world, without male heroism, they can no longer either be "given" or "taken" but must, for better or for worse, rest content with laissez faire?' Would it not be best for us all simply to admit as much? For what was new about the people of Sagan's novels was that they 'have begun to live, no longer in the world that girls dreamed of almost as much as boys, but in this yet strange world, new and of most recent date, which is surely our own and which, as we know, has as its specific characteristic, distinguishing it from all others, the fact that virtually no further wars take place in it nor do true revolutions.' Consequently, it will soon enough be impossible to die gloriously 'except either in a (public or private) bed or under certain conditions, either by confronting (non-gelded and ruminant) beasts with a sword or by risking one's life climbing peaks over 8000 metres in height.' But the problem was that there are not many such peaks left, and of those remaining, either they do not capture the manly imagination as they used to do or they are reached by gondola lifts and helicopters, neither of which is particularly dangerous, and both of which can be used by young and old of either sex. And as for the beasts used to test the manhood of Iberian males, 'the risk is great that a public opinion ... that no longer supports (even in the ex-aristocratic homeland of the last civilian dandies) the idea of putting to death (without pain) a genuine assassin, will soon be moved to put an end to the sufferings (so cruel and so humiliating) that poor vegetarian beasts, who never hurt anyone, are made to undergo.' As for the old gods, of both sexes, who laughed at the manly Achilles, they too are perhaps contented with 'a certain smile.' Like everyone else, they peacefully sip their scotch on the rocks, with the blessings of the most Epicurean sage in the world (707–8). Gods and men, therefore, have regained paradise as members of a genuinely homogeneous, that is, androgynous as well as divine (or animal), tribe.

The inspiration for Kojève's analysis of that aspect of post-historical life corresponding, in Hegel's scheme, to civil society was fiction. Any number of other works could have been chosen, in that fiction is, as it were, inherently naïve. Even where, as with Queneau, it is self-consciously written within a Hegelian atmosphere, the demands of the genre – plot, character development, etc. – mean that a world will simply be presented. This was most obviously true in Kojève's discussion of Sagan who, in all likelihood, was unfamiliar with the father(s) of the new world to which she gave birth. The naïveté and indirection of literature were its great advantage: most of us have become too 'romantic,' as Kojève would have said, to admit of much explicit reality even though we might accept it in larger doses when it has been sweetened in the form of fiction. Whether Queneau and Sagan knew what they were doing (in Kojève's sense) in the end mattered very little: both wrote what they knew.

Kojève's comments on post-historical life were not confined to literary criticism. Earlier we quoted his remark on the harmonization of man and nature resulting in artistic, erotic, playful behaviour that makes human beings happy. In the second edition of *Introduction* Kojève severely criticized this statement. If humans made works of art like spiders, performed musical concerts like frogs, played like kittens, and made love like minks, they nevertheless could not, on that basis alone, be called happy. 'One would have to say that post-historical animals of the species *Homo Sapiens* (who will live in the midst of abundance and in complete security) will be *content* as a result of their artistic, erotic, and playful behaviour, seeing that by definition they will be contented with it.' But their animality would extend to their communication as well: no longer would human beings speak, they would simply react by reflex to vocal or visible signals. Now, if there were no human discourse, there could be neither philosophy nor, what was more serious, could there be wisdom. Existence seemed to have returned to the pre-historic absorption of consciousness in things. In 1946, Kojève said, he saw a return to this sort of animality as a likely prospect. Two years later he decided it was not about to occur but, indeed, had already taken place just as Hegel had said.

In 1806, at the battle of Jena, 'the vanguard of humanity virtually attained the limit and the goal, that is the *end*, of the historical evolution of humanity.' All subsequent 'history' was but a geographical extension of the universal revolutionary force first made actual in France. 'From the authentically historical point of view' world wars and their accompanying revolutions simply brought peripheral and backward areas into line with the position that Europe in principle had achieved. The only difference between the modernization of imperial Russia by way of Stalin and the modernization of imperial Germany by way of Hitler, or even 'the accession of Togoland to independence, or the self-determination of the Papuans,' was that this Eastern, Soviet Hegelianism had obliged the post-Napoleonic West to eliminate more quickly than otherwise it might have done the more or less out-of-date sequels to, and remnants of, its historical and pre-revolutionary past. This catalytic effect was in no way evidence of any fundamental opposition whatsoever. Indeed, Kojève remarked, 'from a certain point of view' the United States has gained, and is continuing to live within, the Marxist 'stage' of final communism, a classless society.[41] Likewise, the Russians and Chinese, to say nothing of 'modernizing' and 'less developed' countries, were only poor Americans. Thus, in 1948, Kojève said: 'I was led to conclude from this that the "American way of life" was the kind of life appropriate to the post-historical epoch; the actual presence of the United States in the World prefigured the "eternal present" that was the future of the whole of mankind' (*IH* 434–6 n1:158–60 n6). The return to animality seemed already to have taken place.

Over ten years passed before Kojève changed his mind. Following a voyage to Japan in 1959 Kojève saw at first hand a society that had for three centuries lived life in isolation and without fighting. Specifically, the embodiment of Japanese civilization, the nobility, had ceased to risk their lives, even in duels, but had not become bourgeois and had not in any way begun to labour. '"Post-historical" Japanese civilization is committed to a road that is diametrically opposed to the "American way."'

While certain parallels exist between Japanese and European 'feudalism,' the Japanese found a far more effective way to negate given-being than could be achieved by fighting or forced labour. This was snobbery. It was true that the commanding heights of Japanese snobbery are the prerogative of the nobility and that there still existed political, economic, and sexual inequalities. Even so, every Japanese, Kojève said, 'is without exception presently in a state of living in terms of totally *formalized* values, that is, values devoid of all "human" contents in the "historical" sense of the term' (*IH* 437 n1; 162 n6). By nature, snobbery was the prerogative of a small minority. The Japanese, however, had succeeded in democratizing it: 'Japan is eighty million snobs.'[42] Snobbery was a useless negativity; in the extreme it was suicidal, though it was not the suicide of a sceptical nihilist, which was a suicide of frustration and despair. It was completely gratuitous. 'Now, seeing as how no animal can be a snob, every "Japanized" post-historical epoch would be specifically human.' In order to maintain human subjectivity distinct from natural given-being (and so avoid the re-animalization of the 'American way of life'), it was necessary that human subjectivity be opposed to given-being, but not in a mode of active negation, that is, not by fighting or labouring. The great achievement of the East was to have achieved this by separating the form and content of action in a most radical manner. Historically, one undertook such a separation in order to alter a specific given content so that it would take on the form one desired: hence the fights and labours. A 'Japanese' separation had as its purpose the exaltation of oneself as pure form and the simultaneous reduction of himself (and all others) to a random, intrinsically insignificant and superfluous 'content.' With respect to others, such an attitude was snobbery; with respect to the disposition of oneself, it was a gratuitous suicide. In neither instance would anything be 'accomplished,' and the 'act' had no meaning at all beyond the attestation that the one who 'does' it was perfectly free not to have 'done' so. But that was entirely enough. One could as easily die for 'reasons' of snobbery as do nothing. Whether one was a kamikaze or one of Queneau's lazy *voyous* apparently was a matter of indifference. Is not that the very height of snobbery?

Conclusion

The result of Kojève's analyses of the principles by which life was lived in post-historical society and in the state, which has been considered as a commentary and amendment of some details of Hegel's *Philosophy of*

Right, was a hierarchy. In ethereal splendour at the top resided the perfect citizen-sage, of whom Hegel was the model and Kojève the avatar, but whose empirical existence was in any event not crucial (so long as one knew what he would have to be). Next came the competent political men, the civil servants, whose serious competition brought forth the leader. His activity, in turn, was correctly understood by the sage. Below them were ranged the lazy, androgynous, comic, animal gods, no less wise in their own ways than the men and women nominally above them. It goes without saying that all were snobs.

8

Consequences

Evidence

This essay began with a few platitudes about modernity. To be modern is to adopt a specific self-understanding or self-interpretation. One sees oneself as autonomous, independent of natural constraints, independent of God, and therefore free to create meaning, equally one's own meaning and the meaning of one's society. The absence of natural constraints is not, however, absolute. Human beings are not angels; they still have bodies. But for modern self-consciousness, one's body, one's gender, for example, does not constrain the meaning of one's sexuality: gay, straight, or kinky, the options of an effectively androgynous existence may everywhere be displayed. Likewise the normal or natural consequences of gender differences have effectively been circumvented by the widespread use of contraception. And finally, what could be more trite than to observe that all this has been described and justified in terms of freedom? Why else would one leave the closet?

Contemporary modes of human liberation are all historical successors to the emancipation of the European bourgeoisie. The basis for bourgeois emancipation, according to Hobbes, lay in a universal and radically equal desire for recognition coupled to the ability, and perhaps the propensity, to murder. Only recognition would bring satisfaction; only fear of violent death would inhibit murder. Death was the greatest evil because it was an absolute dissolution of being. There was no 'after life' to provide recompense for injustice and evil experienced during one's time alive. The hope of divine justice, of divine recognition for virtuous suffering, had been dashed. One may say therefore that bourgeois society and its liberated successors are inherently atheist. Indeed, only an atheist can be truly self-conscious. A believer necessarily is conscious of his own dependence on God and of moral constraints, issuing from a divine source, that bind his conscience. The argument about modernity, however, goes further.

One cannot at the same time remain conscious of one's dependence on another, whether it be nature, God, or another person, at the same time as one is self-conscious. The other upon which one is dependent always appears as a threat to consciousness, a vast mystery, an uncanny enigma, an inexplicable power. To be independent and conscious of one's independence, however, carries with it the temptation of illusion. Self-consciousness must be acknowledged by others if it is to be distinguishable from illusion. Moreover, if the self-consciousness of the other is not to appear to him as dependence upon oneself, the acknowledgment must be reciprocal. One must recognize in the other what the other recognizes in oneself. Self-consciousness, then, if it is to exist in its proper form, implies mutual recognition, a regime that Kojève identified as the universal and homogeneous State.

For the individual modern person, then, self-consciousness is the goal and highest purpose of life. But should one fail in one's quest for self-consciousness, it does not follow that one must fall back into consciousness of dependence. It is not necessarily true that there are no atheists in foxholes. All that failure means, all that prayer before combat means, is that one is not serious or competent enough in one's quest for self-consciousness. Likewise, the actual or alleged failure of the universal and homogeneous State to achieve permanence does not mean it is impossible: it still remains the norm of modernity toward which all modern human beings must strive.

In the course of history Hegel several times brought to light the difficulties of its own making that consciousness raised before itself and subsequently superseded. Eventually every beyond was overcome: human existence came to know itself on its own terms, without the intervention of a natural order, a utopian perfection, or a divine law. Eventually the gap between what men desired, namely recognition of themselves as self-conscious individuals or a regime of mutual recognition, and what they actually happened to experience was closed. Once one had experienced self-consciousness fully, consciousness of dependence is gone forever. When one no longer understands oneself as dependent upon God or nature or any sublimated substitute, one necessarily understands oneself as responsible for whatever meanings actually exist. These meanings, moreover, are completely understood; beyond them, beyond the world, there is nothing to understand. The theoretical and retrospective account of the genesis of modernity is straightforward: history was the process by which freedom, self-consciousness, the regime of mutual recognition, has been actualized. The process itself was moved by contradictions that human beings had overcome through fights and labours until, in the end, they became satisfied with what is, namely the modern, secular, rational world. According to Hegel, everyone lives in, or strives to live in, such a world (cf *RPhil* 7:5). All that is left to do is understand this fact and what it implies.

But is it a fact? Does the entirety of mankind live in Hegelian states or strive to? To be more precise: is it true that the political and social self-interpretation of the contemporary world accords with Hegel's account of the state? For a Hegelian sage who sees his or her task as one of explaining the historical rationality of the actual world, the answer is self-evident. According to Eric Weil, as we have seen, the Hegelian state 'is a modern State, which still exists today everywhere.' Accordingly, 'the Hegelian theory of the State is correct because it correctly analyzes the actual State of his era, and of ours.'[1] The principles of that state, I earlier argued, were set forth in *Philosophy of Right*. Much of the evidence, as has been shown, was deeply embedded in the data of the nineteenth-century European system of nation-states. That is not, however, a limitation.

In some areas of modern life there are clear continuities. Contemporary modern relations of family, society, and state are as Hegel's argument requires. One attains legal majority generally between the ages of sixteen and twenty-one. Thereafter one can take a full part in the legal order of civil society as well as the political order of the state. Generally speaking, children who are legal adults no longer live under the same roof as their parents, so that, once its members are also citizens, love alone, not law, holds the family together. Likewise, generally speaking, social, economic, and political advancement is not legally impeded by 'natural' factors such as ethnicity, religion, or gender. On the contrary, will and competence are the chief factors governing one's position; where they are not, it is commonly held that an abuse exists, sorely in need of correction. The *Polizei* and administration are familiar enough, as are the descendants of Hegel's corporations.

So far as the state itself is concerned, no one dares deny that the slogan of the French revolutionaries is the highest practical wisdom in public affairs. No modern political party could ever hope for office if it denied that the greatest political good is freedom, or that the citizens ought not be recognized as legal equals, or that all people are not really brothers and sisters. The legal structures of Hegel's state are also generally found in existing modern states.

One might, of course, argue that this interpretation is flatly contradicted, for example, by Hegel's insistence upon a hereditary monarchy. But this would be to ignore the fact that Hegel equally insisted that science is not predictive. Hence, the empirical actualization of its truths cannot be foreseen. With respect to hereditary monarchy, therefore, the 'natural' advantage of a royal family, stability of recruitment, has been attained by human artifice – political parties and elections, for instance. One need not, therefore, insist too strenuously that the constitutional monarch be of royal blood: queen, governor general, president, emperor, chairman, and first secretary all serve the monarchical function equally well. They embody the rational freedom of the subject; theirs is the final resolution that makes advice or bills legally binding. The essential feature, which must be preserved if the element of monarchy is to fulfil its proper part, is will. Likewise, one may raise objections from the other end and insist that Hegel defended private property. But again, if we look upon property as the first form in which freedom appears (as Hegel also described it), then its importance lies not in itself but in its being evidence that the givenness of nature has been subordinated to will. This subjection can be achieved equally by possessive collectivism as by possessive individualism. Moreover, the executive – the cabinet and higher civil service – is by and large composed of serious, that is, competitively successful, individuals who are for the most part competent, at least in technical administrative matters. In any event, they are an aristocracy of the robe not of the sword. Likewise, the lower civil servants are state functionaries employed in rule-application and enforcement rather than rule-making. Modern legislatures represent the welfare of citizens, collect taxes, and often are responsible for the declaration of war. They perform the requisite mediating role, preventing gross abuse of power by the executive through their ability to impeach, withhold financial support, and so on. And, of course, they debate, refine, and articulate public opinion rather than simply follow it.

Yet one must also grant that those who would appeal to Hegel's text have a point. To argue that Hegel's is both the last word in political science and an accurate description of our present world, one must make sweeping and ingenious interpretations. Clearly, some things have changed. We, after all, do not live in nineteenth-century European nation-states. The question at issue, however, is whether our present regime is essentially or fundamentally different from its nineteenth-century predecessor, however described. James Doull, for example, has argued that it is: 'The resolution of revolutionary will into objective freedom existed in the national states of the nineteenth century ... The revolution was a fact: the *Philosophy of Right* is not about what might be.' However, 'with the mutual destruction of national States in the great wars of the twentieth century, their power was weakened to dissolve civil society and hold it within their objective purpose, and world power passed to the revolutionary societies of the United States and the Soviet Union, which were founded on the supremacy of civil society.'[2] This is a serious objection, as it appeals to the obvious meaning of Hegel's text. It may be met, however, if one distinguishes the meaning or essence of Hegel's argument from the contingent configuration in which it was cast. This, as has been repeatedly stressed, is Kojève's approach. Accordingly, the state, even in *Philosophy of Right*, is historical in form and so subject to empirical alteration.[3] Thus one must distinguish between nineteenth-century contingencies, such as the difference between the state and civil society, and the essential or fundamental feature that both elements shared, namely the desire for recognition.

This is not wholly wilful or arbitrary. According to Hegel (*RPhil* 262, 262A), civil society provides a limited (not universal) realm for recognition. It is gained through one's 'inner life,' as subjective freedom is actualized in one's choice of occupation, marriage partner, and so forth. Since one cannot at the same time fully enjoy the satisfaction of 'inner life,' taking pleasure in one's family, for example, and also pursue universal recognition, it seems fair to say that civil society (and its twentieth-century equivalent) provide a kind of compensation for drop-outs and incompetent contestants in the more strenuous arena. Even today our politicians often retire for 'family reasons.' In sum, when one resolves the division of civil society and the state into the fundamental question of the seriousness and competence of candidates for the Napoleonic role, one sees that Hegelian elements constitute the substance of contemporary politics even in the two revolutionary regimes Doull mentioned. Since the *Gestalt* of the *Geist* has altered since Hegel's day, one ought not in any case expect the fit between *Philosophy of Right* and contemporary regimes to be perfect.

This is especially true so far as international relations are concerned. Hegel's arguments about foreign affairs were especially bound to the contingencies of the state system. Changes, therefore, have made qualifications necessary. But note: these are qualifications of an essential meaning. And in any event, they all support the process by which the Idea is increasingly actualized. Consider, for example, the amendments that must be made to Hegel's understanding of war. Even if the period 1914–45 is viewed not as a prolonged European civil war, and so not a national or inter-state war in Hegel's sense at all, the names given to those conflicts suggest the ecumenic not national context. Korea was called a 'police action' undertaken by the United Nations. In general, the deployment of nuclear weapons has meant that both Grotius's view of war, that it is the means to maintain law, and Clausewitz's, that it is the continuation of political policy, are obsolete, since even a 'just war' by Grotius's standards can have consequences whose catastrophic injustice far outweighs any other considerations. But such observations simply confirm the contention that war, in the historical sense, has become impossible.

So far as wars of national liberation, proxy wars, terrorism, and high-technology counter-insurgency operations are concerned, several things must be kept in mind. First, Hegel's concern with European states implicitly recognized that they constituted a sort of family. When, therefore, a European state violates the common principles of modern civilization as, for example, Germany did during the Second World War, its leaders are rightly tried as criminals. No such commonality of principle exists between the Western, European, or 'Germanic' states and the rest of the world. In accordance with Hegel's teaching, therefore, the freedom of barbarians has been treated as a formality. Second, the immoderate violence of national liberation movements, terrorists, etc., may simply reflect that unmediated reciprocity which, according to Hegel, is the way of savages. Many of the modernized leaders of, or spokesmen for, these movements, however, justify their activities not in terms of revenge or resentment but, like Fanon, as the 'metaphysical necessity' required to create citizens. The presence of the imperialists is, therefore, as necessary and intelligible as that of the savage natives: the ones must provide the Master's catalytic terror, an enemy against which the others, the several hordes of natives, can respond by struggle and thereby create themselves as a people desiring and deserving a state. Open or covert counter-insurgency is as necessary as insurgents. If the counter-insurgency operatives are technicians and bureaucrats, so much the better for modernity. It goes without saying that, for a Hegelian onlooker, winning or losing the 'war' is a matter of indifference. There are no winners. In an imperialist epoch, when all politics is emulation of Napoleonic expansion, national states are no longer the only significant political units. Consequently, the meaning of public violence is not what was traditionally signified by war: the world is simply conforming more closely to the final regime. It equally goes without saying that, for the participants in the struggle, things may seem quite different. The natives are ridding themselves of oppression, exploitation, capitalism, white men, and so forth. For their part, the imperialists understand themselves to be defending civilization against various more or less oriental despotisms and dark barbarisms.

Finally, one may observe that French, Dutch, British, Belgian, Portuguese, Spanish, and American neo-colonial military activities, unlike earlier adventures of this type, have been neither short, nor inexpensive, nor popular. Consequently, they have not been successful either. And in any event, the revolt of the rest of the world against the West, as Toynbee called the phenomenon, has been less a counter-revolution against westernization or modernization than its continuation under local management. Colonization and decolonization, then, are moments in a single process, 'the painful birth of the modern world itself. None of the former colonial peoples remember it with gratitude, for it was alien rule; but none of them wish to turn back the clock, and this is its historical justification.'[4]

Diplomatic language as well as the course of actual politics also reflects these changes. Hegel's designation of a 'civilized' nation came into common use, so far as European states were concerned, when the older distinction, between Christian and heretic or heathen nations, no longer served the policy interests of European powers. In 1856, when the aid of Turkey, obviously not a Christian nation, was sought by Britain and France in order to frustrate Russian designs, the new term 'civilized nation' was introduced. In 1884 James Lorimer made his famous threefold division of mankind into civilized humanity, to which complete political recognition was accorded, barbarian humanity, to which partial recognition was granted, and savage humanity, which was to receive merely natural recognition.[5] Following the First World War, and especially after the Second World War, civilized nations have been replaced, under article IV of the United Nations Charter, with 'peace-loving nations,' a term first employed in the Moscow Declaration on General Security, 30 October 1943. In short, the changes in Hegel's distinctions have all been in the expected direction, namely toward greater homogeneity.

The three essential elements of the universal and homogeneous state may be summarized as follows. First, it is a regime where natural or quasi-natural factors, that is, inherited status, religious belief, sex, ethnicity, etc, play no public role. In principle, it is a homogeneous social order where recognition is accorded the free, historical, and mortal individual. As Napoleon said, careers are open to talent and every corporal carries a marshal's baton in his knapsack. Second, it is a regime without war, where warriors have been replaced by police, by *Polizei*. In principle, it is a universal empire with no public recognition accorded to nationalist and other collective or common particularities. Third, it is a technological society where production and consumption are understood to result from the wilful imposition of rational form on otherwise formless natural and human being. In contrast to Doull's interpretation, then, a Kojèvian reading of events suggests that both the Soviet and Western power organizations embody (in different combinations or to different degrees) all three essential constituent elements. Accordingly, both are essentially Hegelian states. In characteristically different ways, these power organizations have each achieved a novel institutionalization of the Hegelian idea. One can understand the Soviet Union as an imperial order of the Napoleonic type with a minimum of interpretative creativity. Likewise, the ecumenic claims of the communist movement are beyond dispute. Rather more ingenuity, however, is required to bring out the Hegelian essence of the Western *imperium*.

Modern imperialism

Historically, the national state is an anomaly. One could, in fact, reasonably argue that it has never existed. Of large-scale power organizations in antiquity, one finds empirically three successive sets of empires. First were the cosmological empires such as Egypt and Mesopotamia. Then there were ecumenic empires such as the Persian, the Hellenistic, and the Roman. And third came the orthodox empires of Islam, Graeco-Byzantine orthodoxy, and Western Catholic orthodoxy. Under the impact of modernity, the orthodox empires crumbled and were replaced with what Voegelin has called ideological empires,[6] of which the Napoleonic state was the paradigmatic case.

Voegelin's characterization of modern, Napoleonic empires as ideological is significant but hardly Kojèvian. For Voegelin the meaning of ideology was initially simply empirical and historical. The term itself was coined by Destutt de Tracy to describe what he called the science of ideas. To his enlightened mind, an 'idea' was something that eventually could be traced to sensation. He thought that Descartes had made a serious error. In place of *cogito ergo sum* he fixed a new tag: *sentio ergo sum*.

Ideology was originally intended to be a science that overcame what was seen to be the abstractions of metaphysics and the unreliability of opinion.

Seldom, however, are the circumstances under which the new science was conceived given proper emphasis, namely the Terror of 1793–4. De Tracy had been incarcerated in the town hall at Auteuil and then in a former church at Carmes. Each Monday for several months one or more of his fellow prisoners, some of them his friends, left jail to be sliced into two pieces by the guillotine. He appealed his doom, protesting quite rightly his loyalty to the Revolution. But he was also an aristocrat and something of a snob[7] and grew resigned to his fate. He would, however, gain immortality, and to that end formulated, in the spring of 1794, a discourse that would apply to society the science of Lavoisier, who had been guillotined on 8 May, and the equations of Condorcet, who had died in jail on 27 March. He himself was scheduled to take his last walk on 11 Thermidor. But on 9 Thermidor (29 July), Robespierre was overthrown and citizen Tracy was saved. He was, understandably, upset by the experience. When he finally emerged from jail early in October his hair had turned completely white.[8] According to Kojève, one recalls, terror is what rendered the consciousness of revolutionary freedom amenable to the institution of the Napoleonic state. Historically, that is, ideology and the exemplar of the universal and homogeneous State both appeared in consequence of the Terror.

Imperialism is also a term with French provenance. Originally it referred to the techniques used by Napoleon III to rule his fellow citizens. In the eyes of his British detractors this was a combination of public relations and fraud that badly disguised an authoritarian despotism based upon the army.[9] During the 1870s the meaning of the term in English changed from reference to a federation of British settlement colonies into a military organization not limited to persons of British stock but having British rulers who were, by their own lights, supremely fitted to govern the world.

The origin of this expanded historical horizon lay in the historiography of a century before. Chinese and Persian texts were first extensively published in Western languages in the 1770s; Napoleon's Egyptian expedition in 1798 initiated a serious concern with the ancient history of that country; Gibbon and Niebuhr began the first critical historiography of Rome. 'The result of this outburst was a new view of history revealing the rise and fall of nations, the conquest of one people by another, the organization of a conquered society by its new rulers, the amalgamation of the conquerors and conquered, and the gradual rise of a political society.'[10] The original events that attracted the attention of historians were the Greek and Germanic migrations. By the mid-nineteenth century, however, the impact of the French Revolution and the symbolism of race were both visible.

The two outstanding examples were Gustav Friedrich Klemm's *Allgemeine Kultur-Geschichte der Menschheit* (10 vols, Leipzig, 1843–52) and Joseph Arthur de Gobineau's *Essai sur l'inégalité des races humaines* (4 vols, Paris, 1853–5). Both these large studies argued that racial interaction by distinctive human types, usually by migration, has generated all the important human cultures. The result of the migrations was the initial triumph but eventual dissolution of the conquering élite in favour of an egalitarian society. Both Klemm and Gobineau saw the process begin with the Germanic migrations and, moving through the centuries of dissolution or symbiosis in the forms of medieval Christianity, they agreed that it ended in the French Revolution. Klemm was a liberal democrat and was very pleased with the destruction of the *ancien régime*. According to him, the active races were embodiments of the male principle and the passive ones the female. The acts of conquest were akin to marriage and the final Revolution was the production of androgynous perfection. Gobineau, who saw the flower of human perfection in a strong French aristocracy of which he was a member, saw the Revolution as a disaster for humanity and took a grim satisfaction in predicting its degeneration.

The historiographic conflict of interpretations has continued to the present, though not always within a racial idiom. One may summarize these historiographic conventions as follows: both Klemm and Gobineau agreed that political history on a world scale was constituted by the interaction or symbiosis of active and passive societies. The expansiveness of western European power had brought this knowledge to their attention. A hundred years earlier, for example, Voltaire could still cause a scandal by challenging the historiographic conventions of Bossuet, which were essentially those of St Augustine. Industrial imperialism and the understanding of it by the active Europeans were governed not by the old symbolism of divine creation and the final apocalypse or by the institutions of the medieval *sacrum imperium*, but by secular and internally unlimited power configurations, by national and class interests, and by the activist spirituality induced by ideological commitments.

'Imperialism in the industrial era,' Ronald Robinson has written, 'is a process whereby agents of an expanding society gain inordinate influence or control over the vitals of weaker societies by "dollar" and "gun-boat" diplomacy, ideological suasion, conquest and rule, or by planting colonies of its own people abroad.'[11] That is, the expanding political organization cannot appropriate resources and power simply by force but must provide bribes or threats, governance, religious or ideological conversion, or colonial bodies in exchange. On the European side lay an economic drive to integrate the colonial regions and agrarian empires into the industrial economy, a political drive to secure these areas against other industrial powers, and an ideological drive to convert the non-industrial or non-technological world to the norms of the expansive society. On the non-industrial, non-European, non-technological side, there were collaboration and resistance, sometimes sequential and some-times contemporary.

In Africa and Asia, to use Marx's colourful phrase, European (includ-ing American) capital bashed down the Chinese walls. And then the bargains were struck with the non-commercial élites and from a posi-tion of strength. The terms of the bargain, under what Robinson and Gallagher called the imperialism of free trade,[12] generally permitted tra-ditional native oligarchies and landowners to divert a good deal of politi-cal and economic resources to the preservation of the *status quo* in return for protection of European enterprise and a loose political alliance. The result often turned out to be economic bankruptcy and increased foreign intervention and control. The Europeans, Robinson said, had forced their collaborators to play for high stakes with too few cards. The native élites thereupon found themselves cut off from their own traditional bases of support and eventually were confronted with anti-foreign, neo-traditional uprisings. The European powers responded by switching from a policy of free-trade imperialism to colonial rule or to partition. Not European capitalist interests but the breakdown of native collabora-tive mechanisms signalled a change from early free-trade policies to later policies of partition and direct governance.

These themes are illustrated in great detail in the famous scramble for Africa. It was initiated by the disintegration of the Ottoman Empire, the British need for a secure line to India, French rivalry over Suez, and French strategic requirements for Mediterranean security. Britain in 1882 in Egypt faced the same problem as had France in 1881 in Tunisia. Both had to deal with bankrupt (or, to adopt the high tone of moralism, hope-lessly corrupt) local rulers; both thought that a short, sharp, surgical action would fix things up and they could retire to informal influences. Both were disappointed because they soon had to deal with lower-class, religious-based, fundamentalist rebellions, which they called fanatic. 'No sooner did a European power set its foot upon the neck of the Ottoman rulers of the coastal cities than the nomads of the inland steppes and deserts seized their chance of throwing off the pashas' yoke.'[13] In addition, the British occupation of Egypt was an insult to the French, who were very particular about such points, especially as they regarded the canal as their own and the country as having enjoyed a special relationship with France ever since the Battle of the Pyramids. The French, of course, were happy to accept the 'light soils' of western Africa at Berlin, but they regarded the acquisitions of this Saharan and sub-Saharan real estate not as the result of generous concessions from the British but as strategically necessary to protect the Algerian hinterland and thereby the Mediterranean. During the 1880s, then, turning *res nullis* into *res publica*, and painting vast swaths on a map pink or green or blue, provided employment only for European lawyers and geographers, not Africans.

The paper partition at Berlin was followed by a light occupation but then by resistance. The French army, for example, ran into a reviving and recalcitrant Islam, which it then had to subdue. The sacred, animist, or pagan kingdoms such as the Matebele and Dahomey put up a good fight as well (even Kipling admired the fuzzy-wuzzy because he broke the British square), but once beaten they stayed that way, aided by the zeal of propaganda in favour of the religious truth of the New Testament. Like the Muslims, the Coptic monophysite Christians of Ethiopia were stiffened by their faith to resist conquest by the admittedly inept Italians. By the 1890s, however, a new generation of politicians had come to power. For men such as Chamberlain and Delcassé, light soils were not booby prizes and colonies were not pawns in the great game of European diplomacy, pieces to be sacrificed for traditional interests in the Mediterranean. These new men suffered from 'a kind of geopolitical claustrophobia, a feeling that national expansion was running out of world space, and that the great powers of the twentieth century would be those who had filched every nook and cranny of territory left.'[14] But these men who flourished in the decade around 1900 were late comers, and their anxieties ran deeper than greed. Once colonial administrators began fantasizing over tropical estates and undertaking policy initiatives not on the basis of actual political, diplomatic, or economic interests but on projections and scenarios of future growth that they believed to be tinged with inevitability and full of transcendent meanings, then they were bound to embark upon what would eventually turn out, even for the imperial states, to be foolish and disastrous enterprises. A commonsensical opposition to expansive rashness would be, and would appear to be, based upon caution and prudence as well as inflexibility and fear.

The initial conclusion, then, is that the sequence of Western imperial expansion in the late nineteenth century was precisely the opposite of what the economic interpretation of imperialism demanded.[15] First came the diplomats, carving and slicing and supremely indifferent to those who lived on the ground that their maps imperfectly represented. But people did live there and, for one set of motives or another, which Robinson and Gallagher summarized as proto-nationalist, objected from time to time to the European presence. And so they had to be crushed. Only at the end of the process and in a new psychological atmosphere did the businessmen arrive in large numbers, now heavily subsidized by sunk political and military investments.

A second point concerns the change in attitude. In the 1880s, those who governed in Britain at least were confident and superior. Palmerston, for example, held that poverty and oppression were alike the consequence of illiberal economic and political action. Opening trade to British merchants would open up the country, increase revenues to it and to Britain, and provide the British with opportunities to make friends and allies. But in no case did the partitioners have grand imperial ideas, and they did not feel a need for African colonies. Spheres of influence might provide protection against the activities of other Europeans, but they did not amount to rule over natives. In the event, however, economic penetration set into motion events that did not lead to friendship and prosperity but to rebellions, in Egypt and southern Africa, for example. By 1890, Robinson and Gallagher contended, 'a new age was struggling to be born. To the old men who sat at the head of affairs – as old men usually do – it seemed that imperialism was entering on its greatest epoch. But European expansion was already at odds with the new forces of colonial nationalism which it had goaded into life. The dynasts were beginning to lose their way in history. The shadows were falling over the times and themes they knew best. The end of the European age was in sight. Beset with problems for which their historiography offered no solutions, the old men in the chancelleries came more and more to combat their manifestations rather than to grapple with their causes.'[16] The old liberal self-confidence gave way to fears of subversion and disloyalty; expansion was replaced with harsh measures; Boers and Irishmen had misused their liberties and must be turned into involuntary subjects; progress, freedom, liberalism, a Christian end to slavery, the early Victorian indices of imagination and creative flexibility, dissolved into a defence of prestige and the exertion of administrative control. Liberalism, it seemed, did not always work, especially with pashas, Indian princes, African chiefs, and Boer farmers. Confident and informal expansion, thus, turned first into the cares of consolidation and then into projective fantasies and a deep fear that this great heritage would be lost to others in the inevitable troubles ahead.

A third point is that anti-colonial rebellions could succeed only when the Western rulers ran out of native collaborators and could not bribe, threaten, or seduce any additional ones. The natives had, for their part, to recruit the same political elements that had been on the side of the imperial masters, which in pre-industrial societies meant neo-traditional religious, social, and ethnic units. Accordingly, 'all the nationalist movements that won independence were more or less functions of neo-traditional politics organized in the form of modern political parties.'[17] The parties were coalitions of neo-traditional interests, since the imperial powers had leavened or sheltered tradition, and they maintained their cohesion only so long as the catalyst of colonial power was present. After independence the neo-traditional units often came into conflict with the modernizing party or with its armed or unarmed bureaucracy, led by a Westernized élite. What present stability exists continues to be dependent on an alliance between neo-traditional and modern élites, with the former receiving a good deal of symbolic recognition and the latter receiving various kinds of bribes which the donors call foreign aid. In short, while imperialism has been the major engine of social change, colonial collaboration has been the necessary auxilliary. 'Nationalism,' Robinson and Gallagher said, 'has been the continuation of imperialism by other means.'[18] That is, together, from the 1890s on, European imperialism and local proto-nationalist reaction, whether in the form of resistance, collaboration, or religious hatred, have destroyed tradition and cuffed non-modern societies into the global exchange-economy and the bureaucratic state. The innovations included new social conflicts and new political conflicts, but these were no more than the inevitable sparks thrown off by the rise of a new élite modelled on the reforms of Thermidor.

This discussion of modern imperialism has centred upon three points. First, the Napoleonic empire and the power configurations that succeeded it were not simply extensive real estate holdings but were informed with a spiritual meaning derived from the ideological outburst that accompanied the French Revolution. Second, the context of Western imperialism was partly framed by the increased knowledge that Westerners had of other civilizational units. This knowledge, in turn, exploded the early Christian myth that ordered the events of history on a meaningful time-line starting with God's creation of the world and ending with the Apocalypse. Instead of history being the story of God's way with mankind, it was the story of the rise and fall of power units and civilizations endowed with specific biological or cultural characteristics. Third, the actual expansion of Western power over the rest of the world moved from liberal confidence expressed in Seeley's famous and silly remark delivered in 1881, 'We seem, as it were, to have conquered and peopled half the world in a fit of absence of mind,'[19] to the remarkable sight of Britain and France on the brink of war over Fashoda in 1898. The defensive preoccupations of the late nineteenth century express an anxiety that a decade later erupted into a general war that was without a statement of clear political purpose by any of the participating Great Powers. Yet even these expressions of what might justifiably be called political neurosis were not without their Hegelian meaning. Repression provoked eventual responses that resulted in greater conformity to the Hegelian model of the state and wider dissemination of the appropriate revolutionary ideology. At the same time, however, imperialism in the sense of metropolitan control of colonies was in retreat by the close of the nineteenth century. The actual divestment took another fifty years or so. But by then a new and more flexible instrument of power was in place, the multinational enterprise.

A word of caution is in order. We know from Arendt's interpretation and analysis that imperialism played an important part in the genesis of totalitarianism. But imperialism is not totalitarianism. The presence of Hegelian elements in modern imperialism as well as in the multinational enterprise (MNE) and in the Gulag does not mean that they can all be equated. The purpose of this analysis of Kojève's text, after all, was to make explicit an important thread or aspect of modernity to which Hegel gave the original voice. To evoke these three characteristically different institutionalizations of the Hegelian idea of the state in no way contains an implication that they are interchangeable. It takes very little common sense to distinguish the *Fortune* 500 from the islands of the Gulag. Having made all appropriate empirical qualifications, however, there remains a common Hegelian core. In a final and synthesizing section this topic is considered under the heading of technological society.

Multinational enterprises

Only recently have non-Marxists not been embarrassed to use the term 'empire' to describe the political and economic order centred in the United States. Economic relations have, of course, always been important in the history of empires, and the American one is certainly no exception. Yet the American empire is different. As Samuel Huntington said, it is an empire of functions not territory; it is characterized by penetration and freedom to operate rather than territorial acquisiton and political power or control. The American *imperium*, he said, ought be compared not with prior colonial empires belonging to specific nation-states. Rather, it is a stage in the process of Western expansion that began in the sixteenth century. 'One could speak of Western expansion,' Huntington said, 'but not of *the* Western empire because there were Spanish, Dutch, Portuguese, French, and English empires. Similarly, one can properly speak now of American expansion but not of *the* American empire, because there are so many of them.'[20] Included among these imperial organs are, of course, those controlled from the Pentagon and the Department of State.[21] But also, and perhaps more importantly, are the organizations that perform the 'functions' that 'penetrate' other lands and gain the 'freedom to operate' about which Huntington wrote, namely, multinational enterprises or MNEs.

Before turning directly to a discussion of MNEs, a few preliminary remarks ought to be made. In the last section it was noted that, during the decade around the turn of the century, a new attitude, reflecting a new generation of political men, was manifest in the scramble for tropical estates and in expansive wars. These economic connotations were expanded by Hobson in his famous tract of 1905 into an economic explanation.[22] But an economic interpretation of imperialism is not the same as economic imperialism. Economic imperialism does not necessarily require the acquisition of territory, and territorial acquisition is not invariably undertaken for economic reasons.[23] The activities of MNEs, however, are chiefly economic, and for this reason they may be identified as the most important agent of contemporary capitalist[24] imperialism, the direct descendant of bourgeois emancipation discussed in chapter 1.

In considering MNEs, we largely ignore differences between manufacturing, processing, service, and extractive operations as well as the specific historical contingencies (and competing explanatory accounts) of the origin of European or American direct investment in foreign countries.[25] We focus, rather, on the relation of the MNE to the principles of homogeneity, universality, and technology, all of which, as has been argued, are essential elements of the universal and homogeneous State.

Homogeneity within the MNE is essentially a technical matter of management efficiency. When a firm has reached the point where its central managers no longer think in terms of its North American or European market position but its world position, local executives may constitute an impediment to overall efficiency if they retain a parochial outlook. In fact, patriotism seems always to take second place to company loyalty,[26] but optimal efficiency also means that an organization ought to be able to recruit the best persons for its central executive from any of its subsidiaries. Many executives, however, are unwilling to leave their homelands, so that whether or not they choose to leave the firm rather than be promoted abroad, the effectiveness of the whole organization is impaired. In part, at least, such problems are minimized by changing assignment practices so all national subsidiaries have equal opportunities for recruitment to head office, equalizing compensation and incentives, and standardizing techniques of appraisal and recognition.[27] The hoped-for result, as one advocate lyrically observed, is the advent of the multinational man: 'Mystery has vanished as the searchlight of technology has exposed life overseas ... Suddenly the international man has become nothing more than the rest of us, grinding away at his daily work, wherever he may be.'[28]

The homogenizing effects of MNEs on the behaviour of consumers is familiar to anyone who leaves his or her own bailiwick: Big Macs are available on the Boul' Mich and the Ginza, Pepsis in Magnitigorsk, Cokes in Beijing, digital watches everywhere. Advertising executives, moreover, plan their assaults on the basis of similar buyer motivations even while tailoring their pitch to the peculiarities of specific national and ethnic target groups.[29] That this process of homogenization is a benefit to the world is scarcely open to doubt, at least not by its practitioners.[30]

The absence of war in the style of the nineteenth century has not, of course, meant the establishment of a regime of peace. What has changed, as was argued above, is the meaning of violence. From Homeric times, doing and suffering, violence and action, have been linked; the condition for acting politically was that one was responsible for violating the tranquility of others. But with the end of history has come the end of action in the strong sense of the term, namely the introduction of new consequences. Violence, therefore, has become detached from its traditional relationship to action and is considered simply as an evil to be avoided or a problem to be overcome. The first role of the MNE in this new context, then, is to help achieve the apparently universally desired goals of peace and propserity by ending the violence and suffering inflicted by the politics of the nation-state. Hard evidence that the MNEs are in fact playing their assigned role does not lie thick upon the ground.[31] Rhetoric, however, is abundant.[32] Much of it, no doubt, is self-serving apology, rationalization, or systematic lying. But even lies express a meaning. A second and complementary role, for which there is more evidence and a great deal more talk, is that multinationals discourage 'irrational' beliefs and thereby erode institutions that stand opposed to their operations. Chief among these irrationalities are nationalist and ideological loyalties. That the operations of MNEs are not always in harmony with even the peaceful interests of the nation-state is hardly news to Canadians. For those who have overcome their parochial national sentiments, however, 'the multinational corporation, precisely because it is a threat to the sovereignty and independence of the nation-state, may well be the harbinger of further evolution of human society, out of barbarism towards a more humane, equitable, and non-discriminatory civilization.'[33] The discriminatory aspects of the present level of human evolution that are so vehemently denounced are precisely the natural or quasi-natural restraints indicated earlier: gender, religion, ethnicity, and so on. The conclusion, so far as the future of national state is concerned, is clear: 'To contend that in the present era the state is an anachronistic form of social organization is merely to reiterate the obvious.'[34] Not only have MNEs been instrumental in the demise of the particularist, national state, they have also been praised for their contribution to the end of equally particularist ideology. The proliferation of joint-ventures, turn-key operations, and so on with the communist regimes of eastern Europe (and, presumably, these modes will increasingly be extended to China) is considered to be both mutually beneficial and a sound contribution to a more reasonable and just 'trans-ideological' order.[35] Following the Soviet invasion of Czechoslovakia in 1968, for example, no existing co-production agreements were cancelled. The later U.S. reaction to the invasion of Afghanistan has been widely denounced as irrational and 'ideological.'

The third essential element of the universal and homogeneous State that is central to the operations of MNEs is technology. This topic is considered more directly later in this chapter. In the present context it is enough to note that maximizing long-term profit throughout the world means pursuing the 'one best way' in all areas of activity. The cultural configuration that results places great value (to use one of many such lists) on 'efficiency, productivity, rationality, achievement-oriented evaluation, saving, investment and long-run return, large-scale production, scientific innovation, and a general view of nature as mutable.'[36] The political regime implied is best captured by a slogan used by Harold Geneen when he ran ITT: 'No surprises.' The results can be grotesque if judged by the obsolete criteria of historical rather than post-historical standards: 'I.G. Farben's decision [on 6 February 1941] to locate at Auschwitz was based on the very same criteria by which contemporary multinational corporations relocate their plants in utter indifference to the social consequences of such moves: wherever possible costs, especially labour costs, must be minimized and profits maximized.'[37] Farben built its plant at Auschwitz to produce Buna, synthetic rubber; it was well located in terms of natural resources, transportation facilities, and, of course, cheap labour.

It has become a commonplace for both academic analysts and businessmen to emphasize the importance of technology in initiating and maintaining the MNE and the oligopolistic advantages it enjoys. The role of the telephone and jet aircraft in reducing the importance of time and space is as obvious as the reduction of ambiguity by computers. The constant goal is efficient productivity, which is virtually the meaning of technology. Even among those who see the decline of the MNE as imminent, exception is nearly always made for vertically integrated extractive companies and technologically innovative ones, which in the present context are the most important.[38] And in any event, as Raymond Vernon pointed out, when an MNE surrenders an established product-line to a national firm this is likely to be in response to anticipated profits and growth in a new area. In general, he said, 'casualties are likely in the future, as in the past, wherever multinational enterprises find themselves unable to master the rollover imperative, and these casualties will often signal the broadened opportunities created for national enterprises. Even as the individual subsidiaries of multi-national enterprises are imperiled, however, the multi-national form of enterprise continues to enjoy palpable benefits. The survival prospects of the multi-national enterprise as an institution continue to appear very favourable.'[39]

The continued existence of multinationals is not a decisive fact in any case. What counts is the self-interpretation of contemporary modern human activity. The institutional form of the MNE, like that of the nation-state or of any other ecumenic or parochial 'transnational' movement, is historical. What remains constant is the 'essence,' the 'meaning,' the 'entelechy' of the actual organizations involved. They all seek to actualize the same post-historical principles that constitute the substance of the universal and homogeneous State, and they all do so by the technological domination of nature.

Apart from 'irrational' nationalists who lament the passing of viable national communities[40] or those who see MNEs as an *imperium in imperio* and so a threat even to their countries of origin,[41] much of the criticism of MNEs reinforces the Hegelian principles that have been expounded. Most critics denounce the uneven distribution of profits and the inherent injustice of the already great and now increasing discrepancies in wealth associated with lead/lag costs in development.[42] Now, that is a practical criticism, and practical men have not been wanting in formulating a response. The OECD and Andean Pact countries both have codes of conduct for MNEs. The result has been, as with OPEC and the oil companies, a high degree of organizational co-operation.[43] George Ball, himself a practical man, has provided one of the best-known arguments in favour of a supernational authority to 'oversee' operations of MNEs. His argument is cold comfort to most critics, though quite sensible so far as MNEs are concerned: 'So long as national governments accept no international code of restraints on their own conduct, the freedom of the multinational corporation will be continually challenged.' The benefits of greater freedom are clear enough: 'Freeing world business from national interference through the creation of new world instrumentalities would inevitably, over time, point up the inadequacy of our political arrangements. At least, in a small way, it might thus serve to stimulate mankind to close the gap between our archaic political structure and the visions of commerce that vault beyond confining national boundaries to fulfill the full promise of the world economy.'[44] One expects for example, that the Hughes Tool Company had more than a casual interest in the Law of the Sea Conference, given its apparent capabilities in deep-water resource extraction.

Whether one advocates a spurious reform, or the absence of any control, or one or another variety of Marxism as a desirable successor to the regime of MNEs, certain equivalences of meaning are apparent. Defenders of the MNE, like those of the universal and homogeneous State, can readily admit there exist certain regrettable consequences and unfortunate abuses, but they are, if not inevitable at the moment, at least worth paying. Putting the issue in terms of utilitarian ethics has the happy result for the defender of the MNE that he can always promise that future costs will be less, that things will be reformed, and so on, which is precisely what the more radical critics promise to do. Both sides, apparently, seek and promise to achieve what Harold Laswell most aptly described as 'vast value indulgences.' The commonly sought-for regime would be characterized by 'a common system of identity and a homogeneous life-style' among élites and 'mid-élites.' Eventually this 'life-style' and 'identity' would percolate through to the masses so as to 'mobilize the rank and file of the world community in ways that help to overcome the effects of parochial socialization ... Without fanfare it will be possible to change authoritative and controlling perspectives in such a way as to integrate a world public order of peace, security, and dignity.'[45] It seems only fair to observe that the changes in authoritative and controlling perspectives that are envisaged could be accomplished only without fanfare, that is, surreptitiously and subliminally, which is surely the only practical response to irrational particularisms.

To those still suffering from the after-effects of parochial socialization, Lasswell's vision of peace, security, and dignity seems haunted and eerie. But that, too may be overcome by the 'staff professional' who, ready to 'meet the challenges of the next two decades,' is 'sufficiently well informed and imaginative to introduce human engineering at all levels of a company and in a variety of cultures.'[46] The same attitudes, based on the same principles, recur in the Gulag, only more plainly and more brutally.

Arkipelag GULag

Whatever qualification one may eventually make to the contention made in the last sentence, it cannot simply be dismissed without further consideration. In an interview in 1968, for example, Kojève allowed that he had once thought that Stalin, not Napoleon, had effected the end of history and that he, not Hegel, had been charged with revealing the truth.[47] Moreover, Kojève's interpretation of post-historical political life, the serious struggle of competent individual citizens for universal recognition, may well have been inspired by contemporary judicial events unfolding so dramatically in his hometown, Moscow. The trial of Bukharin, in March 1938, was especially important. Certainly Merleau-Ponty's analysis of it was full of Kojèvian motifs and interpretative insights.[48] Prima facie, then, one has sufficient reason to proceed further.

Virtually all serious analysts of the Soviet government have considered the camps an important constituent element in the operation of that regime. Aleksandr Solzhenitsyn's large book, *The Gulag Archipelago*,[49] was hardly the first to deal with the topic. By the late 1940s evidence had been widely disseminated in the West attesting to the existence of the camps. It was, moreover, overwhelmingly convincing. As early as 1923 a list of sixty-five camps had been published by the Main Administration of Forced Labour in the address directory *All Russia*.[50] Since that time, a trickle of rumours has grown into a vast documentary flood as memoirs, Soviet legal and administrative materials, oral testimony, reports, letters, and so on have been published. The wide range of agreement and consistency of this evidence could fail to convince only a 'compulsive ignoramus' or 'the most purblind or fanatical admirer of the Communist system.'[51] Most accounts have concentrated on the misery and suffering that the prisoners, the zeks, were compelled to undergo, which surely was the most important feature of the camps. Others have reported their origin and operational procedures. None, however, has done so with the dramatic power and thoroughness of Solzhenitsyn. In him are combined magnificent literary gifts and a passionate love for Russia. Indeed, he writes for Russians, even from his New England exile: hence his contempt for those vile fellow citizens who serve to maintain the camps. Of course, there are errors in detail.[52] Most readers, however, would confirm at least the sentiment expressed by George F. Kennan, that *The Gulag Archipelago* is 'the most heavy and relentless book of our time.'[53] But it is neither as a literary text nor as additional testimony to human cruelty that it is examined here: it also expresses the principles of the universal and homogeneous State.

The title of the book, *Arkipelag GULag*, has a certain ugly sonorousness in Russian. The second word, GULag, is an acronym, much beloved by administrators everywhere, and refers to the central prison administration. The first term is the more powerful image: 'Scattered from the Bering Strait almost to the Bosphorus are thousands of islands of the mysterious Archipelago. They are invisible, but they exist' (*GA* I 489).[54] The islands may be as small as a police van scurrying through the darkened streets of Moscow or as large and immobile as the vast camps of Kolyma. They are central to the regime and perhaps its most distinctive feature. 'The Camps are not the "dark side" of our postrevolutionary life. Their scale made them not an aspect, not just a side, but very nearly the very liver of events. It was rare for our half century to manifest itself so consistently, with such finality' (*GA* II 142). The personnel at the top may change, the Archipelago remains: 'It remains because *that particular* political regime could not survive without it. If it disbanded the Archipelago, it would cease to exist itself' (*GA* III 494). The internal imperial organization manifest in the Archipelago is, then, as central to the Soviet regime as the external imperial organization of the MNE is to the American.

As with the account of MNEs, we consider both the internal organization and the external political consequences. So far as the second topic is concerned the importance of the camps for the regime of the universal and homogeneous State appears in several ways. Most of these are familiar and may be summarized briefly. A glance at the Soviet constitution would, as a matter of course, reveal the importance of universality and homogeneity.[55] More important than its beautiful words are the principles actually embodied by the camps. One should note first of all that the camps chiefly served political not economic ends. Thus, in place of the technical ruthlessness of hardware characteristic of the operations of MNEs, one finds the technical ruthlessness of organization in the pursuit of equally unambiguous ends. For example, the first major construction project undertaken by zeks, the White Sea–Baltic canal, did not serve its ostensible military or economic purpose: naval ships and submarines could not use it because it was too shallow, and, as late as 1966, Solzhenitsyn himself reported observing two barges pass, in opposite directions, during a period of eight hours, and carrying identical cargo, firewood (GA II 102). What, then, was its purpose? 'Stalin simply needed a great construction project *somewhere* that would devour many working hands and many lives (the surplus of people as a result of the liquidation of the kulaks), with the reliability of a gas execution van but more cheaply, and that would at the same time leave a great monument to his reign of the same general sort as the pyramids' (GA II:86). But the pyramids were built with contemporary technology: the White Sea canal was built 'with pick and spade – in the flowering of the twentieth century ... Everything was created, as they say in camp, with "fart power"' (GA II 579). Camp production was very inefficient, not simply because of theft, laziness, malnourishment, and *tykhta*, cheating on documentation, but also because of the high supervision costs. However inefficiently produced, the product was the same as in the Nazi camps: death, 'the most basic, the steadiest form of Archipelago output there is – with no norms' (GA II 221). We shall consider the internal significance of death and its organization at great length below.

In a reciprocal relation to the production of death for zeks was the production of recognition for Stalin, his associates, and his successors. Stalin was known to the zeks as *Khozyain*, Master. 'For Stalin's purposes the camps were a wonderful place into which he could herd millions as a form of intimidation. And so it appears that they justified themselves politically' (GA II 578). Under the category of what Solzhenitsyn called 'ideology' (GA I 174),[56] one can also discover a version of the sought-for

Hegelian synthesis of power and wisdom. His respect, of course, was backhanded: 'our obtuse, our blinkered, our hulking brute of a judicial system can live only if it is infallible' (GA III 520). Yet one must admit that the respect was paid and the judicial or administrative order did, indeed, 'live.' Consequently, 'the faultless system was moderated only by the shortcomings of those who carried it out' (GA I 140). Mistakes naturally enough get made, though never by the Organs. Without the Archipelago, 'who can be made to suffer for the errors of the Vanguard Doctrine? For the fact that people will not grow into the shapes devised for them?' (GA III 505). Thus, the infinite flexibility of Soviet law: unpromulgated and secret articles in the criminal code, crimes such as the 'secret exchange of thought,' criminality extended to such recondite socio-historical groups as 'déclassé offshoots' (GA I 66–7, 122; II 329). The consistent purpose of this protean jurisprudence was to ensure that 'every change of course will be shown to be a long-felt need, a logical result of our whole historical development, prophetically envisaged in the One True Doctrine' (GA III 523–4). Solzhenitsyn's rhetoric is assuredly anti-Hegelian. But one cannot fail to observe in his denunciations the long-standing Hegelian theme that blended logical results and the entirety of historical development into the One True Doctrine.

Turning to the internal organization of the Gulag Archipelago, we shall consider the phenomenon, as was done with MNEs, in light of the principles of universality, homogeneity, and technology.

The most obvious and external importance of universality derives from the ecumenic aspirations of communism. In principle, history has endowed the Vanguard with its role; actualizing that role apparently involves the establishment of camps to deal with dying classes and enemies. As the accession of communists to power proceeds, so too does the Gulag accumulate more islands. Presumably the Gulagization of the planet is not impossible. It goes without saying that no respect can be accorded territorial particularity: no 'nation' can claim legitimately to have a quasi-natural or 'traditional' place to live. Evidently the Koreans employed on Siberian railroad construction were the first to learn they could be arrested on the basis of race, after which they were distributed throughout the Archipelago (GA I 72). The only prior example of wholesale and forcible resettlement of peoples that is significant for modern individuals was the African slave trade (GA III 385ff). In both instances, the activity signified that no territory belonged to any people, no real link to the soil existed, there were no ancestral homelands that demanded respect. In short, there exists no 'natural' particularism so far as humans are concerned. The implications were clearly not lost upon those who produced leaky islands of misery and death in the waters of the South China Sea.

Such observations, however, are merely external and commonsensical. To grasp their proper significance one must probe more deeply. Recall that, according to Solzhenitsyn, the camps constitute the 'liver' of the regime; that is, they are an absolutely essential organ of the state, a distillate of the regime as a whole. As Heinrich Böll observed, most of Solzhenitsyn's work has depicted a prison atmosphere, concentrated in the camps, which is to say, diffused through Soviet society. Likewise his use of underworld slang to describe the actions of the regime was intended to reflect its true nature. Furthermore, a stay in camp has become virtually, if not actually, an element of Soviet socialization: 'You go through life from stage to stage – schoolboy, student, citizen, soldier, prisoner, exile – and it is always the same: the bosses are always too heavy, too strong for you, and you must bow down and keep silent' (GA III 426). The camps have become integral parts of Soviet self-consciousness. Less oppressive but more widespread forms of Gulag life would include bread cards, internal passports, residence permits, discharge certificates, work permits, social insurance cards, and all the petty reminders of state power that bother Soviet (and not just Soviet) citizens. A properly socialized example would combine the commandability of a zek with ordinary obedience. 'Wasn't the ideal picture one of prisoners who had no will of their own, nor the capacity to make their own decisions – and of a prison administration that did their thinking and their deciding for them? These are, if you will, the only prisoners who can exist in the new society' (GA I 468). Model citizens, the real New Soviet Men, most perfectly realized within Gulag, were simply without spontaneity, were virtually substitutable bundles of Pavlovian reactions.

Solzhenitsyn found special significance in the flowering of the culture of thieves, *blatnye*, whom Stalin had declared to be 'socially friendly' elements.[57] 'Through its laws the Stalinist power said to the thieves clearly: Do not steal from me: Steal from private persons: You see, private property is a belch from the past (But, "personally assigned" VIP property is the hope of the future)' (GA II 429). Private property may be inherited, is a part of 'nature,' family, tradition, etc. In contrast, personally assigned public property was (in principle) merited, a reward for the historical actions of the individual to whom the apartment, or car, or country residence had been (temporarily, of course) assigned. In Solzhenitsyn's words, the thieves' outlook, expressed in their slogan 'You today, me to-morrow,' which 'initially had conquered the Archipelago, easily swept further and captured the All-Union ideological market, a wasteland without any stronger ideology ... Thus it is that the Archipelago takes its revenge on the Soviet Union for its creation. Thus it is that no cruelty whatsoever passes by without impact. Thus it is that we always pay dearly for chasing after what is cheap' (*GA* II 564–5). Again, if one looks beyond the anti-Soviet tone of Solzhenitsyn's remarks, one may conclude quite simply that the effects of the Gulag are spread throughout Soviet society, which is certainly an empirical approximation of universality.

But then again, one cannot simply overlook the contents of Solzhenitsyn's indictment. As one observer wrote, the effects are like a tumor: when between 8 per cent and 10 per cent of the Soviet population is or has been in jail, the attitudes of camp metastasize throughout the population. 'By teaching young people that it is socially acceptable to inform on their elders or to engage in violence against, for example, religious groups, the state may be creating an inhuman generation which it cannot adequately control.'[58] And yet this too may be reinterpreted along Hegelian lines. According to Kojève, consciousness of death was a 'metaphysical necessity' for the self-formation of fully self-conscious citizens. Now, the chief product of the camps was death, a state of not being there any more, a condition when time, not just history, stops for an individual. Eventually this happens to everybody, hence the genuine universality of death. It would seem, however, that a twenty-five-year sentence, a 'quarter' or even a 'ten ruble note' followed by perpetual exile, was an effective enough simulation of timelessness. Camp terms and exile involved very long periods. Moreover, a zek could be sentenced to an additional term simply by administrative decree. Inside, one must submit to the ceaseless repetition of the same situations: roll call, searches, labour, poor food, cold, mosquitoes, dirt, inadequate sleep, submissive gestures – all this, undertaken by innocent individuals,[59] is as close as one can imagine to the experience of time having come to a stop. Human life gets transformed into a biological rhythm of repetition. In short, the sheer organization of camp routine had the effect of instilling a consciousness of death – first, of course, in the zeks, but also in their guards.

Actual terror was even more effective. To begin with, neither education nor any prior experience was of much help as preparation for being arrested for nothing and interrogated about nothing (*GA* I 121). Thus did there occur the internal melting of consciousness and the disintegration of all stable supports, just as was demanded by Hegel (*PhG* 148:117).

Terror was universal in the sense that everyone knew of it even if they avoided jail: 'That was the way it was in those years: people lived and breathed and then suddenly found that their existence was *inexpedient*' (*GA* I 309). As a consequence of their self-conscious superfluity, the strongest chain binding the zeks to camp 'was the prisoners' universal submission and total surrender to their situation as slaves' (*GA* II 393). In short, the universality experienced by zeks in camp was of their own mortality and finitude. Knowing that their world had been radically transformed for no apparent reason (they were innocent of any crime), the zeks learned that the world as such was utterly contingent. Their compulsory suffering, as close to the pure consciousness of Hegel's slave as it seems possible to get, enforced the same universality represented by the image of an equality of souls before God, which is to say, in death. The Hegelian transformation was obvious: religious universalism, being imaginary and representational, needs be made actual. To the degree this was accomplished by life in the camps, it recapitulated for a new generation the historical meaning of the Terror of the French Revolution. Those who survived, and understood what had taken place, would become self-conscious citizens of the universal and homogeneous State. It has been suggested earlier that Kojève's insights into the meaning of Hegel's text were conditioned by reflections on what he observed taking place in his homeland. As will be indicated below, this was essentially what has happened to Solzhenitsyn himself.

Normally, legal structures ensure a relatively stable and reliable frame within which behaviour is defined as permissible or not. The same arbitrariness and flexibility that resulted from the substitution of administrative decrees for formal, legal procedures also ensured a degree of homogeneity in recruitment. Ilya Ehrenburg has compared arrest to a lottery, and Solzhenitsyn did not entirely disagree. Anyone *could* be arrested: young or old, weak or strong, man or woman, smart or stupid, good or bad. And yet the numbers in the lottery were fixed. 'Those who were bold fell beneath the ax, were sent off to the Archipelago ... All those who were purer and better could not stay in that [i.e. Soviet] society; and without them it kept getting more and more trashy. You would not notice these quiet departures at all. But they were, in fact, the dying of the soul of the people' (*GA* II 642). However skewed and unrepresentative a sample of Soviet society was recruited to the Archipelago, once inside, one's former station ceased to count. 'The Archipelago was a world without diplomas, a world in which the only credentials were one's own claims' (*GA* II 265). Here was created a geuine kind of classless society. 'For the first time in history, such a multitude of sophisticated, mature, and cultivated people found themselves, not in imagination only, but once and for all, inside the pelt of a slave, serf, logger, miner. And so for the first time in world history (on such a scale) the experiences of the upper and lower strata of society *merged* ... Only now could an educated Russian write about an enserfed peasant *from the inside* – because he himself had become a serf' (*GA* II 490–1). Most, of course, never had a chance to tell of their experience of classlessness: 'The experience of the upper and lower strata had merged – but the bearers of the merged experience perished. And thus it was that an unprecedented philosophy and literature were buried under the iron crust of the Archipelago' (*GA* II 491). And yet, even with the ruthless 'compression' and 'atom packing' of individuals into a mass (*GA* III 91), a degree of social differentiation remained: thieves were always above 'politicals' or '58s,' with one exception, to which we shall return.[60] The behaviour of this socially friendly Gulag élite, however, reinforced the pattern of homogeneity.

The thieves' role in the system of oppression is, no doubt, their most important function. They would strip the newly arrested prisoner of whatever few possessions he may have had and give them to the guards in return for favours. 'You are overwhelmed by your unbearable prison term, and you are trying to figure out how to catch your breath, while everyone around you is figuring out how to plunder you. Everything works out so as to oppress the political prisoner, who is already depressed and abandoned without all that' (*GA* I 545). The thieves and their way of life had an impact beyond being the immediate instrument of repression: the gradual blending of the mores of thief and guard resulted in new social categories. 'The *urka* – the habitual thief – who adopted the Chekist faith became a *bitch*, and his fellow thieves could cut his throat. The Chekist who acquired th psychology of the thief was an *energetic* interrogator during the thirties and forties, or else a *resolute* camp chief – such men were appreciated. They got the service promotions' (*GA* II 428).

As has been indicated, the thieves' views slowly but thoroughly permeated the whole society (*GA* II 564–5). It is not the universality of the thieves' psychology that one would emphasize now, however, but the actual content of their outlook. Consider again their slogan, 'You today, me tomorrow.' First of all, it perfectly expressed the attitude of Hobbes's natural man. Life, so long as one has it, is a supremely precarious thing, to be preserved at all costs. It is a fiercely competitive race to out-go all others in order to gain recognition. 'Even when they have a surfeit of everything, they reach out and grab what belongs to others because any unstolen article makes a thief sick at heart' (*GA* II 441). They firmly believed 'that men are rats, that man eats man, and that it can be no other way. Each of them brought a concern for his own fate alone, and a total indifference to the fate of others' (*GA* III 69). In effect they constituted a society of cannibals (*GA* II 520).[61] If life is truly a race, as Hobbes taught, all humans are fundamentally equal, at least in the one thing that counts, the capacity to murder one another. And what, pray, could be more homogenizing than the imagery of cannibalism, genuine anthropophagia? As Solzhenitsyn himself wrote: 'Once I had been brought up on different ideals, but from the thirties cruel life had rubbed us in only one direction: to go after and get' (*GA* II 175). As with MNEs, universality and homogeneity reinforced one another.

In this essay the term 'technology' or 'technique' is meant to indicate not simply the use of machinery, but rather the one best way for doing something. The presence of machinery, then, will depend upon what is to be done. The most important aspect of technolgy, so far as the present topic is concerned, is organization, not hardware. The organizational technique of the Gulag was a combination of administration and violence. According to Solzhenitsyn, an early debate centred on how to obtain the labour-power needed for what E.A. Preobrazhensky had called 'primitive socialist accumulation.' Trotsky favoured drafting a labour army. Stalin, however, 'decided to process the labour army men through the prison machinery' (*GA* II 72). Both, however, would involve a purely administrative apparatus directed at an unambiguous goal.

Reference has already been made to certain non-public elements of Soviet law. Indeed, the entire process by which zeks were recruited amounted to a kind of open secret. Administrative secrecy, it was pointed out in the first chapter of this essay, was an essential constitution of imperial as well as totalitarian rule. Decrees, not laws, are the instrumentalities of such rule, for they have the advantage of being immediately alterable at the whim of the ruler, who thereby appears to those who obey as being irresistible. Secrecy is more than a matter of tactics. In both MNEs and within the Gulag, a maximally efficient drive to ecumenic organization demands that personnel identify completely with the anonymous historical forces that the organization embodies. Now, when one identifies oneself fully with an organization, one becomes, in effect, a function of it. One's persona, as Hobbes said, is absorbed by that of Leviathan. One owes allegiance to no law save the 'law' that demands survival, that is, the continued existence, or better, the expansion, of the regime. In obedience to that 'law' an infinite flexibility is required: human laws, which are intended to provide a stable frame for the community, could not possibly serve that purpose. At its limit, not even decrees ought to be committed to paper. In a regime of command and obedience there can be no opposition and no genuine conflict. Reflecting on the prosecutor Vishinsky's interpretation of the Moscow Trials, Solzhenitsyn observed: 'On the threshold of the classless society, we were at last capable of realizing *the conflictless trial* – a reflection of the absence of inner conflict in our social structure – in which not only the judge and prosecutor but also the defense lawyers and the defendants themselves would strive collectively to achieve their common purpose' (*GA* I 374).

Violence by itself may be considered a technique, and apparently it need serve no further purpose. In the absence of any restraints or moderating influences such as might be provided by the rule of law, it should occasion no surprise that it was widely used. The result was to reinforce the sentiment that everything is permissible (*GA* II 375). The actual contents of that sentiment invariably have turned out to involve chiefly, though not exclusively, the liberation of human beastliness. 'It was an accepted saying that *everything is possible* in Gulag. The blackest foulness, any twist and turn of betrayal, wildly unexpected encounters, love on the edge of the precipice – everything was possible' (*GA* II 468). Torture, of course, is a technique for the extraction of information. Cruelty was not unusual, but it was not really necessary either. In any case, its application ought to be governed by technical criteria: 'When slave-driving became a thought-out *system*, pouring water over a prisoner in subzero temperatures, or putting the prisoner out on a stump to be devoured by mosquitoes had turned into a superfluity and useless expenditure of the executioners' energy' (*GA* II 54). The apparent irrationality of violence, that it was not needed to obtain information since no information was needed to enforce administrative decrees, would evaporate if one ceased to assume that torture must serve some kind of legality, however unusual. In Gulag, torture fulfilled its purpose simply by oppressing zeks. Its sole 'justification' would have been along the lines indicated earlier: it was a 'metaphysical necessity.' Conceivably such an argument would appeal to a Hegelian Sage or to those other votaries of the One True Doctrine, whether manning the watch-towers, handling the dogs, or sitting quietly in the Kremlin. It would hardly be acceptable to anybody else for, as David Rousset, himself a quondam inmate of Nazi camps, said, normal men do not know everything is possible.

There are several conclusions to be drawn from Solzhenitsyn's analysis. First is considered the author's own conclusions, then a Hegelian transmogrification of them. For Solzhenitsyn, the horrors of the Archipelago were the logical result not of Stalin's endocrine imbalances or dark Georgian soul, or of the endemic intolerance that intellectuals, such as Lenin or Marx, so often seem to possess. They do not continue because of a certain pig-headedness or lack of imagination within the present leadership. Rather, he said it was impossible to create 'socialism' in the absence of 'the wholesale robbery of the peasantry, without the enslavement of the working class, without the introduction of mass slave ownership, and without terror.'[62] Whatever else socialism meant and however rich the variants of that doctrine may be, it certainly is not incompatible with the assumptions and purposes of the universal and homogeneous State. And, obviously, Kojève would not dispute the necessity of terror.

For Solzhenitsyn, however, the ideological amalgam of Stalinism-Leninism-Marxism-socialism and all that it implied is The Lie. What is worse, nobody, not even the current crop of Soviet leaders, believes it. 'Although we have had a classless society for so long ... we are used to the idea that crime never ceases, never decreases, and indeed that no one now seems to promise such a thing. In the 1930s they assured us: We're almost there, just a few more years. They don't even make such statements any more' (GA III 522). Ideological lies might have been useful in the 1920s and 1930s, Solzhenitsyn wrote the Politburo, but, 'in our own country today *nothing constructive rests upon it*; it is sham ... It clogs up the whole life of society – minds, tongues, radio and press – with lies, lies, lies. For how else can something dead pretend that it is living except by erecting a scaffolding of lies? Everything is steeped in lies, and *everybody knows it*.'[63] Indeed, totalitarian rule seems to demand that people live lies: 'Our present system is unique in world history, because over and above its physical and economic constants, it demands of us total surrender of our souls, continuous and active participation in the general, conscious *lie*.'[64] And finally, because lying is an integral part of the regime, it is inherently violent. 'Violence,' Solzenitsyn wrote, 'does not and cannot flourish by itself; it is inevitably intertwined with lying. Between them there is the closest, the most profound and natural bond: nothing screens violence except lies, and the only way lies can hold out is by violence. Whoever has once announced violence as his method must inexorably choose lying as his principle.'[65] To follow the summary formulation of Geoffrey Clive, at the heart of the grotesque lies the lie, depravity superimposed upon senselessness. Accordingly, 'for Solzhenitsyn the Soviet state under Stalin is vicious as well as mad in its operations, and thus productive of grotesque acts and policies.'[66] And yet a Kojèvian reading is also possible: our rejection of what presently appears as grotesque is merely prejudice based upon a deficient understanding of the deeper rationality of what is actual.

Within the Archipelago, as without, there exist more and less pure examples of Masters and Slaves. Most, of course, are predominantly servile, what Solzhenitsyn called 'rabbits' (GA I 55), zeks who have become degraded commandable automatons that make the Gulag's finest citizens. The post-historical Master is the 'committed escaper' (GA III 125ff), who behaves, under the circumstances, as one might expect and who, through his own humane shortcomings, most often gets caught. A more effective response, however, was the historical recapitulation of the French Revolution within the Archipelago itself. Rebellion within an atmosphere of terror was not easy. The combination of thieves, informers, and ordinary oppression made it very difficult to obtain sufficient trust in another person to plot concerted action. And even if, for example, a hunger strike could be organized, it would as likely as not be met with machine guns or else the zeks would be allowed to go hungry (GA III 250ff). Yet, in the Kengir camp, a genuine rebellion occurred. It began with the murder (or summary trial, condemnation, and execution) of informers; others of them fled, like the French aristocracy, to safety in special cells (GA III 233ff). A purgative terror continued: information dried up, as potential informers feared more for their lives than they desired favours from the police. 'The bosses could no longer see us, no longer peer into our souls. A gulf had opened between the overseers and the slaves ... This was a hunger strike called by men schooled by decades in the law of the jungle: "You die first, and I'll die later." Now they were reborn, they struggled out of their stinking swamp, they consented to die today, all of them together, rather than go on living in the same way to-morrow' (GA III 258). The result of their audacious creation of power was that the Chekists were compelled to admit 'that far from being a mutiny, this was a conflict between (!) ... between equals ... between the administration and the prisoners!' (GA III 262).[67] With the equality of conflict came a kind of declaration of independence: no longer was Kengir just another island. Thieves, moreover, had joined with politicals in the Kengir rebellion, and at large, 'the massacre of stoolies, the hunger strikes, the strikes, the disturbances in the Special Camps, had not remained unknown to the thieves. By 1954, so we are told, it was noticeable in transit prisons, that the thieves came to respect the politicals' (GA III

290). But these events inside the Archipelago, welcome though they were, must be seen as merely historical. The genuinely post-historical citizens were ex-zeks, living among their uneducated fellows in the less concentrated carceral atmosphere of Soviet society.

A zek either died in the Archipelago or was released, generally into exile in a remote part of the Soviet Union for a specified number of years or in perpetuity. The earlier observation, that the product of the Gulag meat-grinder was death, must therefore be qualified: some survived, and they too were a product. The Kengir rebellion had an obvious effect: 'the social temperature on this plot of land had risen so high that if souls were not transmuted, they were purged of dross, and the sordid laws saying that "we only live once," that being determines consciousness, and that every man's a coward when his neck is at stake, ceased to apply for that short time in that circumscribed place. The laws of survival and reason told people that they must all surrender together or flee individually, but they did not surrender and they did not flee!' (GA III 323). In Hegelian terms, the zeks had overcome, had superseded, consciousness of death. The rebellions, however, came late, not until the 1950s. Years of suffering as slaves, years of 'education' in servitude, of Bildung, were required for the implications of the 'melting' of consciousness to become clear in the last historical acts of the zeks. There was a limit, Solzhenitsyn wrote, to rabbitry, 'and beyond it one is no longer willing, one finds it too repulsive, to be a reasonable little rabbit. And that is the limit beyond which rabbits are enlightened by the common understanding that all rabbits are foredoomed to become only meat and pelts, and that at best, therefore, one can gain only a postponement of death and not life in any case' (GA I 455). Time and Spirit as well as space and bodies had been concentrated in the Archipelago.

Hegel's opinion of the Slavic world would therefore have to be revised. He had found little historical significance there, yet a mere century later a greater number of post-historical individuals had been created in the Soviet Union than anywhere else. The zeks had been a classless society inside; once released they became a 'classless elite.'[68] Of course they had suffered much. How else could their souls have been 'transmuted' or 'purged of dross'? Unless their consciousnesses underwent the experience of liquefaction of all stable supports, how else could they have learned that all things were possible? Of course the rest of Soviet society despised them. How else could one expect the uneducated many to look upon those who had learned different standards, different truths, and who had gained a vastly greater knowledge of human reality? Surely after all that has been said about Kojève and Hegel there is nothing astonishing there: ordinary Soviet citizens, clinging to their parochial bourgeois notions, are bound to despise those who are the truth and perfection of their own ideas, individuals who have experienced at first hand or immediately, without the veil of words, images, or ideologies, the meaning of universality and homogeneity.[69]

One may go so far as to say that the ex-zek is wise. Solzhenitsyn went out of his way to address the Soviet leaders as an equal, as one whose individual acts had a public and, in principle, universal, significance. He addressed them, he said, as 'one who does not stand on a ladder subordinate to your command, who can be neither dismissed from his post, nor demoted, nor promoted, nor rewarded by you, and from whom therefore you are almost certainly to hear an opinion sincerely voiced, without any careerist calculations, such as you are unlikely to hear from even the finest experts in your bureaucracy.'[70] In other words, he wrote like a peer: he recognized the Soviet leaders and gave them the opportunity to recognize him in return. That was why, for example, he persisted in calling his counsel reasonable and practical, and in no way idealistic or utopian. Surely that is the mark of a sage.

Solzhenitsyn is not, however, simply a singular ex-zek, unique in his literary talents, or energy, or patriotism, or religious beliefs. No specific reductive explanation is needed to make sense of his words, for they do no more than express the experiences of millions of others. Some of these are silent because they are dead, others because they have tried to forget the strains of post-historical life, others because they lack the gifts needed to express their wisdom. Any number of reasons could be cited. Their experience as zeks, however, was both personal and common and was, therefore, equivalent in meaning. It was the experience of the totality of history. History, according to Hegel, was the actualization of all human possibilities. When one enters immediately upon a world where all things are possible, one has swallowed, in a concentrated dose, historical experience itself. The rest, one may say, is post-history. Once the experience of history in its totality, namely all possibilities, has been concluded, one becomes if not wise at least a lot wiser than those who have not known history in its entirety. 'It is a good thing to think in prison, but it is not bad in camp either ... A free head – now, is that not an advantage of life in the Archipelago?' (GA II 607). In the ridiculous vocabulary of Soviet penology, this meant quite simply that the rehabilitation of zeks was impossible (GA III 450ff). The wise cannot forget their wisdom. Solzhenitsyn has given this Hegelian insight his own formulation: 'In our day, if you get a letter completely free from self-pity, genuinely optimistic – it can only be from a former zek. They are used to the worst the world can do, and nothing can depress them. I am proud to belong to this mighty race! We were not a race, but they made us one! They forged bonds between us, which we, in our timid and uncertain twilight, where every man is afraid of every other, could never have forged for ourselves' (*GA* III 462). Moreover, Solzhenitsyn knew that, while his wisdom enabled him to address the Politburo as one public man to his peers, the essential feature had nothing to do with action, and everything to do with rational and internal understanding. Solzhenitsyn's imagery was Christian, just as his practical advice was given to Russians; its meaning, however, pointed beyond his own intentions. 'Governments,' he said, 'need victories and the people need defeats. Victory gives rise to the desire for more victories. But after a defeat it is freedom that men desire – and usually attain. A people needs defeat just as an individual needs suffering and misfortune: they compel the deepening of the inner life and generate a spiritual upsurge' (*GA* I 272).[71]

One may conclude, with even more confidence than one could from the example of MNEs, that if the Gulag Archipelago continues (as it shows every sign of doing), the principles of the universal and homogeneous State will be confirmed and will be more fully actualized; if it is wracked by rebellions such as the one at Kengir, those principles will also be confirmed. If Soviet foreign policy consists in the exportation of revolution at the point of a bayonet, one must conclude that Trotsky was exactly wrong. There is no other way to ensure success, especially if it is resisted by the natives. So far as the West is concerned, the implication is obvious: 'Once I used to hope that experience of life could be handed on from nation to nation, and from one person to another ... But now I am beginning to have doubts. Perhaps everyone is fated to live through every experience himself in order to understand ... At the moment the question is not how the Soviet Union will find a way out of totalitarianism, but how the West will be able to avoid the same fate.'[72] Equally one may render Solzhenitsyn's words in a Hegelian idiom: if one is to gain the wisdom of either of those two exiled Russian sages, Kojève and Solzhenitsyn, one must also experience the Gulag. Or perhaps it is enough to recognize the historical rationality of what presently exists in the West. Because we have already experienced the whole of history, whereas the Slavic world, in 1806, had not, it may not be necessary to concentrate historical time so much as to recollect it conceptually. This means, of course, that we must grasp its rationality, a rationality that is common to both MNEs and the Gulag, and most perfectly appears so in the technological society.

Technological society

The term 'technological society' is the English title of a book by Jacques Ellul, *La Technique ou l'enjeu du siècle*.[73] The technological society is the most visible aspect of modernity, the most obvious feature that distinguishes the present age from all prior ages or the now modern peoples from the backward, undeveloped, under-developed, or developing peoples, nations, or states. The technological society is the final consequence of the end of history. The French sub-title, 'the bet (or stakes) of the century,' suggests both that the wager is extremely important since the fate of an entire epoch is involved, and Ellul's fear that the gamble has already been lost. One must take the gaming imagery seriously. In one sense, for Ellul, technological society is 'just' a game; the 'real' meaning of life is experienced in his redemptive faith in a Christian beyond. But in another, it is a very serious game inasmuch as the presence of Christianity in the world might, in the absence of resistance such as his own, forever be eclipsed. In this respect, then, like Solzhenitsyn and many analysts of MNEs, Ellul is a severe critic of existing arrangements.

Ellul described technique in a striking image: 'the head of Apollo set on the body of Dionysius.'[74] More prosaically he defined technique as 'the totality of methods rationally arrived at and having absolute efficiency (for a given stage of development) in every field of human activity. Its characteristics are new; the technique of the present has no common measure with that of the past.'[75] Specifically modern technique, characteristic of the technological society as a whole, is distinct from past techniques because for the first time technique has replaced nature as the 'milieu' or environment of human life. All social phenomena and human activities are to be understood as being situated within technique rather than having become influenced by an external technical factor.[76] Technique is its use. That is, it is a method of action. One can of course use a method properly or not. For example, one can use a car as a means of transportation or as a murder weapon. If used as a weapon it is used badly (= inefficiently) because it was not designed to kill people. A gun would be much better (= more efficient). Accordingly, technical consciousness as a whole excludes *ab initio* any other way of looking at the world. Thus, if technique is the one best way, no one in his or her right mind would ever consciously choose the third best way or the seventh best way.

Heidegger has given his own characteristic account of technique or technology. 'Technology is a way of revealing.'[77] It is not neutral. Indeed, to think of it as neutral is to be delivered over to it in the worst possible way. Technology reveals what is apparently hidden, what does not appear on its own before us. Technology challenges nature to supply energy, for example, which then may be transformed, stored up, distributed, and switched about. Man, moreover, is challenged too, and in a more original way than nature since man must undertake the process of ordering or 'enframing' natural things so they will be useful and at hand as a 'standing-reserve.' An advertisement for a large multinational copper company expressed Heidegger's thought: nature makes ore; Anaconda makes mines. 'Everywhere everything is ordered to stand by, to be immediately at hand, indeed to stand there just so that it may be on call for a further ordering.' Consequently, enframing reveals what is there, reality, as standing-reserve and as nothing else. This is 'the essence of modern technology.' When there are no more objects but only standing-reserve, when all nature has become unified, homogeneous, and ready to be mined, man, who has ordered up this standing-reserve, 'comes to the point where he himself will have to be taken as standing-reserve.' In the mean time, people think they have mastered the earth, with the result that truth can never appear save within the enframing that has been constructed precisely because of a refusal to see what appears on its own. 'The rule of Enframing threatens man with the possibility that it will be denied to him to enter into a more original revealing and hence to experience the call of a more primal truth.' The threat, very simply, is 'the possibility that all revealing will be consumed in ordering, and that everything will present itself only in the unconcealedness of standing-reserve.' Activity and achievement can never dispel this danger; they merely express it.

The replacement of philosophy by cybernetics, as Heidegger also expressed the problem, is a great impiety. According to him, 'only a god can save us. The sole possibility that is left for us is to prepare a sort of readiness, through thinking and poetizing, for the appearance of the god, or for the absence of the god in the time of foundering; for in the face of the god who is absent, we founder.'[78] Ellul has also emphasized the impiety of technique. Violation of the 'natural hierarchy' through the process of enframing is 'fundamentally sacrilegious.'[79] The triumph of technique spells the silence, the death, of God. 'From now on, all that is left is a drab insipid unfolding of implications, an interplay of forces and mechanisms. There will be structures and systems, but we shall no longer be able to speak of "history." Man is now seeing the very purpose of his struggles being removed from him, as well as every opportunity for a more intense life; he may continue to "fight," but his lists will encounter only empty air and unbounded darkness ... The West is dying because it has won out over God.' The world has become a city; nature is a park; the land belongs to Cain.[80]

A Hegelian sage would not simply disagree with Ellul or Heidegger. Technique is an impiety, a challenging of nature as other; eventually it is an overcoming of this otherness. For one whose representational language expresses the experience of 'natural hierarchies' or of 'sacred restraints,'[81] the triumph of technique is nothing less than deicide. But the sage has also overcome representational language and 'poeticizing.' Accordingly, it is impossible to share Ellul's faith and remain a sage. And one could not, of course, travel the prophetic path of Heidegger. But it does not follow that Ellul's analyses are invalid. For the sage, Ellul is a philosopher-theologian. His arguments, however, can be taken over on their own proper terms as phenomenology.[82] And is this not an appropriate synthesis of the constituent elements of Apollo and Dionysius?

Several additional characteristics are implied in Ellul's summary definition of technique as the one best way and in his initial description of technique as a historically novel milieu for human life.[83] Technique is rationally standardized in accordance with explicitly described logical norms. It is artificial and automatic in the double sense of preparing a new generation by training them in technical skills and by replacing unspecifiable criteria of choice with efficiency. It is self-augmenting, an irreversible progress in which means have established an absolute primacy over ends. Any particular obstacle is simply a challenge to the ever more widespread and efficient application of technique. It is unified and homogeneous, with no essential differences among its several branches or regional variations. Not that variations do not exist, but they are variations on the same necessary theme of increasing efficiency: the most perfect technique is precisely the most adaptable and protean. Technique universalizes in the double sense of expanding geographically to create one world on the planet and in the qualitative sense of subordinating all religious hopes, myths, virtues, ethnic particularities, and so forth to its own imperatives. Since it is the primacy of means over goals, it is autonomous with respect to, because unregulated by, any values, opinions, ideas, or human institutions: morality deals with moral problems, technical criteria govern technical ones. It is therefore beyond good and evil insofar as it is the arbiter of morality or the creator of a new one (no one rationally chooses the third best way, etc). In summary, technique is a process of inter-linked totalization, a universal and homogeneous system not of thought but of material reality.[84]

It has become clear that technique is not simply the application of tools to nature. Humans must first see nature as fit to be tooled, as Heidegger insisted, and then they must adapt themselves to the tools in order to get the job done. For example, the creation of waste, 'pollution,' 'externalized costs,' and so forth is no doubt very important in certain respects. But it is also clear that modern, post-historical humans consider these problems as technical challenges. Protests against nuclear power stations, for example, are sometimes the result of a desire on the part of protesters to do without their apparent benefits; more often, however, the protest is itself a propaganda technique in favour of some alternative source of energy that is presumed to be, in the longer term, more efficient. That is, at bottom, one protests against the one technique not because it is 'unnatural' to replicate on earth what 'naturally' takes place only on or in the sun, but because it is inefficient. The consequences for 'nature' do not matter for modern humans because nature itself has no standing, no order, no meaning beyond what appears through technique: pollution is a problem and so subject to a technical solution, not an impiety requiring penance or expiation. Accordingly, the consequences of technique are human, not natural. Moreover, they confirm the contention of Kojève that history is ended.

In the post-historical regime, as has been argued earlier, the elements of mastery and servitude continue to exist, but in a superseded form, as elements of citizenship. This is also true within the technological society.

Consider first the element of slavery. Historically the slave was in bondage to nature, and especially to his natural fear of death. The bondage of technique is historical. 'Obedience to the plow and the plane was indeed the only means of dominating earth and wood. But the formula is not true for our techniques. He who serves these techniques enters another realm of necessity. This new necessity is not natural necessity; natural necessity, in fact, no longer exists. It is techniques' necessity, which becomes more constraining the more nature's necessity fades and disappears. It cannot be escaped or mastered.'[85] In a similar vein, Barrett noted that mankind is called to the pursuit of technical domination of the globe 'strictly as a matter of survival.'[86] The overriding reason for this has already been noted: humans must adapt themselves to techniques if they are to be employed efficiently.[87] There is no escape because technique is a self-augmenting process that tends to universalize means throughout the planet. Accordingly, there exists a new definition of servile citizenship, namely 'serving one's own function well and not meddling with the mechanism.'[88] This outcome, which has been widely observed, has also been widely denounced, often most extravagantly.

It does not appear that way, however, to the technicians, those citizens in whom one may say the element of mastery is most important. Ellul has himself observed that, however unfree and powerless those who are the objects of technique may be, the same cannot simply be said of the technicians.[89] Among themselves, technicians undertake a strenuous comparison of efficiencies through their serious competition. This, too, has been denounced though in fact it is no more than bureaucracy, rationally organized intelligence, the rule of rule. 'A modern state,' Ellul wrote, 'is *not* primarily a centralized organ of decision, a set of political organs. It is primarily an enormous machinery of bureaus.'[90] The great virtue of such a regime is efficiency, 'the necessary form of contemporary politics.'[91] In principle, that is, those who deserve recognition are the efficient not the inefficient. And efficiency, one need scarcely add, is an attribute of a free, mortal, historical individual and is not a reflection of gender, nationality, race, or family.

The efficient, the technicians, the genuine post-historical political class, use a special technique, propaganda, to ensure that their efficiencies are truly recognized, namely by compliance. 'In the midst of increasing mechanisation and technological organization, propaganda is simply the means used to prevent these things from being felt as too oppressive and to persuade man to submit with good grace.'[92] The chief purpose of propaganda, then, is not to transform an opinion but to arouse an active belief so as 'to obtain stable behaviour, to adapt the individual to his everyday life, to reshape his thoughts and behaviour in terms of the permanent social setting.'[93] What is involved is emphatically not an evil conspiracy of ideological fanatics imposing their warped views on uncomprehending multitudes: rather, it is a means of governing that gives the non-political citizens a sense of participation. It is, in any event, unavoidable: 'A modern state, even if it be liberal, democratic, and humanist, finds itself objectively and sociologically in a situation in which it must use propaganda as a means of governing. It cannot do otherwise.'[94] The result is truth, 'in the sense that it creates in men subject to propaganda all the signs and indications of true believers. For modern man, propaganda is really creating truth. This means that truth is powerless without propaganda.'[95] Accepting the truth brings an end to wars and revolutions – though not, of course, to violence and consciousness of death.

This post-historical result, David Lovekin has argued, is the traditional goal of thought, 'the overcoming of the bifurcation between the world and my idea of it.' The actualization of the technological society, therefore, redeems the promise of allowing man 'to live in the world as it really is.'[96] By modifying the deepest recesses of human being, all basic contradictions can be resolved, all fundamental tensions relieved. In a properly technical state 'nothing useless exists; there is no torture; torture is a wasteful expenditure of psychic energy which destroys salvageable resources without producing useful results.'[97] As William Barrett observed, torture is unscientific: it is 'administered after the fact, or the imputed fact, of the crime. Why not prevent the crime of dissent before it arises? The more polished techniques of the behavioural sciences might shape the mind beforehand ... The elaborate "sewage system" for disposing of the rebellious, on which Solzhenitsyn reports, would become unnecessary. All just a matter of finding the right technique.'[98] Political violence, including war, may become inefficient as well. Propaganda, therefore, may be invoked 'to solve problems created by technology, to play upon maladjustments, and to integrate the individual into a technological world.' When the peaceful kingdom has been actualized in plenitude, the police will have nothing to do: 'The civic and technological goodwill and enthusiasm for the right social myths – both created by propaganda – will finally have solved the problem of man.'[99] Thus, once again, history is ended; there is nothing more to do.

Nothing to do, that is, except understand what has taken place; nothing to do but recapitulate conceptually the course of history itself; nothing to do but become wise. And Ellul, despite his protestant language, is wise: 'Technique exists because it is technique. The golden age will be because it will be. Any other answer is superfluous.'[100] Barrett, despite his philosophic modesty, is also wise: since technique is the truth, the revealed reality, of the age, it is impossible to affirm or deny. All one can do is 'try to see where technical and technological thinking, with no other principle but itself, must lead us; and whether some countervailing mode of thought may not be called for.'[101] Technical consciousness is, moreover, uniquely capable of understanding itself completely and perfectly. Lovekin has, with an equally philosophic modesty, put the question correctly but exactly backwards. According to him: 'Technical consciousness ... does not know itself to be a form of consciousness. For it to achieve self-consciousness, it would have to distinguish itself from what it is not, but for this mind the world is as it is conceived, lacking, as it does, a notion of natural object, an object that is separate from itself.'[102]

But this, precisely, is wisdom: the world is as it is conceptually described. Or again, in Ellul's words: 'Technique worships nothing, respects nothing. It has a single role: to strip off externals, to bring everything to light, and by rational use to transform everything into means ... The mysterious is merely that which has not yet been technicized.' The gods are long since dead, and with their passing went any sense of the supernatural. 'The individual who lives in the technical milieu knows very well that there is nothing spiritual anywhere.'[103] One may go further down this Hegelian path. If technical self-consciousness is wisdom, it is also power. Ellul has, much as Arendt, identified this amalgam of power and wisdom with the anonymity of the Grand Inquisitor. This is not, perhaps an error, for such a one has no need to raise questions since the answers are already known.

The Grand Inquisitor ... is faceless. His person eludes every grasp, for he is composed in fact of ten or a thousand individuals, all of them strangers and each of them part of a whole that we never know, but to which, however, we devote ourselves wholeheartedly.' The technological society as a whole, it would seem, is the presence of wisdom. And who could deny its power? 'Thus it is that, after the bloodless planning and the reductive rationalizations, everything falls into place by a process of growth that cannot be called spontaneous since it is the result of calculation (but who does the calculating?) The growth is like the blind growth of a root that makes its way inexorably toward what nourishes it: a growth that is blind, yet guided. In the presence of this reality, which is perhaps the deepest of our age, we must walk with sacred reverence, advancing only on tiptoe. Let no man of the spirit disturb this growth whence man draws all he needs, which works entirely for the greatest good and happiness of this man. The man that you are; the man that I am.
    Why did you come to meddle with us, you with your questions! What right have you?
    Who would stand forth?[104]

Let us then draw together these several Hegelian themes. The first and most obvious is that the technological society is an expression of human will, the cool imposition of form, measure, and line upon an irrational, vibrant, pulsating nature. Technical man, in principle, is liberated from all natural constraints. Obviously, humans are not liberated purely and simply. The regime of pure freedom, Hegel taught, was terror. Rather, the constraints are the constraints of technique itself. Whether these constraints are more severe than those of nature, as many contend, it is idle, for present purposes, to inquire. What can be said is that liberation from natural necessities was coeval with the construction of the technological society and submission to its necessities. Concretely it is peopled by technicians, functionaries who command technique, and by others who consume its results. But all are at home there and know it for what it is. Both the Gulag Archipelago and the regime of the MNEs may be understood without distortion as variations of the technological society. Both, under distinct historical, cultural, geographical, economic, and perhaps even ethical or spiritual circumstances, have put into operation the 'one best way.' They are, therefore, equivalent insofar as they express variations of the same post-historical regime, the universal and homogeneous State.[105]

This Hegelian identity of identity and non-identity exemplified in the Gulag and the MNE is expressed perhaps most directly in the great symbol that overreaches power relations in the conventional sense between the Soviet Union and the United States: The Bomb. The symbolism has its own pre-history. In the operations from Rapidan to Petersburg, in 1864, General Grant initiated a technique of waging war that became the self-conscious strategy of the Western Front. The objective was to produce enemy corpses. The overwhelming image of the Second World War, of course, is the concentration camp. It took nearly five years to produce four and one-half million corpses at Auschwitz; today it can be done in a couple of minutes by a single machine. The imagery of the camps persists not only because, as Arendt said, they were laboratories where it was proved that everything is possible, but also because 'accepting as we do that all things are now effortlessly possible everywhere we see them as a small scale trial run for a nuclear war.'[106] In fact, one nuclear war has already been fought. The effects of it on contemporary consciousness are equal to, if not greater than, those of the camps. The potential Gulagization of humanity would, indeed, actualize the ultimate tyranny, and many sound objections can be raised against the rule of MNEs. Nevertheless, in both cases, rebellions, however futile, would still be possible. Nuclear annihilation, however, is absolutely final.

This difference is reflected in the special spiritual consequences of the A-bomb attacks on Hiroshima and Nagasaki. Atomic war was, and in the future would be, unlike any other. 'Hiroshima gave new meaning to the idea of a "world war," of man making war upon his own species ... For after Hiroshima, we can envisage no war-linked chivalry, certainly no glory. Indeed, we can see no relationship – not even a distinction – between victimizer and victim, only the sharing in species annihilation.'[107] Servile technical cleverness has eclipsed the *raison d'être* of the master. The sheer destructive power of atomic weapons has ensured that not even fraudulent recognition could ever be gained through their employ, and this is known to everybody beforehand. As one *Wibakusha*, or A-bomb survivor, observed: 'Such a weapon has the power to make everything into nothing.'[108] Nuclear weapons do not simply destroy things, they destroy 'the boundaries of destruction ... The destruction reflected by that blast [at Hiroshima] was so nearly total and so longlasting that the survivors of the bomb have experienced a *permanent encounter with death*.'[109] Moreover, as many *Wibakusha*-writers have shown, the massive anonymity of A-bomb deaths no less than the actual catastrophic annihilation involved rendered the event impossible to assimilate into any existing vision of human continuity. A-bomb deaths are neither dramatic nor tragic: the massiveness of the disconnection, its abruptness and arbitrariness, made it impossible for writers to establish any symbolic continuity between vaporized people, corpses, or corpselike survivors, and ordinary psychic life. In this respect the A-bomb experience is more difficult to deal with artistically than the camps. One *Wibakusha*-author summarized the entire death-saturated A-bomb experience as 'the omission of various ceremonies.'[110] A-bomb deaths, like the deaths of the camps, are profoundly inappropriate. They bear no relationship to one's ordinary life-span or life-cycle. No ceremony could be seemly. In short, beginning with *Wibakusha*, nuclear weapons have subsequently imposed upon everyone the 'metaphysical necessity' of terror.

The possibility that the species could annihilate itself with its own machinery fundamentally alters the meaning of what Lifton called 'symbolic immortality.' Biological immortality and national continuity are obviously disrupted. Theological imagery of a beyond is transformed if some kind of earthly survival is excluded. In Japan, after the explosion, Lifton reported that neither Eastern nor Western religious imagery proved sufficient to express the meaning of the event. Hence, the growth of strange cults whose apocalyptic imagery expressed an actual human possibility, not a divine transfiguration. Creative immortality had been undermined: if nothing will last, nothing much matters. Art, therefore, need express no more than the anxious nihilism of the artist's life, an anxiety that resonates in everyone's life. And nature, too, can no longer be trusted to endure. Significantly, the presence of radioactive strontium in milk first impressed this novelty on our contemporary consciousness. The result of the decline of these four traditional modes of symbolic immortality (biological, creative, theological, and natural) has been to increase the importance and incidence of a fifth mode, experiential transcendence. Since it is more immediate and sensuous, 'it is therefore less vulnerable to being impoverished by misgivings about historical durability on which the other modes are more dependent.'[111] In its vulgar forms, this mode of transcendence is denounced, for example, as the culture of narcissism. But it also reflects, perhaps indirectly, that humans are mortal, that their lives are really ordered by the desire for recognition. The Bomb, the symbol of oblivion, of the absence of any beyond whatsoever, is the catalyst for this mode of contemporary consciousness.

Yet we have survived in the atomic age, and in our consciousness of survival one may see another aspect of post-historical wisdom. The survivor has come into immediate contact with death, either bodily or spiritually, and yet has remained alive. The survivor is consciousness of death: death is known, and the deadly one has returned full of its knowledge. Yet he knows he did not 'deserve' to survive. There is nothing logical, or right, or natural in one's surviving, no more than it was natural, logical, or right for Jews, zeks, or Japanese to have died as they did. All survivors attempt to make sense of their encounter with death. Whatever it is that the survivor knows, it is part of the dialectic of life and death, of dying and rebirth. The struggle to articulate this dialectic can derail into guilt, a sense of psychic invulnerability, or psychic numbing. But it can also be re-formed in a context within which the death-immersion and the altered, 'reborn' personality of the survivor can be understood. In the past, catastrophe has often resulted in an 'enlargement of human consciousness. Our present difficulty is that we can no longer be sure of this opportunity. We can no longer count upon survivor wisdom deriving from weapons which are without limit in what they destroy.'[112] Our present difficulty, that is, is that we can enlarge our consciousness no further: we all know the real potential for complete catastrophe. And knowing what it means assures us of our wisdom.

The only problem we have, like the wise *voyous* of Queneau's novels, is to give our lived wisdom its proper form. Of course one must name the constituent elements of our limitless powers of technological violence; of course one must make sense of absurd, unceremonious death. 'The problem, then, is not only calling forth end-of-the-world imagery, but in some degree mastering it, giving it a place in our aesthetic and moral imagination ... In blocking our imaginations we impair our capacity to create the new forms we so desperately require. We need Hiroshima and Auschwitz, as we need Vietnam and our everyday lives, in all their horror, to deepen and free that imagination for the leaps it must make ... The vision of death gives life. The vision of total annihilation makes it possible to imagine living under and beyond that curse.'[113] Making that vision articulate by giving an account of it is to understand what is rational in existing actuality. It, too, is the rose at the heart of the cross.

Epilogue

'"An Epilogue," Garp wrote, "is more than a body count. An epilogue, in the disguise of wrapping up the past, is really a way of warning us about the future."'[1] Garp's remark is especially applicable to a topic such as the present one. If one's self-understanding is indeed post-historical, if one really thinks there is nothing more to do, one must face the implications of boredom and snobbery. Chief among these seems to be the attractiveness of what used to be thought criminal. One must face the implications of the possibility that the technological society will continue indefinitely. Chief among these seems to be an end to what used to be called justice. If what is best in human beings involves their aspirations, but if the eternal things, the highest things, have been eclipsed and if all human possibilities have, in principle, been exhausted, one must be ready to embrace what used to be called degeneration or decadence. The alternatives, that is, are few. And yet after a certain point compromise turns into complicity and the detachment of irony becomes indistinguishable from duplicity, foolishness, or cowardice.

First the body count. At the beginning of this essay I argued that the hermeneutical canon that I would be following postulated a connection between words and deeds. A discourse, that is, could be judged not only by its internal coherence but also as an expression or articulation of a specific and public configuration of consequences. Reciprocally, action can be seen as the actualization of words. Now, this is not a principle of interpretation that is widely held. Most political scientists would not agree with Solzhenitsyn, for example, and connect the teaching of Karl Marx and the promises of socialism with the operations of the Gulag. Marx was a theorist, an analyst, a historian, they would say, and the Soviets were men of action and power, they were revolutionaries or betrayers of the revolution, etc. The usual, normal, conventional, acceptable method of procedure is to make a distinction between power and knowledge. It would take a lengthy argument to show why I believe that power and knowledge form an ensemble or a single configuration,[2] and for present purposes it is not necessary.

Let me recapitulate the logic of the argument of this essay. 1 / *Ex hypothesi*, Kojève has given a sound and definitive explication of Hegel's *PhG*. 2 / This explication and, *a fortiori*, Hegel's text contain a comprehensive account of modern self-consciousness, which is to say, the self-understanding that modern human beings give to their own actions and to what those actions mean. 3 / Thus, modern politics expresses a Hegelian-Kojèvian meaning. I have argued, at quite different lengths, to be sure, in favour of these three points. In terms of space, this has largely taken the form of showing what Kojève's interpretation of Hegel's text was.

In the first chapter I followed Hannah Arendt in arguing that there was a connection between the emancipation of bourgeois spirituality from the constraints of medieval life, experience, and symbolism, and the eventual creation of a novel political regime, totalitarianism. In Hobbes's political science, the connection was explicitly drawn between the liberation of bourgeois spirituality, which resulted in a race to out-go and a propensity to inflict violent death in order to gain recognition, and the evocation of the mortal god, the mighty Leviathan, who would crush the children of pride, snuff the seditious roaring of a troubled nation, and impose order. In the last chapter, I argued that Hegel's regime, called by Kojève the universal and homogeneous State and, I believe, equivalent to Hobbes's Leviathan, was increasingly actualized in the contemporary world, though in characteristically different ways in its several provinces.

Second, the warning. If, as I contend, power and knowledge are constituent elements of an ensemble, the argument of Hegel, Kojève, Hobbes, or anybody else has a component of power to it. Usually this is called truth and is meant to be persuasive because it is rational. But certainly since the early days of modernity, truth has been linked to power: *nam et ipsa scientia potestas est*. The endpoint of this opinion, which I do not for the moment question, is the conjunction of the political science of Hobbes, Hegel, and Kojève with a political regime that has been described in various ways as totalitarian, bureaucratic, technocratic, tyrannical, and so on. Two things, which in the end are equivalent, seem to follow. 1 / If Hegel and Kojève in fact express comprehensively modern self-consciousness, then contemporary life is not simply modern. It contains non- or pre-modern aspects as well. 2 / If there is something unacceptable in living under a political regime that conforms to the political science of Kojève and company, then this may serve as a clue to the limitations of their interpretation, not of modern political life, but of political life as such.

Taking these points together, then, one might make the following summary. If one finds bureaucratic rule repulsive, whether in the form of sheer atrocity as practised most perfectly in the East and with remarkable but primitive enthusiasm in various poor or less developed or 'southern' countries, or in the form of a more benign rule, without terror, by civil servants, mandarins, multinationals, and social insurance numbers, if one finds the higher knowledge of bureaucracy an insult and a violation of one's own sense of person, dignity, or self, a violation of justice, of decency, or of whatever name one gives to the experience, to the real and undeniable experience of such rule – then, the options of Hobbes, Hegel, and Kojève may not be the only ones; the account they give gave may not be complete. But any alternative to the understanding that history is over is enormously difficult to formulate. A more profound warning is to see why this is so.

Religious objections

Emil Fackenheim has argued that after Auschwitz Hegel could not be a Hegelian. Evidently Kojève could. The promise of Hegelian wisdom, both Fackenheim and Kojève would agree, can be redeemed only if two conditions are met. First we must actually be free, historical, mortal, individuals, that is, post-Christian, post-Jewish, and post-French Revolution moderns. And second, we must understand ourselves that way; that is, we must be able to integrate the entirety of our spiritual existence into the sphere of speculative discourse, whose perfection is the system of science. 'In short, while actually at one end of the Hegelian ladder, we are already, potentially, at the other as well.' Now, Fackenheim wrote as 'a Jew committed to Judaism'³ and consequently opposed Hegel on two crucial points. 'Hegel's philosophy seeks to mediate all things, divine as well as human, transforming all absolute into relative distinctions. Jewish religious existence, in contrast, remains stubbornly committed to at least two *absolute* distinctions – between the Divine and the human, and between the one true God and all the false.'⁴ For Fackenheim, Hegel did not make good his promise of wisdom because he did not 'do justice' to

Judaism. Accordingly, he did not provide a compelling answer to the one question a Jew might ask, namely: how does a Jew get into the system? Hegel's answer, at least in its Kojèvian version, would be that he could not do so and yet remain a Jew.[5]

Supposing, however, one were committed not to Judaism (or Christianity, Islam, etc.) but, as Kojève insisted, to self-consciousness, as the highest goal of existence? Implicitly, of course, one also would be committed to the impossibility of any reality experienced as being 'beyond' or 'above' existence, to use a spatial image, or to an 'eternity' that was more than the unsurpassability of the wisdom of the present. However that may be, for such a (to the religiously committed) idolatrous consciousness, there would clearly be no problem of principle involved in gaining access to the system. But what about getting out of the system once one got in? So far as the Kojèvian interpretation was concerned, this was a non-problem: if the system is, or strives toward being, comprehensive, then there is no outside to which one could conceivably seek to go. The force of the logic is as inescapable as it is unsettling. One seems to have returned to the position of Koyré in 1934, before the Kojèvian juggernaut started to roll. Koyré's summary objection, which was reported in chapter 2, was that 'the synthesis is unforeseeable,' that the end of history both destroyed philosophy of history and constituted its purpose. This self-cancelling aspect of Hegel's argument was evidently what made the system 'dead.'[6] What killed it, what made it no longer persuasive or true, apparently, was the actual course of world history itself, that *Weltgericht* from which there was no appeal. Fackenheim, for example, asked: 'Could any *occurrence whatever* in the "actual world" force me out of it [i.e. the system]? Is the system hospitable to all *conceivable* empirical realities and immune to all *possible* threats?'[7] His answer was that there was one threat that Hegelian science could not accommodate: radical evil, radical anti-spirit.

Moreover, Fackenheim maintained that such a threat was actual, and that in consequence of Hegel's inability to foresee such actualization – indeed, his error in thinking it was impossible – the Hegelian claim had been shattered. 'Serious about history, he would have scorned the current liberal pretense that nothing except a "relapse into tribalism" has occurred. Serious about religion, he would have scorned every form of secularist frivolity about idolatry, including above all the current left-wing Hegelian pretenses that Nazism is a mere species of "fascism," which in turn is but "the last stage of capitalism."' Necessarily, Hegel would have been unprotected by less than comprehensive claims; he would have remained 'radically self-exposed to the realities – at the price that his "modern world" and his own philosophical comprehension of it both lie in shambles. His "modern world": constituted by "the identity of the divine nature and the human," it can survive anything except an idolatrous identification of the two. His own philosophy: requiring a "modern world" in which, except for comprehension, universal mediation is already actual, it cannot survive the demise of that world.'[8] Whereas for Hegel, even the worst state was better than none, because, even if in a perverted way, it yet fulfilled human aspirations. Consequently there would be 'no room in Hegel's philosophy for an idolatry that revels in the defilement of everything human and blasphemes against everything divine; nor for an anti-society whose factories are geared to but one ultimate produce, and that is death. Leaving room for no absolute evil anywhere, his thought leaves room for it, least of all, in the Christian Europe of modern times. Yet precisely this was the space and time of Auschwitz and Buchenwald.'[9] Fackenheim's argument was more serious than the remarks of Koyré for having been made after 1934. A similar objection has been raised by Leo Strauss.

Some of the questions touched upon in the course of debate between Strauss and Kojève were dealt with above.[10] Here we are dealing with Strauss's more or less pragmatic and commonsensical objections to the actual and anticipated consequences of the universal and homogeneous state as reflected in Kojève's political science. First, Kojève, Strauss said, had 'an insufficient appreciation of the value of utopias,' which are, strictly speaking, descriptions of 'the simply good social order.' More broadly, according to Strauss, 'one can speak of the utopia of the best tyranny.' Kojève, however, 'denies our contention that the good tyranny is a utopia' by pointing to the example of Salazar's Portugal and alluding to Stalin. Strauss considered it highly questionable that Stalin was a good tyrant (OT 300–2:200–2). Second, Kojève was of the opinion that tyranny cannot be understood on the basis of classical political science, which reflected only the morality of masters. But Strauss argued that, according to classical political science, the master was by no means the highest human type. On the contrary, the highest was the sage. No Hegelian would disagree; consequently, classical political science was self-sufficient and there was no need to supplement the classical teaching with any servile morality based on the Bible. Nevertheless, 'the desire for honour is the supreme motive of men who aspire to tyrannical power.' Where Kojève thought that men were attracted to tyranny because it was a means to accomplish the highest tasks, the classics did not believe one could accomplish the highest tasks by using the lowest methods, and they knew that tyranny involved very low methods indeed. To look upon tyranny as a means, Strauss said, a person must be blinded by passion. 'By what passion? The most charitable answer is that he is blinded by desire for honour or prestige' (306–7:204–5). And finally, Kojève's synthesis of pagan and biblical morality 'effects the miracle of producing an amazing lax morality out of two moralities both of which made very strict demands on self-restraint.' The result, therefore, was not sincere: Kojève encouraged others through his speech to perform base acts that he himself would never undertake. He did so, according to Strauss, because he wished to overlook 'the untrue assumption that man as man is thinkable as a being that lacks awareness of sacred restraints or as a being that is guided by nothing but a desire for recognition' (307: 205). Since that assumption is untrue, the satisfaction that all human beings desire can never be gained by recognition alone, not even by universal recognition.

Strauss and Kojève both agreed that recognition is sought by tyrants. Satisfaction, according to the classics, however, is identified with happiness, at least in the absence of 'an omniscient God who demands from men a pure heart' (OT 318:211). Since Kojève's synthesis was miraculous (and reasonable men do not trust miracles) the question truly at issue is whether happiness comes from recognition (and the tyrannical life) or from understanding (and the philosophical life). According to Strauss, there is an inherent conflict – at one point he called it a tragic conflict – between the philosopher and the political man, including the tyrant: the one seeks happiness through his specific desire to understand the eternal things, the other through his specific desire for recognition. Moreover, this conflict will exist within the universal and homogeneous state. Even if no one has any good reason to be dissatisfied in such a state it does not follow that it will provide satisfaction, since men do not always act reasonably. In addition there are good reasons, Strauss said, to oppose such a state. There is no guarantee that the leader deserves his position to a higher degree than others. Equals treated unequally is a recipe for sedition. Both of these objections have in fact been met: those who are not reasonable are criminals in need of reform, and strenuous, serious competition among competent equals is the pith and substance of higher post-historical politics, the struggle for recognition unimpeded by the restraints of law.

Fighting and labouring constitute the humanity of existence. But, according to Kojève, there is none in the universal and homogeneous state: all wars are over, there is nothing new to do. This seems to mean that the fulfilment of reasonable satisfaction implies the evaporation of man's humanity. 'It is the state of Nietzsche's "last man,"'' which therefore confirms 'the classical view that unlimited technical progress and its accompaniment, which are indispensable conditions of the universal and homogeneous state, are destructive of humanity' (OT 337:223). Thus, Strauss concluded, while such a state may be fated to come, it is impossible to say it will bring satisfaction. Rather, it will bring a return 'as in a cycle, to the prehuman beginnings of History. Vanitas vanitatum. Recognitio recognitionum.' For Kojève one suspects that these Nietzschean themes would be interpreted differently. There are, to be sure, last men, consumers who labour, blinking their way through boring tasks and evenings of television. They observe no rules; they revere no limits because they are not conscious of any. But in addition to post-historical servility there exists post-historical mastery in the form of what Nietzsche called nihilists, men of power who know there are no limits, no rules, because they know themselves free to make up their own. And from this dialectic of nihilists and last men is it too fanciful to see emerge, if not the Nietzschean over-man or super-man, perhaps one of the followers of Zarathustra?

Strauss had a response to this implicit reply of Kojève as well. Supposing that thinking, not labouring or fighting, really does constitute what is specifically human in people, it does not follow necessarily that the universal and homogeneous state, which is the precondition for actualizing wisdom, would be justified. According to Strauss, this would mean that the most important distinction, between the wise and the unwise, had been superseded. Whereas the classics did not believe in universal happiness because they thought only a few could pursue the highest things, Kojève claims that this defect or weakness in human life has been overcome. Man is not so weak as that or, what is the same thing, the demands of virtue are not so high. According to Strauss, therefore, Kojève simply replaced 'moral virtue by universal recognition' and 'happiness by the satisfaction deriving from universal recognition' (OT 340:225). The universal and homogeneous state, then, is inherently immoral. Worse, the leader will have to suppress all activities, including thought, that might lead people to doubt that it is final and perfect. In the interests of homogeneity the leader will suppress any thought that indicates 'there are politically relevant national differences among men that cannot be abolished or neutralized by progressing scientific technology' (OT 341:226). Philosophers will be forced to defend philosophy even before the leader, who presents himself as the final interpreter of the final philosophy and so justified in prosecuting the criminally false philosophers. Under similar circumstances in the past philosophers fled to other lands, philosophy went underground and became esoteric. But there can be no escape from the final tyrant; philosophy will be extinguished, not realized, in the universal and homogeneous State.

Kojève would no doubt accept the facts and probabilities of Strauss's argument, though certainly not its tone. For him, as for Hobbes, tyranny was simply a name used by those who mislike a government. Philosophy had no purpose beyond a pedagogy for wisdom. For Strauss and for the classics, philosophy was a search for an eternal order. 'I assume, then, that there is an eternal and unchangeable order within which History takes place, and which is in no way affected by History' (*OT* 343). In Kojève's language, which Strauss on this occasion accepted, he assumed that 'Being is essentially immutable in itself and eternally identical with itself.' In contrast, Kojève held that 'Being created itself in the course of history' or that 'the highest Being is Society and History, or that eternity is nothing but the Totality of historical Time; that is, eternity is limited.' According to Kojève the distinction between the conditions for philosophy and the objects of philosophy is not fundamental; according to Strauss it is. According to Kojève the origin of philosophical knowledge is radical attachment to human things; according to Strauss it is radical detachment. According to Kojève man is absolutely at home on earth, is absolutely a citizen of the earth; according to Strauss, 'man must not be absolutely at home on earth, but must be a citizen of the whole' (344). But this means that Strauss and the classics must remain unhappy. Man must be a citizen of the whole; the whole includes a beyond, a not-here. But man is here and not any place else. To long to be at home in another place while knowing it is elsewhere is to be forever unhappy. In short, according to Kojève, all Strauss has done is turn pagans into Christians. Since this happened historically there is no reason why it should not be easily enough accomplished conceptually. Perhaps it would be more accurate to say that Strauss, who also lived post-historically, is simply a beautiful soul longing not for a transcendent beyond but for an idealized past. After the horrors of this century this attitude may be understandable, but it does not bring understanding. It may lead to philosophy but it does not bring wisdom, not even the wisdom of a survivor.

Both Fackenheim and Strauss have raised equivalent religious objections, the one ostensibly on the basis of revealed religion, the other on the basis of pagan philosophy. They may have cast doubt on the comprehensiveness of the system, but they have hardly shattered it. Indeed, they may simply have displayed their piety. For a Hegelian this presents merely a practical problem: *credo ut intelligam*. If Fackenheim would renounce his religious commitments, if Strauss would do the same for his philosophical ones, then, perhaps, they might become wise. In short, the religious objections to Hegel are, at best, inconclusive. A second kind of objection is developed from within the claim of having attained wisdom.

Aporias of wisdom

Stanley Rosen has provided the clearest exposition of the formal implications of Hegel's claims concerning the actualization of Wisdom. As his arguments are uncommonly clear and straightforward no more than a summary is required.

According to Kojève, wisdom began with philosophy; the sage was a satisfied, complete philosopher. And philosophy, by all accounts, begins in wonder. But where, or in what, does wonder begin? If wonder has a beginning it cannot itself be wonder but non-wonder, which is either subjective certainty or actual knowledge; in either case doubt is absent and so is the difference between opinion and knowledge. But under these circumstances wonder would never arise because it seems to be a response to an awareness of the difference between knowledge and opinion or perhaps a knowledge of the inadequacy of one's opinions or of their grounds. In Rosen's words, 'to begin in wonder, philosophy must begin with knowledge, which is to say that knowledge and wonder do not begin at all but are coeval with man ... The idea of a chronologically "first" thought is unintelligible, since it would be incomprehensible.'[11] The conclusion one must draw is that philosophy has no beginning, not in the sense that there was not a 'first' philosopher but that, for example, the sayings of Thales are intelligible only in philosophical terms. If to have no beginning is to be eternal, then philosophy must be eternal.

Philosophy also means friendliness toward, or, more strongly, love of, wisdom. It is, then, an expression of human eroticism, of the desire to possess things immediately, and eventually to possess all things. But eroticism is not just the desire to get more things but also to understand things; according to Plato in *Republic*, at least, eroticism also takes the form of anger or spiritedness. The relationship between the passionate desire for things and the rational desire for knowledge is suggested by the 'structure' of desire itself as it is exhibited in the world. Every desire for a thing is also a tacit desire that it be available. At a minimum we may raise the tactical or technical question concerning the activity needed to be done to achieve the desired object, but this questioning is quickly extinguished as the desired object is obtained. And yet satisfaction is temporary; the same desires recur or, once secured, the objects of satisfaction serve as the basis for new, more exotic, complex, 'interesting' desires. This experience, which so far follows the Hegelian story resulting in sentiment-of-Self, may lead to reflection on the conditions for satisfaction. This reflection is more than tactical or technical because the meaning of satisfaction is called into question, which is to say that, so long as it remains problematic and under discussion, it remains illusive and the one doing the reflecting (or thinking or speaking) is necessarily not satisfied but in quest. The asking of questions, then, is the articulation of our wonder.

Rosen answered the objection of Kojève, that such a position results either in frustration or madness and is, in any case, unhappy, with remarks in the same spirit. Consider what the achievement of wisdom would mean: wisdom, all agree, is complete speech. Complete speech entails complete satisfaction. Complete satisfaction means the extinction of desire. No desire means no desire to speak, reason, think. Hence one falls silent; indeed one becomes like a beast or a god. In fact, there is no way to tell apart the two: beasts are mute and gods, while they may speak or act, exhibit by so doing what they have in common with humans. Kojève accepted that consequence, but not, evidently, what it implied, namely, that 'there is no complete speech (since it would then be the same as, or indistinguishable from, silence), but only speech *about* complete speech or speech which articulates, renders intelligible, and is accompanied by desire.'[12] Just as desire is evidence of human dissatisfaction or incompleteness, so is speech evidence of human imperfection; speech, in obedience to desire, attempts to bridge the disjunction between humanness and thingness, but in such a way that the distance between the two is maintained.

Alternatively one may say that man is a problem standing in need of a solution that, if attained, would be a final solution, a disaster, a holocaust to a dead god. One must therefore reconcile oneself to the paradox of an accessible but unaccomplishable goal; one must deflect the desire for an unaccomplishable complete speech to speech about complete speech, 'that is, speech which has grasped the truth about human nature, and so which functions in a healthy or sane way to articulate desire, guided by the ideal of perfection, but which, for that reason, avoids pressing any element in the situation beyond what it can bear, or which is guided by the ideal to avoid all unbalanced attempts to achieve it, [which] is *philosophy*.'[13] Wisdom is accessible as a rationally visible, formal, necessary model by which philosophically partial speeches can be distinguished from non-philosophical ones. Wisdom is something like a Kantian regulative ideal so far as speech is concerned; it is not, therefore, itself a speech. Yet it is precisely the claim that wisdom is complete speech that is its greatest strength, for, once having refuted the claim to a complete speech about the whole, we seem to be thrown back upon the no less satisfactory alternative of endless speech or chatter.

Let us restate the problem and Hegel's solution to it. The discursive account of the whole resulted from the weaving together of completed but finite stages, the several historical worlds and their discursive and representational self-articulations. Every particular stage P gave rise to a successive stage non-P, a more comprehensive version of P. Now, non-P is not the same as Q; rather Q was the supersession, the *Aufhebung*, of P and non-P. Moreover, it was Q alone, not R or W, that was the *Aufhebung*, which is to say that the succession was not arbitrary. Eventually the logical alphabet was complete, and one returned to P. Thereafter the circle of wisdom may be repeated. Each logical letter was itself incomplete. Now, 'so far as the human thinker is concerned, the logic can only be thought one step at a time. What guarantees the validity of each step as it is taken? Certainly not the Whole, which is not visible or present until the *end* of discourse.'[14] The fundamental contradiction therefore may be summarily stated: 'Hegel claims that the actual is brought into being by discourse, and by a discourse which can occur only after the actual presents itself.'[15] Hegel's reply was that, from the standpoint of wisdom, or eternity, or absolute knowledge, the actual was fully developed; thus, any temporal discourse explained an aspect of eternity by articulating itself. But if this were so, all philosophical discourse must be a projection; the sense of any particular discursive or representational articulation of reality could only appear afterwards. Accordingly, the logical appropriateness of the discourse must be unknowable. Or, considering the validity of the sequence of the logical alphabet one may ask: was the order of succession a matter of good luck? That is, did each world-historical actor just happen to utter the correct world-historical speech at the correct time? And even if this were so, how did he or she do so unless he or she had a vision of the whole prior to the utterance? This alternative having been rejected by Hegel, one is left to conclude that the sequence as a whole was, in fact, predetermined – by Hegel.

To summarize the formal aporias of actualized wisdom: desire gives rise to speech, which in turn expresses the desire for completeness, for wisdom, which appears as the end of speech. If every speech is partial, and thus not complete but accompanied by desire, its partiality must appear in the context of something that is not partial but complete or whole. And if wisdom is an 'ideally' complete and rational speech, it can only appear that way to an incomplete and rational speech. To try to close (rather than bridge) the gap between completeness and incompleteness, between words and things, theory and practice, necessarily results in unintelligibility. Alternatively, the gap, the 'absence,' between the two corresponds to a desire that must be present and therefore strains toward completion at the same time that it is aware that the attainment of completion would mean its own extinction, which is precisely what it does *not* desire. It follows from this that the one person who could not feel satisfied would be the sage. If one were completely satisfied one would feel no desires at all, not even the desire for complete satisfaction. 'The wise man does not desire to be wise, because he *is* so.' He does not desire anything because desire is privation, and he is complete, especially if the Concept is identical with Being. Therefore, the wise man cannot be satisfied at all: "satisfaction" is a term having significance only for an incomplete man who still dwells within history. The "complete" man is not a man at all.'[16] Perhaps he has become a mortal god, as Kojève playfully suggested. But if so, he must either display his humanity by speaking or else remain silent and so indistinguishable from a beast.

Anxiety and alienation

Fackenheim and Strauss have provided what, to Kojève, would appear to be religious objections undertaken from a position that they think is external to the system but that he knows is a constituent element of it. Both sides seem to be agreed that, in the end, one is called to choose one or another standpoint. Rosen, in contrast, has made a logically impeccable objection from within the context of the system, not outside. He has not, however, raised the question of choice and irrationality precisely because he has been concerned with logic. No doubt reasonable people would find it persuasive; no doubt believers in the religious views of Fackenheim or Strauss would find their criticisms persuasive. Politics, however, is a public expression of the whole of human being, not just its rational part, and not just its religious part. Modernity is at the core of our experience of the world, not pagan philosophical nature or the historical faith in the God of Abraham and of Isaac. One should not, therefore, expect the many to be persuaded to abandon their claims to be wise. Indeed, one may well anticipate a rigorous enforcement of those claims either in the form of technological imperatives or ideological politics. To understand what the politics of wisdom entail one must treat the logical aporias and religious impieties not as final refutations but as clues to the spiritual attitude of the sage, or of the one who claims to be wise. One must look to the fundamental experiences of reality, that is, and not remain content simply to show that the claim to wisdom is logically self-cancelling or religiously offensive. Only then can one say one has understood what the wise man means.

In these concluding sections, then, we consider the motivations that inform the attempt to account fully for the end and the beginning of philosophy. The purpose is certainly not to turn away from philosophy toward psychology, but to avoid the inconclusiveness of the critical objections raised so far. One must deal with motivating experiences, not with the discursive results, since philosophers too write what they do on the basis of their reality experienced.

The beginning of philosophy, Rosen argued, is no initial start, the end no final achievement. If this is so, the attempt to account fully for both beginning and end would seem to conclude in the destruction of philosophy. End and beginning are not states of affairs but symbols that make less unintelligible our experience of wonder by providing a direction for our questioning to take as it is attracted to, or measured by, the end.

> What we call the beginning is often the end
> And to make an end is to make a beginning.

Eliot's lines from Little Gidding express the mystery of beginning and end as precisely as do the logical aporias of discursive analysis. To insist upon the mysteriousness of beginning and end is not the same as declaring them radically unintelligible. One knows at least that they are mysterious. The corresponding state of the psyche is a precarious balance between a knowledge that one does not know the beginning and the end, and a desire to explore this ignorance further. In Eric Voegelin's words, 'Man, when he experiences himself as existent, discovers his specific humanity as that of the questioner for the Where-from and the Where-to, for the ground and the sense of his existence.'[17] The desire to account fully for the ground, the beginning, or the origin, as well as the sense, the end, or the limit, is, then, a modification of the philosophical balance of desire for knowledge and knowledge of ignorance.

One may characterize the experience of philosophical balance as a dialectic of restless questioning and soothing answers insofar as the movement of the search is guided by the immobility of that of which the questioner is in search. Or again, the answer becomes manifest as a presence experienced within the searching desire to know. To philosophize, then, is to respond by questioning the source of one's wonder; in that questioning one is drawn toward the origin of it. In addition, of course, this experience of questioning response is itself symbolized in an analysis of the psyche, which uses terms such as wonder, eros, reason, trust, spiritedness, and so on. The context of these terms in philosophizing is, precisely, the philosopher's exploration of the structure of reality as experienced in (or by) the psyche. The requirement of personal participation by the philosopher in the exploration of his own psyche serves formally at least to guard against any misunderstanding that philosophizing is simply intellectual assent to a series of propositions about properties of things that, altogether, are taken to be reality. The other side of participation, which in part explains the substitution of propositions for philosophical symbols, concerns its precariousness.

If the locus of participation in reality is the psyche, which expresses its exploration in thought, it is clear that it has nothing else to rely upon for the truth of its existence than the process of exploration itself. Thinking, as Hannah Arendt has said, is done without a banister. The move from the mood of wonder and questioning uncertainty to anxiety and paralysis is easily enough understood. Instead of the process of motion and rest, trial, error, correction, and further trial, we look only to the motion of the process, its *Unruhe*, as Hegel said. That is, we consider only the apparently endless succession of desires, ceasing only in death. We trust the cosmos no further but take our experience of unsatisfied desire, which is one moment of the dialectic, as the meaning of the whole. It would be better to say that the whole, the cosmos, is replaced by chaos. 'We become self-conscious about the apparently infinite character of our eros; we lose the naïve (no pejorative here) identification with ourselves which permits us to direct our eros, profiting by experience and knowledge. We panic at what we are; in the face of what we desire, what we have won becomes meaningless.'[18] Whatever the cause for the change in mood it occurs during the phase of questioning and restlessness; it is an alteration in one's attitude toward existence, not an intellectual operation or sheer act of will. What has been lost from the questioning unrest is a sense of direction: instead of an exploration of reality, there is alienation from it.

Once the experience of reality is lost and life is lived in a mood of alienation rather than participation, the erotic content of existence is likewise altered. Anxious in the uncertain truth of ignorance, the psyche takes refuge in the certain untruth of an imaginary knowledge of the beginning and the end. In place of love for, or friendliness toward, wisdom is the desire to dominate. This is perfectly understandable on its own terms: if reality is chaotic, the psyche that knows it is at least not quite so chaotic. Accordingly, it senses itself warranted in undertaking whatever measures are necessary to restore order.

But what can it do? Seeking to overcome the restlessness of erotic anxiety, the alienated psyche seeks to control the restlessness of erotic wonder as well. From anxiety at its own unlimitedness, eros tries to stifle itself. But inasmuch as eros is constitutive of existence, the attempt cannot be a success, short of death. The first thing to be said, therefore, is that accounts of the beginning and end that are formulated in such a way that the one who makes the account secures imaginative control over what is taken to be the source of restlessness are death warrants (written as epitaphs) for desire. Second, then, the contradiction between the attempt to overcome desire and the origin of this attempt in a particular and perverted mood of desire, namely anxiety, leads to resistance. To the alienated psyche, this experience simply confirms the chaotic nature of reality as given and intensifies the desire to change it. The alienated psyche does not desire to abandon the mood of anxiety. Rather, anxiety projects its mood on its surroundings so as to confirm the certainty of its own alienation. The image of these surroundings, following Robert Musil, we may call 'possible reality' or 'second reality.' The conflict between the alienated world projected by the anxious desire of the psyche and the actual reality of existence thereby becomes generalized.

Eric Voegelin has described this process as the eclipse of reality.[19] The first level of the analysis focuses on the contrast in contents between the imaginary possible reality and the reality of common experience. Here the projected reality eclipses (but does not obliterate) the reality of common experience. Second, one considers the act of intending to eclipse reality. The manifestation of this act can take the form of factual lies, rhetorical duplicity, 'the construction of a system that, by its form, suggests its partial view as the whole of reality,' a refusal by the author to discuss the premises of the system in terms of reality experienced, and so on. And third, one must consider the actor's commitment to his own projection, his denial of any alternatives, and his attempts to alter common reality so that no alternatives are possible. 'In this aggressiveness,' Voegelin commented, 'there betrays itself the anxiety and alienation of the man who has lost contact with reality.'[20] The ostensible purpose of these imaginative projections designed to eclipse reality is to shield the alienated psyche from the source of its anxieties. In fact, they constitute a disturbance within reality.

Merleau-Ponty once observed that a cripple expresses his deformity to the extent he tries to hide it. In much the same way, the eclipse of reality by an imaginative projection expresses the projector's resistance to reality. But reality eclipsed is not reality abolished; if it were abolished, there would be nothing to resist, nothing in relation to which the psyche could be alienated. Indeed, it is the persistent tedium of reality that constitutes the great problem for the alienated psyche, a problem that it tries to surmount through its imaginative projects. Yet reality remains, a nameless pressure behind the possible reality that vainly tries to destroy it. The initial act of eclipse must, therefore, be followed by subsequent acts of repression. The political formula, in Solzhenitsyn's phrase, is that lies are enforced by violence. The resulting pattern of alienated existence may be specified as follows. 1 / When people act on the basis of their imaginative projections so as to make the world conform to their image of it, the areas of contradiction and resistance will increase in number and intensity. 2 / As the world eclipsed is not abolished, discrepancies between the two realities appear and these inspire revisions in detail or new projects. 3 / An increasing number of revisions inspires a concern with logical rigour and persuasiveness. 4 / Once a logically coherent second reality has been achieved, interest shifts from the act of construction to the expression and analysis of alienated existence within the imaginative project. Historically speaking, one moves from the naïve exuberance of the projections of the eighteenth century to the sombre despair of twentieth-century disorientation and boredom. The process can be seen in Hegel's commitments as well. Necessarily this account is sketchy.

Boredom and diremption

If 'all that moveth doth in Change delight,' the closing of the circle of wisdom cannot, on its own terms, avoid boredom. The secret of boredom, according to Voltaire, is to say everything. And if everything has been said, because everything has been done, how much more boring would it be to repeat everything. Now, if the satisfaction of the imaginative experience of wisdom spells the extinction of desire in the form of wonder and the expression of desire in the form of anxiety, it is clear that the discursive claim of wisdom cannot be taken on its own terms. It also seems clear that the real experience of boredom, melancholia, and world-weariness may well derive from an atrophy of wonder gained through the projected integration of all prior discourse into one's own system. Indeed, the effort of constructing the system, the sheer intellectual and physical labour of writing all the words on paper, may serve the function of diverting the author from a frank confrontation with the source of his ennui, namely his own refusal to give up his imaginative projection.

First among the causes of melancholia in Burton's great *Anatomy* was God or, by God's permission, the devil and his ministers. Hegel would not disagree: the boredom of the world, he said, characterized the spirituality of a society whose gods have died (*Dok* 318).[21] Ecumenic boredom occurred in antiquity with the establishment of the Roman Empire at the price of obliterating the spiritual substance of the conquered peoples; their gods and cults became equally meaningless members of the Roman pantheon. Only Christianity could redeem the world from such diremption. But the Church, we have long ago learned, externalized its reconciliation in dogma and rite; with the Reformation, the great advantage of representation, its poetic sacrality, was replaced by a division between inward and individual spirituality, on the one hand, and external, spiritless activity, on the other. To overcome this second boredom, a second sacralization must be achieved, this time not in an external representational form but in an internal conceptual form, proper to spirit. Under this aspect Hegel would complete the work of Luther and, like Christ, heal the fragmentation of the age.

The text just summarized, *Fortsetzung des 'Systems der Sittlichkeit'*, was written during the period when *Phenomenology* was composed. In one sense there is nothing extraordinary in Hegel's argument. No philosopher could diagnose properly the disorders of the day without having gained the initial psychic stability and insight necessary to undertake such an analysis. A concern with the question of historical disintegration, then, is less remarkable than the appearance of a complex of sentiments that allowed Hegel to conceive of integrating his own intellectual speculations, taken to be a salvific enterprise, with the process of history. Here one may quote a key passage (*Dok* 324): 'Every particular man is merely a blind link in the chain of absolute necessity by which the world advances itself. The particular man can raise himself to dominate a part of this chain only if he knows the direction in which the great necessity wishes to move, and if he learns from this knowledge how to speak the magic words to evoke its shape.' Voegelin has provided an exegesis of this remarkable text.

First, he said, it revealed the intensity as well as the cause of Hegel's anxiety. He saw himself as a blind link in a necessary process of world history beyond which or outside which no meaning existed at all. To cease to be blindly submissive to necessity one must raise oneself at least to the extent of being able to see the direction in which history is moving and then magically call up its *Gestalt*. The knowledge of the magic words, evidently, will put the seal on all subsequent meaning because it accounts for all the suffering, disorder, and boredom of the present and in this way affects the sought-for reconciliation. The empirical text that constitutes the imaginative project is, of course, *Phenomenology*.

As Dempf pointed out, Voegelin had analysed the form of Hegel's project under the heading of 'historiogenesis.'[22] By this term was indicated a speculative complex embracing the order of a particular society, its origin, and its subsequent development. Usually historians dismiss as legendary or mythical the accounts of the origin of a society – the foundation of Rome by Aeneas, of Britain by Brutus, and so forth – without further inquiry as to why anyone would bother to create such legends. Voegelin argued that 'the mythical part of historiogenetic speculation is not a piece of unhistorical fabulation, but an attempt to present the reasons that will raise the *res gestae* of the pragmatic part to the rank of history.' The motives for undertaking the speculation arise from the experience of historical change and continuity. This experience is to be distinguished from that of cosmic rhythms for which suitable rituals and rites may be developed in order to ensure the arrival of spring, the flooding of the Nile, and so on. Historiogenetic speculations, however, place events, extending back to an absolute point of origin, upon a single line of irreversible time where change is not rhythmic but final. Moreover, the individuals who undertake the historiogenetic speculation invariably conclude by integrating a manifold of discontinuous events into a single story, their own. 'To the aggressive overtones ... there corresponds an undercurrent of obsessive anxiety above which the authors attempt to rise by the imaginative conversion of a temporal gain into a possession forever.' The invention of a single story is, clearly, an attempt to endow the contingency of historical change with the dignity and serenity of cosmic or other ultimate order.

Historiogenetic speculations, then, are undertaken in a mood of anxiety, not trust. Historical reality is deliberately distorted so that the story comes out right, that is, in conformity to the imaginative projections of the author. The object of the projection is to eclipse the unsettling reality of historical contingency with a second reality, the comforting meaning of which is the finality of the author's present. The technical problem Hegel faced concerned the breakdown of the Christian historiogenetic construction, which proceeded from the creation of the world through the history of Israel to Christianity, Rome, the Western sacred empire, down to the present. Voltaire's attack on 'theology of history' in the name of 'philosophy of history' had the undoubted merits (whatever its shortcomings in other respects) of putting the Christian historiogenesis into perspective as an imaginative construction. Henceforth it would be impossible for a conscientious historian to ignore the developments of India, China, Islam, or Russia as parallel to, though independent of, Western history. Rather than abandon what Merleau-Ponty called the 'historical authority' of the West, Hegel undertook to reinterpret Christian historiogenesis in terms of the dialectical unfolding of the *Geist* to its maximal articulation in his own reflections on the final events of his day.

I have presented Hegel's historiogenetic story already and here need only refer to a few of the more spectacular distortions. Since the history of the world moved from east to west, the chronological priority of the ancient Near Eastern empires had to be ignored: China, the farthest east, had to get the ball rolling. Egypt and Mesopotamia were demoted to phases of the Persian empire, which was located suitably to the west of India but to the east of Greece. We have already mentioned Fackenheim's objections to Hegel's reading of Israelite and Jewish experience; there is also the startling inclusion of Islam within the Germanic World. By such 'ingenious devices,' Voegelin remarked, 'he manages to herd the errant materials on the straight line that leads to the imperial present of mankind and to himself as its philosopher.'[23]

In addition to this historical creativity, Hegel also undertook an elaborate discursive obfuscation. We have already considered some of the logical implications of the attempt to replace philosophy as love of wisdom with 'actual knowledge.' In addition one may observe that the only discussable reality was consciousness, whose phenomena range from sense experience to absolute knowledge. Consciousness itself, however, seems to belong to nobody, not human beings, not God, not the cosmos, not society. 'The reader ... [might] justly ask what a consciousness that is nobody's consciousness could possibly be? And if he received no answer at all, or were more or less politely put off with the suggestion that it was his fault, if he did not understand what is crystal-clear, he might become suspicious.'[24] If it is true, as was argued above, that the questioning search of philosophizing constitutes a noetic symbolization of a common human experience of reality, the incompleteness of the series of questions and answers is not a defect or imperfection of existence but an expression of what it means to be human. Conceiving of a perfected knowledge that puts an end to the tiresome business of living as a human being who asks questions is, then, an aggressive attack on human dignity. The aspect we have been considering may be specified as follows: Hegel sought to end the diremption and boredom of history by gaining power over it and bringing the whole gruesome, dreary *Schlacht-bank* to an end. Henceforth history would be abolished, and the last age, bearing the imprint of Hegel's evocation of meaning, would commence. The element of compulsion could not be more clear.

Magic words

Let us now combine the arguments of the preceding sections. Rosen's analysis brought to light the formal aporias of the claim to have actualized wisdom, turning the argument once again toward philosophy and its informing desires. Philosophical balance is experienced as a dialectic of restless questioning and soothing answers; it is a search guided by an immobile goal. Inasmuch as the answers one gains are always also part of the search, there is never the complete repose of having attained one's goal and so becoming immobile. Hence, there may arise changes in mood, an alteration of desire from friendliness and trust to anxiety and distrust. Accompanying this emotional change is a cognitive one. Thus one may speak of the creation of an imaginary or 'possible' second reality intended to eclipse the experience of common reality (because, existing in a mood of anxiety, that common reality is experienced as alien).

Hegel's speculation was cast in a historiogenetic form; accordingly, it was locally concerned with the origin and development of a specific concrete society. In any such argument, the history of a given society is taken to reflect the whole of cosmic meaning, its stability as well as its instability. Historiogenetic speculation is also a quest for beginning and end and in this respect is a symbolism equivalent to that expressive of philosophical experience. Hegel's erotic shift from trust to anxiety evident in the claim to have actualized wisdom is, then, perfectly complimented by his cognitive deformations. By forcing historical events into place along a single line of meaningful time, by forcing the evidence of common reality to conform to the second reality of the system of science,

Hegel could appear to gain power over real history and thereby overcome his anxiety concerning its instability.

The beginning, both pragmatic and spiritual, was the dialectic of
Master and Slave, which was taken to be both a 'pre-historic' originating
event and a saving tale introduced as the source of meaning. Under
either aspect, it is the initial historiogenetic moment. The pragmatic end
was the Napoleonic Empire as revealed by Hegel's system, that is, the
ecumenic organization of humanity under the power of the Idea. The
circle of beginning and end has a rationale of its own even while it
appears arbitrary or nonsensical when examined by the cognitive procedures of common experience and logic. On the basis of the end, the
Empire and system whose 'in-the-beginning' is found in the dialectic of
Master and Slave, the common realities of power politics, and pragmatic
history are rendered into symbolic events of an apocalyptic drama, the
author of which is Hegel. In that experiential context alone can one find
a consistent, although hermetic, intention.

The hermeticism involved may be illustrated by recalling Kojève's
treatment of the 'dualism' of Hegel and Napoleon (*IH* 153–4). There
Kojève wondered whether the final dyad of *Bewusstsein* and *Selbstbewusstsein* was to be suppressed by Napoleon recognizing Hegel, presumably to be followed by Hegel's removal from Jena to Paris. On the basis of
the argument just made, we should look to understand the relationship
between Hegel and Napoleon in terms of the *Zauberwörter* that Hegel
alone pronounced. Hegel did not, therefore, wish simply to be one of a
succession of healers of the diremption of the age to be followed in later
ages by further diremptions and further healers. This is why, in the
preface to *Phenomenology*, we find that *Geist* 'wins its truth only when,
in absolute diremption, *in der absoluten Zerissenheit*, it finds itself.' That
is, diremption as well as healing is a property of *Geist*, so that when
ages of diremption occur historically, they are not healed by the activities of men such as Jesus, Luther, or Hegel. They are healed by the *Geist*
itself. In this same passage Hegel explained that spirit is the absolute
power of the self-enclosed circle of wisdom because it looks negativity
in the face and dwells with it. 'This dwelling with the negative is the
magic power that transforms it into being, *Sein*,' and is, moreover, identical with the subject who knows it (*PhG* 30:19). Thus, by arguing that
it is *Geist* that achieves its *Gestalt* in the system of science, Hegel avoids
the problem of the system ever being superseded. As was mentioned
earlier, it is as if the system wrote itself using Hegel as its agent. All

honour being paid to the *Geist*, his responsibility was negligible (*PhG* 59:45).

Placing the problem of Kojève's dualism in the context of Hegel's circle of science, in the second reality created from his imagination and anxious desire, means that one does not have to deal with the German philosopher or the French soldier. Since the dyad 'Napoleon-Hegel' does not refer to the historic individuals known by those names but to constituent elements of Hegel's consciousness, itself conceived as nobody's consciousness, the sought-for reconciliation can take place with comparative ease. The *Zauberwort* in this instance was the 'reconciling "Yes,"' whereby the two constituent elements 'Hegel' and 'Napoleon' give up their separate and opposed existence in response to the invocation of 'the existence of the Ego that has expanded into a duality and remains there identical with itself and in its complete externalization and antithesis knows itself with complete certainty.' The single Ego has been verbally (or, if one prefers, magically) expanded into a pair of now reconciled, but once opposed, Egos. The results of the successful incantation, of the real uttering of the *Zauberwörter*, in representational imagery, are nothing less than 'the revealed God in the midst of those who know themselves in the form of pure Knowledge' (*PhG* 472:409). Those who know themselves in this way are, of course, Hegelians privy to the *Zauberworte*. By pronouncing the magic words, the absolute diremption of the *Geist* is reconciled, the age is healed, history is over.

Throughout this essay I have tried simply to present Kojève's political science, proceeding upon the assumption, nowhere proven save by the argument itself, that his reading of Hegel is the most comprehensive and coherent account of contemporary modern political life. I assumed that, in principle, Kojève has provided an exhaustive account of our own post-historical existence. He has brought to coherent form the several incoherences of the present world. He has made sense of what others have denounced and criticized as exploitative, tyrannic, chaotic, nihilist, self-destructive. He has shown why the only thing to which one can reasonably aspire, the only excellence remaining, is to become wise, to enact imaginatively the Hegelian system. In this way the unexampled horrors of the present – the widespread slaughter of human beings by other human beings and the threat of complete annihilation of life on the planet – might be understood and so 'forgiven.' It is a hard teaching that directs one to see these things as 'metaphysical necessities' whose being makes possible the creation and preservation of the universal and homogeneous State, which is itself required for the actualization of wisdom. Then everything, Kolyma and McDonald's, Auschwitz and Disneyland, Hiroshima and Sony, is rendered rational.

Common sense rebels at this. Fackenheim's faith finds it an abomination. Strauss and other philosophers find it shocking and unnatural. Voegelin exposes a magical compulsiveness at the heart of the enterprise. And yet, even if we are not wise the way Solzhenitsyn's ex-zeks are wise, we are all, as Lifton reminds us, survivors. We have survived in the modern world, the world that for over a generation has been threatened with man-made extinction, the world that surely has grown dirempted, melancholy, and boring. Whether the miseries of the present can be overcome may be doubted. Certainly they cannot be overcome by pronouncing magic words. Not that magic words are without effects: actions taken on the basis of magic are still actions; the imaginary conflict of second with common reality is still a conflict within common reality. To the extent that others are bewitched by Hegelianism, these consequences will be part of the disorders of common reality. The dilemma of Kojève's or Hegel's political science is this: it is at once an expression, an account, and an overcoming of our present discontents. It is, therefore, an appropriate articulation of the spectacle of modernity: great but vulgar, exhilarating but nauseating, vital but devastated. Hegel could not heal the diremptions of his age by writing a book. Even less could Kojève heal the diremptions of our age by negotiating the GATT. Yet by bringing those diremptions to light perhaps they told a saving tale. However, perhaps Heidegger was right: only a god can save us. Perhaps, indeed, a logos that has turned into technique must fall silent to leave room for regeneration.

Notes

INTRODUCTION

1 Gérard Lebrun, *La Patience du concept: Essai sur le discours hégélien* (Paris, Gallimard, 1972), 14

2 Eric Voegelin, 'On Hegel: A Study in Sorcery,' *Studium General*, 24(1971), 363ff. See also Georg Lukács's remarks, *The Young Hegel*, tr Rodney Livingstone (Cambridge, MIT Press, 1975), 462.

3 Otto Pöggeler, 'Zur Deutung der *Phänomenologie des Geistes*,' *Hegel-Studien*, I (1961), 267 (emphasis added)

4 Henri Lefebvre, *La Fin de l'histoire* (Paris: Minuit, 1970), 151

5 See, for example, Jean-Michel Rey, 'Kojève ou la fin de l'histoire,' *Critique*, 264 (1969), 437–59; Eric Weil, 'La fin de l'histoire,' *Revue de métaphysique et de morale*, 75 (1970), 377–84; E. Clémens, 'L'Histoire (comme) inachèvement,' *Revue de métaphysique et de la morale*, 76 (1971), 206–25. See also R.K. Maurer, *Hegel und das Ende der Geschichte* (Stuttgart, Kohhammer, 1965), 139–56; Eric Gans, 'Meditation Kojèvienne sur la critique littéraire,' *Critique* 294 (1971), 1009–17.

6 Kostas Axelos, 'La Question de la fin de l'histoire,' *L'Homme et la société*, 20 (1971), 193–4

7 Hans-Georg Gadamer, *Hegel's Dialectic: Five Hermeneutical Studies*, tr P. Christopher Smith (New Haven, Yale University Press, 1976), 36. See also Paul Ricoeur, *Freud and Philosophy: An Essay on Interpretation*, tr Denis Savage (New Haven, Yale University Press, 1970), 60ff.

8 Judith Shklar, *Freedom and Independence: A Study of the Political Ideas of Hegel's 'Phenomenology of Mind'* (Cambridge, Cambridge University Press, 1976), 14

9 *Hegel's Dialectic*, 101–2

10 Lebrun, *La Patience du concept*, 17–18; Roger Garaudy, *Le Problème hégélien* (Paris, Centre d'études et de recherches marxistes, 1963), 28
11 For details see Kenley R. Dove, 'Hegel's Phenomenological Method,' *Review of Metaphysics*, 23 (1970), 627–41.
12 *Liberalism Ancient and Modern* (New York, Basic Books, 1968), vii
13 Amié Patri, 'Dialectique du Maître et de l'Esclave,' *Le Contract social* V (1961), 234. As usual, an exception must be made for those who soldier on the intellectual front for the French Communist Party. The definitive line was established, appropriately enough, by a committee. See La Commission de Critique du Cercle des Philosophes Communistes, 'Le Retour à Hegel,' *La Nouvelle Critique*, 20 (1950), 43–54. Equally amusing polemics are E. Bottigelli, 'A propos du retour à Hegel,' ibid, 21 (1950), 73–81; J.-T. Desanti, 'Intervention du Cercle des philosophes,' ibid, 45 (1953), 138–45.
14 Stanley Rosen, Review of Kojève *Essai* in *Man and World*, 3 (1970), 120
15 Otto Pöggeler, 'Hegel Editing and Hegel Research,' in J.J. O'Malley et al ed, *The Legacy of Hegel: Proceedings of the Marquette Symposium, 1970* (The Hague, Martinus Nijhoff, 1973), 14
16 This information was supplied by M. Jean Cassou, who at the time was Commissioner for the Comité directeur des mouvements unis de résistance in charge of the Toulouse region where Kojève undertook these operations.
17 'Interview,' *Encounter*, 41:6 (December 1973), 82. Aron also described him as 'one of the most intelligent men I have met, perhaps *the* most intelligent ... Kojève gave me the impression of genius.' Kojève was the author of the compromise formula agreed to during the 'Kennedy round' of the General Agreement on Tariffs and Trade, GATT.
18 Hegel said this twice, once in the preface to *Philosophy of Right* and once in paragraph 6 of the third edition of his *Encyclopedia of Philosophical Sciences* where he added that it was a 'simple' statement.

CHAPTER ONE: THE LEGACY OF HOBBES

1 Tilo Schabert, *Gewalt und Humanität: Uber philosophische und politische Manifestationen von Modernität* (Freiburg and Munich, Verlag Karl Alber, 1978)
2 New edition (New York, Harcourt, Brace and World, 1966), originally published in 1951 as *The Burden of Our Time*
3 Arendt distinguishes the social and the political with great conceptual rigour in *The Human Condition* (Chicago, University of Chicago Press, 1958).

4 *Origins of Totalitarianism*, 25
5 In addition to Arendt's analysis, J.A. Hobson's standard *Imperialism* (1905), John Gallagher and Ronald Robinson, 'The Imperialism of Free Trade,' *Economic History Review*, 2nd series, 6 (1953), 1–15, D.K. Fieldhouse, '"Imperialism": An Historiographic Revision,' ibid, 14 (1961), 187–209, and Benjamin J. Cohen, *The Question of Imperialism: The Political Economy of Dominance and Dependence* (New York: Basic Books, 1973) all provide useful accounts of the issues involved.
6 *Origins*, 130
7 They were not an unprecedented type of political man. Evidently the bureaucrats of Augustus Caesar were men of similar temperament and behaviour. See F.W. Walbank *The Awful Revolution: The Decline of the Roman Empire in the West* (Toronto: University of Toronto Press, 1969).
8 The same blending of nature (race) and history (expansion), and the same contradictions, can be found in the continental imperialism of the pan-German and pan-Slav movements.
9 During the early 1950s, when the Soviet camps were becoming widely known and their significance debated, this was a common topic for discussion. See, for example, Maurice Merleau-Ponty, *Signes* (Paris, Gallimard, 1967), 330ff.
10 André Glucksmann, *La Cuisinière et le mangeur d'hommes: Essai sur les rapports entre l'Etat, le marxisme et les camps de concentration* (Paris, Seuil, 1975), 72
11 Arendt, *Origins*, 123
12 Glucksmann, *La Cuisinière*, 97
13 The first term is Arendt's. The second is from Gil Elliot, *Twentieth-Century Book of the Dead* (London, Allen Lane, 1972), 41.
14 Aleksandr I. Solzhenitsyn, *The Gulag Archipelago, 1918–1956. An Experiment in Literary Investigation*, tr Thomas P. Whitney (New York, Harper & Row, 1973), I, 66–7.
15 Bernard-Henri Lévy, *La Barbarie à visage humain* (Paris, Grasset, 1977), 185
16 Solzhenitsyn, *Gulag Archipelago*, I, 468, 145
17 Kojève's version of ideology agrees with this aspect of ideology, though hardly with any additional ones. According to him it is a partial account which is held to be complete: '*My* perspective (it makes little difference whether it be individual or collective) necessarily gives rise to an "ideology" insofar as *my* theory of the World is not *the* theory of the World, that is, insofar as it does not imply *all* possible theories in general' (*IH* 311). Hence, all discourse that is not complete discourse or Wisdom is

ideological. That is, everything but Hegelian Science is, in the end, ideological.

18 Arendt, *Origins*, 470ff
19 Solzhenitsyn, *Gulag Archipelago*, I, 174
20 Lévy, *La Barbarie à visage humain*, 138
21 Leo Strauss has been instrumental in reminding political scientists of this 'forgotten' kind of writing. See his *Persecution and the Art of Writing* (Glencoe, The Free Press, 1952).
22 Thus, Gadamer wrote that Kojève's 'way to Hegel, which is determined by the blood letting of the Russian October Revolution and by the ensuing wish to acquire a better understanding of Marx, led him to apply Hegel historically in ways that are not entirely convincing' *Hegel's Dialectic*, 66 n10.
23 Arendt, *Origins*, 139
24 Lévy, *La Barbarie*, 62
25 *The Political Philosophy of Hobbes: Its Basis and Genesis* (Chicago, University of Chicago Press, 1952), first published by the Clarendon Press, Oxford, 1936. Strauss and Kojève knew one another well. They both published reviews in *Recherches philosophiques*, both were associated with the Ecole pratique des hautes études, and during the 1930s they planned 'to undertake a detailed investigation of the connexion between Hegel and Hobbes' (*Political Philosophy of Hobbes*, 58 n1).
26 Strauss explained in the preface to the American edition that modern political philosophy began not with Hobbes but with Machiavelli. He argued this at length in his *Thoughts on Machiavelli*. This is a very complex argument, a consideration of which must be avoided here. What is of significance for present purposes is an exposition of certain characteristically modern premises or presuppositions given clear and outspoken form by Hobbes and accepted by Hegel.
27 Reference is given in the text to *Leviathan*, ed M. Oakeshott (Oxford, Blackwell, n.d.). Roman numerals refer to the chapter, Arabic to the page.
28 *Political Philosophy of Hobbes*, 94
29 Hobbes's arguments concerning a Christian commonwealth and the kingdom of darkness are of minor importance for our purposes.
30 According to Deutscher, Stalin assiduously read *Leviathan* (quoted in Lévy, *La Barbarie*, 171).
31 Hobbes, *The Elements of Law, Natural and Politic*, ed Ferdinand Toennies, (Cambridge, Cambridge University Press, 1928), I 9.21, p. 48
32 At *Leviathan*, XIII 84, Hobbes adds to fear of death 'desire of such things as are necessary to commodious living; and a hope by their industry to obtain

them.' In *De Cive*, I 2–3, it is clear that violent death is the greatest evil. The significant difference is that the knowledge one has, that one will someday die, is rational; when reason mediates behaviour, the result is uncertain. Fear, however, is an immediate experience, with no meddlesome interposition of particular human faculties. The results, therefore, are certain.

33 Strauss, *The Political Philosophy of Hobbes*, 20
34 Ibid, 22
35 Religion, as shall be shown, seems to have been generated from ignorance and fear, which gives rise to anxiety, especially concerning the future. See *Lev* XII. One might say that Hobbes gets rid of religion in order to make room for worship.
36 Eric Voegelin, *The New Science of Politics: An Introduction* (Chicago, University of Chicago Press, 1952), 159–60. For evidence, see *Lev* XXXI 233; XXXII 242.
37 Strauss, *The Political Philosophy of Hobbes*, 127–8, 135
38 Ibid, 152
39 Voegelin, *The New Science of Politics*, 186
40 'You don't know informers face to face, and then you are surprised that the omnipresent Organs could know that during the mass singing of the "Song of Stalin" you merely opened your mouth and didn't waste your voice? Or that you didn't enjoy yourself at the November 7 demonstration?'; Aleksandr I. Solzhenitsyn, *The Gulag Archipelago*, tr Thomas P. Whitney, II (New York, Harper & Row, 1975), 354.
41 Arendt, *Origins of Totalitarianism*, 140
42 Ibid, 143
43 Voegelin, *The New Science of Politics*, 189

CHAPTER TWO: HISTORICAL CONSCIOUSNESS

1 *Nihilism: A Philosophical Essay* (New Haven, Yale University Press, 1969)
2 See Emil Fackenheim, *Metaphysics and Historicity* (Milwaukee, Marquette University Press, 1961), 4ff.
3 Friedrich Engel-Janosi, 'The Growth of German Historicism,' *Johns Hopkins University Studies in History and Political Science*, 62 (1944), no. 2; D.E. Lee and R.N. Beck, 'The Meaning of "Historicism,"' *American Historical Review*, 59 (1954), 568–77; Calvin G. Rand, 'Two Meanings of Historicism in the Writings of Dilthey, Troeltsch, and Meinecke,' *Journal of the History of Ideas*, 25 (1964), 503–18.
4 *What Is Political Philosophy? And Other Studies* (Glencoe, Free Press, 1959), 57

5 As no specific analysis is devoted to the work of Jean Hyppolite, who in the opinion of many is co-responsible for the rebirth of Hegelianism in France, a short word of apology is required. It is true that no account of contemporary French intellectual history is even remotely adequate that ignores his importance. But that is not the goal of this essay. To those who nevertheless would rebuke an author who presumed to speak about a topic such as French Hegelianism without giving Hyppolite pride of place, one must point out, with the English translator of his principal work, that Hyppolite excused himself by deliberately refusing to attend Kojève's lectures. He was, therefore, untouched by our present concern. See John Heckman, 'Hyppolite and the Hegel Revival in France,' *Telos*, 16 (1973), 135, reprinted as the introduction to the English translation of *Genèse et structure de la phénoménologie de l'esprit de Hegel* (Paris, Aubier, 1946), published by Northwestern University Press, 1974, xxvi.

6 For details see M. Janicaud, 'Victor Cousin et Ravaisson face à Hegel,' *Recherches Hégéliennes*, Bulletin d'information du CRDHM, Université de Poitiers, no 5 (March 1972), 5–6; Jean Aler et al, ibid, no 10 (December 1974); Marcel Méry, 'L'Hégélianisme dans la littérature française du XIXe siècle,' *Etudes philosophiques* (Nice) 20 (1973), 77–9; D.D. Rosca, *L'Influence de Hegel sur Taine* (Paris, Gamber, 1928); René Serreau, *Hegel et l'Hégélianisme* (Paris, PUF, 1965), 89–96; J.L. Dumas, 'Renouvier, Critique de Hegel,' *Revue de métaphysique et de morale*, 76 (1971), 32–52. See also Léon Brunschvicg's majestic (and anti-Hegelian) treatise, *Le Progrès de la conscience dans la philosophie occidentale* [1927], 2nd edn (Paris, PUF, 1953), II 379–80, 395 et seq, 410–11.

7 'Rapport sur l'état des études Hégéliennes en France,' originally published in *Transactions* of the First Hegel Congress, The Hague, 1930, reprinted in *Etudes d'histoire de la pensée philosophique* (Paris, Gallimard, 1971), 228

8 See for example the appeal by Taine and Renan, reprinted in *Archives de philosophie*, 33 (1970), 673–4. An editorial note appended recorded that their proposals were ignored. See also Emile Beaussire, 'Le centenaire de Hegel en 1870,' *Revue des deux mondes*, 91 (1871), 145–61; Ernest Hello, *L'Homme* (Paris, Palmé, 1872), 140.

9 According to Charles Andler, Hegel's son and executor, Karl, wished a German to be the first to examine his father's manuscripts and so had them sent to the Royal Library in Berlin, with the notice of restrictive access attached. As a result, Dilthey's study, *Die Jugendgeschichte Hegels* (Leipzig and Berlin, Teubner, [1905] 1921), was not published until a full

24 years after Herr made his first approach to Karl Hegel. See Andler, *Vie de Lucien Herr* (Paris, Rieder, 1932), 42–3.

10 See, for example, G. Noel, *La Logique de Hegel* (Paris, Alcan, 1897) and the discussion of the Société française de philosophie, 31 January 1907, *Bulletin de la Société française de philosophie*.

11 This is the picture presented by the neo-Kantian Victor Delbos in his course on Kantian elements in German philosophy delivered in the Sorbonne in 1909 and published after the war. See, in particular, 'La méthode de démonstration chez Hegel,' *Revue de métaphysique et de morale*, 32 (1925), 271–81.

12 *De l'Explication dans les sciences* (Paris, Payot, [1922] 1927). See also Meyerson's essay, first published in 1923, 'Hegel, Hamilton, Hamelin et le concept de cause,' in his *Essais* (Paris, Vrin, 1936), 28–58. So far as I have been able to determine, only one article appeared in a major philosophical journal during this period, Bernard Groethuysen's study, which followed Dilthey's historical methods, on 'La conception de l'état chez Hegel et la philosophie politique en Allemagne,' *Revue philosophique*, 97 (1924), 180–207.

13 *Les Doctrines politiques des philosophes classiques de l'Allemagne* (Paris, Alcan, 1927), vi, 323; also ix, 296 et seq, 332. The same problem was not tackled in English until 1940 with the debate between Knox and Carritt in *Philosophy*, reprinted in W. Kaufmann ed, *Hegel's Political Philosophy* (New York, Atherton, 1970), 13–52.

14 Andler, 'Langue et littérature d'origine germanique,' *Annuaire*, Collège de France (Paris, Vuibert, 1929); ibid, 1931; *Revue de métaphysique et de morale*, 38 (1931), 277–510. See also the study of Alain, *Idées* (Paris, Hartmann, 1932), 205–99.

15 G. Canguilhem, 'Hegel en France,' *Revue d'histoire et de philosophie religieuses*, 27 (1948–9), 282–97; P. Dubarle, 'La philosophie française depuis 1940,' *La Vie intellectuelle*, 15 (February 1945), 155–7.

16 François Châtelet wrote recently: 'Since Hegelianism has become integrated into academicism, Part B, IV, A [the dialectic of Master and Slave] of the *Phenomenology of Spirit* has become summarized, controlled, clarified – the high point of all resolutely progressive education ... Upon it is conferred the virtue of revealing at the same time all the dimensions of the human condition'; *La Philosophie des professeurs* (Paris, Grasset, 1970), 72–3.

17 Roberto Salvadori, *Hegel in Francia: Filosofia e Politica nella Cultura francese del Novecento* (Bari, De Donato, 1974), 83. Cf Paul Asveld, 'Zum Referat

von Walter Biemel über die *Phänomenologie des Geistes* und die Hegel-Renaissance in Franckreich,' *Hegel-Studien*, Beiheft 11, Stuttgarten Hegel-Tage, 1970 (Bonn, Bouvier, 1974), 657 et seq.

18 Jean Wahl, *Le Malheur de la conscience dans la philosophie de Hegel* (Paris, PUF, [1929] 2nd edn 1959), 7–8

19 Ibid, 31. The expression 'boredom of the world' was used by Hegel to characterize both his own times and those of Jesus, in *Dok* 318.

20 Ibid, 71–2, 36

21 Ibid, 44, 48

22 Ibid, 49–50. Thus, for Hegel, Christ the 'hinge of history' was followed by other 'world-historical individuals' and eventually by the greatest tragedy of all, the 'world-soul' Napoleon and his self-destructive actions. Cf the famous letter to Niethammer, 13 October 1806 in J. Hoffmeister ed, *Briefe von und an Hegel* (Hamburg, Meiner, 1953), I I 28.

23 Wahl, *Le Malheur*, 54–5. See also Kojève's comments in his *Kant* (Paris, Gallimard, 1973).

24 Wahl, *Le Malheur*, 57

25 Ibid, 77

26 Ibid, 91 et seq

27 Ibid, 51, 111

28 Alexandre Koyré, Review of Wahl *Le Malheur*, in *Revue philosophique*, 110 (1930), 140–1

29 Wahl, *Le Malheur*, 52; cf above note 19.

30 Wahl, *Le Malheur*, 146–7

31 Salvadori, *Hegel in Francia*, 23; Wahl, *Le Malheur*, v

32 Koyré, Review, 142

33 Ibid, 142–3

34 Consider also Koyré's remarks in his review of Dilthey, 'Histoire de philosophie,' *Revue philosophique*, 113 (1932), 481–91, and his comments in *Etudes d'histoire de la pensée philosophique* (Paris, Gallimard, 1971), 150–1. Wahl did not agree and attributed Koyré's criticism to his lack of appreciation for literature. See Jean Wahl, 'Le Role de A. Koyré dans le développement d'études Hégéliennes en France,' *Hegel-Studien*, Beiheft 3, Hegel-Tage, Royaumont, 1964 (1977), 19.

35 Bergson, it is true, was at the Collège de France, but, as Raymond Aron remarked, he was read as if he were already dead, and he influenced hardly at all the philosophy curriculum; *History and the Dialectic of Violence* tr B. Cooper (Oxford, Blackwell, 1975), x.

36 Ecole pratique des hautes études, Section des sciences religieuses, *Annuaire, 1927–1928* (Melun, Imprimerie Administrative, 1927), 61–2.

37 'Les recherches philosophiques d'Alexandre Koyré,' *Critique*, 206 (1964), 684–5. A partial bibliography is in F. Braudel et al, *Mélanges Alexandre Koyré*, 2 vol, (Paris, Hermann, 1964).

38 Koyré, 'Note sur la langue et la terminologie Hégélienne' (originally in the *Revue philosophique* [1931] and republished) in *Etudes d'histoire de la pensée philosophique*, 206.

39 Ibid, 212–13

40 Ibid, 220–1

41 He was equally non-committal in his study of Boehme, allowing only that numerous Boehmian 'signatures' were found upon Hegel's thought without saying whether Hegel had, so to speak, forged them. *La Philosophie de Jacob Boehme: Etudes sur les origines de la métaphysique allemande* (Paris, Vrin, 1929), 506–7.

42 EPHE, *Annuaire*, 1933–1934, 57–8

43 Both papers are entitled 'Hegel à Iéna,' the first being published in *Revue philosophique*, 118 (1934), 274–83, and the second in *Revue d'histoire et philosophie religieuses*, reprinted in *Etudes d'histoire de la pensée philosophique*, 147–89.

44 *Revue philosophique*, 281

45 Ibid, 282–3

46 Ibid, 283

47 Koyré, *Etudes d'histoire de la pensée philosophique*, 160

48 Ibid, 188

49 Ibid, 153. The obituary, like that pronounced by Charles Taylor a quarter-century later, was premature. See Taylor, *Hegel* (Cambridge, Cambridge University Press, 1975), 537–8, 545–6. Indeed, according to Stanley Rosen (*Political Theory*, 7 [1979], 146), there exists a veritable 'Taylor Syndrome,' namely, 'the rictus of the liberal who wishes to appropriate Hegel for contemporary purposes, while at the same time trimming Hegel's sails to the winds of contemporary fashion.'

50 Koyré, *Etudes*, 189. A few years later, Wahl reached the same conclusion: 'Note sur l'espace et remarque sur le temps,' *Revue de métaphysique et de morale*, 46 (1939), 421.

51 Koyré, *Etudes*, 177

52 Ibid, 189

53 Conférence de M.A. Kojevnikoff, diplôme de la section, suppléant, EPHE, *Annuaire*, 1934–35 (Melun, Imperie Administrative, 1935), 54–5, reprinted in *IH* 57

54 Koyré published two collections of papers on Russian philosophical thought; Kojève published two papers on the same person, V. Solovyov,

one in German and the second, four years later, in French. In addition, his thesis at Heidelberg was on Solovyov. The recent study by Guy Planty-Bonjour, *Hegel et la pensée philosophique en Russie, 1830–1917* (The Hague, Martinus Nijhoff, 1974), 101, 229, and incidental remarks made by Koyré and Kojève in their studies of Russian thought, suggest similarity, if not the direct influence, of Slavophil and materialist readings of Hegel as an atheistic anthropologist or 'humanist,' in the left-Hegelian or Feuerbachian sense, with their own interpretations.

55 A. Kojevnikoff, 'Phénoménologie' (a series of book reviews), *Recherches philosophiques*, 2 (1932–3), 473–4

56 Ibid, 475

57 Kojevnikoff, 'Phénoménologie' (a series of book reviews), *Recherches philosophiques*, 5 (1935–6), 417–18

58 Kojevnikoff, *Recherches philosophiques*, 2 (1932–3), 474. In this respect Kojève continued Wahl's approach by giving due weight to the 'warmth' of the concrete.

59 See Kenley R. Dove, 'Hegel's Phenomenological Method,' *Review of Metaphysics*, 23 (1970), 615–41, for an exhaustive discussion of the issues involved. Eric Weil wrote: 'Method? Certainly, but on condition that one does not see there a pre-existent or pre-developed procedure, a way of doing that would stem from the needs, the preferences, the decisions of an empirical subjectivity. The method exists, but it is the consciousness of a path which has been trod, not one of those methods which are applied to objects taken to be given and immediate'; 'The Hegelian Dialectic,' in J.J. O'Malley et al ed, *The Legacy of Hegel*, 62.

60 We shall consider Kojève's correction of Hegel below. If Horace forgave Homer for nodding off (*verum operi longo fas est obrepere somnum*), surely one can do as much toward Hegel, whose works were also rather lengthy.

CHAPTER THREE: HOW HISTORY ENDED

1 After the war Kojève was persuaded by one of his former auditors, Robert Marjolin, to join the civil service, a fitting end, as has been observed, for a Hegelian. Kojève also must have enjoyed following Hegel in having his lecture notes published by devoted pupils.

2 The first chapter, 'En guise d'introduction,' was published separately in *Mesures* in 1939.

3 This can be observed, for example, in Kojève's vocabulary. In 1933–4, he spoke of 'absolute philosophy' (*IH* 34); a year later it was 'true philosophy' (*IH* 65). Or again, he identified the atheist who has overcome God

by knowing that he has been recognizing himself in God as 'the-man-of-Reason.' None of these terms would be used later: Hegel would not be described as a 'man-of-Reason' who composed any sort of philosophy whatsoever, but as a Sage, a Wise Man who wrote The System of Science or Wisdom.

4 See Gadamer, *Hegel's Dialectic*, 72.

5 Fritjof Capra, *The Tao of Physics* (Boulder, Col, Shambhala, 1975)

6 See Emil Fackenheim, *The Religious Dimension in Hegel's Thought*, chapter 4, 'The Hegelian Middle,' for an alternative, and more faithfully Hegelian, discussion of the three-fold mediation involved in Hegel's thought. See also Stanley Rosen's comments on Hegel and Aristotle in his *G.W.F. Hegel*, 80–8.

7 We will leave aside any consideration of whether Kojève's understanding of 'human nature' in terms of immutable essences is, in fact, to be found in Greek philosophy. What is indisputable is that, among his contemporaries across the Rhine, there was a great deal of very loud talk concerning a master race whose innate mastery was a consequence of their genetic, natural being. See also the remarks of one of Kojève's auditors, Gaston Fessard, SJ, *Pax Nostra: Examen de conscience international* (Paris, Grasset, 1936).

8 Jacques Monod, *Chance and Necessity: An Essay on the Natural Philosophy of Modern Biology*, tr Austryn Wainhouse (Toronto, Random House, 1971), 112 et seq

9 This is audaciously argued by Julian Jaynes, *The Origin of Consciousness in the Breakdown of the Bicameral Mind* (Boston, Houghton Mifflin, 1976), II 2. We do not assume that Jaynes is correct but that, even if he is, Hegel's argument, amended by Kojève, still stands.

10 Most comments on Kojève's work assume him to be an academic commentator. See, for example, Charles Taylor, *American Political Science Review*, 64 (1970), 627; George Heiman, *Journal of Politics*, 41 (1979), 275. A more adequate but still one-sided account is Patrick Riley, 'Introduction to the Reading of Alexandre Kojève,' *Political Theory*, 9:1 (1981), 5–48.

11 *Essai d'une histoire raisonée de la philosophie païenne* (Paris, Gallimard, 1968), 9

12 'Self-Consciousness and Self-Knowledge in Plato and Hegel,' *Hegel-Studien* 9 (1974), 122

13 Ibid, 129. See also his *G.W.F. Hegel*, 159.

14 Gadamer made the point (*Hegel's Dialectic*, 62 n7) that Kojève's (and Hyppolite's) translation of Hegel's *Begierde* as *désir* is not always correct, as the connotations change according to the stage reached in the transi-

tion to self-knowledge. No doubt the same objection could be made with respect to the English *desire*.

15 See Gadamer, *Hegel's Dialectic*, 64.
16 See Rosen, *G.W.F. Hegel*, 152, 155.
17 Ibid, 158, called the dialectic of master and slave 'a mythical representation of the historical recognition of the self in its relation with others.' See also: E. Clémens, 'L'histoire (comme) inachèvement,' *Revue de métaphysique et de morale*, 76 (1971), 221. The significance of a mythic representation, as with all representational or religious forms, is that it is not a fully articulate, logical, discursive account: it appeals to more immediate sentiments, such as belief, rather than to conscious understanding or reason.
18 *Dok*, 314
19 In his *Lectures* of 1803–4, Hegel evidently denied the humanity of the Slave. See *Jenenser Realphilosophie I: Die Vorlesungen von 1803–04*, ed J. Hoffmeister (Leipzig, Felix Meiner, 1932). See Kojève's remarks, *IH* 571. The Hobbesian resonances, indicated in chapter 1 of this essay, are obvious enough.
20 'Truth' for Kojève always had the meaning, most forcefully argued by Heidegger, of 'revealed reality.' This interpretation, although widely accepted, is not philologically unshakeable (cf P. Friedländer, *Plato*, I, tr H. Meyerhof [New York, Bollingen, 1958], chapter 11) and, philosophically, amounts to a *petitio principii*.
21 This is why, moreover, the corruption of the Master, who manifests the pure universality of death, takes place in the form of sheer particularity, the privatization of life first expressed by the Slave and then by money. For details see Judith N. Shklar, *Freedom and Independence*, 46.
22 *Hegel's Dialectic*, 65
23 In his *Early Theological Writings* Hegel wrote: 'The heroes of all nations die in the same manner, for they have lived and in the course of their lives they have learned to recognize nature's power'; *Theologische Jugendschriften*, ed Herman Nohl (Tübingen, Mohr, 1907), 46.
24 *Hegel's Dialectic*, 67. 'For us it is clear that such a Master is no Master. But is it clear for the Master? Is he not comical precisely because he feels himself to be a Master, yet in truth he is afraid? We who recognize the dependency of the Master know as well that his dependency is actually that of desire, and does not come from his failure to be recognized.'
25 It can, however, very easily be underestimated. See, for example, Riley, 'Introduction to the Reading of Kojève,' passim; George Armstrong Kelly, *Hegel's Retreat from Eleusis: Studies in Political Thought* (Princeton,

Princeton University Press, 1978), 31–4, 51–3; and Shklar, *Freedom and Independence*, 60–1, 72–3, 93–5.

26 Rosen, *G.W.F. Hegel*, 154–5
27 Ibid, 155
28 One finds an identical sentiment and very nearly identical language in Marx's third manuscript of 1844, *Frühe Schriften*, ed H.J. Lieber and Peter Furth (Stuttgart, Cotta, 1962), I 604–5.
29 Hegel's observation that he completed the text of *Phenomenology* on the eve of the 'last' battle, at Jena and Averstädt, was eloquent evidence as to just how cunning history actually was.
30 One should add that Africa, according to Hegel, is properly speaking still deep in the darkness of Nature, on the other side of the threshold of World History (*VPG* 129:99).
31 Here special mention should be made of the Crusades. This curious search for the material presence of the divine in a particular piece of territory, a 'Holy Land,' shiploads of which were subsequently exported to Europe along with other odd relics, was not, Hegel said, entirely senseless. The West learned, after Palestine was reconquered, that the actual embodiment of the Infinite for which it had been searching 'was to be sought only in subjective Consciousness and not in any external or naturally existing thing, that the actual embodiment in question, as the conjunction of the secular and the eternal, is the spiritual self-consciousness of the person' (*VPG* 472:393).
32 Hence Hegel's sarcasm in his discussion of those medieval nobles who insisted upon ancient privileges. See *HPW* 275ff.

CHAPTER FOUR: APOLITICAL AND POLITICAL ATTITUDES

1 One must emphasize that, according to Kojève, the polis was no more than the first state and was bound to be superseded by its historical successors. There was, in short, no 'nostalgia for Hellas' as has often been alleged. See, for example, Judith Shklar, 'Hegel's Phenomenology: An Elegy for Hellas,' in Z.A. Pelczynski ed, *Hegel's Political Philosophy* (Cambridge, Cambridge University Press, 1971), or her *Freedom and Independence*, chapter 2 and passim. See also Charles Taylor, *Hegel*, 387–8, and Georg Lukács, *The Young Hegel*, chapter 4.
2 If he did not leave the family but had sons of his own, there would arise a 'grandfather problem.' The father, as head of the family, must be absolutely superior to his son, which now includes the son of his son. But then, since the son is not absolutely superior to his own son, he cannot be

a true father. Of course, there could be extended families, but they were not the families of warrior-citizens – or, if they were, the headship was honorific.

3 See Thucydides, *Peloponnesian War*, II 42.

4 If the presentation I have been making reads as a peculiar plot summary of Sophocles' *Antigone*, this is doubtless because of the great importance Hegel attached to that play. Yet the conflict of laws was not confined to the relations of a pious sister toward her criminal brother. According to Kojève, Aeschylus's *Oresteia* carved the same meaning. Iphigenia had been killed in sacrifice by her father, Agamemnon, that the Greek fleet might leave Aulis and proceed to Troy. Upon his return to Argos he, in turn, was killed by his wife, Clytemnestra, and his cousin, her lover, Aegisthus. Orestes, Agamemnon's son, under orders from Apollo, took revenge by killing Aegisthus and his own mother. As he was justifying his actions the Erinyes, the avenging ones, appeared to him, and he fled. In Kojève's words, 'the sacrifice of Iphigenia manifests the contradiction between the State and the Family. By the murder of Agamemnon, the very principle of Royalty (= State) is suppressed and the Family entirely takes the place of the State. (Aegisthus is not a King.) By destroying the family (by killing his mother), Orestes wishes to restore Royalty to his father by becoming King himself: for Agamemnon would then become father of the King and would be himself King. Orestes will be killed by the infernal gods [i.e. the Erinyes]. There is no solution' (*IH* 253). At least none appears by the end of *Agamemnon* and *Choephoroe*.

A 'solution' was offered by Aeschylus in the third part of the trilogy, *The Eumenides*. There Athena persuaded Apollo and the Erinyes to treat the matter legally and refer it for judgment to an Athenian court, established on this occasion, the Areopagus. The division was equal. Athena cast the deciding vote and Orestes was acquitted; she then conciliated the now enraged Erinyes by persuading them to accept as compensation a permanent sanctuary in Attica. Kojève said of *The Eumenides* that 'Aeschylus disavows *The Agamemnon* ("domestication" of the Erinyes = transformation of Tragedy into Comedy)' (*IH* 253). Kojève (and Hegel) seemed to have ignored the importance of persuasion, *peitho*, as the instrument by which the order of Zeus imposed itself on the demonic divinities of the older law. Athena did not simply crush the claims of the Erinyes even while she reminded them (827ff) that she could unlock Zeus's thunderbolt. The point that Aeschylus was making, that justice, *dike*, had evolved from the rigid legality of revenge to the flexibility of persuasion, had apparently been lost, and the institution of a court of citizens who would 'diagnose *dike'* was transmogrified into a comic occasion. According to Aeschylus, the jurors were inspired by 'reverence and fear' (698ff). But we, as good Hegelian Sages, must forget about *The Eumenides* and Aeschylus's intentions and retire to the dilemma he transcended, the conflict of absolute laws.

5 One should, perhaps, make the obvious Hegelian point that Alcibiades and Alexander were both pupils of philosophers. Whether they were faithful pupils is a separate question, though Hegel and Kojève would doubtless say that they realized their teachers' thoughts (or, in the case of Alcibiades, tried to).

6 Cf Robert Musil, *The Man without Qualities, The Like of It Now Happens (II)*, tr E. Wilkins and E. Kaiser (London, Secker and Warburg, 1967), II 143.

CHAPTER FIVE: THE DIALECTIC OF HISTORICAL IDEOLOGIES

1 We will not survey the controversy here. An intelligent discussion may be found in Georges van Riet, 'Le problème de Dieu chez Hegel,' *Revue philosophique de Louvain* 63 (1965), 353–418. See also Eric Weil, *Hegel et l'état* (Paris, Vrin, 1950), 49ff.

2 *Freedom and Independence*, 56. Earlier, she wrote that 'biblical religion especially is never allowed to speak in its own voice at all. Christianity is interpreted, given its "real" meaning, explained and criticized without a moment's respite' (49). This was also the burden of Fackenheim's *The Religious Dimension in Hegel's Thought*. Even Taylor, who was usually so noncommital, was moved to remark that Hegel's Christians would find it impossible to pray (*Hegel* 493). Here one might recall one of Hegel's youthful aphorisms, that reading the daily newspaper was the modern man's morning benediction.

3 Hegel referred here to the colossal statues of Amenhotep III, erected near Thebes. In 27 BC an earthquake partially destroyed one of them, and the ruined stonework made the sound mentioned. It was the voice of Mennon, King of the Ethiopians, responding to his mother, Eos (Dawn). An alternative explanation held it to be the result of the passage of air through the porous stone as a consequence of a sharp change in temperature with the heat of sunrise.

4 The aforementioned obscurity of the text makes any more definite interpretation difficult. That it is not wildly eccentric is shown by the widespread agreement that the French Revolution was, in Hyppolite's words, a

'metaphysical event' for Hegel (*Studies on Marx and Hegel*, tr John O'Neil [New York, Basic Books, 1969], 58). Contemporary scholars as distinct in their approach as H.S. Harris ('Hegel and the French Revolution,' *Clio*, 7 [1977], 5–18) and Georg Lukács (*The Young Hegel*, 454) are agreed on the philosophical importance of the Revolution. A full discussion of the issues can be found in Joachim Ritter, *Hegel und die französische Revolution* (Köln und Opladen, Westdeutscher Verlag, 1957).

5 This assumption does not mean that Hegel's text is not also a discussion of the internal self-development of consciousness, as Hyppolite argued in his great commentary, or a discussion of an individual act of forgiveness for a transgression, as Shklar suggested.

6 Napoleon was simply the first exemplar of Napoleonic existence, just as Hegel was the first exemplar of the Sage. See Lukács, *The Young Hegel*, 306, for a similar interpretation.

7 In 1938–9 Kojève nevertheless repeated his remarks on the obscurity of the passage and speculated again that Hegel may have been awaiting a reciprocal 'official' recognition from Napoleon. He added, however, that none of their personal relations much mattered. See *IH* 311 n1.

CHAPTER SIX: THE POST-HISTORICAL ATTITUDE

1 The most comprehensive account of the problems involved is H.F. Fulda, *Das Problem einer Einleitung in Hegels Wissenschaft der Logik* (Frankfurt, Klostermann, 1965). A historical account of various interpretations of the relationship is Otto Pöggeler, 'Zur Deutung der *Phänomenologie des Geistes*,' *Hegel-Studien*, Beiheft 3 (1964), 27–74; see also Heinz Kimmerle, 'Zur Entwicklung des Hegelschen Denkens in Jena,' *Hegel-Studien* Beiheft, 4 (1965), 33–47. Joseph C. Flay, 'The History of Philosophy and the *Phenomenology of Spirit*,' in Joseph J. O'Malley et al ed, *Hegel and the History of Philosophy* (The Hague, Martinus Nijhoff, 1974), 47–61, argued that, indeed, *Phenomenology* did resolve the vexing problem of how to begin to enter the System, namely with the history of philosophy understood as the phenomenology of Spirit. This was more or less what Hegel himself indicated in his *Wissenschaft der Logik* I 29–30 (Miller tr, 48–9). Other summaries and dissents are in Rosen, *Hegel*, 128ff, and Fackenheim, *The Religious Dimension*, 31ff and 73ff.

2 Hegel made some very witty remarks in *Logic* about 'possibility' as a rhetorical subterfuge. Of course it was always 'possible' for the Sultan to become pope, but it would be rather stupid to argue anything on the basis of this 'possibility.' See *Logic* para 261.

CHAPTER SEVEN: THE POST-HISTORICAL REGIME

1 References to the preface to the *RPhil* are given first for the original and then for the Knox translation. Other references are to numbered paragraphs and Additions.

2 A thorough analysis of this apparently baffling sentence, which Hegel repeated almost unchanged in *Enz* para 6, and which he pronounced a commonplace, can be found in Emil Fackenheim, 'On the Actuality of the Rational and the Rationality of the Actual.' See also Joachim Ritter, *Hegel und die französche Revolution*, chapter 1.

3 Compare Hobbes, *Leviathan*, XVII 109.

4 Ritter, *Hegel et la Révolution française*, 53

5 Or, if one prefers, the laws of 'bourgeois' economics. In this context, however, the phrase bourgeois economics is redundant: what is bourgeois is, precisely, what is economic, namely the system of needs within civil (or bourgeois) society, *bürgerliche Gesellschaft*.

6 For a thorough discussion of Hegel's use of the term see Richard L. Schacht, 'Hegel on Freedom,' in Alasdair MacIntyre ed, *Hegel*, (Notre Dame, Notre Dame University Press, 1972), 324–6.

7 Expositors and critics of Hegel, beginning, no doubt, with Marx, have argued that Hegel did not say anything very helpful about the poor. Poverty is said to result from the *smooth* working of civil society that resulted in the over-production of goods, which the poor could not buy (cf *RPhil* 244A). At the same time, however, Hegel argued that only the state could overcome the imbalance that would result when the economy was unfettered (*RPhil* 185). He did not, however, provide details as to how this could be done, leading a modern critic, S. Avineri, to declare that this showed Hegel's 'rare and astonishing grasp of the nature of civil society as well as his ultimate inability to cope with the problem of poverty.' Indeed, according to Avineri, this was 'the only time in his system where Hegel raises a problem – and leaves it open'; *Hegel's Theory of the Modern State*, 154. Eric Weil, *Hegel et l'état*, 88–100, made essentially the same point. A Hegelian response would emphasize that, while poverty may be a fact, the eradication of it was, in principle, advocated by Hegelian politics. To overcome poverty was a technical operation made possible by the domination of nature (cf *RPhil* 236).

8 For details, see G. Heiman, 'The Sources and Significance of Hegel's Corporate Doctrine,' in Z.A. Pelczynski ed, *Hegel's Political Philosophy*.

9 Solange Mercier-Jola, 'La notion de besoin chez Hegel,' *Recherches Hégéliennes*, no. 5 (March 1972), 75

10 If it were not already plain enough, Hegel went out of his way again to explain that he was not concerned with the genesis of historical states but with the idea of the (universal and homogeneous) state, to which all existing contemporary historical states more or less conformed, going so far as to call it an 'actualized God' (*RPhil* 258A). Walter Kaufmann has expended a good deal of energy trying to clarify Hegel's (to him) unfortunate phrase. See Kaufmann, 'The Hegel Myth and Its Method,' in Alasdair MacIntyre ed, *Hegel*, 25 (and elsewhere). Following Kojève's interpretation, however, the scandal evaporates. The state, obviously, was the actualization of what was once imagined to be God. Consider, for example, *RPhil* 270 or 272A in this regard.

11 Cf Strauss, *On Tyranny*, 335:222.

12 See Eric Weil, 'Hegel et la concept de la Révolution,' *Archives de philosophie*, 39 (1976), 3–19, for an elaboration of this contention.

13 See *HPW* 217 for Hegel's explicit statement on the unimportance of 'strict monarchical form.' For supporting arguments, see Weil, *Hegel et l'état*, 59–60, and Lukács, *The Young Hegel*, 307.

14 Weil, *Hegel et l'état*, 64

15 The great man exacted the truth from public opinion and informed the age of its own rational will by accomplishing what the age truly demanded. Then, after having initially defied the prejudice of public opinion, but having through his accomplishments informed the public of its true will, the public would make of his great accomplishment their own prejudice and so accord the great man the recognition that was his proper due (*RPhil* 318, 318A). Hegel made substantively the same point regarding himself as a great man of science at the end of the preface to *Phenomenology*. At the same time, however, the great man who was truly self-conscious knew that the substance of 'his' great deeds was not his own but rather the doing of the world spirit. Here compare *RPhil* 348 with *PhG*, 57–9:44–5.

16 For a spirited defence of Hegel's reputation as a 'modern' political thinker insofar as he favoured representative political institutions, a relatively free press, etc., see Avineri, *Hegel's Theory of the Modern State*, 176ff.

17 See Knox's note to para 322 and reference.

18 Weil, *Hegel et l'état*, 74

19 The chief defect of social contract 'theories' was that they reduced the state to its conditioning element, civil society, and made of the state an inessential, epiphenomenal result. See Hegel's remarks at *RPhil* 183, 258, 281, 337.

20 See Weil, *Hegel et l'état*, 77–8. Cf Lukács, *The Young Hegel*, 504.

21 Emil L. Fackenheim, 'Hegel and Judaism,' 161–85, suggested that the Jews could play their part twice. Perhaps; but then we should be Nietzschean enough to extend the same privilege to the Germans too.

22 Hegel here referred readers, if it were not already obvious, to paras 331 and 57, which in turn referred to the master-slave dialectic of *Phenomenology*.

23 Consider here Hegel's remarks on Machiavelli, *HPW* 220–3; on the need of Germany for a Theseus, *HPW* 234, 241; and on the difference between the response of the Wurtemburgers and the French when a heroic personality arose in their midst, *HPW* 251, 281–2. The result showed that the right of heroes was not an empirical right, but the right of reason. The Wurtemburgers, as distinct from the French, were simply unreasonable. Kojève made the same point rather more crudely: true moral actions supported the universal and homogeneous state (*IH* 95), which meant that they must be successful (*IH* 465:189–90). Consider on this point as well Lukács's remarks, *The Young Hegel*, 310 and reference.

24 And they are not, one should add, of concern in this essay. If anything is clear about the traumas of the non-European world it is that they are modernizing traumas, not returns to barbarism, however bloody they may be and however inconvenient for the rest of the world. Cf Weil, *Hegel et l'état*, 73, and chapter 8 below.

25 Kojève referred to Nietzsche, *Gay Science*, ɪ 24.

26 Emil Fackenheim wrote: 'Hegel's philosophy seeks to mediate all things divine as well as human, transforming all absolute into relative distinctions. Jewish religious existence, in contrast, remains stubbornly committed to at least two *absolute* distinctions – between the Divine and the human, and between the one true God and all the false'; 'Hegel and Judaism,' 161–2. Such an agument in terms of actual Jewish religious practice was open to the equally practical response of the exuberant Hegelian to the silent 'sage.' If there were no such people who were stubornly committed ...? We consider this below in the Epilogue.

27 And neither, for that matter, had 'contemplation.' The 'contemplation' of the sage did not simply recapitulate the 'contemplative' absorption of primordial desire in things. On the contrary, the sage only appeared inactive since he neither changed anything nor introduced novelty. In fact his 'contemplation' actualized the circular, perpetual, conceptual movement of complete thought (*IH* 410). And the 'secular arm,' so to speak, was busy forcibly actualizing what already was.

28 Compare Plato *Phaedrus* 278d or Aristotle *EN* 1178b 25.

29 That Kojève's reading is not wildly idiosyncratic may be confirmed by

Hegel's remarks in *Logic* 161 and in *Philosophy of History* 126-7:70-1 and 177:111.

30 'In the Nazi murder camps no effort was spared to make persons into living *things* before making them into dead things. And that the dead had been human when alive was a truth systematically rejected when their bodies were made into fertilizer and soap ... The Holocaust Kingdom was an end in itself, having only one ultimate "produce," and that was death ... The dead Jews of the murder camps ... were not the "waste product" of the Nazi system. They were *the* product'; Emil Fackenheim, 'The Human Condition after Auschwitz,' in his *The Jewish Return into History*, 89, 90, 93.

31 Kelly's charge, that Kojève distorted Hegel's teaching by emphasizing what Kelly called the exterior and political rather than the internal and psychological, may be called into question here, where the two external elements have been fused in the shape of the citizen, and the external has been fused to the internal in the shape of the sage. That is, what Kelly called the 'psychological' Kojève treated under the heading 'wisdom.' Thus one could maintain that Kojève, by bringing the external (citizen) together with the internal (sage), had already answered Kelly's criticism: Kelly's reading of Kojève, not Kojève's of Hegel, was 'one-sided and needs correction.' Cf 'Notes on Hegel's "Lordship and Bondage,"' in MacIntyre, *Hegel*, 192-4.

32 See also Weil, *Hegel et l'état*, 54.

33 According to Hegel, monarchy was to be hereditary. Elective monarchy was a foolish dream (*RPhil* 281). Kojève's position seemed to favour something like an elective monarchy in the sense that the leader of the universal and homogeneous state was he who was most competent and serious. It was argued above, moreover, that strict monarchic form was less important than genuine monarchic function, namely the articulate human speech: 'I will it.' For references, see note 13, above.

34 Leo Strauss, *De La Tyrannie*, contains Kojève's review 'Tyrannie et sagesse,' 215-80, originally published as 'L'action politique des philosophes,' *Critique*, 6 (1950), 41-2, 46-55, 138-55. Leo Strauss, *On Tyranny*, contains a translation of Kojève's review and a slightly shortened version of Strauss's reply. Citations in the text are given as *OT*, with the French pagination first and the English second.

35 Kojève used the terms tyrant, leader, and political man interchangeably. His reasoning was as follows: until recent times tyranny was invariably a term of condemnation referring not to despotism (which, strictly speaking, existed only within the family) but to the rule by terror of a minority, guided by an exclusive authority, over a majority. Contemporary

political experience, such as the 'polemic' between Eastern and Western democrats, Kojève's way of referring to the cold war, had made a more adequate definition possible. A tyranny may be said to exist when any fraction of the citizenry, a majority or not, imposed its will and ideas on the rest without trying to come to terms or compromise with them and without taking into account their ideas or desires or any authority that they recognized. The tyrannizing fraction could do this, in the end, only by playing on the 'natural' fear of death experienced by the tyrannized, who 'behave in fact like slaves who are ready to do anything to save their own lives. And it is this situation that certain of our contemporaries qualify as "tyranny" in the pejorative sense of the term' (*OT* 230–1: 153–4).

36 The procedure of 'asking for the hand' of a daughter, for example, is at best a quaint formality among adult citizens of the modern state.

37 *Pierrot mon ami, Loin de Rueil,* and *Le Dimanche de la vie.* The review is entitled 'Les romans de la sagesse,' *Critique,* 60 (1952), 387–97. Page references are given in the text. Any connoisseur of post-historical litera-ture would enjoy Queneau's work. According to Queneau, 'Literature is the projection on the imaginary level of the real activity of man; labour, the projection on the real level of the imaginary activity of man. Both are born together. The one is a metaphorical outline of Paradise Lost and measures the unhappiness of man. The other progresses towards Paradise Regained and tests the happiness of man ... Thus, the normal occupation of human life is to labour and imagine'; *Une Histoire modèle* (Paris, Galli-mard, 1966), 103–4.

38 A *voyou* is someone who hangs about in the street (*voie*), in order to see (*voir*) what is going on, a *voyeur.* See Raymond Queneau, 'Philosophes et voyous,' *Les Temps modernes,* 6:63 (1951), 1193–1205.

39 *Bonjour tristesse* and *Un Certain Sourire.* The review is entitled 'Le dernier monde nouveau,' *Critique,* 111–12 (1956), 702–8. Page references are given in the text.

40 Argus Panoptes or Argus, the dog of Odysseus? The first was beheaded by Hermes, the second died of joy when his master returned. Or did Kojève have the builder of the *Argo* in mind? In any event, Sagan was not amused: see Kojève's letter to his friend Georges Bataille, editor of *Critique,* 10 October 1957, Bibliothèque nationale, NAF, 15854.

41 See Jean-François Revel, *Ni Marx, Ni Jésus.* As one wit remarked, to tell the Toronto proletariat they had nothing to lose but their chains would be a waste of time; they all use snow tires.

42 Gilles Lapouge, 'Entretien avec Kojève,' *La Quinzaine littéraire,* 53 (1 July 1968), 18–20.

CHAPTER EIGHT: CONSEQUENCES

1 *Hegel et l'état*, 56, 71
2 James Doull, 'Hegel and Contemporary Liberalism, Anarchism, Socialism: A Defence of the *Rechtsphilosophie* against Marx and his Contemporary Followers,' in J.J. O'Malley ed, *The Legacy of Hegel*, 248
3 See Weil, *Hegel et l'état*, 74, for additional arguments along these lines. See also Avineri, *Hegel and the Modern State*, 106ff.
4 Herbert Lüthy, 'Colonialization and the Making of Mankind,' *Journal of Economic History*, 21 (1961), 494. For an account of the pre-history of the claims and demands of 'have-not' nations, see Douglas Rimmer, 'Have-Not Nations: The Prototype,' *Economic Development and Cultural Change* 27:2 (1979), 307–25. What the original 'have-nots' didn't have were colonies.
5 'La Doctrine de la reconnaissance, fondament du droit international,' *Revue de droit internationale et de législation comparée*, 16 (1884), 333–59.
6 R. Eric O'Connor ed, *Conversations with Eric Voegelin* (Montreal, Thomas More Institute Papers, No. 76, 1980), 117.
7 Before the Revolution he had commissioned a genealogy that traced his origin to 1419, when four Scottish brothers named Stutt crossed the Channel to serve as archers in the army of the Dauphin against the English during the Hundred Years' War.
8 This information (and many additional anecdotes) can be found in Emmet Kennedy, *Destutt de Tracy and the Origins of 'Ideology'* (Philadelphia, American Philosophical Society, 1978).
9 Richard Koebner and Helmut Dan Schmidt, *Imperialism: The Story and Significance of a Political Word* (Cambridge, Cambridge University Press, 1965), 1.
10 Eric Voegelin, 'The Growth of the Race Idea,' *Review of Politics*, 2 (1940), 297–8.
11 'Non-European Foundations of European Imperialism: Sketch for a Theory of Collaboration,' in William Roger Louis ed, *Imperialism: The Robinson and Gallagher Controversy* (New York, Watts, 1976), 129
12 Their initial thesis was published as 'The Imperialism of Free Trade,' *Economic History Review*, 2nd series, VI (1953), and is reprinted in Louis, *Imperialism*, along with some critical response to it, especially as it was developed at length in *Africa and the Victorians: The Official Mind of Imperialism* (London, Macmillan, 1961). This book may be compared with the analyses of Arendt and Schumpeter; it can be warmly recommended for its brilliant prose style alone.

13 Robinson and Gallagher, 'The Partition of Africa,' *New Cambridge Modern History* XI, reprinted in Louis, *Imperialism*, 82
14 'The Partition of Africa,' 110
15 See Richard Koebner, 'The Concept of Economic Imperialism,' *Economic History Review*, 2nd series, II (1949), 1–15; D.K. Fieldhouse, 'Imperialism: An Historiographic Revision,' *Economic History Review*, 2nd series, XIV (1961), 187–9.
16 Robinson and Gallagher, *Africa and the Victorians*, 287
17 Robinson, 'Non-European Foundations of European Imperialism: Sketch for a Theory of Collaboration,' in Louis, *Imperialism*, 146
18 Robinson and Gallagher, 'The Partition of Africa,' 125
19 J.R. Seeley, *The Expansion of England* (London, 1883), 8
20 Samuel P. Huntington, 'Transnational Organizations in World Politics,' *World Politics* 25 (1973), 343–4. One should add that Huntington is by no means a radical, left-wing intellectual; indeed, he is just the opposite. His contribution to *The Crisis of Democracy, Report on the Governability of Democracies to the Trilateral Commission* (New York, New York University Press, 1975) heaped scorn upon 'value-oriented intellectuals who often devote themselves to the derogation of leadership, the challenge of authority, and the unmasking and delegitimization of established institutions' while singing the praises of 'policy-oriented intellectuals' such as himself (6–7). His analysis of governmental instability revealed that it was caused by 'an excess of democracy,' the remedy for which was abundantly clear (113). One finds a compatible economic analysis from a quite different political standpoint in Stephen Hymer, 'The MNC and the Law of Uneven Development,' in J.N. Bhagwati ed, *Economics and World Order* (New York, Macmillan, 1972), 113–40.
21 Even American military expansion, with a few conspicuous exceptions, has not followed the traditional method of occupying vast tracts of real estate. Instead, the power to operate military installations on foreign soil (and more or less isolated from the host country) has been divorced from the right to exercise political control. The Guantanamo naval base in Cuba is an excellent example.
22 D.K. Fieldhouse, '"Imperialism": An Historiographic Revision,' *Economic History Review*, 2nd series, XIV (1961), 187–9
23 For examples and details, see, inter alia, David S. Landes, 'Some Thoughts on the Nature of Economic Imperialism,' *Journal of Economic History* 21 (1961), 496–512; Richard J. Hammond, 'Economic Imperialism: Sidelights on a Stereotype,' ibid, 582–98; Richard D. Wolff, 'Modern Imperialism: The View from the Metropolis,' American Economic Association, *Papers*

and Proceedings, 60 (1970), 225–30. One must also mention the classic paper, now over a quarter-century old, by John Gallagher and Ronald Robinson, 'The Imperialism of Free Trade,' *Economic History Review*, 2nd series, VI (1953), 1–15.

24 By capitalism I mean no more than a developed market economy, to be contrasted, according to the United Nations classification, with developing countries and centrally planned economies. Reasons such as economies of scale, research and development costs, and other barriers to entry mean that most MNEs are large integrated organizations enjoying an oligopolistic market position and so are able to avoid many of the disciplines classically associated with a competitive national economy. Hence their greater freedom of operation; hence too, the concern of national governments. Figures vary: generally it is said that about 90 MNEs have greater gross corporate/national products than half the states in the world.

25 An account of the issues involved is in Robert Gilpin, *U.S. Power and the Multinational Corporation: The Political Economy of Foreign Direct Investment* (New York, Basic Books, 1975), chapters 1–4. The most widely accepted non-Marxist theory was developed by Raymond Vernon in 'International Investment and International Trade in the Product Life Cycle,' *Quarterly Journal of Economics*, 80 (1966), 190–207. See also his subsequent works, *Sovereignty at Bay: The Multinational Spread of U.S. Enterprises* (New York, Basic Books, 1971) and *Storm over the Multinationals: The Real Issues* (Cambridge, Mass, Harvard University Press, 1977), and the applications of the product-cycle theory by Theodore H. Moran, 'Transnational Strategies of Protection and Defence by MNCs: Spreading the Risk and Raising the Cost for Nationalization in Natural Resources,' *International Organization*, 27 (1973), 273–87, and his 'Foreign Expansion as an "Institutional Necessity" for U.S. Corporate Capitalism: The Search for a Radical Model,' *World Politics*, 25 (1973), 369–86. For criticism of specific details, see Ian H. Giddy, 'The Demise of the Product Cycle Model in International Business Theory,' *Columbia Journal of World Business*, XIII:1 (spring 1978), 90–7. Several different definitions of the MNE can be found in Foreign Investment Division, Office of Economics, Dept of Industry, Trade and Commerce, *Notes on Some Definitions of the Multi-National Enterprise*, (Ottawa, mimeo, August 1971).

26 Jack N. Behrman, *Some Patterns in the Rise of the Multi-national Enterprise* (Chapel Hill, University of North Carolina Graduate School of Business Administration, 1966), 109, reported: 'When pressed for instances in which local nationals displayed concrete evidence of a higher loyalty to

the host government and a disloyalty to their own company, no official interviewed could provide one.' See also 110–11.

27 H.V. Perlmutter and D.A. Heenan, 'How Multinational Should Your Top Managers Be?,' *Harvard Business Review*, 52 (November–December 1974), 127–9

28 Thomas Aitken, *The Multinational Man: The Role of the Manager Abroad* (London, George Allen and Unwin, 1973), 13

29 James Killough, 'Improved Payoffs from Transnational Advertising,' *Harvard Business Review*, 56:4 (July–August 1978), 102–10

30 Howard V. Perlmutter, 'The Multi-national Firm and the Future,' American Academy of Political and Social Science *Annals*, 403 (1972), 150–2; David A. Heenan, 'Global Cities of Tomorrow,' *Harvard Business Review* 55:3 (May–June 1977), 79–92

31 A plausible case can be made for the efforts of the major oil companies during the 1973–4 oil crisis to hold down talk of a Western invasion of the Middle East oil fields. That such a course would have been economically useless as well as politically dangerous seems clear. See Edith Penrose, 'OPEC's Importance in the World Oil Industry,' *International Affairs*, 55:1 (1979), 18–32. 'If OPEC did not exist, it would be in the interest of the industrial world to promote its creation in some form' (18) because of the need to manage oil prices in a weak market.

32 More or less academic remarks along these lines, as distinct from propaganda pumped out by public relations departments, can be found in John Fayerweather, 'The Internationalization of Business,' American Academy of Political and Social Science *Annals*, 403 (1972), 1–11; John Kenneth Galbraith, 'The Defense of the Multinational Company,' *Harvard Business Review*, 56:2 (March–April 1978), 83–93. J. Brown ed, *World Business: Promises and Problems* (New York, Macmillan, 1970), celebrates the glories of the MNE. A Canadian contribution is E. Hugh Roach, *In Defence of Multinationals: The Myths, the Realities, and the Future*, (Toronto, CIIA, 'Behind the Headlines,' 35:5, 1977).

33 Harry Johnson, 'Economic Benefits of the Multinational Enterprise,' in H.R. Hahlo et al ed, *Nationalism and the Multinational Enterprise: Legal, Economic, and Managerial Aspects* (Leiden, Sijthoff, 1973), 166–7. See also George W. Ball, 'Cosmocorp: The Importance of being Stateless,' *Atlantic Community Quarterly*, 6 (1968–9), 163–70.

34 Gerald A. Sumida, 'Transnational Movements and Economic Structures,' in C.E. Black and R.A. Falk ed, *The Future of the International Legal Order*, IV, *The Structure of the International Environment* (Princeton, Princeton

University Press, 1972), 567. See also Peter P. Gabriel, 'Management of Public Interest by the Multi-national Corporation,' *Journal of World Trade Law* 11 (1977), 23–5.

35 James A. Ramsey, 'East-West Business Cooperation: The Twain Meets [sic],' *Columbia Journal of World Business* V:4 (July–August 1970), 17–20; Howard V. Perlmutter, 'Emerging East-West Ventures: The Transideological Enterprise,' ibid, IV:5 (September–October 1969), 39–50

36 D. Osterberg and F. Ajami, 'The Multinational Corporation: Expanding the Frontiers of World Politics,' *Journal of Conflict Resolution*, 15 (1971), 462

37 Richard L. Rubenstein, *The Cunning of History: Mass Death and the American Future* (New York, Harper and Row, 1975), 58

38 Sanford Rose, 'Why the Multinational Tide Is Ebbing,' *Fortune*, XCVI:2 (August 1977), 111

39 Vernon, *Storm over the Multinationals*, 101. See also Stephen D. Cohen, 'Changes in the International Economy: Old Realities and New Myths,' *Journal of World Trade Law*, 12 (1978), 273–88.

40 For example, Kari Levitt, *Silent Surrender: The Multinational Corporation in Canada* (Toronto, Macmillan, 1970)

41 For example, Gilpen, *U.S. Power and the Multinational Corporation*; Vernon, *Sovereignty at Bay*; Andrew Hacker, 'Politics and the Corporation,' in Hacker ed, *The Corporation Take-Over* (New York, Harper and Row, 1964), 246–70; Anthony Sampson, *The Sovereign State of ITT* (Greenwich, Fawcett, 1974); Arthur Selwyn Miller, 'The Global Corporation and American Constitutionalism: Some Political Consequences of Economic Power,' *Journal of International Law and Economics*, 6 (1971–2), 235–46; idem, 'Toward the Techno-Corporate State? An Essay in American Constitutionalism,' *Villinova Law Review*, 14 (1968), 1–18

42 For example, Stephen Hymer, 'The Multinational Corporation and the Law of Uneven Development,' in J.N. Bhagwati ed, *Economics and World Order*, (New York, Macmillan, 1970); Bernard Mennis and Karl P. Sauvant, *Emerging Forms of Transnational Community: Transnational Business Enterprises and Regional Integration* (Toronto, Heath, 1976), 161–71

43 Vernon, *Storm over the Multinationals*, 202–3; Jack N. Behrman, 'Governmental Policy Alternatives and the Problem of International Sharing,' in John H. Dunning ed, *The Multinational Enterprise* (London, George Allen and Unwin, 1971), 301–2

44 George Ball, introduction to Richard Eells, *Global Corporations: The Emerging System of World Economic Power* (New York, Interbook, 1972), 7–9

45 Lasswell, 'Future Systems of Identity in the World Community,' in Black and Falk ed, *The Future of the International Legal Order*, 26

46 R.L. Desatnick and M.L. Bennett, *Human Resources Management in the Multinational Company* (New York, Nichols, 1977), 311–14
47 Gilles Lapouge, 'Entretien avec Kojève,' *La Quinzaine littéraire*, 53 (1 July 1968), 18–20
48 Merleau-Ponty's analysis is in *Humanisme et terreur* (Paris, Gallimard, 1947). I have provided an extensive analysis of the issues involved in *Merleau-Ponty and Marxism: From Terror to Reform* (Toronto, University of Toronto Press, 1979), chapter 3.
49 Aleksandr I. Solzhenitsyn, *The Gulag Archipelago, 1918–1956, An Experiment in Literary Investigation* (New York, Harper and Row, 1973), I, tr Thomas P. Whitney. Volume II, also translated by Whitney, was published in 1975, and volume III, translated by Harry Willetts, was published in 1976. All references, with minor changes, are to these editions and are indicated in the text as *GA*, with the Roman numeral indicating the volume, the Arabic the page. The secondary literature, at least on *GA*, is still fairly manageable. Particularly helpful are Stephen Carter, *The Politics of Solzhenitsyn* (London, Macmillan, 1977), and the collection edited by John B. Dunlop et al, *Aleksandr Solzhenitsyn: Critical Essays and Documentary Materials*, 2nd ed (New York, Collier, 1975). A fascinating account of the difficulties and drama connected with the publication of *The First Circle*, tr Thomas P. Whitney (New York, Harper and Row, 1968), Solzhenitsyn's account of life in a *sharashka*, akin to Dante's limbo, where interned intellectuals and technicians are turned into accomplices of the oppressors, as well as *GA*, is found in Olga Carlisle, *Solzhenitsyn and the Secret Circle* (New York, Holt, Rinehart and Winston, 1978). Claude Lefort's *Un homme de trop: Réflexions sur 'l'Archipel du Goulag'* (Paris, Seuil, 1976) was also helpful.
50 Robert Conquest, *The Great Terror: Stalin's Purge of the Thirties* (London, Macmillan, 1968), 335
51 Robert Conquest, 'Evolution of an Exile: *Gulag Archipelago*,' reprinted from *Saturday Review* (20 April 1974) in Kathryn Feuer ed, *Solzhenitsyn: A Collection of Critical Essays* (Englewood Cliffs, NJ, Prentice-Hall, 1976), 90
52 Thus, for example, Roy Medvedev, a Marxist Soviet 'dissident' and author of *Let History Judge: The Origin and Consequences of Stalinism*, tr Colleen Taylor, ed David Joravsky and Georges Haupt (New York, Vintage, 1973), while allowing that he could not accept Solzhenitsyn's assessments or conclusions, nevertheless declared 'emphatically that all the basic facts in his book, and especially the details about the life and torments of prisoners from their arrest until their death (or in rarer cases, until their release) are completely authentic'; 'On Solzhenitsyn's *Gulag Archipelago*,'

reprinted from *Intercontinental Press* (25 March 1974), in Kathryn Feuer, *Solzhenitsyn*, 97.

53 George F. Kennan, 'Between Earth and Hell,' reprinted from the *New York Review of Books* (21 March 1974) in Dunlop, *Aleksandr Solzhenitsyn*, 502

54 Michael Heller reported the extent to which Soviet leaders were impressed by the imagery: *GA* 'foretold the future and revealed the outlines of that future measures of the gravest kind have been taken in the fight against the book. The most radical of these is the banishment of the word "archipelago" from the Russian language. Even geographers are obliged to substitute for it the expression "group of islands"; 'The Gulag Archipelago, Volume III: Outlines for the Future,' *Survey*, 98 (1976) 176.

55 Section X of the Constitution of the Soviet Union, which details fundamental rights and duties of citizens, includes: the right to work, to rest and leisure, to maintenance in old age or sickness, and the right to education. Women have equal rights with men; there is no discrimination in terms of nationality or race; the church is separated from the state and from school so as to ensure freedom of conscience. There is freedom of speech, of the press, of assembly (including the holding of mass meetings), and freedom of processions and demonstrations. Likewise trade unions and similar professional societies are guaranteed. Privacy of persons, homes, and mail are all protected by law, and the Soviet Union affords the right of asylum to foreigners struggling on behalf of workers and for national liberation. These rights are outlined in twelve articles. Duties are outlined in four: citizens must obey the law, act honestly, respect the rules of socialist intercourse, safeguard public property, perform military service, and defend the country. The principles of the Soviet Fundamental Law are, in effect, those of a Hegelian state. The universality of its quickening spirit, the communist movement, is, as Stalin would have said, 'well known.'

56 See also Aleksandr Solzhenitsyn, *Letter to the Soviet Leaders*, tr H. Sternberg (New York, Harper and Row, 1975) 10, 55ff, 62ff.

57 See Yuri Glazov '"Thieves" in the USSR: A Social Phenomenon,' *Survey*, 98 (1976), 141–56.

58 Carter, *The Politics of Solzhenitsyn*, 53

59 One of the bitter jokes of camp life reported a conversation between a guard and a zek. 'Guard: How long are you in for? Zek: Twenty-five years. Guard: What did you do? Zek: Nothing. Guard: Filthy liar! For nothing you only get ten years.'

60 '58s' were political prisoners sentenced under article 58 of the Criminal Code.

61 This is the dominant image in André Gluksmann's book, *La Cuisinière et le mangeur d'hommes: Essai sur les rapports entre l'état, le marxisme et les camps de concentration* (Paris, Seuil, 1975).

62 *Radio Liberty Research Supplement* (Munich, Radio Liberty, 3 June 1975), 10–11

63 Aleksandr I. Solzhenitsyn, *Letter to the Soviet Leaders*, 62. As John B. Dunlop observed, Solzhenitsyn's point in his much publicized disagreement with Andrei Sakharov was that 'even if they do not believe in Marxism, the Soviet Leaders are *forced* to believe as if they do. And so, consequently, is all of Soviet society'; 'Solzhenitsyn in Exile,' *Survey* 96 (1975), 135.

64 Alexander Solzhenitsyn, 'As Breathing and Consciousness Return,' in Solzhenitsyn et al, *From under the Rubble* (Toronto, Little, Brown, 1975), 24

65 *Nobel Lecture*, tr F.D. Reeve (New York, Farrar, Straus and Giroux, 1972), 32. As Hannah Arendt said, 'All these [political] lies, whether their authors know it or not, harbor an element of violence; organized lying always tends to destroy whatever it has decided to negate, although only totalitarian governments have consciously adopted lying as the first step to murder'; 'Truth and Politics,' in *Between Past and Future: Eight Exercises in Political Thought* (New York, Viking, 1968), 252.

66 Geoffrey Clive, *The Broken Ikon: Intuitive Existentialism in Classical Russian Fiction* (New York, Macmillan, 1972), 142

67 The result for the reader of Solzhenitsyn's book is equally astonishing: after 1,500 pages of senseless, stupid, and brutal killing, finally one encounters a justifiable homicide.

68 The term is taken from John Bayley, 'The Gulag Archipelago,' *The Listener*, 91 (14 February 1974), 195.

69 In any particular individual, specific psychological explanations may well be applicable. The aggregate meaning, however, is political, not psychological. A thorough account of the psychology of the German response to the Nazi camps is found in Bruno Bettelheim's famous study, *The Informed Heart: Autonomy in a Mass Age* (Toronto, Collier-Macmillan, 1960). No doubt a study of the Soviet Union would turn up similar evidence.

70 *Letter to the Soviet Leaders*, 1

71 One can always rely upon the committed (or perhaps just dim) Marxist to add a light touch. Francis Baker, for example, denounced the transformation of Solzhenitsyn's consciousness as a result of his journey through the Archipelago as a mystification; *Solzhenitsyn: Politics and Form* (London, Macmillan, 1977), 100–1. Solzhenitsyn had already made his reply, having encountered such an attitude, along with everything else, on the inside:

'He is imperturbable. He speaks in a language which requires no effort of the mind. And arguing with him is like walking through a desert' (GA II 341).

72 Solzhenitsyn, *A Warning to the West* (London, Bodley Head, 1976), 8, 14
73 (Paris, Colin, 1954), tr John Wilkinson, *The Technological Society* (New York, Vintage, 1964)
74 *The Betrayal of the West*, tr Matthew J. O'Connell (New York, Seabury, 1978), 166
75 *Technological Society* xxv
76 Ellul, 'The Technological Order,' *Technology and Culture*, 3 (1962), 394. In the words of Norbert Wiener, 'We have modified our environment so radically that we must now modify ourselves in order to exist in this new environment'; *The Human Use of Human Beings* (New York, Doubleday, 1956), 46.
77 This and the following quotations are from 'The Question Concerning Technology,' tr William Lovitt, *The Question Concerning Technology and Other Essays* (New York, Harper and Row, 1977).
78 Heidegger, 'Only a God Can Save Us,' *Philosophy Today*, 20:4 (1976), 277
79 *Technological Society*, 49
80 *Betrayal of the West*, 81
81 Strauss, *On Tyranny*, 205; cf Gadamer, *Hegel's Dialectic*, 73.
82 According to his translator, *The Technological Society* may usefully be compared to *PhG* inasmuch as it contains a 'phenomenology of the technical state of mind' (*The Technological Society*, xiii). Kojève has likewise observed that the transformative labours of historical slaves have been responsible for rendering the deadly and dangerous world of nature into a specifically human and technical one (*IH* 499–500: 228). Even a critic of Ellul was moved to admit that *The Technological Society* 'remains to this date the only comprehensive treatment of modern technology as a distinct and unique phenomenon in the history of man'; William Kuhns, *The Post-Industrial Prophets: Interpretations of Technology* (New York, Weybright and Takkey, 1971), 84. Other accounts of Ellul's argument are: Carl Mitcham and Robert Mackey, 'Jacques Ellul and the Technological Society,' *Philosophy Today*, 15:2 (1971), 102–21; David C. Menninger,' Jacques Ellul: A Tempered Profile,' *Review of Politics*, 37 (1975), 235–46; H.T. Wilson, 'The Sociology of Apocalypse: Jacques Ellul's Reformation of Reformation Thought,' *The Human Context*, 7 (1975), 474–94; David Lovekin, 'Jacques Ellul and the Logic of Technology,' *Man and World*, x:3 (1977), 251–72.
83 These characteristics are set out in detail in *The Technological Society*, 79–147, and in *Le Système technicien* (Paris, Calmann-Levy, 1977), 129–

279. The similarities with Hegel's account of the growth of self-consciousness to wisdom are obvious.

84 As William Barrett wrote, technology has created 'one world out of our
planet for the first time since humans appeared upon it. In so doing it
transforms world history itself from an abstract and daring idea in the
minds of philosophers and historians two centuries ago into an actual
and pressing reality'; *The Illusion of Technique: A Search for Meaning in a
Technological Civilization* (New York, Anchor, 1978), 179. Likewise Ellul:
'Philosophy has tended to totalize in its search for an intellectual system,
a master key to universal reality. Today the same tendency prevails, not
in the intellectual sphere ... but in the sphere of reality, all parts of the
social body being so conjoined and interconnected as to make that
organism all-encompassing and uniform,' *Autopsy of Revolution*, tr Patri-
cia Wolf (New York, Knopf, 1971), 257. These quotations are adduced
not as irreproachable interpretations of the nature or history of philosophy, but as expressing an appropriately Hegelian sentiment concerning
the technical rationality of the technically actual.
85 *The Technological Society*, 146
86 *The Illusion of Technique*, 207
87 *Le Système technicien*, 347; *The Technological Society*, 320
88 Langdon Winner, *Autonomous Technology; Technics out-of-control as a
Theme in Political Thought* (Cambridge, MIT Press, 1977), 207
89 *Le Système technicien*, 359. We shall consider the case of self-conscious
technicians below.
90 *The Political Illusion*, tr Konrad Kellen (New York, Knopf, 1967), 141
91 Ibid, 70
92 Ellul, *Propaganda: The Formation of Man's Attitudes*, tr Konrad Kellen and
Jean Lerner (New York, Knopf, 1971), xvii
93 Ibid, 75
94 Ibid, 138
95 Ibid, 235. See also *The Political Illusion*, 112, 116.
96 'Jacques Ellul and the Logic of Technology,' 251, 263
97 *The Technological Society*, 287; cf *The Political Illusion*, 220ff.
98 *The Illusion of Technique*, xii
99 *Propaganda*, xvii
100 *The Technological Society*, 436 (closing sentences of Ellul's book)
101 *The Illusion of Technique*, 208
102 'Jacques Ellul and the Logic of Technology,' 259
103 *The Technological Society*, 142–3
104 *The Betrayal of the West*, 191–2

105 Let there be no misunderstanding. An equivalence of meaning does not imply an identity of all constituent elements. In Ellul's words: 'Technique does not lead to general Uniformity. In fact, it creates a certain diversity. Its objectives are always the same, and so is its influence on man ... Therefore we shall continue to have the appearance of different civilizations in India and Greenland. They will indeed be different in certain aspects. But their essence will be identical: they will be techniques'; *The Technological Society*, 130. Living in an archipelago of Disneylands and Macdonalds will always be more sybaritic than an archipelago of Gulags. Any fool knows that, even without a visit to the Soviet Union. We are dealing, however, with equivalent meanings.

106 A. Alvarez, 'The Concentration Camps,' *Atlantic*, 210:6 (December 1962), 70

107 Robert Jay Lifton, *Death in Life: Survivors of Hiroshima* (New York, Random House, 1967), 541

108 Ibid, 79

109 Robert Jay Lifton and Eric Olson, *Living and Dying* (New York, Praeger, 1974), 23. The Vietnam war reinforced this experience in a number of diffuse ways expressed in the ambivalent views of the American civilian population toward Vietnam veterans. See Lifton, *Home from the War: Vietnam Veterans, Neither Victims nor Executioners* (New York, Simon and Schuster, 1973).

110 Quoted in *Death in Life*, 477

111 *Living and Dying*, 127

112 *Death in Life*, 541

113 Lifton, *The Life of the Self: Toward a New Psychology* (New York, Simon and Schuster, 1976), 132–3

EPILOGUE

1 John Irving, *The World According to Garp* (New York, Pocket Books, 1979), 567

2 This has been done at great length by Foucault. I have given an interpretation of Foucault's argument in *Michel Foucault: An Introduction to His Thought* (Toronto, Edwin Mellen, 1982).

3 Emil Fackenheim, 'Would Hegel Today Be a Hegelian?,' *Dialogue*, 9 (1970), 223; *The Religious Dimension in Hegel's Thought*, 12

4 'Hegel and Judaism,' 161–2

5 One should add that a Christian or a Muslim, to say nothing of an animist or Zen master, must equally cease to hold to whatever initial religious commitments they have if they are to become wise. This was stressed

repeatedly in our presentation of Kojève's exegesis of *Phenomenology*. We rely on Fackenheim's argument here because he so cogently describes the alternatives.

6 See Taylor, *Hegel*, 537–8, for details.
7 'Would Hegel Today Be a Hegelian?,' 224
8 Fackenheim, *Encounters between Judaism and Modern Philosophy: A Preface to Future Jewish Thought* (New York, Basic Books, 1973), 158
9 Fackenheim, *The Jewish Return into History: Reflections in the Age of Auschwitz and a New Jerusalem* (New York, Schocken, 1978), 239. Likewise, Edgar Morin observed: 'In his analysis, Hegel forgot about torture to the death, a sort of horrible synthesis between the desire to nihilate and the desire to humiliate the other, where the torturer obtains enjoyment similar to assassination and enslavement'; *L'Homme et la mort dans l'histoire* (Paris, Corrêa, 1951), 53.
10 See also George Grant, *Technology and Empire: Perspectives on North America* (Toronto, Anansi, 1969), 79–110.
11 Stanley Rosen, 'Wonder, Anxiety, and Eros,' *Giornale di Metafisica*, 6 (1957), 649
12 Rosen, *Nihilism*, 209
13 Ibid, 217–18
14 Ibid, 274
15 Ibid, 273
16 Ibid, 258
17 Voegelin, 'Reason: The Classic Experience,' *Southern Review*, new series 10 (1974), 241
18 'Wonder, Anxiety and Eros,' 652
19 'The Eclipse of Reality,' in Maurice Natanson ed, *Phenomenology and Social Reality: Essays in Memory of Alfred Schutz* (The Hague, Martinus Nijhoff, 1970), 183–94
20 Ibid, 186
21 The analysis and argument that follow are indebted to Voegelin's polemical analysis, 'On Hegel: A Study in Sorcery,' *Studium Generale*, 24 (1971), 335–68, and to Alois Dempf, 'Die aktuelle Bedeutung einer korrekten Hegelinterpretation,' *Bayerische Akademie der Wissenschaften* 5 (1971), 1–18.
22 'Die aktuelle Bedeutung,' 17. The final text of Voegelin's on the topic is in *Order and History* IV, *The Ecumenic Age* (Baton Rouge, Louisiana State University Press, 1974), 59–113. A more complete account of the concept than can be provided here is in my 'Voegelin's Concept of Historiogenesis: An Introduction,' *Historical Reflections/Réflexions historiques*, IV: 2 (1978), 231–51.
23 *The Ecumenic Age*, 63–7
24 'On Hegel,' 343

Index